GRAMMAR OF THE ENGLISH LANGUAGE

John Wallis, aged 85, painted by Sir Godfrey Kneller
by courtesy of The Trustees of the Bodleian Library, Oxford

JOHN WALLIS

GRAMMAR OF THE ENGLISH LANGUAGE

with an introductory grammatico-physical

TREATISE ON SPEECH

(or on the formation of all speech sounds)

A new edition

with translation and commentary by

J. A. KEMP

LONGMAN

LONGMAN GROUP LTD
LONDON
Associated companies, branches and representatives throughout the world
© Longman Group Ltd 1972

First published 1972
ISBN 0 582 52492 X

*Made and printed by offset in Great Britain by
William Clowes & Sons, Limited
London, Beccles and Colchester*

PREFACE

In his monograph *Die Grammatik des englischen Sprachmeisters John Wallis* which appeared in 1936 Martin Lehnert expressed surprise that no systematic research had been done on Wallis's Grammar, in spite of constant references to it in histories of English sounds, and the fact that more was known about Wallis's background than about almost any other early writer on English. Morel's dissertation (1895) was, as Lehnert pointed out, merely 'eine gutgläubige Inhaltsangabe' – an uncritical contents list – which did virtually nothing to explain or interpret. Lehnert provided a thorough and penetrating survey of Wallis's life and work and of his description of sounds in general, and of English sounds in particular. Any new edition of Wallis must be heavily indebted to him, and the extent of this debt will be apparent in the present edition. However, as part of a series concerned with the development of linguistics its emphasis is different. Lehnert's book concentrates on Wallis's description of the sounds of speech, and especially on his evidence for the pronunciation of English, which is of great importance. This edition, it is hoped, will complement Lehnert by taking in also Wallis's description of the parts of speech in English (Chapters II–XIII of the Grammar), and by concentrating more on the success or otherwise of Wallis and his contemporaries and predecessors in finding suitable frameworks for their descriptions of languages.

It has not been possible to include Chapters XIV and XV of the English Grammar (*De Etymologia* and *De Poesi*); Wallis expanded them more than any other part of his book in his later editions, and their inclusion would have required a much larger edition than this. In comparison with their length they are less directly of interest for the main purpose of this book than the earlier chapters; a summary of their contents is given in the introduction (*pp* 28–9). Also excluded are the *Praxis Grammatica* – grammatical comments on the Lord's Prayer, the Apostles' Creed, and a short poem – which Wallis first introduced in the 4th edition, and the letter written by him to Thomas Beverley, which was appended to the 6th edition (see title-page on *p* 75, and introduction *p* 13).

The facsimile text is that of the 6th edition, 1765 (see *p* 73), which is virtually identical with the text of the 5th edition, 1699 – the last that Wallis himself supervised. The notes on the text indicate how this text differs from that of earlier editions; most of the differences are the result of additions rather than alterations. Wallis appears to have made little attempt to revise his description in the course of the forty-six years which separate the publication of the 1st edition (1653) and the 5th. Hence the danger, pointed out by Lehnert, of using late editions as evidence for the pronunciation of their time. However, for the purposes of this edition it seemed better to start from the fuller text.

The translation is a new one, written in a modern idiom. It is true that virtually a complete translation of Wallis may be found in the grammars of Greenwood (1711) and Brightland (1711) – see *pp* 68–9 – but in places they are inaccurate or incomplete, and sometimes Wallis's text is inextricably mixed up with material from other sources, so it seemed more satisfactory to start afresh. As far as possible I have tried to avoid using technical terms of modern origin, which might have the effect of reading more into the text than is in fact there. In most cases the spellings of English words given in the 6th edition have been retained, but long ∫ has been changed to *s*, and some alterations have been made to the punctuation and capitalisation, to bring them into line with modern usage. Where letters appear in italics they are orthographical symbols; phonetic symbols are always enclosed in square brackets, and are taken from the alphabet of the International Phonetic Association. The phonetic terminology follows Abercrombie (1967).

It remains for me to thank all those who have assisted in the production of this edition. The idea of it was originally given to me by Professor David Abercrombie, and I owe him a great deal for his advice and encouragement. I have also been greatly helped by discussions with colleagues at Edinburgh University; and I am grateful to Professor A. C. Gimson of University College London and Professor R. H. Robins of the School of Oriental and African Studies for valuable comments. However, the responsibility for what is contained in this book is entirely my own. My task was made easier by the co-operation and assistance given to me by librarians, particularly those of the Edinburgh University Library, the National Library of Scotland, the Signet Library, the British Museum, and the Bodleian Library. Finally I wish to thank my wife for her help in typing and criticising the drafts, and for her patience and encouragement throughout the preparation of this edition.

Edinburgh University   J. A. KEMP

CONTENTS

INTRODUCTION

1 There has been no edition of John Wallis's *Tractatus De Loquela* and *Grammatica Linguae Anglicanae* since the 6th edition was published in 1765, and no complete translation. Yet it represents a very important landmark in the history of phonetics and English grammar. The number of editions published (see *p* 71 *f*), and the amount of the text incorporated into Greenwood's and Brightland's grammars (see *p* 68 *ff*), are evidence of its wide influence in the seventeenth and eighteenth centuries. In the nineteenth century A. J. Ellis and Henry Sweet both held Wallis in high regard and grammarians and phoneticians today can still find in his work much that is of interest. In this introduction the intention will be to give some idea of what kind of a man Wallis was, and to assess his contribution to the study of phonetics and grammar, his debt to his predecessors, and his influence on later generations.

2 Sources for Wallis's life

The sources for what we know of Wallis's life can be divided into three types: [*a*] autobiography, [*b*] biographies, [*c*] others.

[*a*] The fullest and most authoritative account, though clearly not the most impartial, is contained in a letter from Wallis to Dr Thomas Smith. It was written in Oxford on 29 January 1697, in response to a request from Smith for details about his life to be used in a biography, but the biography never appeared. The original letter and Dr Smith's reply are in the Bodleian Library (MS Smith 31 and MS Smith 66, *f* 31). Wallis's letter was subsequently printed in Thomas Hearne's Works, Vol III, in the foreword to Peter Langtoft's Chronicle, Oxford, 1725.

[*b*] (i) Bodleian MS Smith 31, *ff* 58–9 also contains a manuscript copy of the short biography of Wallis which appeared in Collier's Dictionary (2nd edition, London, 1727) written by Dr David Gregory

(1661–1708), Savilian Professor of Astronomy in Oxford from 1691 to 1708.

(ii) A biography of Wallis was written by John Lewis, Minister of Margate, in 1735 (Bodleian MS Rawl. C.978, Brit. Mus. MS 32601, and on microfilm in Edinburgh University Library). It appears to be very largely based on Wallis's letter to Thomas Smith.

(iii) A memoir of John Wallis, written by his great-grandson William Wallis, appears as a preface to an edition of his sermons first published in London in 1791. This has some interesting details not included in the other biographies.

[c] The remainder of the sources consist of (i) letters written by Wallis or his contemporaries; (ii) mentions of him by contemporary writers – notably Anthony Wood, Thomas Hobbes, Henry Stubbe, Thomas Hearne, John Aubrey, Samuel Pepys, William Holder, John Davys; (iii) other works by Wallis himself – for example *A Defence of the Royal Society*, 1678. These sources are all listed in the bibliography.

3 A chronological summary of his life

1567 John Wallis, his father, born in Thingdon (Finedon) Northants. Educated Trinity College, Cambridge. Minister of Ashford, Kent, from 1602 until his death on 30 November 1622. After the death of his first wife he married Joanna Chapman of Godmersham, Kent (*b* March 1581), daughter and heiress of Drew Sanders, an eminent London merchant, on 12 March 1612, and had by her five children – Sarah, Ellen, John, Henry and William – John being the eldest of the sons. His second wife died 26 September 1643.

1616 23 November John Wallis born. Educated in Ashford till 1625, when occurrence of the plague caused him to be sent to Tenterden, Kent. Attended a private school at Ley-Green kept by a Scotsman, James Mouat, until 1630, when the school closed down.

1630 Sent to Felsted School, Essex, under Martin Holbech. Continued there for two years; in 1631 made his first acquaintance with mathematics. Learnt Latin, Greek and some Hebrew.

1632 Christmas. Sent to Emmanuel College, Cambridge, and chosen as Foundation Scholar. Became skilled in logic.

1637 BA.

1640 MA. Left Emmanuel, there being no vacancy for a fellowship at this time. Entered Holy Orders. Chaplain to Sir Richard Darley at Buttercramb, Yorks.

1641 Chaplain to Lady Vere in London and Castle-Hedingham, Essex, for two years. In 1642 made his first decipherment of a document relating to the capture of Colchester, 27 December 1642.

1643 Minister of St Gabriel's, Fenchurch Street, London. On the death of his mother inherited a substantial estate in Kent.

1644 Fellow of Queens' College, Cambridge. Appointed a secretary to the Assembly of Divines at Westminster. Gave evidence against Archbishop Laud (Prynne, *Canterburies Doome*, 1646, *p* 73).

1645 Married Susanna Glyde of Northiam, Sussex (*b* January 1622). About this time attended meetings to discuss scientific matters in London. Vacated his fellowship at Queens' College, Cambridge.

1647 Minister of St Martin's, Ironmonger Lane, London.

1648 Signed a paper remonstrating against bringing the King to trial and executing him.

1649 Appointed by the Parliamentary Commissioners to replace Peter Turner (1586–1652) as Savilian Professor of Geometry at Oxford. Took up residence at Exeter College.

1650 His son John born – later educated at Trinity College Oxford, and became barrister-at-law, married Elizabeth Harris of Nettlebed, 1 February 1682 and had three children: John, Mary and Elizabeth.

1653 First edition of *Tractatus de Loquela* and *Grammatica Linguae Anglicanae* (Oxford).

1654 Received DD degree, subsequently confirmed by Convocation after the Restoration in 1662. Dispute with Professor Seth Ward, Savilian Professor of Astronomy, over seniority (Wood, 1691–2, *p* 627).

1656 Published *Arithmetica Infinitorum*, which made his name as a mathematician. Beginning of his dispute with Hobbes over mathematics. His daughter Anne born, 4 June – married John Blencow, 23 December 1675 (barrister-at-law and later one of the Barons of the Exchequer) and had seven children: John, Mary, Anne, Thomas, William, Elizabeth and Susanna.

1657 Published *Mathesis Universalis*, based on his lectures.

1658 Appointed to succeed Gerald Langbain as *Custos Archivorum* of Oxford University, provoking a dispute over his eligibility for the post, and an attack on him by Henry Stubbe (*The Savilian Professor's Case Stated*, 1658). His daughter Elizabeth born – married William Benson, 21 February 1682, who died 5 November 1691. No children survived.

1660 The Restoration. Confirmed in his posts as Savilian Professor and *Custos Archivorum* and made King's Chaplain. Royal Society formally constituted (December), Wallis being a founder member.

1661 Taught Daniel Whaley to speak. Served on Commission to review the Book of Common Prayer as one of the Presbyterian members.

1662 Royal Society given its first Charter by the King (15 July). Wallis taught Alexander Popham to speak.

1663 Royal Society given its second Charter as *The Royal Society of London for improving Natural Knowledge*, 22 April.

1664 2nd edition of the Grammar (Oxford).

1668 Correct theory of inelastic bodies put before the Royal Society and published in *Philosophical Transactions* III, 1864. Later expounded in *Mechanica* (1669–71).

1670 Beginning of controversy with Holder over deaf-teaching.

1672 3rd edition of the Grammar (Hamburg).

1674 4th edition of the Grammar (Oxford).

1685 Accession of James II. Wallis's enemies renewed their accusation that he had deciphered Charles I's letters at Naseby. Wallis defended himself in a letter to Dr Fell, Bishop of Oxford (see *p* 11).

1687 Death of his wife, 17 March.

1688 4th (pseudo) edition of the Grammar (Hamburg).

1689 Accession of William III. Wallis took oath of allegiance; appointed Royal decipherer.

1691 Supported the doctrine of the Trinity (*De Sacra Trinitate*).

1692 Consulted on the Gregorian calendar and advised against it, so that it was not adopted. Published *A Defence of the Christian Sabbath*.

1693–99 Published *Opera Mathematica et miscellanea*, in 3 volumes, dedicated to William III, including 5th edition of the Grammar (1699).

1697 Published *A Defence of Infant Baptism*.

1703 Died in Oxford aged 86, 28 October.

4 Aspects of Wallis's life

Wallis's range of interests was extraordinarily wide, as can be seen from an examination of the titles of his published works (Niceron, 1745). For the greater part of his life he was a professional mathematician, but he found time to take an active part in the religious controversies of his day and was one of the founder members of the Royal Society, publishing numerous articles in the *Philosophical Transactions* on the tides, the barometer, the thermometer, ancient and modern music, the memory, the resistance of air, the veins of plants, etc. Outside mathematics his most influential work was the *Grammatica Linguae Anglicanae*, his only venture into grammatical studies. He edited works by Ptolemy, Archimedes and Aristarchus of Samos on music, mathematics and astronomy; and many of his religious commentaries and sermons were published. He became famous, even notorious, as a breaker of ciphers, and as a teacher of the deaf. Some of these aspects of his life will now be considered in more detail.

[a] Education

Wallis showed an early aptitude for academic work, and has no hesitation in proclaiming, in his letter to Thomas Smith (see *p* 1), how he excelled at the various studies he embarked on;[1] he says 'it was always my affectation even from a child, in all places of learning or knowledge, not merely to learn by rote, which was soon forgotten, but to know the grounds or reasons of what I learn'. Under James Mouat he learnt 'the technical part of grammar'. At Felsted School Martin Holbech 'used to say I came to him the best grounded of any scholar that he received from another school'. There he learnt Latin and Greek, and 'had been used in both the schools to speak Latin'; he also learnt some Hebrew, and 'in a few years had

[1] See Hearne (1725), III.xcliii *ff*.

read over all the Hebrew Bible'. At Christmas 1631, during his vacation, he became interested in his younger brother's books on 'how to write and cipher, or cast account', and his brother showed him what he had been doing 'which was the Practical part of Common Arithmetick in Numeration, Addition, Subtraction, Multiplication, Division, The Rule of Three (Direct and Inverse), the Rule of Fellowship (with and without Time), the Rule of False Position, Rules of Practise and Reduction of Coins'. He worked over all the examples his brother had previously done and 'found no difficulty to understand it. . . . This was my first insight into Mathematicks and all the teaching I had.' (See further on this in section [c] below.) 'At this time also', he says, 'I learnt the rudiments of Musick and of the French Tongue.'

At Cambridge University he improved his Latin, Greek and Hebrew but, he continues, 'my first business was to be the study of Logick. In this I soon became Master of a Syllogism'. He stresses the value of this in disputations in which 'I was able to hold pace with those who were some years my Seniors'. Wallis then went on to Ethics, Physics and Metaphysics, and 'the Speculative part of Physick and Anatomy, and . . . was the first of his [Dr Glisson's] Sons who (in a publick Disputation) maintained the Circulation of the Bloud (which was then a new Doctrine), though I had no design of practising Physick'. He also studied astronomy and geography, as part of his theory that any knowledge acquired could do no harm, and might come in useful. Lastly but not least he 'became timely acquainted with Systematick and Polemick Theology. And had the repute of a good Proficient therein.'

Lehnert (1936, § 8) remarks, comparing him with Leibniz, 'man kann fast behaupten dass . . . er zu den letzten universalgebildeten Menschen zählt, die das Wissen ihrer Zeit in sich vereinigten'.[1] No doubt it was his astonishing versatility, and facility in attaining a high standard in whatever he attempted, that contributed to his impatience with the work of lesser men and led to fierce controversies, as we shall see.

[b] Religion

The son of a well-respected minister, he was himself ordained in 1640. In his autobiographical letter to Thomas Smith he gives a long

---

[1] 'One can almost say that . . . he is to be counted among the last "wholly-educated" men, who embodied in themselves the state of knowledge of their times.'

account of the Westminster Assembly of Divines, which lasted from 1643 to 1653, and which he attended as one of the secretaries.[1] Its purpose was to abolish the Episcopacy, if possible, and to revise the liturgy, in order to preserve peace in the Church of England and greater agreement with the Church of Scotland and other churches abroad; he says he benefited a great deal from hearing the debates. Wallis showed great sympathy with the Presbyterians then and later, and represented them in the Commission to revise the Book of Common Prayer in 1661. However, he appears subsequently to have complied with the terms of the Act of Uniformity, and to have been firmly loyal to the Church of England during the latter part of his life. His attitude to Dissenters was liberal and tolerant; in a letter to George Keith, written in Oxford, 3 June 1700 (quoted in W. Wallis, 1791), he said 'they dissent only from the declaration required by Parliament of unfeigned assent and consent to all and everything contained and prescribed in and by the Book of Common Prayer'. In his letter to Thomas Smith[2] he says of himself: 'As to Divinity (on which I had an eye from the first) I had the happiness of a strict and Religious Education, all along from a Child. Whereby I was not only preserved from vicious Courses, and acquainted with Religious Exercises; but was early instructed in the Principles of Religion, and Catachetical Divinity, and the frequent Reading of Scripture, and other good Books, and diligent attendance on Sermons. (And whatever other Studies I followed, I was careful not to neglect this.)' The biographer of *Biographia Britannica* (1766) hints at the slight Wallis must have felt when his friends and contemporaries Seth Ward and John Wilkins both received bishoprics, while he himself did not (see *p* 17). However, he seems to have reconciled himself to this; in a letter (W. Wallis, 1791, cviii-cix) he explained his reasons for declining the Deanery of Hereford in 1692: 'It was a proverb when I was a boy: Better set still than rise to fall; if I have deserved no better I shall doubt whether I have deserved this, it being but equivalent to what I have, and with which I am contented. I know it is easily said, He that will not accept a small preferment does not deserve a better, and if so I am content. I am an old, old man and am not like to enjoy any place long.' In the latter part of his life he published works supporting the doctrine of the Trinity (1691), the traditional Christian Sabbath (1692) and the practice of infant baptism (1697).

[1] Hearne (1725), III.clii *ff*.
[2] loc cit, *p* cl *ff*.

[c] *Mathematics*

Wallis relates how he first made the acquaintance of mathematics by reading some books belonging to his brother (see *p* 6). Subsequently he studied it by himself 'as a pleasing Diversion, at spare hours; as books of Arithmetick, or others Mathematical fel occasionally in my way. For I had none to direct me, what books to read, or what to seek, or in what Method to proceed. For Mathematicks (at that time, with us) were scarce looked on as Academical Studies, but rather Mechanical; as the business of Traders, Merchants, Seamen, Carpenters, Surveyors of Lands, or the like; and perhaps some Almanack-makers in London. And amongst more than Two hundred Students (at that time) in our College, I do not know of any Two (perhaps not any) who had more of Mathematicks than I (if so much) which was then but little; And but very few in that whole University. For the Study of Mathematicks was at that time more cultivated in London than in the Universities.'[1] One of the books which chiefly influenced him was Oughtred's *Clavis Mathematica*. He made a high reputation for himself from the year 1642 onwards as a cipher-breaker (see Section [e] below) and in 1649, when the Parliamentary Commissioners relieved Peter Turner of his post of Savilian Professor of Geometry at Oxford, they chose Wallis to be his successor; he remained there until his death, fifty-four years later. His most significant mathematical works were *Arithmetica Infinitorum* (1656) and *Mechanica* (1669–71). The former made his reputation, laying the foundations of differential and integral calculus. The latter put forward the correct theory of inelastic bodies, surpassing all previous work on the subject. His fame spread throughout Europe, and he is recognised by mathematicians as the greatest precursor of Newton, with whom he corresponded in his later years, at one point taking him to task for his reluctance to publish the results of his research (Brewster, *Memoirs of Sir Isaac Newton*, I.455–6). One often-quoted story illustrates his extraordinary mathematical memory. In the *Philosophical Transactions* (1685, xv. 1269) he relates how he extracted the square root of 3 while in bed at night and found it: 1.73205,08075,68877,29353; and at a foreigner's request he took another number consisting of 53 places of figures and 'in the dark of the night extracted its root to 27 places'. Both of these numbers he retained in his mind, till he afterwards wrote them down by daylight.

[1] Hearne (1725), III.cxlvii *ff*.

Other discoveries for which he was responsible were: the way of expressing the quadrature of the circle by an infinite fraction, the properties of the cycloid, cyssoid, conchoid, parabola, spiral, etc, and the existence of continued fractions. The symbol for infinity is also of his invention and he found a new value for π. In *Tractatus Algebrae Historicus et practicus* (1685) Wallis gave credit to the Englishman Thomas Harriot for discoveries made by the French mathematician Vieta (who incidentally was also a decipherer) and was later attacked for this national bias by historians of mathematics (for example, by Montucla, *Histoire des Mathematiques*, Paris (1758), II.82). He quarrelled with Pascal and Fermat, and described Descartes as a plagiarist, showing a zeal for controversy and an aggressive spirit which was to appear in many facets of his life. He and Thomas Hobbes (1588–1679) had a bitter quarrel dating from Hobbes's publication of mathematical theories which Wallis considered wholly inaccurate. Each took it in turn to refute the other's argument in a series of publications between 1655 (*Elenchus geometriae Hobbianae*) and Hobbes's death. In a letter to Mr Tenison, 30 November 1680, after Hobbes had died, Wallis talks of him as 'morose, supercilious, highly opinionated of himself and impatient of contradiction, which put him upon great passion and foul language', and quotes similar comments made by Doctor Seth Ward in his *Vindiciae Academiarum* (1654). He goes on to say that Hobbes's knowledge of mathematics, which was little, made him think himself a great man, but when he began to write he betrayed himself (Bodleian MS Add. D.105, *ff* 70–71). However, in the edition of his Collected Works in 1693–99 Wallis omitted his attacks on Hobbes, not wishing, he says, to prolong the quarrel after his death. A letter of Hobbes's written in 1678 is printed in Clark's edition of Aubrey's *Lives* (I.378); it is concerned with the controversy over deaf-teaching between Wallis and Holder (see below *p* 12) but also goes so far as to assert that Wallis was ignorant of mathematics – a charge that he could well afford to leave unanswered. For further treatment of Wallis's mathematical work see Scriba (1966) and Scott (1938, 1958).

[*d*] *The Royal Society*
'About the year 1645' while in London he attended meetings to discuss problems of 'what hath been called the New Philosophy or

Experimental Philosophy'.[1] The subjects for discussion included 'Physick, Anatomy, Geometry, Astronomy, Navigation, Staticks, Magneticks, Chymicks, Mechanicks and Natural Experiments' (expressly excluding Theology and State Affairs). The meetings were held in various places, one being Gresham College, and were attended, among others, by John Wilkins, later Bishop of Chester, and Samuel Foster, Professor of Astronomy at Gresham College. These meetings continued weekly till 1649, when Wallis, Wilkins and Dr Goddard moved to Oxford. From then on meetings were held in both places and culminated in the foundation of the Royal Society in 1660 (incorporated by Royal Charter in 1662). Subsequently Wallis took a regular part in discussions and published many articles in the *Philosophical Transactions* (see Niceron); for a time he was president of the Oxford Philosophical Society (Wood (1891), III.78). See Weld, 1848; McIntosh, 1956.

[e] Deciphering

While chaplain to Lady Vere in London in 1642, at the beginning of the Civil War, Wallis relates[2] that he was shown a letter in cipher which had been intercepted, and was asked, half in joke, if he could make anything of it. Though he had never seen a cipher before he succeeded in deciphering it within two hours. This success, he says, 'was then looked upon as a great matter' and from then on his services were much in demand and 'I afterwards ventured on many others . . . and scarce missed of any that I undertook, for many years, during our Civil Wars and afterwards'. Indeed he became famous throughout Europe for this skill. His German contemporary, the famous philosopher and mathematician Leibniz (1646–1716), wrote to him asking for his method (29 December 1698) but Wallis in his reply refused to disclose it (16 January 1699): see Davys (1737). Leibniz described Wallis's decipherments as 'the greatest instance ever known of the force and penetration of the human understanding' (quoted by W. Wallis, *Sermons*, 1791). The correspondence with Leibniz is printed in Vol III of the Collected Works (1699): *Epistolarum quarundam Collectio, rem Mathematicam spectantium*. Wallis was involved for many years in a controversy about certain letters of King Charles I, captured at Naseby, which he was alleged to have deciphered for the Parliamentary forces. He himself

---

[1] Hearne (1725), III.clxi *ff*.
[2] Hearne (1725), III.clviii *ff*.

strenuously denied the charge and is supported by contemporary evidence, but his enemies were all too ready to press the matter; see Barwick (1724), *pp* 60–61, 251, 504; Stubbe (1657); A. Wood (1891), *pp* 507–8; Davys (1737), *pp* 6–7; Wallis (1685), *p* clxx *ff.* He deposited some deciphered or partly deciphered letters in the Bodleian Library in 1653, where they can still be seen (MS e Mus. 203, also published in Davys, 1737). Wood asserted that Wallis was subsequently allowed to 'scratch out many foul things', with the collusion of the librarian. Wallis had reserved the right to alter what he wished when he deposited the collection, but that the deletions were of 'foul things' is quite unsubstantiated, and they are very slight.

In his memoirs on his great-grandfather, published in 1791, William Wallis gives a further account of some of his deciphering, quoting from Wallis's letters (1689 onwards) to Lord Nottingham, Secretary to William III. Wallis complains: 'It is hard service and I am quite weary. If your Honour were sensible how much pains and study it cost me you would pity me – and there is a proverb of not riding a free horse too hard.' Other hints of lack of appreciation come in later letters to the Earl of Shrewsbury – Nottingham's successor. In one he mentions studying eight or ten hours a day for seven weeks (*p* xxxiii) which 'is hard service for my years, unless I would crack my brains at it'. In a letter written 23 November 1689, he complains of failing eyesight. Nor was he very well rewarded – he mentions receiving two amounts of £50 each as payment for 'some hundred sheets', some of very great importance, and compares it to 200 guineas received earlier from Lord Arlington for less than one tenth of the work (*p* xl–xli). He also worked for the Elector of Brandenburg deciphering some '200–300 sheets of very difficult and different ciphers with no reward'. He was promised a rich medal and a gold chain, but only received it long after; it can be seen in the portrait of him by Kneller (in the Examination Schools at Oxford and reproduced here as a frontispiece). He was finally granted a pension of £100 per annum in 1700 with survivorship to his grandson, William Blencow, whom he had instructed in his method of deciphering (see Pepys–Tanner I.172 – letter from Pepys written to Dr Charlett, 15 May 1699).

[f] Teaching the deaf
The art of teaching deaf-mutes was known before Wallis's day, though it is not clear how far it was known in England. In Spain it

had been successfully practised by Pedro Ponce de León (1520–1584) and after him by Juan Pablo Bonet (*Reduction de las letras*, 1620) who claimed to have founded the art, and taught the son of the Constable of Castile (see Holder, 1678, *pp* 5–6). Kenelm Digby witnessed this while on a visit to Spain (*Of bodies*, 1669, *p* 320) and it was known to Dr John Bulwer (*Chirologia*, 1644; *Philocophus*, 1648). Wallis (1678, *p* 20) maintained that he knew nothing of Bonet's method nor of Digby's account of him, but had worked out his own method, based on the description of sounds contained in the first edition (1653) of the *Tractatus de Loquela* and the Grammar (see Author's Preface *p* 117 and the letter to Robert Boyle, 14 March 1662 – published in *Philos. Trans.*, 18 July 1670, 1087–1097). However this may be, he claimed to have taught two deaf-mutes to speak, namely Daniel Whaley, son of the Mayor of Northampton, in the years 1661–2, and Alexander Popham, son of Lady Wharton by her previous husband Admiral Popham, in the year 1662. Whaley, then about twenty-six, had lost his hearing when he was five years old. Popham was about twelve and had been deaf and dumb from birth. Wallis made much of his achievement, producing Whaley before the Royal Society on 21 May 1662 to demonstrate his success, and also before the King. He implied in a postscript to his letter to Robert Boyle that he had been the first to teach Popham to speak. This letter, though written in 1662, was not published until 1670. Meanwhile Wallis's contemporary, William Holder (1616–1698), rector of Bletchington near Oxford and later successively Canon of Ely and of St Paul's, had published his *Elements of Speech* (1669), to which he appended his own method for teaching the deaf, and claimed he had been the first to teach Popham to speak. He had also published an article (*An Experiment concerning Deafness*) in *Philosophical Transactions*, May 1668, 665–668. The publication of Wallis's letter to Boyle sparked off a fierce quarrel with Holder; in a Supplement to the *Philosophical Transactions* of July 1670, publication of which was for various reasons delayed till 1678, Holder again claimed priority in teaching Popham (in 1659), and said Wallis knew this perfectly well and had witnessed the result at Bletchington. The Supplement contained a Preface by Oldenburgh, publisher of the *Philosophical Transactions*, making it clear that he associated himself with Holder's remarks and deplored Wallis's conduct. Holder was further incensed by the fact that Wallis's achievement had been extolled again in Dr Robert Plot's *History of*

Oxfordshire (1677), in a passage which Holder alleged had been written by Wallis himself. Wallis hastened to reply to Holder's charges and in 1678 published *A Defence of the Royal Society* where, in more than thirty pages, he attempted to justify himself and to refute Holder's allegations. The truth of the matter is not easy to assess. It was certainly true that Holder had taught Popham first, but Wallis claimed that by the time Popham came to him he had lost any abilities that he might have had two years before. Wallis's detractors had splendid ammunition here. Anthony Wood (1891, I.309–10; 1691–2, II.815–16) condemned him, and so did John Aubrey in his *Lives* of Holder and of Wallis, though one must remember that Aubrey was a very close friend of Holder's, so his evidence is suspect; and Wood was one of Wallis's most bitter critics. Thomas Hearne also joined in the criticism (26 April 1711 – Hearne (1711), III.155) but admitted himself that he was prejudiced against Wallis. There is little doubt that Wallis knew of Holder's teaching Popham; his protestations are over-elaborate and lack the ring of truth. It is possible to find witnesses who will testify to the honesty both of Holder (Aubrey's *Life*, which calls him 'a perfect good man') and of Wallis (Lewis's *Life*, and *Biographia Britannica*, Vol VI, Part II, 4128, 4135), but the evidence in general is in favour of Holder. His *Elements of Speech* was an improvement on Wallis's description of speech sounds and Wallis was not one to delight in the achievements of others. Aubrey claims that the famous mathematician William Oughtred in the preface to his *Clavis Mathematica* (1667 edition) gave Wallis a worthy character, but that, unknown to him, Wallis as editor contrived to add a section praising his own ability as a decipherer, which Oughtred only saw when the book was printed. Stories of this kind may be exaggerated but the fact remains that here was a man who liked to have his own achievements, which were many, made known as widely as possible.

The main accounts of his own methods of teaching the deaf are contained in three letters: (i) to Robert Boyle, (see *p* 12); (ii) to Dr Thomas Beverley, 30 September 1698 (to be found [*a*] in *Philos. Trans.*, October 1698, [*b*] in Vol III of Wallis's Collected Works, 1699, *pp* 696–700, [*c*] appended to the 6th edition (1765) of the Grammar); (iii) to Conrad Amman, 1669–1724 – a Swiss-born doctor living in Holland, who had formulated his own method for teaching the deaf – January 1700 (to be found prefaced to Amman's *Dissertatio de Loquela*, 1700; this was later published jointly with

Wallis's *De Loquela* in 1727 and 1740). Lehnert (1938) describes the seventeenth-century situation with regard to deaf-teaching, and shows that success in teaching the deaf to speak was still commonly regarded as a kind of miracle.

[g] The Oxford Don

Wallis moved to Oxford when he became Savilian Professor of Geometry in 1649 and lived there for the rest of his life. From Lewis's *Life* we gather that as Professor he was expected to lecture twice a week, on Wednesday and Saturday at 8 am. All scholars of two years' standing had to attend until they had been Bachelors for one year, on penalty of paying a fine of sixpence! He took an active part in university life, as can be seen from his letters. In 1658 he was elected *Custos Archivorum*, which involved looking after the archives of the University, and defining the University's rights and privileges in law suits (for example, in the dispute with the Stationers' Company of London over printing rights – see Bodleian MS Rawl. A.171, letters to Pepys dated 20 April 1688, *ff* 26–27 and 36). His rival for election was Dr Richard Zouch, who had been Assessor in the Vice-Chancellor's Court for thirty years and was well versed in the Statutes, etc. Wallis was attacked, after his election, by Henry Stubbe – *The Savilian Professor's Case Stated* (1658). Stubbe alleged that Zouch had been defeated only through the connivance of the Vice-Chancellor and the Senior Proctor, who wanted to keep Zouch out because of his Royalist sympathies. He also claimed that it was illegal for a Savilian Professor to hold this office. Wallis had stated his case (*Reasons showing the consistency of the place of Custos Archivorum with that of a Savilian Professor*, 1657) and the appointment continued, but it rankled with his opponents, particularly Anthony Wood (1691–2, II.415, 627). He considered himself ill used by Wallis who later, as *Custos Archivorum*, Wood alleges, took away all the writings and registers which he, Wood, had had in his keeping for eighteen years (Wood, (1891), II.424), and in February 1681 refused to let him have any books out of the archives and took away his key by a trick (Wood (1891), II.517, III.84). The quarrel continued, and eventually Wallis threatened an action against Wood (August 1692) because of references made to him in *Athenae Oxonienses* II. In *Life and Times* (II.507–8, December 1680) Wood describes Wallis as an enemy of King and Church and indifferent to what master he served, 'a liver by perjury . . . ambitious and impudent . . . impaling his wife's arms with his, whereas she was but a poor wench and came in her blew pettycote and green stockings to Oxford . . . Cozning and cheating the University by spending their money in his owne business at London.' But Wallis continued to be Keeper of the Archives till his death, and his portrait, presented to the university by Samuel Pepys in 1702, hangs in the Examination Schools in Oxford, a gift for which Pepys received a fulsome tribute from the university, containing a generous appreciation of Wallis's services.

5 Wallis's character

[a] Contemporary views

It has already become apparent that many of the contemporary accounts were written by men who had come to blows with Wallis for various reasons: Hobbes (mathematics), Stubbe and Wood (the post of *Custos Archivorum*), Holder (deaf-teaching). They all agree that he was a proud, arrogant man who liked to claim credit for other people's work. John Aubrey, a friend of Hobbes and Holder, said: 'To give him his due prayse he hath exceedingly well deserved of the commonwealth of learning, perhaps no mathematical writer so much. Tis certain that he is a person of real worth, and may stand with much glory upon his own basis, needing not to be beholding to any man for fame, of which he is so extremely greedy, that he steals flowers from others to adorne his own cap.' Holder (1678, *p* 10) speaks of him in very similar terms. Hobbes and Wood had nothing good to say about him.

Pepys often met and corresponded with Wallis in his later years and obviously had a great affection and admiration for him, though the first time they met he had not been impressed (Diary, 16 December 1666). His correspondence with Dr Charlett, Master of University College Oxford, and others, shows Wallis in a good light (references are to Tanner, 1926):

(i) Charlett to Pepys, 31 March 1699 (I.171): 'This good old gentleman is now as fresh and vigorous for any new understanding (of any sort) as if he had never put pen to paper and I know he longs to be at Euclid, though he pretends to me he intends to play all the Easter holidays if I do not find him work.'

(ii) Charlett to Pepys, 15 May 1699 (I.172): 'Dr Wallis complains often of decays but none else can perceive them . . . He says 83 is an incurable distemper. I believe Death will no more surprise him than a proposition in Mathematicks.'

(iii) Kneller to Pepys (II.255): 'I can show I never did a better picture nor so good a one in my life, which is the opinion of all that has seen it, and which I have done meerly for the respect I have for your person, fame and reputation, and for the love of so great a man as Dr Wallis.'

(iv) Pepys to Kneller, 28 March 1702 (II.256): 'I have long determined . . . upon providing as far as I could by your hand towards immortalising the memory of the person (for his name can never dye) of that great man and my most honoured friend, Dr Wallis.'

In 1695 Wallis presented Pepys with a copy of his Collected Works (I.107). Pepys died before him (26 May 1703) and the last letter in his own hand is a reply to the letter Wallis wrote thanking him for the portrait by Kneller (presented to the University of Oxford in 1702).

Dr Gregory, Savilian Professor of Astronomy in Oxford during the latter part of Wallis's life, wrote a short biography (see Introduction *p* 1). It includes a description of Wallis: 'He was of low stature, well shaped, black-haird, but by reason of age, before he dyed, very white. He enjoyed a very uninterrupted health, which he maintained rather by sobriety than exercise, which he very little favoured. He preserved the solidity and the quickness of his judgement and eye-sight to the last, even without spectacles.'

George Hickes in the preface to his *Anglo-Saxon Grammar* (1689) wrote 'quantum domi forisque celebratur consummatus ille Geometer ac Theologus Johannes Wallisius noster, qui infra gloriam suam non duxit Grammaticam Linguae Anglicanae nova prorsus methodo scribere'.[1]

Lewis's *Life* (1735, see *p* 2) is clearly biased towards Wallis but worth quoting: 'Though while he lived he was looked on by the most rigid and zealous party men in the University with a jealous eye, and suspected as not thoroughly well affected to the Monarchy and Church of England, he was yet very much honoured and esteemed by others of a better temper and judgment and of more knowledge and larger thoughts. By these, both at home and abroad, was he reckoned the glory and ornament of his country and of the University in particular.'

---

[1] 'How widely famous, at home and abroad, is that peerless geometer and theologian of ours, John Wallis, who thought it not beneath his reputation to write a Grammar of the English Language, using a totally new method.'

The article in *Biographia Britannica* (Vol VI, Part II, 1766) described him as having 'impartiality and candour' and being endued with 'a comprehensive latitude of temper which gave each party in any controversy room enough to be easy in his decision' (4128). It goes on (4135) 'the easiness of his temper will never be questioned by any who, reflecting on that merit that made him the boast of his own country, as well as the envy of the rest of Europe, sees him showing no kind of discontent at being neglected, though he saw his two co-rivals, Ward and Wilkins, equally obnoxious to the government with himself, get raised to the highest dignity in the Church.'

Finally his own view of himself. He writes (letter to Dr Smith, 1697): 'It has been mine endeavour all along to act by moderate principles, between the extremities on either hand, in a moderate compliance with the Powers in being, in those places, where it hath been my lot to live, without the fierce and violent animosities usual in such cases against all that did not act just as I did, knowing that there were many worthy persons engaged on either side and willing ... if things could not be just, as I could wish, to make the best of what is; and hereby (thro' God's gracious Providence) have been able to live easy, and useful, though not great.'

[b] Later views

There has been no complete biography of Wallis, but many writers since his time have praised his works. For mathematicians' views one may consult histories of mathematics (*eg* Scott, 1958), and his fame as a grammarian will be the subject of a later section. Morel in his dissertation (1895) did not attempt to assess Wallis's achievements. Lehnert (1936, § 18) counts him among the greatest intellects of his time; he pays tribute to Wallis's remarkable ability to reconcile opposing views and factions, his clear self-knowledge – 'I have been able to live easy and useful, though not great' – and his astonishing versatility, manifest in the titles of his works. Several times in his book he talks of Wallis's practical outlook as typical of Englishmen.

Some have criticised his facility in transferring his loyalties from King to Parliament, from Parliament to King, from James Stuart to William of Orange, from Presbyterian to Anglican, as showing weakness and lack of conviction. But he was not afraid to stand out against Charles's execution (see Lewis's *Life*), and his views on religion were tolerant rather than vacillating. Apparently, however, he could not tolerate ignorance masquerading as knowledge, for his attack on Hobbes was merciless. As to his arrogance, it may well be that this is accentuated by his rivals to vent their jealousy on him for being better than they were. Academic jealousy has always been a stimulus to fierce and unreasoning feuds in which supposedly philosophic and intelligent men show an astonishing blood-lust and parochiality of mind. Wallis's achievements were many, and he had no need to exaggerate them, but he liked to think of himself as a pioneer; for example, in taking up mathematics when others despised it (Hearne (1725), III.cxlvii–viii); in promulgating new ideas (Circulation of the Blood – ibid, cl); in forsaking the common road (same page); in deciphering (clix–clx); in the New Philosophy (clxii–iii); in the description of sounds and grammar, and teaching of the deaf (clxv–clxvi). He was indeed a pioneer, but where he found himself not after all first, as in his dispute with Holder, his ambition was frustrated. In his old age he appears to have been respected and admired in his own university circle, but had outlived most of his friends and contemporaries. He was buried in St Mary's, Oxford. Ralph Thoresby (*Letters of Eminent Men* (1832), III.43) quotes a letter from the Rev Cavendish Nevile written on 13 December 1703, containing the following passage: 'Dr Wallis, I suppose you hear, is dead, and buried by an ungrateful son, unworthy the character of so learned and so rich a person, there not being above eighteen scholars at his funeral.'

6 Wallis the grammarian

In his letter to Dr Thomas Smith (1697) Wallis says:[1] 'In the year 1653 I was persuaded to publish a Grammar of the English Tongue; chiefly to gratify strangers, who were willing to learn it . . . but complained of its difficulty for want of a Grammar, suited to the propriety and true Genius of the Language. To this I prefixed a Treatise of Speech (*de loquela*) wherein I have philosophically considered the Formation of all Sounds used in Articulate Speech (as well of our own, as of any other Language that I know); By what Organs, and in what Position each sound was formed; with the nice distinctions of each, (which in some letters of the same Organ, is very subtil:) so that, by such Organs, in such Position, the Breath issuing from the Lungs, will form such Sounds, whether the Person do or do not hear

[1] Hearne (1725), III.clxv.

himself speak. Which was, I think, a new attempt, not before undertaken by any (that I know of) before that time. For tho' it were observed, that some letters were Labials, some Dentals, some Palatines, and some Gutturals; and some Grammarians have in some few shewed a different Formation of the same Organ; yet it is but of very few they have so done; and very imperfectly; None (that I know of) had before attempted it, as to all; whatever may have been done since in pursuance of what I had then taught.' In the Author's Preface to the Grammar he had made a similar claim to be the first to have attempted to describe English in terms of its own characteristic structure, instead of in terms of Latin, and also the first to have made a systematic description of the whole structure of speech in terms of the various articulations involved (*p* 109 *ff*).

Before we examine Wallis's Grammar itself it may be helpful to consider briefly some aspects of the Western tradition of grammar writing which he inherited. That part which concerns the description of sounds is dealt with in section 7 of this Introduction. Fuller accounts of the history of early grammars are to be found in Arens (1955), Dinneen (1967), Jeep (1893), Jellinek (1913), Kukenheim (1932, 1951, 1962), Robins (1967), and Steinthal (1890–91).

[*a*] *Aspects of the Western grammatical tradition before Wallis*
The origins of grammar in the West go back to Greece. For the Greeks grammar was, on the one hand, closely associated with philosophy – important contributions to its early development came from Plato, Aristotle and the Stoics – and on the other hand with literary criticism; the elucidation and interpretation of early Greek writers such as Homer was the main concern of the Alexandrian scholars, whose work was codified by Dionysius Thrax (*c* 100 BC).

The Greek philosophers associated grammar closely with logic. The Greek word ὄνομα (*onoma*) in addition to its common meaning *name* is used in the sense of *word, noun, subject*, and *logical subject*, and Plato's terms ὄνομα and ῥῆμα (*onoma, rhēma*), sometimes translated *noun* and *verb*, correspond more closely to *subject* and *predicate*. Aristotle used the same two terms but added a third, σύνδεσμοι (*syndesmoi*), comprising words lacking the syntactic independence of *onoma* and *rhēma*: article, pronoun, conjunction and perhaps preposition. The Stoic philosophers devoted considerable attention to language analysis, but unfortunately their works survive only in secondary sources. They split Aristotle's *syndesmoi* into two groups – inflected and uninflected – and divided his *onoma* into proper and common nouns. The grammatical category of case (πτῶσις) was restricted to nouns and similarly inflected words (see also note 108, *p* 319), and the importance of aspect (completion/non-completion) in the verb was recognised. However, it was the Alexandrian tradition as codified by Dionysius Thrax which had the major influence on subsequent grammatical developments. The *Τέχνη γραμματική* of Dionysius Thrax is the earliest surviving grammar of Greek. It shows a number of differences from the Stoics' description, most notably in the increase of the number of word-classes to eight: noun, verb, participle, article, pronoun, adverb, conjunction, preposition. Attributes of the various word-classes included gender, number, case, person, mood, voice, tense, conjugation. The scope of the grammar includes the sounds, and the inflections and derivations of the word, but no syntax. This deficiency was remedied by the works of Apollonius Dyscolus (second century AD).

In spite of the efforts of such individual thinkers as Varro (116–27 BC) to modify the classifications of the word-classes and grammatical categories so as to suit the Latin language better, most Latin grammarians followed Dionysius Thrax and Apollonius Dyscolus. The grammars of Donatus (fourth century AD) and Priscian (sixth century AD) represent the cumulated expression of this tradition; through them it was transmitted to the medieval grammarians and to Renaissance Europe. Priscian's order of description – *litterae* (sounds), *syllabae* (syllables), *dictio* (word), *oratio* (sentence) – is reflected in the medieval scheme: *orthographia* (letters and pronunciation), *prosodia* (prosody), *etymologia* (grammar of the word), and *syntax*. The grammatical categories of Greek were translated into Latin, and in most instances the difference was not great enough to require changes. To the Greek cases (nominative, vocative, accusative, genitive, dative) it was necessary to add ablative, but, to take one example, the Greek optative mood was preserved in spite of the lack of a distinctive paradigm for it in Latin. We shall find examples of a similar inclination to accept earlier descriptions uncritically when we come to consider the early grammars of the European vernacular languages.

The grammarians of the Middle Ages were particularly concerned with the logical basis for grammar, and sought to discover common features in all languages, based on the mental 'affections' common to all men. Some advances were made in syntax: the idea of government (*rectio*, *regimen*) is treated more fully (see *p* 38) and the noun class is subdivided into noun-substantive and noun-adjective, on the basis of the syntactic independence of the former, not shared by the latter. The separation of noun and adjective as independent parts of speech did not take place, however, until the eighteenth century (R. Johnson, 1706).

In the fourteenth century the literary masterpieces of Dante, Boccaccio and Petrarch and Dante's treatise *De vulgari eloquentia* (On the eloquence of the vernacular) stimulated the study of the vernacular language in Italy and other European countries. However, the revival of interest in the ancient classics which came with the Renaissance served to strengthen the conviction that Greek and Latin had reached a perfection of expression which could not be equalled by any vernacular language. Latin remained the language of scholarship and an essential requirement for all educated men, though it was now the Latin of Cicero that was to be acquired, not the Vulgar Latin which had served as a second language throughout Europe in the Middle Ages. The rise of the vernaculars also received a stimulus from the discovery of printing, and their value as a unifying factor was perceived by many of the rulers of the time. Increasingly they were taken as a symbol of patriotism, and in England Robert Mulcaster (*c* 1530–1611), headmaster of St Paul's School and an educational reformer, was not slow to extol the merits of English, which he considered had already reached its zenith and had no need to give precedence to any other language. But until it was shown that the vernaculars could exhibit grammatical regularities reducible to rules in the same way as Latin there could be no real challenge to the classical languages. It was only to be expected, therefore, that early grammars of the vernaculars should model themselves on Latin; where there were inescapable differences various expedients were resorted to in order to preserve an appearance of similarity.

In the fifteenth century one of the most pressing problems was the establishment of a satisfactory orthography for vernacular languages. Historical changes in the sounds had led to a situation in which the words as written were often far from conveying the phonetic value in any consistent way, and in many countries attempts were made to reform the spelling. For this reason the first section of grammars, *orthographia*, tended to be the longest. *Etymologia* was usually the next in length, but prosody and syntax were often virtually ignored. In England two notable early spelling reformers were John Hart (see Hart, 1955) and Sir Thomas Smith, 1568 (see Introduction *p* 40); and on the Continent spelling reformers included Nebrija in Spain (see *p* 213), Trissino in Italy (1524)[1] and Meigret in France (1542).[2] There was considerable confusion of sound and symbol (see *p* 63), and most of these early grammars of the vernaculars took the written and not the spoken language as their basis. The choice of which dialect to describe in some cases presented a problem, but in general the pronunciation with most prestige was that used by the Court of the rulers. It is noteworthy that grammars of Catalan and Provençal were written long before grammars of Italian, Spanish or French.

Petrus Ramus (1515–72) was strongly opposed to the scholasticism of the Middle Ages, with its abstract approach to language description and dependence on Aristotelian philosophy. His Latin grammar (1559) adopted a new division into only two parts which he called *Etymologia* and *Syntaxis*. He regarded *Orthographia* and *Prosodia* as aspects which permeate the whole of a language, not to be confined to a description of letter and syllable as if totally separate from word and sentence. He had considerable influence on later writers, and in particular on Franciscus Sanctius of Spain (1554–1628) who published his *Minerva, seu de causis linguae Latinae* in 1587, and on the English grammarians Paul Greaves (1594) and Ben Jonson (1640). However, the main stream of the Donatus-Priscian tradition is represented in the Latin grammars of Thomas Linacre (*De emendata structura Latini sermonis*, 1524), and Lily (*A shorte introduction of grammar*, 1557 edition and later), whose influence in England was very strong; Lily's Grammar was certainly used as a basis by Bullokar in writing the first grammar of English (1586). In Germany the early grammars of German, for example those of L. Albertus (1573)[3] and Johannes Clajus (1578),[4] followed the pattern of Latin, and were written in Latin, chiefly with a view to enabling foreigners to learn German (Jellinek, 1913, *pp* 60–63).

The influence of Latin is chiefly obvious in the treatment of the parts of speech and grammatical categories such as case, number, gender, tense, mood. All educated men knew Latin, and were at

[1] *Epistola delle lettere nuovamente aggiunte nella lingua italiana a papa Clemente* VII (ed Daelli, Milano, 1864).
[2] *Traite touchant le commun usage de l'escriture françoise.*
[3] *Teutsch Grammatick oder Sprach-Kunst.*
[4] *Grammatica Germanicae linguae.*

home with the traditional Latin terminology. However, there were those who felt that the traditional priority of Latin in schools and the whole idea of learning languages by grammatical rules was based on the wrong principles. In Germany Wolfgang Ratke (Ratichius, 1571–1635), a schoolmaster, made it his aim to reform existing methods. His comparative lack of success appears to have been due in no small part to his arrogance and tactlessness, though his ideas were in advance of his time. Like another great educational reformer of the seventeenth century, Johann Amos Comenius (1592–1670), he urged the advantages of using the mother tongue as a basis for instruction in all subjects, and the teaching of its grammar before that of any other language. Again like Comenius he was strictly against the standard method of teaching languages through rote learning of grammatical rules, and strongly advocated the use of all possible means to arouse the pupils' interest. Another of Ratke's ideas was that all grammars would have something in common, so that German grammar could form a basis for any other language, with suitable modifications. His dictum was *omnia docenda per notiora* – 'all things should be taught through what is more familiar'. He did not himself publish a grammar, but an account of his method is given in the preface to Eilhard Lubinus's translation of the New Testament (1615) and in *In Methodum Linguarum generalis introductio* (ed P. Stotzner, in *Neudrucke Pädagogischer Schriften* XII.38);[1] see also Ising (1959). Among books based on his method were the *Grammatica universalis pro didactica Ratichii* (*c* 1619) which appeared both in Latin and in German, and Helwig's *Libri didactici Grammaticae Universalis*, also published in Latin and German editions, posthumously, in 1617 (see Jellinek, 1913, *pp* 90–94).

In England similar misgivings about methods of language teaching had been expressed by Ascham and Mulcaster, but the first man to propose a radical change, along very much the same lines as Ratke in Germany, was Joseph Webbe (see Salmon, 1961). His important publications fell within the period 1622–29, when it seems likely that he was already advanced in years. Like Ratke he deplores the use of rote learning of rules and isolated words and emphasises the advantages of learning groups of words in their customary collocations.

[1] I am indebted for these references to V. Salmon's article (1961).

The parts of speech remained at the traditional eight in most vernacular grammars of the time. There were some exceptions; somewhat earlier Fortunio (*Regole grammaticali della volgar lingua*,
1516) had restricted the parts of speech in Italian to four – noun,
pronoun, verb, adverb – and Nebrija (1492) in Spain had increased
them to ten, including the gerundive and the 'nombre participial
infinito', an invariable participle (Kukenheim, 1932, *p* 99). Meigret
(*La Tretté de la grammere françoeze*, 1550, *p* 26) has eight parts, but
adds the article as an extra, outside the scheme. Petrus Ramus in his
Latin grammar (1559) followed the Aristotelian scheme (see *p* 19);
he groups noun and verb together, separating them from his second
class by their possession of the category *number* (see Funke (1941),
and Greaves (1594) ed Funke, introduction). Two English grammarians, P. Greaves (1594) and Ben Jonson (1640), chose to adopt
Ramus's scheme, and Hume (1617) was also influenced by him,
though he substitutes *person* for *number* as his criterion for division
into word-classes. Bullokar wrote the first English grammar in
English (1586) and in this we see an example of the tradition inherited from Priscian through Linacre and Lily (see *p* 22). The eight
parts of speech of Latin are preserved intact, and the article is
treated simply as a 'sign' of the substantive, not as a separate part
of speech. The influence of Latin on the classification into word-
classes is paralleled by its influence on the grammatical categories
used for describing the vernaculars. The most obvious way in which
they differed from Latin was in their comparative lack of inflectional endings. A strict consideration of this alone would in many of
them have resulted in the disappearance of such categories as *case*
in substantives and adjectives, *gender* (as distinct from sex) in substantives, adjectives and pronouns, *number* in adjectives, and many
of the Latin *mood* and *tense* distinctions in verbs. However, in most
grammars, other considerations are introduced in order to preserve
the Latin categories.

Of English grammars before Wallis only Greaves (1594) excludes
the category of case from substantives. Bullokar (1586) has five
cases, which correspond to Latin nominative, accusative, genitive,
dative and vocative; none of them, except for the genitive, has a
distinct termination. In the sentence 'John gives Richard the book'
Richard is taken to be the equivalent of the Latin dative (which
Bullokar calls 'gainative'). However in 'he gives the book to
Richard' *Richard* is accusative, because according to Bullokar all

prepositions are followed by the accusative case. The adjective too, though invariable in form, is said to have cases. Hume (1617) and Gil (1619) also keep the Latin cases, but regard them as marked by syntactic position (nominative before the verb, accusative after it), or by the use of certain prepositions – *of* being a sign of the genitive, for instance, *to* of the dative, *in* of the ablative, and *O* of the vocative. A distinction between 'termination cases' and 'sign cases' is made in the earliest Italian grammarians. In *Regole della lingua fiorentina*, which was published before 1495, the various combinations of article or preposition + article with noun are taken as different cases: *el cielo, del cielo, al cielo, O cielo, dal cielo* (see Kukenheim (1932), *p* 108 *ff*, 140). Fortunio (1516),[1] however, reserves the term *case* for the pronouns, which show changes of termination, while Bembo (1525)[2] suggests a possible distinction between the particles *di, da* and *a*, which he calls case-signs (segni de' casi) and prepositions. Of the later sixteenth-century Italian grammarians Castelvetro (1563)[3] rejects this distinction, and Ruscelli (1581) wishes to separate *di, da* and *a* as case-signs in some uses (*eg: padrone di casa*) and prepositions in others (*sono partito di casa*). In France Meigret (1550) (see *p* 24) and Cauchie (1570) admit case only in pronouns, where indicated by different terminations, and Ramus (1562) omits any discussion of it. Robert Estienne (1558) does not use the term 'case-sign', but regards the words *de, du, à, au, les, aux, des* as indicators of cases. In Germany the situation was somewhat different, in that the article and noun still retained distinctive case terminations. Early grammars of German accept the Latin cases, but later Helwig (1617)[4] restricts them to four in number. In England Hume extended the idea of 'signs' to cover other features of English grammar. For example, the personal pronoun is taken to be a 'sign' of gender, number and person, and the article a 'sign' of the difference between substantive and adjective. Hume is no doubt influenced in this by Ramus, who concedes that words that show no formal change of termination may still be held to exhibit a particular category (for example, indeclinable nouns in Latin, such as *nefas*, can still be regarded as having the category *number*, by analogy with other nouns).

---

[1] see *p* 24.
[2] *Prose della Volgar Lingua* (ed Sonzogno, Milano, 1927).
[3] *Giunta fatta al Ragionamento degli Articoli et de' Verbi de messer Pietro Bembo.*
[4] see *p* 23.

It was recognised in many early writers (see Chomsky, 1966 *pp* 44–5; Salmon, 1969) that though semantically similar relationships may be expressed in quite different ways in different languages, these languages may often be said to possess the same underlying structure. Chomsky (loc cit) writes: 'It is important to realise that the use of the names of classical cases for languages with no inflections implies only a belief in the uniformity of the grammatical relations involved, a belief that deep structures are fundamentally the same across languages, although the means for their expression may be quite diverse.' *Cf* Lyons (1968, *p* 302): 'Although the category of case is traditionally restricted to inflexional variation, it is clear that both the "grammatical" and "local" functions . . . are logically independent of the way in which they are realised in particular languages. Furthermore, these "grammatical" and "local" functions may be realised in the same language partly by case inflexions and partly by other means – most commonly by prepositions or postpositions, or by word-order. This means that the category of case cannot be discussed solely from a morphological point of view.' This is not to say, however, that all the early grammarians were aware of this; many, perhaps most, were motivated simply by a wish to find a way of retaining the Latin framework, and often the equivalences drawn are too precise and rigid.

What has been said of case applies also to the other Latin categories. In Latin *number* is formally marked in adjectives, as well as in nouns, pronouns and verbs, and so one finds early English grammarians attributing number to the English adjective, in spite of its invariable form, by virtue of its association with substantives in the singular and plural. In Greek and Latin three, or more, *genders* were distinguished on the basis, at least in part, of distinctive terminations. In English the distinction of the different sexes is often equated by early grammarians with Latin gender, which frequently does not correspond with sex (see *p* 279 *f*). Bullokar (1586) has six genders, Hume and Gil three; sometimes the personal pronoun is taken to be the formal mark of gender in English, though Greaves is one of the few who excluded gender even from pronouns. Descriptions of the verb mostly take over the full Latin tense system, but Jonson recognises that in English there is no formal mark of a difference between present and future in the verb itself. The auxiliary verbs *will, shall, have, had* are taken as markers of the tenses corresponding to Latin future, future perfect, perfect and pluperfect.

Similarly in the case of the Latin moods: Greaves and Jonson, following Ramus, exclude the category of mood, but Bullokar has all five (indicative, imperative, subjunctive, optative, and infinitive). Gil and Butler omit subjunctive and optative, but introduce a *potential* mood instead. As with tenses, auxiliary verbs (and the particle *to*) are regarded as 'signs' of the moods, *eg: let* and *shall* for imperative, *may, might, can, should, would, could* for potential.

Some English grammarians of this period retain declensions and conjugations; in the classical languages these were based on formal differences in the paradigms of nouns and verbs respectively. English having no case terminations, we find differences in the plural form of substantives used as a criterion for declensions: Gil has three – (i) substantives which show a vowel change or no change at all in the plural, *eg: foot, sheep*; (ii) those with plurals in [s] or [z]; (iii) those which are imparisyllabic in singular and plural, *eg: house/houses*. Jonson's two declensions are also based on plural formation: (i) those that end in *s*; (ii) those that end in *en* (*oxen* etc). Gil's conjugations are distinguished by characteristics of the stem-vowel in present and past tenses: (i) no changes, or change only of length – *love, bite, leave, cast*, etc; (ii) vowel shows one change in imperfect past and past participle – *come, run, think*; (iii) vowel shows two changes, one in imperfect past and another in the past participle – *swim, swam, swum*, etc. Bullokar's three conjugations have quite a different basis: (i) active and neuter verbs – there is no category of passive verbs; (ii) the verb substantive – *to be*; (iii) the verb neuter imperfect – comprising verbs that require an infinitive of another verb to complete their construction – *may, can, might, could, would, should, must, ought*, and (sometimes) *will*.

For a more detailed account of these early grammars of the vernacular languages see Funke (1941), Jellinek (1913), Kukenheim (1932), Poldauf (1948), Vorlat (1963), Michael (1970).

[*b*] *Wallis's Grammar*

If we consider first the overall layout of Wallis's Grammar we find that it resembles the traditional plan, starting with a chapter on pronunciation, though without any proposals for spelling reform, and continuing with a description of the parts of speech, which corresponds to the section traditionally called *etymologia*, with a few remarks on syntax added (Chapters II–XIII, the syntactical remarks being mostly within Chapters IV and XI – *pp* 289 *f*, 349–55).

Chapter xv, *On Poetry*, is a brief account of English prosody. Chapter xiv is entitled *On Etymology*, but uses the word in the classical and modern sense of word-formation and derivation. Since Chapters xiv and xv are not included in this edition a summary of them at this stage will help to give an idea of the work as a whole. In the 4th edition (1674) Wallis almost doubled the length of Chapter xiv; in the 5th edition (1699) it is again expanded and is more than three times as long as in the 1st edition. For sound symbolism *cf* Bloomfield (1935), *p* 245; Bolinger (1965), Part ii; Jespersen (1922), *pp* 312 *ff*, 396 *ff*.

Chapter xiv, On Etymology

Section I. Regular word formation (Analogice formata): Possessive adjective, etc in *r(e)*; *you/your, they/theyre*; *husband-ry*, *forge-ry*, etc. Formation of verbs from substantives: *a house/ to house*, etc; *haste, to hasten*, etc. Adjectives formed from substantives: *louse/lousy*; *wealth/wealthy*, etc; *joy/joyful*, etc; *delight/ delightsome*, etc; *worth/worthless*, etc. Prefixes *un-, in-, en-, dis-, mis-*. Adjectives in *-ly*. Diminutive adjectives in *-ish*. Diminutive substantives in *-ock* (*hillock*), in *(r)el* (*cockrel, satchel*), in *-ling, -kin*. Augmentatives *sup/sip*; *top/tip*; *swallow/swill*; *little/lee-tle*. Abstract substantives in *-ness, -head, -hood, -th* (*depth*, etc), *-ship, -dom(e), -ric(k), -wick* (*bailywick*). Occupational substantives in *-monger*. Substantives in *-ment, -age, -tion*.

Section II. Remoter derivations: Beat/bat/battle/batter, etc; *twig/twitch/twinge*, etc. He tries to find common meanings in consonant clusters: for example, *sn* – the nose (*sniff, snuffle, snarl*, etc); *sh* – subterfuge and protection (*shun, shame, shade*, etc); *bl* – breath (*blow, bleak, bluster*, etc); *str* – power (*strength, strive, stress*, etc); *thr* – violent motion (*throw, thrust, throb*, etc); *wr* – distortion (*wry, wrestle, wriggle*, etc); *cr* – something broken, bent or displaced (*crack, crumb, crush*, etc); *shr* – stronger contraction (*shrunk, shrivel, shrimp*, etc); *gr* – something hard, troublesome (*grate, grind, grief*, etc); *sw* – silent or soft movement (*swing, swim, sway*, etc); *cl* – adherence (*cleave, clasp, clot*, etc); *sp* – scattering (*spread, split, spill*, etc); *sl* – silent movement (*slip, slide*, etc). Also in terminations: *-ash/-ush, -ing, -ink, -ingle, inkle, -umble, -amble* in which he says the vowels signify different types of action, *i* being slighter, *a* next, and *u* more ponderous. He then goes on to list words derived from Latin (via French) and words shared with the Germans, which, he says, may have come from Latin or Teutonic; also words derived directly from Greek. There follows a long list of derivations, showing how in the transition words have lost initial or final segments. Finally there is an attempt to show how some words have originated from a combination of two others; for example, *gruff* from *grave* and *rough*.

Chapter xv, On Poetry

This chapter is comparatively brief. Wallis says that the prime factor is the *number* of syllables, though quantity also plays its part. Poetry is distinguished from prose particularly by its freer word order. He regards the iambic metre as most suited to English, but gives examples also of trochaic and dactylic metres. Psalm 2 is rendered in dactylic hexameters, and also in sapphics. There is no attempt to formulate a general theory of English prosody. All he says is that many syllables may be either long or short, but that it is vital for the syllables bearing most emphasis, whether because of the 'accent of the voice or the meaning of the sentence' (*sive pro accentu vocis, sive pro ratione sententiae*), to have the greater length. He compares

> The mán is blést that háth not bént,
> to wícked réad, his eár

with

> Bлесséd is thé man, thát hath nót
> bent, tó wickéd read, hís . . .

as examples of iambic metre, the second being '*versus . . . plane horridus*', because of the lack of observance of this rule.

In general, then, Wallis adheres to the traditional scheme of presentation. Moreover, he states in the Author's Preface (*p* 113) that he intends to keep the terminology of Latin, in spite of the fact that it is not entirely suited to English, because of its familiarity and his unwillingness to make innovations unnecessarily. Since all educated men could be assumed to know Latin, the use of it as an approach to English grammar was normal, though, owing to the efforts of such men as Ascham, Mulcaster and Joseph Webbe (see *p* 23), the idea of reversing the order and using English grammar to approach Latin was becoming increasingly common. But Wallis warns the reader against assuming that Latin grammar has *exact* equivalences in English, and gives the lack of case endings in English as an example. He excludes case from his description of English, while accepting that word-order and prepositions perform a similar function in English to that of case in Latin (*p* 289 *ff*). By analogy he uses the terms 'nominative words' and 'accusative words' to refer to the syntactical relationship conveyed by the position of nouns before or after verbs. He compares the use of the preposition *of* in English with the Latin genitive, the use of *to* with the Latin dative and of *by* with Latin ablative (*p* 295), but points out that Latin has several equivalences of these words: *to* may also be expressed by *ad* with the accusative, and *by* may be equivalent to *per, iuxta* or *praeter* with the accusative. Wallis even avoids using the word 'case' (*casus*) where different terminations are found in English – in the personal pronouns – though he talks of different 'forms' or 'states' and compares the 'rect state' with the Latin *casus rectus* (*ie* nominative). He excludes case elsewhere on formal grounds – because of the absence of overt markers in the form of terminations; as we have seen (*p* 26) this interpretation of 'case' is a narrower one than many linguists would give it today (*eg* Fillmore, 1968). Wallis's rejection of categories not overtly marked by inflections typifies his attempt to avoid complications which might stand in the way of the would-be learner, while using analogies with Latin where possible. The crucial point about his decision to exclude these categories is not so much whether it can be seen to be right or wrong in hindsight, as the fact that it challenged the traditional assumption that they were universal features of language, rather than just characteristics of Greek and Latin.

Gender is also excluded. Pairs of words such as *man, woman*; *horse, mare*, etc (*p* 279) and the pronouns *he, she, it* (*p* 321) are regarded as distinctions of *sex*; he points out the inconsistencies in Latin as between sex and gender. Gil (1621, *p* 40) had retained three genders, including under masculine such things as *sun, stars,* and *winds* and under feminine *moon, islands, cities,* and *regions*, by virtue of the personal pronoun used to refer to them. Wallis makes no mention of these, but like Gil would no doubt have treated them as personifications.

The *number* category is admitted for substantives but not for adjectives (which show no formal sign of it – *p* 303). However, Wallis forsakes his formal principle when describing the pronouns;

the interrogative is said to be *who* 'in both numbers' (*p* 323), just as *sheep, hose* are said to be used 'for both numbers indifferently' (*p* 283). Clearly the category of number is extended by analogy to these examples from the bulk of substantives and the personal pronouns which do show a formal mark of it, whereas no adjectives do so. It is not clear whether Wallis would attribute number to *learned* in a phrase such as *the learned*; on *p* 327 he describes it as an adjective with substantive understood, but on *p* 315 he says 'adjectives which are used substantivally (their own substantive being omitted) are re-garded as substantives'. The distinction of different types of sub-stantives as *countable, uncountable, collective* or *mass* is not found explicitly in Wallis, though it is not unusual to have a list of the uncountables in late seventeenth-century grammars (see *p* 35). Person and number in verbs are accepted by Wallis, as by all early grammarians. Hume (1617) had been the first to emphasise the function of the personal pronoun as a marker of person and number, but Wallis gives in addition a clear statement of the part played in this by terminations (*p* 335).

Wallis does not use the terms declension or conjugation, but divides verbs into two broad categories: independent (*absoluta*) and auxiliary (*auxiliaria*); the auxiliaries are divided into 'complete' (*integra*) and 'defective' (*mutila*). The 'complete' ones are the verbs 'to have' and 'to be' and the 'defective' comprise *do, will, shall, may, can* with their imperfect past tenses, and *must*. This grouping is quite similar to Bullokar's three conjugations (*p* 27), and the broad division corresponds to Butler's *absolute* and *supple-tive* verbs.

Tenses are reduced to two, present and past, on formal grounds, and moods disappear altogether. Instead of regarding combinations of various auxiliary verbs with the independent verb as equivalent to the formally distinct Latin tenses and moods, he deals with the auxiliaries separately, but draws comparisons with the Latin usage (*eg* on *p* 333 – 'in this respect it is exactly like the Latin infinitive mood'; *p* 335 – 'the terminations are left out in commands and after the conjunctions *if, that, although, whether* . . . namely where Latin would have the imperative or subjunctive mood'). He rigorously confines his use of the terms *tense* and *mood* to instances where the independent verb shows formal variations. The fact that semantic and syntactic correspondences can be found, for example, between Latin verbs in the future tense and the combination of *shall* or *will* with independent verbs in English, or between Latin subjunctive and combinations involving the auxiliary verbs *may, might* etc had led many of his predecessors to adopt the Latin verbal paradigms *en bloc*; this Wallis thought unjustified. As in his description of case and gender, he shows his unwillingness to use terminology taken from Latin which seemed to him misleading if not wholly superfluous, though he does not deny the fact that many parallels may be found between Latin and English usages.

His treatment of syntax is very scanty, amounting to a few remarks: in Chapter IV on relations expressed by word-order and the use of prepositions (*p* 289 *ff*); in Chapter V on the position of adjectives; and in Chapter XI on variations in word order in questions, commands, concessions etc, and the construction corresponding to Latin impersonal verbs.

Wallis's claim that he avoids describing English in terms of Latin is justified. Superficially his retention of the Latin terminology, including the traditional eight parts of speech, tends to obscure the extent of his departure from tradition. One must remember that his chief concern was to provide an easy introduction to English for foreigners; he therefore wished to avoid introducing new terms, where the traditional ones could be made to serve his purpose. Although he was not the first to exclude categories such as case and gender from English (Greaves had done so in 1594), his Grammar was the first substantial work to do so, and had a much wider influence. In the Author's Preface (*p* 111) he refers to the fact that his method has been imitated since its first publication by certain Frenchmen in their *Grammaire Universelle*. The famous *Grammaire générale et raisonée de Port-Royal* was published in 1660 (Lancelot and Arnauld, 1660) and proclaimed as its purpose the discovery of what is common to all languages and what is characteristic only of specific languages. French, Latin, Greek and Hebrew are the main languages used to illustrate this theme. Its scope extended beyond the purely practical aims of Wallis; but the idea of a grammar that would extend over language boundaries was not a new one. The medieval grammarians, with their concern for the logical basis of language, approached it from one direction; the seventeenth-century rationalists, inspired by Descartes, from another. The attempt to probe beneath the surface of languages and so to find a common core underlying many or even all of them has its parallels in the recent history of linguistics. Chomsky (1966) examines the Port-

Royal Grammar in an attempt to illustrate the similarities of approach that he believes it shows to modern transformational generative grammar, with its postulation of a 'surface structure' and an underlying 'deep structure' (see Salmon, 1969). In Chapter VI of Part II of the Port-Royal Grammar, for instance, the authors recognise that different languages have different ways of expressing what are essentially the same relationships; where Greek and Latin use case terminations and Hebrew an internal modification the vernaculars express these relations by a different word-order or the use of prepositions (*cf: p* 26). If Wallis believed that Lancelot and Arnauld had borrowed his method it could only have been in ceasing to make Latin the point of departure. He had the practical aim of making English as simple as possible to learn, and this led him to do away with the complexities of Latin paradigms which he felt gave it an unduly forbidding appearance. Lancelot and Arnauld were also led to cut away the superficial exterior in order to find something more logical and universal underneath. Wallis claims universality only in his *Tractatus de Loquela*, which he believed provided a basis for the description of the *sounds* of all languages. It was not his intention that the Grammar should be anything more than a grammar of English, though he several times associates English with other vernaculars of his time in their points of difference from Latin.

Wallis, as we have seen (*p* 9 *f*), was very closely involved in events that led up to the founding of the Royal Society. He numbered among his contemporaries William Harvey, Christopher Wren, Robert Boyle, Leibniz and Newton, to mention only a few illustrious names; many of these men were his personal friends. With the stimulation of such friends and the breadth of his knowledge of mathematics, anatomy, physics and many other subjects he was well equipped to make a break with tradition. In comparison with the many striking developments in language studies in the seventeenth century, including attempts to create a new universal language (see McIntosh 1956) and to reform teaching methods, Wallis's achievement may seem less startling than one might expect. But his Grammar, taken in the context of its day, marked a turning-point. Even though some of his claimed innovations were not entirely new, his authority and clarity of exposition was responsible for making their dissemination wider and for increasing their impact, with the result that his influence both at home and abroad surpassed that of any other contemporary grammarian. It does Wallis's reputation no good to pretend, as some have done, that he was head and shoulders above all previous or contemporary grammarians or that he revolutionised the approach to grammar writing. Nevertheless, within the practical limits that he set himself he succeeded handsomely and deserves credit for removing some of the blinkers that had been obscuring the view of grammarians of English prior to his time.

[c] Wallis's description of the parts of speech
The major innovations which Wallis introduced have already been mentioned (*p* 30 *f*). This section deals with some further points regarding particular parts of speech.

(i) *The noun* Wallis does not give any definition of the noun, or of the other parts of speech; this is in accordance with his assumption expressed in Chapter II of the Grammar (*p* 277) that his readers, being familiar with Latin, would find it superfluous. For this reason also he omits the division into proper and common nouns, referring to proper nouns only in passing (*pp* 287, 309). He retains the division of nouns (*nomina*) into noun substantive and noun adjective, which had been hinted at in the Roman grammarians and became firmly established in the Middle Ages. It was not until the early eighteenth century that these two categories were made separate parts of speech (R. Johnson, 1706), but by dealing with them in separate chapters Wallis gives them a degree of independence. Funke (1941, *p* 79) notes that he carried the substantive/adjective division through other parts of speech too; demonstrative and relative pronouns are classed as *nomina adjectiva*, personal pronouns as *nomina substantiva*; forms in *-ing* (*eg: burning*) may be participle (adjective) or verbal noun (substantive) – *p* 333. There is no subdivision into countable, uncountable, collective, abstract (see *pp* 31, 35).

(ii) *The articles* In Ancient Greek the article was in origin a demonstrative pronoun, and in early Greek (*eg* Homer) still retained much of its demonstrative force. In Attic Greek it had lost this force, and in many of its uses is comparable with English *the*; Greek had no article corresponding to English *a*. Latin had no articles, but the Stoics when listing the parts of speech applied the name *articulus* to some of the pronouns (Priscian II.iv.16; XVII.iv.27). The *pronomen articulare* was divided into (i) *finitum* (for example, *hic* – this), and (ii) *infinitum* (for example, *aliquis* – someone), and the name *articulus* was applied particularly to the second category. Eventually the term *finitus* (translated as 'definite') was applied to German *der*, French *le* and English *the* and *infinitus* (translated 'indefinite') to *ein*, *un*, *a*. These terms were not used in English grammars before Greenwood (1711), though Jonson uses the words *finite* and *infinite*. With respect to the status of the articles, Bullokar regards them not as a part of speech but simply as a sign of the substantive (see *p* 24). Butler also takes this view. Jonson puts them with the pronouns, Greaves and Wallis with the noun adjective, and Gil and Hume with prepositions and adverbs. Greaves and Wallis both regard them as less emphatic forms of *that* (demonstrative) and *one* (numeral).

According to Wallis both *a* and *the* signify that a generic word is being applied to some particular thing, whether species or individual. The difference, he says, is that *the* may signify application to more than one (unlike *a*) and indicates that whatever it is applied to is a closely specified thing or things, *eg*:

Numeral Article		Demonstrative Article
A man	is beating	the woman
Men	are beating	the women

whereas *man is beating woman* would presumably be an example of Wallis's unapplied generic term. However, it is quite possible to use the article before a noun without giving it a specific application, except in the case of material nouns (*earth*, *wood* etc) or abstract nouns (*history*, *wealth*, etc). These material and abstract nouns are usually grouped together as *uncountables*, and cannot take the article; the same applies to *man* and *woman* when used in a generic sense. Wallis is probably referring to the uncountables when he uses the expression *voci generali generaliter significanti* – 'a generic word with a generic application', but he gives no examples, whereas Cooper (1685, *p* 117) describes them as *voces quae significant res homogeneas, quae dividi non possunt in distinctas partes et differentes, ideoque carent plerumque numero plurali* – 'words which signify homogeneous things, which cannot be divided into distinct parts, and so mostly have no plural number'. Cooper's examples are such things as herbs, crops, liquids, metals, virtues, vices. Most eighteenth-century grammars include similar lists. Greenwood (1711) amplifies Wallis's account of the articles, adding (i) *what* to the words that can be followed by the indefinite article, (ii) the use of articles with adjectives used as substantives, (iii) the use of *the* with *same*, *self*, *he, she* where a substantive is to be understood, (iv) abstract and material nouns which do not take the article, (v) exceptions, other than rivers, where the article is used with proper names: *the Marlboroughs, the Albemarle* (a ship).

(iii) *Prepositions* Wallis deals with prepositions immediately after the substantive and the articles because of the intimate relationship they have with the substantive, supplying a link which had often been provided by the cases alone in Latin (see *pp* 24–5, 38). He says that prepositions are in a sense properties of the noun, in that they affect its relationships with other words. Of English grammarians he was the first to stress the similar function of prepositions to that of case inflections in Latin, and in the same chapter he relates the function of word-order in English to uses of the Latin nominative and accusative cases. In most grammars of the seventeenth and eighteenth centuries prepositions are classed with adverbs, conjunctions and interjections (see *p* 37).

(iv) *Pronouns* These are variously classified by early grammarians. Priscian, following Apollonius Dyscolus, had confined the term *pronomen* to the personal and the demonstrative, on the grounds that interrogatives, relatives and correlatives do not take the place of proper nouns, and are best classed as *nomina*. Donatus, however, used *pronomen* for interrogatives and relatives also but made them a special group – *pronomina infinita*. Priscian's influence predominated in the Middle Ages, but Petrus Ramus classed all pronouns under the heading *nomen*, dividing them into substantives (personal pronouns) and adjectives (the rest). This classification was adopted by Greaves, Gil, Jonson and Wallis. Gil seems to have been the first English grammarian to use the term *nomina personalia*, which Wallis uses as an alternative to *pronomina*. Wallis, like Greaves, does not speak of the gender of pronouns, making the forms *he, she, it* simply relate to the sex of the noun they refer to. Bullokar and Gil followed Lily and Ramus in giving pronouns all the five Latin cases, but most other grammarians of this period confine them to two – Wallis's *rect* and *oblique* (see *pp* 25, 30). He gives a general rule for their use, according to their position in relation to the verb, but this is modified in a later chapter (Chapter XI).

(v) *Adjectives* Almost all other grammarians of the sixteenth and seventeenth centuries give adjectives a category of *number*, in spite of their invariable form, but Wallis adheres firmly to his formal criterion (see *pp* 26, 30). Bullokar and Jonson also gave them genders, though, conscious of the lack of formal marks, they appeal to the Latin usage as their justification. Jonson even distinguishes adjective from substantive by its possession of more genders. Bullokar accepts the same six cases for the adjective as for the substantive and Butler also retains the same two – *rect* and *oblique*. Wallis excludes number, gender and case. He introduces two types of adjectives which he says are immediately derived from substantives and can take the place of almost any prepositional phrase. The first – *possessive* adjective – is what most grammarians called the genitive of the substantive; Wallis classes it as an adjective because of its similar position before the substantive it qualifies, but he does not account for the fact that the possessive adjective can itself be qualified by an adjective, unlike other adjectives, as in *old John's hat*. The second type he calls *respective* adjectives; in combinations of two substantives such as *sea-fish, wine-vessel* he describes the first half as an adjective (see note 103, *p* 315), rather than calling the whole a compound substantive (*cf* Bradley, *The Making of English* (1904), *p* 64: 'In speaking English we feel that the elements of such a combination are as much distinct words as are the adjective and the following substantive').

(vi) *Verbs* As we have seen (*p* 31) Wallis dispenses entirely with conjugations, and with other categories that are not formally marked in the principal verb, such as moods (formed with auxiliaries), all but two tenses, and voices. In this he differs from most earlier grammarians, at least in the degree of his adherence to formal criteria. It was more usual to retain the Latin moods, tenses and conjugations, equating them with English constructions made up of auxiliary and main verb, or with weak and strong verbs (see *p* 27). Wallis devotes a chapter to what he calls *verba anomala*, which includes all verbs that do not form their imperfect past tense and past participle in *-ed*. He is careful to point out (*p* 363) that some of the 'anomalous' or 'irregular' forms are earlier in origin than the 'regular' forms in *-ed*, and that others (the substitution of *t* for *d* – *p* 357) are better regarded as a contraction than as an irregularity.

(vii) *Adverbs, conjunctions, prepositions and interjections* Although he has already dealt with prepositions in a separate chapter (see *p* 36) Wallis mentions them again in Chapter XIII, presumably because they were so frequently associated with adverbs, conjunctions and interjections. The Aristotelian tradition divided parts of speech into

(i) noun and verb, (ii) linking words (σύνδεσμοι). The second of these groups was translated into Latin as *syncategoremata* or *consignificantia* (Quintilian I.4; Priscian II.iv.15). In the sixteenth century Petrus Ramus adopted a similar grouping, using formal, not semantic, criteria. He divided parts of speech into *voces numeri* (words having the category of *number* – noun and verb) and *voces sine numero* (adverbs and conjunctions – adverbs including prepositions and interjections). In England he was followed by Greaves, Jonson, Hume and Butler, though Butler keeps the preposition as a separate part of speech. Wallis was probably influenced by this tradition here. Wilkins (1668) has two groups (*p* 304 *ff*) which he calls *integrals* (substantive, adjective, participle, derived adverb, verb) and *particles* (pronoun, underived adverb, conjunction, preposition, interjection, article), and Cooper (1685) follows this division closely, except that he includes all adverbs under particles. Another markedly different grouping is to be found in the Port-Royal Grammar (1660), where parts of speech are divided according to whether they signify the *objects* of our thoughts (noun, article, pronoun, participle, preposition, adverb), or the *manner* of our thoughts (verb, conjunction, interjection).

(viii) *Government (rectio) and agreement (convenientia)* These are the two syntactical relationships most often mentioned in early grammars. The former, in Greek and Latin, had to do with the relationships shown by case differences, preposition or verb being said to govern the nouns etc with which they were linked syntactically by case. *Agreement* concerns relationships between adjective and substantive, noun and verb, relative and antecedent, where it is *identity* that is indicated, not *determination* of one by the other (see Lancelot and Arnauld, 1660, Chapter XXIV). Gil was the first grammarian of English to devote much of his work to syntax, though Bullokar has some remarks on the case of nouns and word order. Wallis uses the idea of government in Chapter V (*p* 303) rather in the same way as Jespersen uses *rank* – to express the hierarchical relationship of words to one another within a close group. The substantive is said to govern the adjective applied to it, and the adjective to govern a further qualifying phrase that is applied to it. The terms *governing, governed* in this sense correspond to Jespersen's relationship between *primary* and *secondary*, or *secondary* and *tertiary* (*M.E.G.*, II.§ 1.21). Otherwise Wallis's remarks on syntax are few, and occur mostly in Chapters IV and XI.

7 Wallis the phonetician

Descriptions of the sounds of Greek and Latin are to be found in many ancient writers; very few of them give any clear evidence which would allow us to identify the sounds positively. None were trained to observe speech in detail, and often they blindly followed their predecessors, or were persuaded by theoretical assumptions concerning the structure of the language to exclude certain sounds from their consideration. Some of the more dependable accounts are to be found in the works of Aristotle, Dionysius Thrax, Cicero, Quintilian, Dionysius of Halicarnassus and Terentianus Maurus (see further on the value of the evidence in Sturtevant, 1940, Chapter 1). None of these ancient writers put forward anything that one could regard as a systematic description of speech sounds; in most cases descriptions were based on the nature of the sounds as perceived by the ear, and not on the mechanism of their production – that is, they were auditory, not articulatory – and it is notoriously difficult to find sufficiently precise terms for an adequate auditory description.

During the Middle Ages no substantial improvements in phonetic description were made by grammarians of Latin. Out of the main stream, and remarkable for its perceptiveness of phonological principles, was the so-called *First Grammatical Treatise*, written in the twelfth century by an Icelandic scholar with a view to adapting the Latin alphabet for use in Icelandic. Unfortunately his skill as a phonetician, which was of a high order, did not benefit his contemporaries or immediate successors, for his treatise remained unpublished until 1818 (see Haugen (1972) and Robins (1967), *pp* 72–4). In the sixteenth century the interest in spelling reform led to some advances in phonetic observation, and a more rigorous distinction of sound from symbol (see *pp* 62–3). Noteworthy descriptions of particular languages are to be found in Salviati[1] for Italian, in Meigret[2] and Sainliens[3] for French, and Ickelsamer (1534) for German. Ickelsamer gives a brief description of the vocal organs, the vowels and the consonants, but provides no overall system for classifying sounds; Ramus (1559) described the sounds of Latin in some detail, but borrows a great deal from Priscian, and his description of French sounds (1562) is sparse. In England the spelling

---

[1] *Degli Avvertimenti della Lingua sopra'l Decamerone*, 1584.
[2] *La Tretté de la Grammere francoeze*, 1550.
[3] *De pronuntiatione linguae Gallicae*, 1580.

reformers Thomas Smith (1568) and John Hart (1551, 1569, 1570) made some interesting phonetic observations, including descriptions of the syllabic consonants (see *p* 61) of the voiced/voiceless distinction in consonants, weak forms, and assimilations; Hart also introduced a sophisticated phonetic transcription. However, it was Jacob Madsen, of Aarhus in Denmark, who first presented (in 1586) a system of description based on direct observation which he hoped would be adequate for any language. Unfortunately, like his predecessors, he allowed himself to be unduly influenced by the descriptions handed down by classical writers; in attempting to describe Danish he failed to record accurately sounds which he must have been hearing all the time – for example [ð], [ɣ]. One important contribution that he made, however, was in taking articulations as the basis of his description rather than sounds (see *pp* 43, 45, 51).

In the seventeenth century a more scientific attitude manifested itself. In Madsen's tradition, and greatly influenced by him, was Petrus Montanus of Delft. *De Spreeckonst* (1635) gives a complicated and sophisticated account of the vocal organs and speech in general which deserved to be widely known; in fact he had little influence, owing to his highly complex terminology and method, and the fact that he wrote in Dutch (see Vos (1962), *p* 7 *ff*). There is certainly no evidence that when Wallis wrote *Tractatus de Loquela* he knew of Montanus, though he may possibly have been acquainted with Madsen's book, which was written in Latin. In England the most interesting attempt at a systematic classification before Wallis was that of Robert Robinson (1617). Robinson's vowel classification was based on tongue position, but it had only one dimension – front/back (see below, *p* 43). The consonant classification has several points of resemblance to Wallis's (see *p* 51), but his work is on a much smaller scale, and the descriptions of articulations somewhat sketchy.

Wallis was therefore not justified in claiming to be the first to put forward a complete articulatory system for describing speech, but his classification by place and manner of articulation was an advance, and has quite a modern look about it, as we shall see.

Aspects of early phonetic descriptions will now be briefly considered, under the following headings: [*a*] The mechanism of voicing and pitch variation; [*b*] vowels; [*c*] consonants; [*d*] non-segmental characteristics of speech; [*e*] sound and symbol; [*f*] syllable division.

[a] The mechanism of voicing and pitch variation

Wallis's account of the pitch mechanism used in speech (*p* 133) provides for two different types of pitch variation: (i) differences in the characteristic range of pitch used, whether between two different people, or in one person's voice at different stages of his life; see Abercrombie (1967), *p* 99 – tessitura; (ii) variations of pitch in any one person's voice at a particular stage of his life. The first of these, he says, is attributable to the trachea; the longer and narrower it is the higher the pitch will be, and vice versa. He compares it with a tube in its acoustic characteristics, very reasonably, but his knowledge of acoustics lets him down, for in fact an increase in the length of a tube has the effect of lowering, not raising, the pitch. Differences of type (ii) he attributes to the action of the larynx; the slit (*rimula*) of the larynx widens to produce a low pitch and narrows to produce a high pitch. Wallis's account may well be based on Galen's description (*De usu partium* VII.13), which also gives prominence to the function of the trachea. Another early anatomical description of the larynx which he may have known is that of Fabricius ab Aquapendente (*De larynge* 5). The word *rimula* which Wallis uses of the narrow chink within the larynx is one Latin equivalent of the Greek word γλῶττις; this is used by Galen of the top of the trachea and occurs in Lucian (*Harm.* 1) referring to the mouthpiece of a musical wind instrument. By the sixteenth century it had come to be used in the sense of a small opening within the larynx; Latin synonyms used for it include *fistula, rima, rimula, lingula, lingua parva*. The fact that air forced through a narrow gap may produce musical tone was familiar from wind instruments and from whistling. Van den Berg (1968, *p* 278), in the course of his excellent succinct account of the mechanism of the larynx, points out how the analogy with whistling misled Dodart, and no doubt others before his time were similarly led to the theory that a narrowing of the passage through the larynx will lead to a rise in the pitch of the voice.

Voice was said by Aristotle to be caused by air striking the edge of the trachea (*De Anima* 420b). Galen (*De plac. Hippoc. et Platonis*, Lib.II) calls it 'breath beaten by the cartilages of the larynx', and Fabricius (loc cit *p* 36 *ff*) says that air passing through the *narrowed* glottis is made vocal and sonorous. Wallis leaves his exact explanation vague; voice, he says, is due to vibration of the larynx and trachea, caused by tension (*p* 135), but he does not state the direction of the tension, or how it is caused. Compare Holder (1669) 'the

Larynx both gives passage to the Breath and also . . . by the force of Muscles, to bear the sides of the Larynx stiffe and near together, as the Breath passes through the *Rimula*, makes a vibration of those Cartilaginous Bodies which forms that Breath, into a Vocal sound or Voice . . .' (*p* 23); a remarkably modern sounding description, typical of Holder's keen insights into the mechanism of speech. Cooper (1685, *p* 23) closely follows Wallis. Amman (1700a) gives a much fuller description of the larynx, and specifically denies that narrowing in itself can produce voice – there must, he says, be a regular widening and narrowing, caused by a balance of force between muscles and cartilages (*p* 22 *ff*). This regular vibration is conveyed to the air. He likens the effect to the vibration of the tongue which occurs in producing *r*, and of the lips in soothing a baby. The *rimula*, or slit, is responsible for pitch changes – when narrow it gives a high pitch and when wide, a low pitch. But he also mentions other factors which affect the pitch: (i) the length and thickness of the cartilages, (ii) the raising and lowering of the larynx by muscles connected with the hyoid bone, breast bone etc. Raising will involve simultaneous narrowing of the *rimula* and vice versa. The first tentative descriptions of the vocal cords appeared between 1700 and 1707 in Denis Dodart's articles in *Mémoires de l'Academie Royale des Sciences de Paris* (see Bibliography). In these *Mémoires* for the year 1741 we find Antoine Ferrein calling them *cordes vocales* or *rubans*, and his account of the mechanism of voicing stresses the importance of the vibratory action as opposed to the width of the aperture. For a recent account of the mechanism of voicing and pitch variation see Van Riper and Irwin (1958), *pp* 443–56.

[b] *Vowels*

Wallis does not attempt to give a definition of vowels or consonants; he accepts them as familiar traditional categories. When early grammarians do define them the vowels are said to have greater sonority, to involve little or no obstruction of the air-stream and to be capable of being pronounced by themselves, whereas the opposite is said to be true of the consonants (see also *p* 50). Robinson (1617) introduced a third category, called 'the vital sound' which was formed in the throat, and could accompany other sounds. By this he meant 'voice', and is thus one of the earliest writers to envisage the possibility of *voiceless* vowels as well as voiceless consonants. Madsen (1586) distinguished the consonants as having a definite articulatory movement in the mouth, and in general more noise than vowels (*maiore motu et strepitu editur*). Montanus (1635) apparently made sonority his criterion. As early as 1568 Smith had recognised that consonants can be uttered without any accompanying vowel or diphthong; this is also noted by Hart (1569), Gil (1619 *p* 19) and Holder (1669, *p* 28), but we find Greenwood in 1711 (*p* 249) still repeating the old definition – one of his own additions to the text of Wallis (see *p* 69 below).

Articulatory descriptions of vowels in the sixteenth and seventeenth centuries vary considerably in the categories they start from and the total number of vowels that they allow for. An account of some of them will provide a standard of comparison.

Hart (1551) – 3 degrees of mouth aperture (no lip-rounding); 2 degrees of lip-rounding (no tongue position specified). The vowels may be long or short, giving a possible total of 10.

Madsen (1586) – *3 lingual:* 3 degrees of mouth aperture (no lip-rounding). *5 labial:* 3 degrees of lip-rounding (*o* is divided into three types, but the articulatory basis for this is not made clear). He says (editor's translation): 'the tongue has a fixed position for labial vowels which we could only observe if the mouth had a glass cover, but it is not necessary to describe it because nature determines its position'. He observed the longer and narrower shape of the mouth cavity in the labial vowels; the 5 labial vowels are needed to describe the front rounded vowels of his own language – Danish.

Robinson (1617) – 5 places of articulation, each being assigned a short and a long vowel; no degrees of mouth aperture or changes in lip position. His short and long vowels are differentiated by 'short and long organs', which apparently refers to a contraction or extension of the tongue, at each place of articulation.

Montanus (1635) – 3 degrees of mouth aperture, 8 places of articulation and a further division of snap/steady based on the type of onset of the breath. He believed that the resulting 48 vowels could be found in languages. Lip-rounding he believed to be a secondary and 'accidental' feature.

Newton (c 1660) – 8 different vowel qualities are arrived at, the 'greatest cavity in the mouth' being progressively moved forward from the throat to the lips. 6 of the vowels may be long or short, giving a total of 14.

Dalgarno (1661) – 4 degrees of mouth aperture (no lip-rounding) – *4 gutturals*. 3 degrees of lip-rounding (no tongue position specified) – *3 labials*. Each vowel may be long or short, giving a total of 14.

Wilkins (1668) – *3 linguals:* 3 tongue positions (more concave, less concave, somewhat convex). *2 labials:* 2 degrees of lip-rounding (the closer rounded one is said to have a concave tongue position longways). He adds 3 ambivalent sounds which *may* act as vowels, and each of which may be voiced or voiceless: *1 labial* (lips still more rounded), *1 lingual* (tongue still more convex; no lip-rounding), *1 guttural* (with free emission from the throat and no lip-rounding). Like Wallis he emphasises that the size of the aperture ('measure of apertion') is infinitely divisible, so that in theory the number of vowels cannot be limited. He also allows for each of his vowels to be short or long.

Holder (1669) – Cavity shape determines the vowel quality and in determining this he says that the tongue is the main factor, lips and throat playing a subsidiary part. While recognising the theoretical possibility of a large number of vowels, he thinks 9 enough, but emphasises the difficulty of description and (perhaps with an eye on Wallis) adds that it is foolish to expect a nice tidy classification. His description contains elements that anticipate modern oppositions such as open/close, front/back, tense/lax and long/short. He groups the vowels into: *3 gutturals* (no lip-rounding) – 1 has a completely open passage, and the other 2 require 2 different degrees of lowering of the larynx. *4 palatic* – involving progressive fronting and raising of the tongue (no lip-rounding). *1 labio-guttural* – the guttural vowel which has the larynx most lowered, with lip-rounding added. *1 labio-palatic* – the highest palatic vowel, with lip-rounding added. He adds that any vowel may have lip-rounding, but the closest and frontest and the openest and most retracted most frequently have this modification. 2 of the vowels have strong tension of the lips and 1 vowel strong tension of the tongue; these 3 vowels may act as consonants (*ie* semi-vowels). Any vowel may in theory be voiced or voiceless, nasalised or non-nasalised, short or long. He does not have a category of central vowels, but in other respects is remarkably near modern analyses.

Cooper (1685) – *4 lingual* vowels with progressive raising and fronting of the tongue (no lip-rounding). *2 labials*, with slight and close rounding respectively (no tongue position specified). *2 gutturals* (no lip-rounding), one requiring a wide open mouth, and the other formed in the throat with 'a simple murmur' being the 'basis of all other vowels'. (*cf* Robinson's 'vital sound', *p* 42, though that is not classed as a vowel.)

Amman (1700a) – 3 places of articulation (guttural, dental, labial); 2 degrees of mouth aperture for the dentals (no lip-rounding); 2 degrees of lip-rounding for the labials (low tongue position specified); 1 guttural (several variants possible). He also has a category of *mixed vowels*; for these, he says, the tongue takes up the position for dental *e* and the other vocal organs position themselves for *a, o, u,* respectively, giving three mixed vowels, å, ŏ, ŭ (see also *p* 47).

In these descriptions many of the modern categories already appear; Holder's classification comes nearest to modern schemes. Lack of any instrumental aids meant that tongue position was difficult to determine and Madsen, Hart and Montanus all recommend the use of the finger to check articulatory positions.

The division of vowels into *lingual* (determined by mouth aperture or tongue position) and *labial* (characterised by varying degrees of lip-rounding and excluding all non-rounded vowels, which would be *lingual*) was made by Hebrew grammarians to describe the three Hebrew vowels, two being lingual and one labial. It also sufficed for the three vowels of Arabic (see note 16, *p* 137). However, when it was applied to European languages, for instance by Madsen (1586), certain difficulties arose. *Labial* is adequate as a place category for vowel articulations as long as there is no contrast between rounded vowels with front and back tongue positions respectively, for example between [y] and [u]. Madsen's labial vowels included both [y] and [u]; he describes them both as having lip-rounding and protrusion, and distinguishes them not by their difference of tongue position on the horizontal axis, but by their different degree of aperture on the vertical axis. The difficulty of observing tongue positions in labial vowels contributed to this incorrect analysis. Robinson (1617) put forward quite a new scheme (see *p* 43) involving five basic horizontal positions for the tongue and no labial modification. Montanus (1635), by increasing the number of places of articulation horizontally to eight and having three vertical divisions for each, increased the possibilities of differentiation considerably, but he also ignored lip-rounding as being inessential.

Wallis's scheme for the vowels has been compared with the nineteenth-century schemes of Melville Bell and Henry Sweet because he adopts a 3 × 3 division horizontally and vertically. But he differs from the Bell-Sweet classification in the crucial fact that he retains the traditional *labial* category as one of his places of articulation on the horizontal axis. Their horizontal axis specifies three different categories distinguished by tongue position – back, front, and mixed (back and front), each of which can be modified by rounding or unrounding of the lips. So the labial modification has become quite a separate factor, whereas for Wallis it is still an *alternative* to his two categories of lingual vowels. We have seen that his contemporary, Holder, had a much better grasp of the determining features of vowel quality (see *p* 44), and we find Amman (1700b) pointing out the weaknesses in Wallis's scheme; for example the differentiation of [u] and [y] by degree of lip aperture, instead of by different tongue positions. Amman is also critical of the exact symmetry of Wallis's scheme, a criticism which is repeated frequently by Lehnert (1936). Wallis starts by assuming the three horizontal places of articulation exemplified by the Arabic and Hebrew vowels (*p* 137), and goes on to divide each of these into exactly three categories, according to the size of the mouth aperture (larger, medium, smaller); the nine resulting articulatory postures he regards as enough to account for all the vowel sounds 'which can be heard today'. Later he concedes (*p* 151) that it is quite possible to divide the mouth aperture vertically into more categories, and may be thought necessary, to account for other vowels as yet unheard. Finally (*p* 153) he states that each of his nine vowels may have both a long and a short form, though certain of them are rarely long and certain others rarely short. In his description of the nine vowels in detail (*pp* 139–151) he quotes examples from English, French, Italian, Spanish, Welsh, German, Hebrew and Greek. We know that he had studied French before going to Cambridge, but there is no evidence to show how well he knew the various modern languages which he quotes from. In describing the consonants he makes some mistakes in identification (for example, Spanish *ll* – *p* 183), which suggest that his acquaintance with them may have been from reading rather than from direct aural observation. One apparent inadequacy of his system is its mention of only one of the front rounded vowels

[46]

of French, namely [y]. As Amman pointed out, he does not provide for the mixed vowel *ŏ* which occurs in German and Dutch, unless he is assuming its identity with the French vowel in the last syllable of *serviteur*, which he puts in his guttural category, so suggesting that it is unrounded – an analysis which Amman hotly disputes. One is therefore bound to be somewhat wary of placing too much confidence in Wallis's foreign examples. Lehnert (1936) and Dobson (1968) both attempt to make deductions as to the quality of *thin a* from Wallis's comparison with French and Italian sounds, but are forced to assume either that it is an untypical identification or that it applies to the short form and not to the long one (Lehnert, § 93; Dobson, *p* 238). Similarly with Wallis's *round o* (*p* 147); the comparison with French *au* and with Greek *ω* is taken by Lehnert (§ 122) and Dobson (*p* 240) to mean quite different things. As phoneticians well know, the precise description of vowel quality is very difficult and depends on the existence of some unvarying reference point or points (such as Daniel Jones's Cardinal Vowels – see Jones, 1962, § 131 *ff*). The use of sounds from a particular language as a reference point may lead to confusion and ambiguity because of the wide variations in vowel quality that are usually found in different accents of the same language; the specific accent referred to must be very clearly specified, and Wallis's descriptions leave much to be desired in this respect. His articulatory categorisation into nine vowels, each of which may be long or short, is intended to act as a framework for the vowels of all languages with which he was familiar. However, the English-based nature of it is suggested by the fact that the fourteen vowels which he exemplifies, out of a possible eighteen, are all English vowels; the long forms of *obscure u* and *feminine e*, and the short forms of *round o* and *thin u*, he says, rarely occur 'at any rate in English' (*p* 153). The articulatory framework does allow some deductions to be made as to the quality of the vowels, in combination with other evidence from contemporary writers, but only in broad terms; attempts to reach a precise specification must be speculative to a large extent. The scope of this edition does not permit any detailed discussion of the problems presented by Wallis's and other writers' evidence concerning English vowel sounds. These are fully treated in Lehnert (1936), Zachrisson (1913), Horn-Lehnert (1954), Dobson (1968), Chomsky and Halle (1968) and elsewhere. The following table summarises Wallis's evidence, with some of his examples for each vowel:

Name and articulatory category	English examples	Foreign examples
thin a (palatal, wide)	short: bat, Sam, bar long: bate, same, bare	French *em* or *en*; Welsh and Italian *a*
masculine e (palatal, medium)	short: sell, set, best long: seal, seat, beast	French, Italian and Spanish *e*
feminine e (guttural, medium)	short: vertue, liberall, liberty long: ——	French feminine *e*
thin i (palatal, narrow)	short: fit, fill, sin long: feet, feel, seen	French, Spanish and Italian *i*, Welsh *i* or final *y*
open o (guttural, wide)	short: folly, lost, cost long: fall, laws, cause	German open *â*, French *a*, Hebrew long and short *camets*
round o (labial, wide)	short: —— long: one, whole, boat, those	Greek ω, French *au*
obscure o, u (guttural, narrow)	short: turn, dull, cut long: ——	French *-eur* in *serviteur* etc, Welsh *y*, except finally
fat u (labial, medium)	short: full, pull, wood long: fool, pool, woo'd	German *fat u*, Spanish and Italian *u*, French *ou*, Welsh *w*
thin u (labial, narrow)	short: —— long: muse, tune, dure, new, lieu	French *u*, and similar to Spanish *iu* and Welsh *iw, yw, uw*

The names which Wallis gives to the vowels are in some cases based on their articulations (round, open), but in others it is less easy to know the meaning he attached to them (for example, *exilis*, *pinguis* which have been translated *thin*, *fat*). Wallis was following classical tradition in naming vowels in this way, but the meaning attached to *exilis* and *pinguis* in classical authors varies. Terentius Scaurus (18.12) contrasts them apparently as *short* and *long* respectively whereas Sergius in Donatum (525.24) uses *tenuis* and *pinguis* for *non-aspirated* and *aspirated*. In general it seems to be the case that *exilis*, *tenuis*, *angustus* are opposed to *pinguis*, *latus*, *crassus*, *plenus* – the former group being associated with the quality of what would now be called *front* vowels and the latter with that of *back* vowels. For instance the front vowel [y] in Wallis has the label *exile* whereas the back vowel [u] is called *pingue*, both having the same place of articulation – the lips. *Cf* note 28, *p* 237.

Comments on Wallis's description of particular vowels will be found in the notes. Three which require somewhat lengthier comment are dealt with here:

(i) *Feminine e,* and *obscure o, u* (*pp* 139, 141) These two vowels are both described as 'obscure', and distinguished from each other only by a difference in mouth aperture. The description of feminine *e* suggests that it was a contextual variant of masculine *e*, retracted through the influence of a following *r*. It is not necessarily true, as Lehnert suggests, that only a retroflex American type *r* could have this effect. Wallis differs from other sixteenth- and seventeenth-century writers in distinguishing obscure *u* from feminine *e*. In *A Defence of the Royal Society* (1678, *p* 18) he remarks that Wilkins thought these two vowels the same, but maintains that obscure *u* is a 'broader' sound. The use of an unrounded vowel in the words that he quotes as containing obscure *u* was widespread in the seventeenth century, especially where the preceding consonant was not labial – *cf: pull, wood,* which had rounded vowels (see Dobson, 1968, *pp* 585 *ff*, 720 *ff*). Lehnert (§ 105) refers to Ellis (v.638), who quotes with approval a description of the 'North-Northern' pronunciation of *u* as 'slightly approaching German *ö* and French *eu* in beuf, fleur etc'. For evidence as to pronunciation of *eu* in sixteenth-seventeenth century French see Thurot (1881–3), II.442–4, and Amman's comment (quoted on *p* 47).

(ii) *Thin u* Wallis's description of both French and English *u* as monophthongal conflicts with other contemporary evidence. Wilkins (1668) calls the monophthong *whistling u* or *u Gallicum*; because of its difficulty for English speakers he says he will omit further consideration of it. Cooper (1685, *pp* 27–28), like Wilkins, gives a diphthongal pronunciation for the English sound, and sometimes for the French sound also, though he notes that the monophthongal pronunciation is particularly French and difficult for English people. However, Holder's description of *u* clearly refers to the monophthong [y], and he quotes the word *rule* to exemplify it. In the Grammar (*p* 265) Wallis admits the diphthongal character of *eu, ew, eau* as opposed to *u*, and it may well be that his frequently shown tendency to relate differences in the orthography to differences in the sounds is at the root of his description of *thin u* (see also Lehnert (1936), § 140–47, Dobson (1968), *p* 239).

[c] Consonants

The earliest known division of speech sounds to be made in Europe is that recorded by Plato (*Cratylus*, 424c; *Philebus*, 18b; *Theaetetus*, 203b). The letters (γράμματα, στοιχεῖα) are divided into three groups: (i) those with 'voice'[1] (φωνή) – the vowels, τὰ φωνήεντα; (ii) those with neither 'voice' nor sound (φθόγγος), the stop consonants;[2] (iii) those between, τὰ μέσα, having sound but no 'voice' – [l m n r s] and the double consonants [dz ks ps]. Aristotle took over these three categories, using the term ἄφωνα (*without 'voice'*) to refer to the stop consonants, Plato's second group, and ἡμίφωνα (*half-voiced*) for Plato's third group. He also introduced the word προσβολή (*approach* or *application*) to refer to the movement of the articulators in forming the consonants. This word was translated by the Latin grammarians as *appulsus*, and we find it in Holder (1669) as *appulse*.

Dionysius Thrax (*c* 100 BC) kept the same three categories and gave the general name τὰ σύμφωνα (*accompanying 'voiced' sounds*) to the consonants as opposed to τὰ φωνήεντα (*the 'voiced' sounds* or *vowels*). Latin grammarians translated σύμφωνα into *consonantes* (consonants) and φωνήεντα into *vocales* (vowels). Aristotle's ἡμίφωνα became *semivocales* (half-voiced) which now included *l m n r s x f*, and ἄφωνα became *mutae* (mutes) which comprised the letters *b c d g h k p q t*.[2] The *semivocales* were sometimes identified as those whose *names* began with a vowel, whereas the names of the *mutae* began with their own sound.

This division persisted through the Middle Ages, and it is not seriously challenged until the sixteenth century. Madsen (1586) was one of the first to criticise the largely auditory basis of the classification and to put forward an articulatory one in its place; he could quote the authority of Aristotle's προσβολή for this. He divided the consonants into two main groups: (i) *lingual* – formed basically by the tongue, and (ii) *labial* – having the lower lip as the active articu-

---

[1] 'Voice' is used here to render Greek φωνή; this should not be identified with the technical term 'voice' in modern phonetics. In Plato φωνή is a distinguishing feature of vowels as opposed to consonants, and in Aristotle it characterises vowels and also consonants which are audible on their own, in contrast with the stops, including [b d g], which have no 'voice'. It is partly a phonetic term, which might be rendered 'sonority' and partly functional, roughly equivalent to 'syllabicity'. This phonetic/functional definition is found also in the Latin grammarians – *vocales* and *semivocales* can both be pronounced on their own, but only the former can constitute syllables, whereas neither of these properties is possessed by *mutae* (Donatus I.1.1–2).

[2] For the threefold division of stops in Greek and Latin see Robins (1967), *p* 32; Sturtevant (1940), §§ 90, 93–4; Allen (1968), *p* 12 *ff*.

lator. The *lingual* consonants are divided into: (a) *linguopalatine*, which involves the blade of the tongue articulating against the palate, and includes *s r l n*, and (b) *linguodental*, in which the blade articulates against the teeth (upper teeth – *t d*, lower teeth – *c h j g*; for the latter group Madsen says that the inner tongue approaches the palate and teeth, and the tongue is convex, but he is not satisfied that he has determined the place of articulation correctly). The *labial* consonants are divided into (a) *labiodental* – *f v*, and (b) *labiolabial* – *p b m*. He is very unsure about the function of the nasal cavity, and appears to believe that it plays a part in the formation of his linguodental stops.

Hart (1551, 1569) has a detailed description of English consonants in articulatory terms, but does not provide an overall scheme of classification or technical terminology, though as an observer he rates high among early phoneticians. Smith (1568) also has some valuable remarks on English consonants, but he starts from the traditional classical division into *mutae* and *semivocales*. Robinson (1617) divided up the consonants into *mutes*, *semimutes*, *greater obstricts*, *lesser obstricts*, and the *peculiar* [l]; his classification is based on articulation – greater and lesser obstricts are differentiated by the extent of the mouth aperture (*cf* modern *fricatives* and *approximants*), the name *mute* is applied to letters without any escape of the air stream, and *semimute* to those with no escape through the mouth. His three divisions of place of articulation – *inward*, *middle*, and *outward* – are very similar to Wallis's *guttural*, *palatal*, and *labial*.

Wallis starts with the same three categories that he has already used for the vowels – *labial*, *palatal* and *guttural*; these relate to the point at which the air-stream is stopped or compressed (modern *place of articulation*). Those consonants involving a complete stoppage of the breath at one of these three places are described as *primitive* or *basic*. The rest he regards as derived from these; they have the same place of articulation, but air is permitted to escape, though under strong compression. In modern terms these *derivative* consonants differ in *manner* from the primitive consonants. Both primitive and derivative are divided further, according to the *direction of the air-stream:* (i) escaping entirely through the mouth – *mutes*; (ii) escaping entirely through the nose – striking the air in the mouth cavity only in passing – *half-vowels*; (iii) escaping half through the mouth and half through the nose – *half mutes*. Of these three categories the half-vowels, he says, have no *derivative* forms in languages.

The following table summarises the classification so far (the symbols represent tentative phonetic interpretations of Wallis's own symbols – see *p* 197):

Manner of articulation
(modification of the air-stream)

	complete stoppage (*primitivae, clausae*) 'primitive', 'closed'			strong compression, no stoppage (*derivativae, apertae*) 'derivative', 'open'			
Escape via:	mouth only (*mutae*)	both equally (*semi-mutae*)	nose only (*semi-vocales*)	mouth only (*mutae*)	both equally (*semi-mutae*)	nose only (*semi-vocales*)	others
Place of articu-lation — labial	p	b	m	f ʍ	v w	lowing	
palatal	t	d	n	s θ	z ð	groaning	l r
guttural	k	g	ŋ	x h	ɣ j	groaning	

In many ways this table has a modern look, but several of its features require comment:

(i) The factor which he uses to distinguish what are today classed as pairs of voiced and voiceless consonants (p/b; s/z, etc) from each other is the direction of the air-stream. Wallis recognised that any letter, other than the total mutes and their corresponding open forms, could be pronounced either with or without a simultaneous vibration of the larynx. The former resulted in normal speech and the latter in whispered speech (see *p* 135 and note 10); but he denied that whispered *b*, *z*, etc were the same as *p*, *s*, etc. In describing the letters *l* and *r* (*p* 181) he talks of their affinity to *d* and *n* rather than to *t*, in having a vibration of the larynx *and* an air-stream with escape, at least partly, through the nose. In other words he consciously rejected voice/voicelessness as a feature capable by itself of distinguishing segments from each other. Why?

Lehnert attributes it to a concern to preserve the three-way classification of air-streams in addition to the triple place of articulation and mouth-aperture. This may have been the motive, but one must assume that Wallis based the division to some degree on observations. In the production of a voiced stop, before it is released, vibration is likely to be felt in the nose; perhaps it was this that gave him the idea. It is an interesting fact that the traditional stipulation that in oral sounds the velum must be firmly closed against the pharynx wall, so as to prevent air entering the nasal cavity, is not correct. Modern research into nasality has shown that in normal speech it is only necessary for the opening into the nasal cavity to be *substantially smaller* than that into the oral cavity for oral sounds to be perceived (Van Riper and Irwin, 1958, *p* 241). However, Wallis's equal division of the air-stream between nose and mouth would certainly result in a nasal segment being perceived, not an oral one.

It may be significant that Wallis remarks (*p* 157) that the total mutes 'have no sound . . . because the breath does not escape into the outside air'; because *b d g* have a sound of their own he may have felt impelled to allow for air to escape somewhere. *Cf* Smith (1568), who states that every letter, if it is to sound, must have an *efflatio* (escape of breath), or the result would be simply a compression of the breath.

In *A Defence of the Royal Society* (1678, *p* 18) Wallis refers to criticisms of him made by Wilkins (1668), who had analysed consonants as *sonorous* or *mute* according to their accompanying larynx vibration, or lack of it. He rejects this analysis on the grounds that *sonorous* and *mute* correspond to voice and whisper 'which respect the whole Tenor of Speech, not the Formation of particular Letters' and which he compares with loudness, pitch and length. To whisper a word, he says, does not change the essential character of the letters – this would require a different articulation, and whisper is not an articulation. For example, he denies that whispering the words *ved*, *bed* turns them into *fet*, *pet*. Phoneticians today would agree that the word *bed* (if we take it to be the English word) when whispered does not become *pet*. The difference lies in the fact that, in English, vowels followed by final voiced consonants are regularly longer than when followed by voiceless consonants; this distinction is preserved even when one whispers them. In some languages it may be necessary to postulate a further distinction involving force of articulation; the terms *fortis* and *lenis* have been used to refer to this (Heffner, 1949, *p* 121 *ff*; Kim, 1965). Wallis regarded larynx vibration as *one* of the normal features of [b d g v w z ð ɣ j l r], but not a significant feature. He does not include [m̥ n̥ ŋ̊] among the sounds he describes, because they differ from [m n ŋ] only in having no larynx vibration; that is to say, they would be whispered sounds with no separate articulation of their own. Similarly Welsh *ll* is distinguished from *l* not by its lack of larynx vibration, but by its greater breath force (*p* 183).

The comparative 'softness' of the voiced member of paired consonants had long been recognised. Madsen quotes Quintilian's authority that *d* was softer than *t*. Hart mentions a difference of 'inward sound' and of breath force, but seems to regard the former as more important. Wilkins contrasts *p t k/b d g* as hard/soft, but says that the second group have a 'vocal murmur' unlike the first. He carries the voiced/voiceless distinction through all his consonants, admitting voiceless nasals and liquids (*cf* Holder, 1669 – see *p* 56). In his letter to Wallis (1700b) Amman criticises his failure to notice that the pairs *v/f*, *z/s* are distinguished from each other not by any difference of articulatory position, but simply by the fact that *v* and *z* are accompanied by '*sonus quidam vocalis*'. This criticism has often been repeated since then, and most recently by Dobson (1968, *p* 231), but, as we have seen, factors other than voicing do play their part. Wallis deserves some credit for perceiving this, even though it leads him to postulate an even less satisfactory explanation.

(ii) Nasals are classed as 'closed' consonants. It is more common to group them with *l* and *r* as continuants, but their oral closure and release link them with the stops, and some modern analyses have called them 'nasalised stops' (Bloch and Trager, 1942).

(iii) There is no separate category for labio-dentals – *f* and *v* are classed as labials. We saw earlier (*p* 51) that Madsen also had a general class of labials which he subdivided into labio-labial and labio-dental. Presumably Wallis has the same thing in mind, though it is surprising that he does not make it explicit. In *A Defence of the Royal Society* (1678, *p* 19) he criticises Wilkins's analysis of *f* and *v*, and says that these two letters may be formed *either* 'by the two lips' *or* 'between the neather lip and the opposite teeth'. In modern notation, he seems to be describing [ɸ] and [β] as well as [f] and [v] (see note 49, *p* 165).

(iv) The restriction of the places of articulation to three also leads to problems in the classification of the other open consonants. Hart had recognised at least five places of articulation, and Madsen six. Holder (*p* 53) had separate categories of *lingua-dental* – *th dh* – and *gingival* – *s z l r* – and Cooper (table, *p* 37) subdivides both palatal and dental, giving a total of seven places. Wallis has to introduce another type of subdivision. *V/w* (in modern terms, labio-dental/labial-velar), *s/th* and *z/dh* (in modern terms, alveolar/dental), *ch/h* (in modern terms, velar/glottal), and *gh/y* (in modern terms, velar/palatal) are each distinguished by Wallis according to the *shape* of their aperture, as *thinner (subtiliores, tenuiores)/fatter (crassiores, pinguiores)* respectively. He contrasts a long thin aperture (*rimula*) with a rounder and broader one (*foramen*). Lehnert (1936, *p* 67) takes *rimula* to refer to the aperture of the glottis, as it does in Section I of the *Tractatus*, but there can be no doubt that Wallis means the aperture in the mouth cavity; in describing *w* and *s* he specifically says that the cheeks, mouth and tongue are involved in determining the shape of the aperture.

If Wallis means by *v*, *ch* and *gh* the fricatives [v] [x] and [ɣ], these do have a narrower mouth aperture than *w*, *h* and *y* respectively, (if he means by *y* the frictionless continuant [j]) – see further the comments on pp 58–9 and in note 83, *p* 189. But *s/th* and *z/dh* differ not so much in the shape of the apertures involved as in the fact that for the first of each pair the air-stream characteristically strikes the edge of the teeth, whereas in the second it does not. The employment of more categories of *place* would have resulted in a clearer analysis, though it would have upset the symmetry of Wallis's 3 × 3 basis for classification.

(v) An important criticism of the analysis of the total mutes (*p t k*) was made by Amman in his letter to Wallis (Amman, 1700b). He pointed out that there is no mention anywhere of the release of the stop closure. The nature and timing of the release can be important in distinguishing different types of stop consonants (see Abercrombie, 1967, Chapter 9).

Wallis's consonant classification is summed up in the following table (the symbols used are Wallis's):

	Primitive (closed)			Derivative (open)							
	mutes	half-mutes	half-vowels	mutes		half-mutes		half-vowels		others	
				slit	round hole	slit	round hole	slit	round hole		
labials	p	b	m	f	f	v	w	lowing			
palatals	t	d	n	s	th	z	dh	groaning		l	r
gutturals	c	g	ñ	ch	h	gh	y	groaning			

Of grammarians who wrote later in the seventeenth century Wilkins (1668) uses a place and manner classification, but groups the nasals with the open consonants, unlike Robinson, Dalgarno (1661) and Wallis. Holder (1669) comes nearest to modern analyses. He distinguishes nine different articulations by place and manner. These articulations can accompany four different *material* states to give a total of thirty-six consonants, divided into (i) voiceless, non-nasal [p t k f θ s ʃ ʃ ʀ]; (ii) voiceless nasal; (iii) voiced nasal; (iv) voiced non-nasal. He concedes that many of these are not used in languages, some (for example, voiceless nasals) being 'harsh and troublesome', so that only nineteen out of the thirty-six are regarded as regular. He is one of the few early writers on speech to mention the glottal stop.

Further comments on Wallis's analysis will be found in the notes; a few of the problems are discussed here in more detail:

(i) *Guttural n* (*p* 159 *ff*) As Wallis points out [ŋ] was known and identified in classical times as having the same place of articulation as *k* and *g*. The Greek use of γ to represent its occurrence before velar stops was copied by some Roman writers; Priscian (I.vii.39) quotes Varro, and Gellius (*Att. Noct.* XIX.14.7) mentions the words *anguis, increpat* and others, describing the *n* as 'not a true one but a counterfeit' (*adulterinum*); he identifies it as between the letters *n* and *g* in its character. This passage is quoted by Madsen (1586). Greaves (1594), Robinson (1617) and Hodges (1644) all recognised that it was a simple sound, distinct from *n*, but Wallis was the first to give such a full description. Dalgarno (1661 and 1680) also discusses it in considerable detail. Newton (*c* 1660) thought that Hebrew **y** represented [ŋ], but neither Wallis nor Wilkins are inclined to accept this identification. Holder and Cooper interpret it rather as a *voiceless* velar nasal – [ŋ̊]. Petrus Montanus (1635) gives a detailed and accurate description (see Vos, 1962, *p* 206); Vos points out that according to Diringer (1958, *p* 182) in Anglo-Sephardi Hebrew **y** is pronounced *ng*. Amman (1700b) praises Wallis's description; he elsewhere (1700a) says that Hebrew **y** is the only symbol for [ŋ] which exists in any language. Sixteenth-century writers appear to have ignored it, which may be an indication of the fact that it had not yet become a separate phoneme at that time.

(ii) *w and j* (*pp* 167 *ff*, 189 *ff*) The question of how, if at all, the consonants [j] and [w] differ phonetically from the vowels [i] and [u] is an old one. Wallis allows that the difference may only be one of relative length, [w] and [j] being shorter, but he insists that these are to be interpreted as consonants. He follows Gataker, who had himself followed Madsen, in analysing the second elements of *ai, ei, oi, au, ou*, as consonants rather than vowels. In *Tractatus*, Section IV, p 199 *f* (4th edition and later) he argues that *yee* and *woo* differ from *ee + ee* and *oo + oo* in having a definite movement of the articulators in the course of their pronunciation. It is certainly the case in English to-day that the consonants [j] and [w] tend to have a closer stricture when they precede the vowels [i] and [u] respectively (Jones (1962), §§ 803, 814), but in other environments they differ from the vowels in phonological function rather than in articulation. *w* or *j before* a vowel are classed as vowels by Hart, Smith, Wilkins and Amman, and as consonants by Gil, Daines, Hodges, Montanus, Wallis, Holder and Cooper. Cooper says that the consonants do not differ in articulation, but have more compression of the breath than the vowels. *w* and *j after* a vowel are classed as vowels by Hart, Smith, Wilkins, and Amman, and also by Gil, Daines, Hodges and Cooper. Madsen, Montanus, Gataker, Wallis and Holder make them consonantal. In recent times Trager and Smith (1951) have analysed them as consonantal post-vocalically, but this analysis is phonologically based and the phonetic evidence they present is not convincing. (See also Lehiste, 1964, Chapter 4.)

(iii) *Latin v* (*p* 169 *ff*) In the course of his description of the consonant *w* Wallis disagrees with Gataker's opinion that the Latin consonant *v* always had this sound, *ie* [w], though in a paragraph added in the 5th edition, 1699, (see note 61, *p* 171) he changed his mind. He cites as evidence of two different values for the Latin consonant *v* the fact that in Latin names it is transliterated into Greek sometimes as *ου* and sometimes as *β*. From this he deduces that, if *ου* represents [w], *β* must stand for another sound, probably digamma, which according to Wallis had the sound [v] (see note 53, *p* 167). In fact digamma represented [w], so his theory falls down. However, it is true that both *ου* and *β* occur in Greek representing Latin *v*; the former is the earlier usage, but by the second century AD both are frequent. In one Greek inscription the name Nerva appears both as *Νέρβα* and as *Νέρουα* (*Inscriptiones Graecae* IX.1.200). This fluctuation of *ου* and *β* is sometimes taken as evidence that the Latin consonant *v* was by then acquiring a fricative pronunciation –

either bilabial [β] or labio-dental [v], and certainly it had done so by the third century A D. But, as Sturtevant points out (1940, *p* 142, note 5) the use of Greek transliterations as evidence for the pronunciation of Latin *v* in fact does not get one very far, because Attic and Hellenistic Greek had none of the sounds [w], [v], [β] before the first century A D. There is no doubt that the Latin consonant *v* represented [w] or [ʋ] in classical Latin up to the first century A D. (Quintilian I.iv.6–7, I.vii.26, XII.x.29; Velius Longus VII.58.17K; Priscian I.iv.20–21; for a summary of the evidence see Sturtevant, 1940, *pp* 140–43). Another question raised by Wallis (*p* 167 *ff*) is the relation between the vowel [u] and the consonant [w]; he cites some Latin examples. It is necessary to distinguish carefully here between sounds and symbols. In the original classical Latin script the same symbol, V (or in cursive script *𝒰*), was used to represent both the vowel [u] and the consonant [w]. The need for a separate symbol for the consonant was realised by Roman writers (Quintilian I.iv.6–8), and the Emperor Claudius tried to introduce the symbol Ⅎ for it, but without success. For the distinction between the symbols *u* and *v* see note 1, *p* 213.

(iv) *Guttural ch* (*p* 185) The examples Wallis gives to illustrate this sound are conflicting, but it seems that he is describing [x] or [χ]. Ancient Greek χ was an aspirated stop, [kh], in the classical period (Sturtevant, 1940, § 90), though in Modern Greek it stands for either [ç] or [x] according to the context, like German *ch*. Classical Arabic *Cha* and Hebrew *Caph* with *raphe* are voiceless velar/uvular fricatives, but *Cheth* is a pharyngal fricative. The alternation between [ç] and [x] occurred also in Old and Middle English, [ç] occurring after front vowels, and [x] after back vowels; *cf* modern Scots *dreich*, with [ç] and *loch*, with [x]. Guttural *ch* is described by Wallis as 'midway between *c* and *h*' because of its narrow aperture, compared with the complete closure of *c* and the wide aperture of *h*. Descriptions of it are given by Gil, Montanus, Newton, Dalgarno, Wilkins, Lodwick, Holder and Amman; Montanus's description is especially accurate (Vos, *pp* 201–3).

(v) *Guttural h* (*p* 185) The sound Wallis is describing is [h], which in modern phonetic terms may symbolise a glottal fricative or a voiceless vowel – that is, a segment with the articulatory posture of a vowel but without vibration of the vocal cords. Its association by Wallis with *guttural ch* (a velar/uvular fricative) is confusing, but an inevitable result of his restriction of the places of articulation to three. Owing partly to the similarity of [h] to a simple expulsion of the breath, with no apparent articulation of the vocal organs in the mouth, its status as a letter has often been called into question. The fact that it was not written on the same line as other letters in classical Greek (though it was in early Greek, as Wallis says) is sometimes taken as evidence of its peculiar status. Quintilian (I.iv.9; I.v.19) doubted if it could be called a letter, and Priscian (I.iv.16) definitely rejected it. In sixteenth- and seventeenth-century descriptions its breathy nature is emphasised, but Madsen pointed out that breath was an essential part of all letters (*cf* Smith's *efflatio* – see *p* 53), and that *h* could distinguish one word from another. Like Wallis he rejected arguments based on the fact that elision occurs before it, on the grounds that similar arguments apply to other letters, for example *s* and *m*. Hart (1569) described *h* as 'breathes two' *cf* Wallis's *aspiratio duplex*, which, however, he applies to *ch* as opposed to *h*. Gil (1621, *p* 10) noted the use of *a*, *my* (not *an*, *mine*) before it as proof of its consonantal nature. Montanus (1635) gives a very full and interesting description (Vos, *pp* 197–9); he says that he first of all identified it with a voiceless vowel, but subsequently realised that it was a throat letter, and so wishes to retain both descriptions; he also recognised the possibility of voiced *h*. Wilkins (1668) and Cooper (1685, *p* 35) noticed its affinity with the vowels following it, apart from its lack of voicing. Holder (1669, *p* 68) denied it the status of a letter, but goes on 'yet in that it causes a sensible, and not incommodious discrimination of sound, it ought to be annexed to the alphabet'. His description of it indicates a voiceless vowel, but since for him all vowels are 'vocal' he cannot class *h* with them. Like Amman (1700a) he recognises that there may be a narrowing of the passage through the larynx during its production. Compare modern descriptions of *h*, for example Jones (1962 §§ 776–778): 'The letter *h* denotes the sound of pure breath having a free passage through the mouth. This letter is used in transcribing English and many other languages to represent any one of the sounds produced when the mouth is held in a vowel position and air is emitted through the wide open glottis. The different varieties of *h* are known as *breathed glottal fricative* consonants, since the friction produced by the air passing through the glottis is the feature common to all of them. . . . There are as many varieties of *h* as there are vowels. . . . The English *h* phoneme comprises a great many members, the variety used in each particular

[59]

case being that which corresponds to the vowel immediately following.'

(vi) *Guttural gh* (*p* 187) Wallis is presumably referring to [ɣ], the voiced counterpart of [x], but in the examples he gives *gh* had the sound [ç] or [x]. Dobson (1968, *p* 232) is probably right in assuming that Wallis is confusing the sounds [h] and [ç] when he quotes the Northern pronunciation of *light* etc as containing 'the sound *h*'. Hebrew *Ghimel* with *raphe* and Arabic *Ghain* both represent voiced velar or uvular fricatives in the Classical languages (*cf* note 43, *p* 159). [ɣ] is described by Montanus as a sound of Low Dutch, and so also by Lodwick and Amman. Wilkins follows Wallis in his incorrect supposition that it was the original sound of *gh* in *right, daughter*, etc and that it occurred in Irish; in fact *gh* in Irish also represents a *voiceless* fricative.

(vii) *The ' compound' sounds sy, zy, ty, dy* (*p* 201 *ff*) Wallis's analysis of the initial consonants in English *jar, shame* and *chew* and French *je* as *dy, sy, ty*, and *zy* respectively differs from that of other sixteenth- and seventeenth-century writers (see Dobson (1968), *pp* 957–9; Lehnert (1936), §§ 83–5); the majority analyse them as [dʒ], [ʃ], [tʃ] and [ʒ]. The foreign sounds Wallis quotes do not support his analysis; Lehnert cites Ickelsamer (1534) as evidence that German *sch* represented a simple sound. In the 4th and later editions Wallis mentions the criticisms made but rejects them (*pp* 203–5). Lehnert (loc cit), as so often, attributes the analysis to Wallis's *Schematisierungstendenz*; he suggests that it fits in too neatly with the analysis of the diphthongs, which have *y* or *w* as their second element. This may well be the reason; in recent times phonemic analyses have used similar devices for purposes of symbol economy (see *p* 57 on *w* and *j*), but here Wallis claims to be describing what is *heard*, and hotly disputes whether the introduction of an *s* into these groups (*tsy, dsy*) gives an acceptable pronunciation. It is possible that he based his analysis on pronunciations of words like *nation, nature, orchard, soldier* with [sj] [tj] [dj] instead of [ʃ] [tʃ] [dʒ], and extended this identification to other words where the former pronunciation did not occur.

(viii) *Palatalised and labialised stops* (*p* 207 *ff*) Wallis's record of the pronunciations *cyan, gyet, begyin* is very interesting, both as additional evidence of the palatal nature of *thin a* and also possibly as evidence of differences in the pronunciation of this vowel in the

North and South of England (see Lehnert (1936), § 185; Dobson (1968), §§ 379, 432). His description of *y* as 'having something in common with the preceding consonant and the following vowel' exposes one of the inconsistencies of his analysis; he has classed *y* as guttural, but the related vowel *i* is classed as palatal (see *p* 189, note 83). The spellings *pw*, *bw* probably represent [p̆] [b̪] rather than [pw] [bw]; that is, labialisation of the initial stop, with a resulting *w*-like glide on to the vowel, just as *cy*, *gy* represent palatalised stops. Russian provides a good example of this labialisation before back rounded vowels (Jespersen, *M.E.G.*, I.§12.64). Lehnert, 1936, § 169 points out that Gil (1621, *p* 15) gives triphthongal *buoi* for *boy*, calling *boi* a *dialectus Borealium* and Butler (1633) has *bwoë*. Lehnert also quotes examples from the Cely-papers, 1475–88: *pwoynte* (*p* 85), *apwoyntyd* (*p* 100). By the eighteenth century it was frowned upon; Nares (1784) regards *bwoile* as an undesirable imitation of French. Wright (1896) records *bwile* (boil) in the dialects of Northants, Shropshire and Oxfordshire, and *bwoy* (boy) in Shropshire, Berkshire and Devonshire. (Wallis analysed the first element of the diphthong in *boil* as either *obscure ò or open o*, but on *p* 209 the insertion of *w* is said to occur 'especially before *open o*'.)

(ix) *English syllabic consonants* (*p* 219) In calling *needles* and *lightnes* monosyllables Wallis does not observe that the *l* in the former and the *n* in the latter are syllabic. Hart (1570) said of words such as *able* that they did not constitute two syllables, even though they seemed to; *l m n r* according to him have half the sound of a vowel, and so, when used next to one or two consonants without a vowel, make half a syllable – usually at the end of words. Smith (1568) recognised them as syllabic only when they occurred after stops. Gil (1621, *p* 20) thought that in English, though not in any other language, consonants could make up a syllable; he quotes *bridle, title, oxen, bidden, open, saddle* as examples. Daines (1640) calls *l m n r* 'three-quarter vowels' when final, and says that they form an imperfect syllable; his examples include *l – fable, uncle, fiddle, trifle* etc; *r* (usually after *c g w*) – *acre, maugre, tower* – but he concedes that in these there may be an intervening vowel; *m – prism*; *n – benign*. Hodges has a section in his spelling tables for words in which the last syllable is vowelless, such as *feeble, needle*. However, Dalgarno (1661) and Cooper (1685), like Wallis, regard such words as *riddle* (Dalgarno) and *strengthen* (Cooper) as monosyllables; Cooper (1685, *p* 48) says that *le* and *en* are sounded like *l n* when final, but adds that *bl* in *grumble* has the same sound as in *blame*. See further in Dobson, 1968, *p* 887 *ff*.

[*d*] *Non-segmental characteristics of speech* (*p* 209 *ff*)

Wallis's account of the speech habits of different communities is imitated by Wilkins (1668, *pp* 380–81), who also mentions variations in style of speech between individual members of one speech community. Basic 'settings' for different languages have been suggested by Sweet (1932, §§ 184–188), who calls them the 'organic basis', and by Honikman (1964), who calls them 'articulatory settings'. Sweet made German the mean between English and French, describing French as having the most front articulation, which appears to conflict with Wallis's description. However, in describing the English pronunciation as at the front of the mouth Wallis is not referring to the place of articulation, but rather to the comparative lack of interference with the air-stream at this point. Cooper (1685) attributed the different *toni*, or accents, of different sexes, ages and localities to variations in the size of the vocal tract and vocal organs, and in the forcefulness of the articulation and of the air-stream (*pp* 18–19). Wallis's passing reference to pitch differences which characterise 'the sentence taken as a continuous whole' is typical of the inadequate treatment of intonation in early grammars of English. Hart (1551) mentions the falling tune, and Butler (1634) both falling and rising; *cf* also Butler's *Rhetoricae*, London (1629), Book II, Chapter IV.

[*e*] *Sound and symbol*

Wallis's use of the word *litera* (letter) requires some comment. Following the ancient tradition he defines it as 'uncompounded and indivisible' (*p* 129); *cf* Aristotle, *Poet.* 1456b 20, στοιχεῖον . . . ἐστιν φωνὴ ἀδιαίρετος. Aristotle and his contemporaries used the terms στοιχεῖον (*stoicheion*) and γράμμα (*gramma*) interchangeably for either 'sound' or 'written symbol'. The Stoics gave γράμμα a threefold meaning: (i) τὸ στοιχεῖον; (ii) ὁ χαρακτὴρ τοῦ στοιχείου – the symbol, or letter in its narrow sense; (iii) τὸ ὄνομα οἶον "Αλφα – the name of the letter, *eg* Alpha (Diogenes Laertius, VII.56). Sextus Empiricus (*Math.* I.99) added that the first of these – στοιχεῖον – in its narrowest sense signified δύναμις τοῦ χαρακτῆρος – the sound; *cf* Boethius, *De interp.* II.23.16, and Diels (1899), *pp* 59–60.

The same relationship existed in Latin between *elementum* and *litera*; at first both are used equally of sound or symbol, but later *elementum* is sometimes confined to 'sound' and *litera* to 'symbol' (Boethius, loc cit II.22.27 *ff*; Priscian I.ii.4). Diels, 1899, and in recent years Burkert, 1959, investigate the origin and occurrence of the words στοιχεῖον and *elementum*, which were also used by classical philosophers to refer to the basic elements underlying everything, just as the letters of the alphabet can be said to be the basic elements of speech. The threefold interpretation of γράμμα by the Stoics is also applied to Latin *litera*: (i) *nomen* – name, (ii) *figura* – symbol, (iii) *potestas* – sound (see Abercrombie, 1949).

Wallis recognises the ambiguity of meaning of *litera* as either 'sound' or 'symbol', and for the most part succeeds in avoiding the pitfalls into which confusion of these two meanings had led many of his contemporaries. On the whole he seems to use *litera* to signify one of the phonemes of a language, having a distinctive symbol associated with it; phonetically similar phonemes in different languages, although their symbols may differ, *eg* P and Greek *Π*, are the same *litera*. In describing vowels he seems to avoid using *litera*, perhaps because particular symbols, such as A E I O U, are more ambiguous in their realisation as sounds than are the consonant symbols. In some instances he is certainly using *litera* to mean written symbols, *eg* in the Latin text *pp* 146, 17; 160, 7; 166, 16; 174, 16; 178, 18; 186, 4; 204, 26; 206, 5. However, on *p* 192, 5, where the discussion is specifically concerned with the confusion of symbols, he uses *characterem literae z* (the symbol for letter *z*). In the Grammar (*p* 220, 10) he calls *x* a letter, though earlier (*Tractatus, p* 131) he regards it as a combination of two letters. In describing mute *e* (*p* 250, 30) he says that it becomes a 'sounding *e*' so as to avoid 'an inadmissible combination of letters' (*concursus literarum illigabilium*), where *literae* must refer to sounds, not symbols. The *Tractatus* starts from the sounds, whereas Chapter I of the English Grammar starts from the letters of the alphabet which are used in English, and goes on to describe the sounds associated with each.

[*f*] Syllable division (*p* 229 *ff*)
The long digression on vowel length and syllable division was introduced into the chapter on English vowels in the 5th edition. It is noteworthy as the first real attempt to formulate a rule for the occurrence of long and short vowels in English. Wallis was obviously in-

fluenced by his knowledge of the Hebrew syllable division. In order to explain the occurrence of the long vowels in words such as *take*, *make* he puts forward the theory that in these words the final *e* was originally pronounced, so that the preceding consonant was not functioning as an arresting consonant to the first syllable, but a releasing consonant to the second. Therefore the first syllable, being open, was long. This theory is an over-simplification; some of the examples he quotes were in fact never dissyllabic – *one, bone, stone* – and other words of similar appearance – *come, some* – never had long vowels. Nevertheless it is an intelligent attempt to find an explanation. Cooper (1685, *p* 20) maintained that a vowel in an open syllable cannot be short, because shortness results from 'a sudden appulse or collision of the speech organs, which compresses or wholly stops the breath-stream' (*subito appulsu vel collisione instrumentorum, comprimente spiritum vel totum intercipiente*). Attempts to relate the syllable as a unit to physiological processes involved in speech production have been only partially successful (see Stetson, 1951; Twaddell, 1953; Fry, 1964; Ladefoged, 1967, Chapter 1). No wholly satisfactory general phonetic definition of the syllable has yet been found, and questions of syllable division are usually related closely to the phonology of the particular language under examination. Wallis talks of 'vowel length' being determined by the syllable structure, except at one point (*p* 235) where he refers to the length of the *syllable*. In English there is a reciprocal relationship between vowel and following consonant in a (C)VC type monosyllable. Greater length in the vowel is compensated by a shorter arresting consonant, and vice versa. Abercrombie (1961, *p* 33) quotes the words *sleep* and *slip* as examples of this. He goes on: 'It is not so often pointed out that in *slipper*:*sleeper* the difference here too manifests itself over most of the word: it is true that the first vowel in *slipper* is shorter than the first in *sleeper*, but the second vowel in *slipper* is longer than the second in *sleeper* (at least in my pronunciation and that of others who speak like me). The use of the terms "short vowel" and "long vowel" for V^1 and V^2 is thus to some extent misleading, and it is better to think of V^1 as producing, when in the first syllable of a structure (C)VCV(C), the quantities $\cup -$, and of V^2 as producing, in the same structure, the quantities $\cap \cap$.' His symbol $\cap$ represents a syllable quantity intermediate between $\cup$ and $-$, and on *p* 31 he defines V^1 as 'the so-called "short" vowels (*ie* in the traditional Jones numbering, numbers 2, 3, 4, 6, 8, 10)' and V^2 as 'the so-called "long" vowels and the diphthongs (numbers 1, 5, 7, 9, 11, and 13–21)'. Abercrombie's article examines the relationship between syllable quantity in English and the 'phonematic structure' of the syllable, showing that although in some dissyllabic feet the structure determines the quantity, in others it is quite irrelevant (op cit *p* 31).

Wallis's comments on syllable division in Welsh may be compared with those of Sweet (1932, § 159), who talks of CVC–V syllable division as *close stress* and CV–CV as *open stress*. Unlike Wallis he believes that Welsh resembles southern European languages in having *open* stress. It was the same phenomenon, no doubt, that both were describing; Sweet says that to the unaccustomed ear open stress suggests doubling of the consonant, and explains this as due to the fact that the consonant receives a new force impulse, which makes it more prominent. Wallis accounts for this apparent length by making the intervocalic consonant an arresting one, shortening the preceding vowel (*cf* note 36, *p* 153). It has been suggested that in a word of CVCV structure the syllable division could be assumed to occur *within* the medial consonant, rather than before or after it, this consonant then being regarded as both arresting and releasing (see Hockett, 1955, *p* 52 – interludes; *cf* Anderson, 1969).

The Greek and Latin grammarians' practice in dividing syllables (see *p* 231 *ff*) was not based on phonetic observations but was simply a convenient way for breaking up words when writing them. From the prosody it is clear that consonant groups which could form a releasing cluster initially in a word – *eg* [mn] [kt] – were divided when following a vowel, whether within a word or not; the first of these consonants was regarded as closing the previous syllable, making it long in quantity, and the second as releasing the next syllable (as in τέμ-νω). Exceptions to this rule were combinations of plosive and liquid (λ ρ or a nasal), at least in Attic Greek – see Allen (1968), *p* 100 *ff*. The length of the *vowel* before the consonant group (as opposed to that of the *syllable*) was not affected by the syllable division. Allen (op cit *p* 97 *ff*) recommends the use of *heavy/light* for syllable quantity, and *long/short* for vowel length.

Wallis's proposals for indicating vowel length involve showing the syllable division by means of a hyphen (*p* 235) – before the medial consonant to show a long vowel (*la-ter*) and after the medial consonant to show a short vowel (*lat-er*). For a comparable use of the hyphen in modern phonetics see Jones (1962), Chapter XXXII. Cooper (1685, *p* 45) followed Wallis in pointing out the discrepancy between written syllable division in English and the actual division that occurs in speech.

8 The accent of English described by Wallis

In Chapter I of the Grammar (*p* 273) Wallis makes it clear that he was concerned to describe what he calls 'a pure and authentic pronunciation of the English language'. He expressly excludes dialectal variations in different parts of the country, affected speech and other such "barbarisms' (Latin *barbarismus* was originally used to refer to the introduction of foreign words and phrases into classical Latin; later it came to mean also the use of words or expressions not in accordance with the classical standard of the language). He also excludes 'the careless pronunciations of certain sounds' to be heard both among the mass of the people and in polite circles. He may have included in this category such features of English as assimilation and weak forms, which had been described by Hart (1569); certainly Wallis does not mention them. From time to time he refers to alternative pronunciations, for example on *p* 237 '*Walk, talk* etc are better pronounced with English *a*, though careless speakers say *wau'k, tau'k*, etc copying the French . . .'; *p* 263 '*Au*, or *aw*, if properly pronounced, would represent a sound made up of short English *á* and *w*. But many people nowadays pronounce it as a simple vowel . . .'; *p* 265 '*Eu, ew, eau* are made up of *clear é* and *w* . . . though they are given a rather sharper pronunciation by some. . . . However, the first pronunciation is more correct.' Frequently Wallis seems to be taking the spelling as an indication of the more 'correct' form (see note 27, *p* 145). Although Wallis was born in Kent and spent the first fourteen years of his life there, there is no doubt that as a preacher and later as a university teacher he would have spoken the accent of English current in Court circles and in the universities. This, then, is what he is referring to as 'a pure and authentic pronunciation'. Only in one or two cases does it seem likely that his Kentish origin may have led him to record a dialectal pronunciation (see note 82, *p* 283; *cf* Introduction, *p* 60 – *gh*, *p* 61, and note 28, *p* 147 for other mentions of dialectal pronunciations).

Hart (1570) contrasted the language of the Court and of London with that of the 'far West or North Countries'. Gil (1621, Chapter 6) gave many examples of dialect forms, dividing them up into North, South, East, West and Poetic as opposed to the pronunciation which he takes as the basis for his description – the 'common' dialect (*communis dialectus*). He regarded the dialect of the West as most barbarous: '*et maxime si rusticos audias in agro Somersettensi: dubitare enim quis facile possit utrum Anglice loquantur, an peregrinum aliquod idioma*' – 'in particular if you hear the countrymen in Somerset: for one might easily be at a loss to know whether they were speaking English or some foreign tongue'. Gil also criticises *Mopsarum fictitias* – affected pronunciations (Preface *p* 7) and savagely attacks the language of the 'wandering beggars' (*p* 19). Cooper (1685), headmaster of a school demanding a pure form of speech, has a chapter entitled *De Barbara Dialecto*, which includes forms to be avoided either because they are dialectal or because they are *facilitatis causa* – simplified forms of pronunciation; for example *possable* for *possible*, *'ent?* for *is not?* Jones (1701), who intended his book primarily as an aid to spelling, recorded a wide variety of different pronunciations, but took that of London, the universities and the Court as his standard.

9 Wallis's influence on later writers

Wallis's fame as a mathematician no doubt helped to make his Grammar more widely known – see *p* 71 *f* for an account of the editions published (ten in all). His immediate successors were certainly influenced by him. Dalgarno (1661) gives a very similar consonant system, and Owen Price (1665) adopts Wallis's description of the vowels (Zachrisson (1913), *pp* 182–3). Wilkins (1668, *p* 357) says of him 'amongst all that I have seen published (he) seems to me with the greatest accurateness and subtlety to have considered the Philosophy of Articulate sounds'. Cooper (1685) names Wallis and Wilkins as the most helpful of his predecessors, and says Wallis was the first to attempt to adapt the grammatical art to suit English; he followed him in many respects both in classification of sounds and in grammar. His work is ordered in a similar way: (i) sounds in general; (ii) English letters and their sounds; (iii) grammar – which includes much of what Wallis deals with in the chapter *De Etymologia*. Like Wallis he associates prepositions closely with substantives, and virtually quotes Wallis's exact words in parts. He takes over the terms *possessive-* and *respective-*adjectives and borrows many examples. This is not to say that he plagiarised Wallis; he added much that was new, for example, chapters on syntax and on accents.

The same cannot be said of the early eighteenth-century grammar by Greenwood (1711) and that commonly known as Brightland's Grammar (1711). The relationship between English grammars of the seventeenth and eighteenth centuries is discussed, mostly with reference to sounds and not to grammar or syntax, by Zachrisson (1914 and 1917), Lehnert (1937–8) and Sundby (1952). Lehnert's article is concerned chiefly with the dependence of Greenwood and Brightland on Wallis for their description of sounds and with the authorship of Brightland's Grammar (quoted in this edition as Brightland, for convenience). He shows that this grammar is in fact a compilation from various sources probably put together by Charles Gildon (1665–1724) and published by John Brightland anonymously, because of its plagiarisms (see also Scheurweghs and Vorlat, 1959). The sources, recognised earlier by Ellis, are Wallis (1674), The Expert Orthographist (1704) and Ben Jonson (1640). Another source, not mentioned by Lehnert, is Lancelot and Arnauld (1660).

Greenwood's *Essay towards a Practical English Grammar* went through five editions between 1711 and 1753 and his shortened *Royal English Grammar* nine editions between 1737 and 1780. *A Grammar of the English Tongue* (Brightland) had eight editions published between 1711 and 1759. So they equalled Wallis's Grammar in their popularity, which is not surprising considering that a very large proportion of both consists of a literal translation of it. Greenwood admits his debt, but Brightland incorporates most of the *Tractatus* as notes to the text, with only an occasional acknowledgement, describing the notes as (i) more difficult enquiries into grammar in general; (ii) a defence of details in the text; (iii) pointing analogies to Latin. In the preface to Brightland it is suggested that both Brightland and Greenwood were misled by Wallis, who specifically wrote for men well acquainted with Latin grammar and so could assume many things as obvious. *Cf* Greenwood's preface: 'I have in this book taken in everything that was material from Dr Wallis, but he writing for foreigners and in Latin, I have not pursued his method, as not being every way answerable to my design.' Greenwood also borrows from Wilkins (1668) and Hickes (1689) and says in his preface 'in two or three places I have made use of Mr Lock's expressions, because I liked them better than my own'. His illustrative examples are much fuller than those in Wallis, who relied on the Latin equivalents to convey the meaning, in many cases. A careful comparison of the texts of Greenwood and Brightland with that of Wallis shows that Greenwood translated virtually the whole of Wallis, though in describing the parts of speech he introduced a great deal of other material, so that it is not always easy to separate what he took from Wallis, apart from the Author's Preface and *Tractatus*, which are acknowledged. Brightland (see Lehnert 1938, *p* 200) translates virtually the whole of the *Tractatus* and Chapter I of the Grammar, but in his grammatical section also quotes large portions of Lancelot and Arnauld (1660) and Jonson (1640). His description of the auxiliaries, the distinction of shall/will, and the account of irregular verbs and prepositions are all taken from Wallis. The section on sentences is culled from various chapters of Wallis, combined with Lancelot and Arnauld (construction of names = Wallis, Chapter XI; construction of affirmations = Chapter VIII; construction of qualities = Chapters III and V; construction of particles incorporates Chapter IV; etc).

On the Continent Theodor Arnold (1718) and Thomas Lediard (1726) both translated parts of Wallis literally, though on a smaller scale; for example Arnold took the sections on *e mute*, syllabic consonants, and the pronunciation of *th* (see W. Müller, 1909) and Lediard took the section on the formation of vowels (see Ellis, E.E.P., 1044). Both these grammars were influential, particularly Arnold's. In England, later eighteenth-century grammars were mostly rigidly traditional, ignoring Wallis's innovations. Among the best are Joseph Priestley's *Rudiments of English* (1761) and Dr Robert Lowth's *Short Introduction to English Grammar* (1762), both of which followed Wallis in trying to free English from the influence of Latin. Lowth's grammar was very popular. John Nichols (1828) quotes some letters from Joseph Cockfield which refer to these grammars and to Wallis (Vol V, 1828, *p* 797):

(i) 6 July 1769. 'Did Dr Wallis's grammar of our language ever fall into the hand of my correspondent? It is written in Latin, and was reprinted in 1765 at the expense of the very liberal and ingenious Mr Hollis of Pall Mall. A bookseller the other day talked about a translation, and lent it me for my opinion.'

(ii) 27 July 1769. 'I have read as yet but little of the English grammar mentioned in my former letter; it appears to me a work of learning and judgment and certainly deserves a translation.'

(iii) 21 August 1769. 'I believe a new translation of Wallis would be a work of considerable utility. Dr Lowth's performance, though an excellent one, is not complete in all its parts, nor can it be thought to have precluded further attempts. Since my absence from home I have met with Priestley's improved edition of his grammar which is also good in its way.'

In the nineteenth century Ellis (*Early English Pronunciation*, Vol I) made great use of Wallis as evidence, and Sweet (1888) in turn borrowed much from Ellis. Lehnert (1938, 165–70) suggests that the basis of the English vowel quadrilateral goes back to Wallis and Robinson (1617), though as he admits there is no evidence that Bell knew Robinson's work, and the basis of Bell's vowel classification is different in important respects (see *p* 46).

In the twentieth century the study of grammar and phonetics has made great strides forward, but within the last decade linguists have increasingly been emphasising the fact that traditional grammar foreshadowed in important respects the insights of modern linguistics (*eg* Chomsky, 1966). In the study of language, no less than in other disciplines, the works of early pioneers often contribute considerably to our knowledge and understanding of the subject. Wallis's Grammar together with his introductory *Treatise on Speech* undoubtedly deserves a high rank among such works in the field of linguistics and of English grammar.

10 Portraits

The most famous portrait of Wallis is that by Kneller, showing him full length in a skull cap, bands and robes, with the medal and chain given to him by the Elector of Brandenburg (see frontispiece). This was painted in 1701 when Wallis was eighty-five, at the instigation of Pepys, and was presented by Pepys to Oxford University (see Introduction *pp* 11, 15, 16). It was engraved by J. Faber, Senior (less than whole length), who dedicated it to the Rev A. Charlett (see J. Chaloner Smith, *British Mezzotint Portraits*, 76.I). The original portrait hangs in the Examination Schools at Oxford. Another portrait, by Soest, is in the possession of the Royal Society. W. Faithorne did a half-length portrait of Wallis; his engraving of it was used as frontispiece to Wallis's *Mechanica* (1670). Loggan painted a half-length portrait of Wallis in his skull cap and gown in 1678. An engraving of this, by G. B. Cipriani, appears as frontispiece to the 6th edition of Wallis's Grammar (1765) (see *p* 74). There is also a half-length portrait by Sonmans of Wallis aged eighty-three, in wig, gown and bands, which appears as frontispiece to Vol III of Wallis's *Opera Mathematica et Miscellanea* (1693–99), engraved by Michael Burghers.

11 Editions of the Tractatus de Loquela and Grammatica Linguae Anglicanae

Of the following, the 1727 and 1740 editions are of the *Tractatus de Loquela* only. The rest also contain the *Grammatica Linguae Anglicanae*. Locations of these editions in libraries are given in Alston (1965). Pseudo-editions are those not authorised by Wallis.

(i) 1st edition, Oxford, Leon. Lichfield, 1653. 8° (24), 128 *pp* (facsimile edition, Scolar Press, 1969).

(ii) 2nd edition, Oxford, L. Lichfield, 1664. 8° (24), 128 *pp*. According to the title-page 'priore auctior', but the additions are very few (see notes on the text).

(iii) 3rd edition, Hamburg, Apud Gothofredum Schultzen, 1672. 8° (20), 144 *pp*. *Pace* Lehnert, who says this is an exact re-print of the second edition, there is one important correction (see note 44, *p* 255).

(iv) 4th edition, Oxford, L. Lichfield, 1674. 8° (12), 190 *pp*. There are numerous additions in this edition. The notes on the text indicate those up to Chapter XIII. Chapter XIV was expanded from 16 pages in the 1st edition to 31 pages, and Chapter XV from 1 to 2 pages. Wallis added a *Praxis Grammatica* in 3 sections, which analyses the grammar and etymology of the Lord's Prayer, the Apostles's Creed and some pieces of verse, totalling 55 pages.

(v) 4 (pseudo) edition, Hamburg, 1688. An exact copy of the 3rd edition. Bound together with John Podensteiner's *Clavis Linguae Anglicanae* and William Perkins's *Fundamentum Christianae Religionis*, 1688. (These 3 works were also bound together with an edition of Mauger-Festeau's *New Double Grammar*, published at the Hague, 1696.) In the preface the edition number has been changed from 3rd to 4th, but the 1st edition is still referred to as '*novendecim abhinc annis*' (19 years ago).

(vi) 5th edition, Oxford, 1699; contained in the 3rd volume of *Opera Mathematica et miscellanea.* Folio, (6), 80 *pp.* The last edition published during Wallis's lifetime. Many additions, especially to Chapter xiv (almost twice as long) and Chapter xv.

(vii) 6th (pseudo) edition, Leiden, J. Langerak, 1727. This contains only the *Tractatus de Loquela,* bound with Conrad Amman's *Dissertatio de Loquela* and 2 letters exchanged by Wallis and Amman. The text is almost identical with that of the 1699 edition; 1 complete sentence is omitted however: 33.31–34.2, Et ab Anglo-Saxonum . . . vel *enough.* There are 1 or 2 other small omissions: 8.31 Italique suum; 33.14 olim. 8° (8), 54 *pp.*

(viii) 7th (pseudo) edition, Leiden, J. Langerak, 1740. An exact reprint of the 1727 edition, except for edition number and date.

(ix) 6th edition, London, G. Bowyer, 1765; London and Leipzig, Io. Dodslei et Casp. Moseri, 1765. 8°, xxxv, 281 *pp.* A well printed octavo edition, commissioned by Thomas Hollis. Hollis consulted the London bookseller Millar with proposals for the edition and Millar in turn invited the printer, William Bowyer, to ask the opinion of Dr Lowth. Lowth replied that in his opinion 'the reprinting of this grammar would be for the benefit of Natives as well as of Foreigners'. However, when asked to write a preface to it he refused, without giving any reason (see Nichols, 1812, *pp* 445–448). Nichols remarks 'to say the truth Mr Hollis was not in those days fit company for Orthodox Divines . . . he was procuring a new edition of Locke's letters concerning Toleration'.

Two other editions are listed, but have not been examined by the present editor:

(i) An abridged edition, edited by Carl H. Rappolt, Königsberg, 1731 (see Lehnert, 1936, § 39). This reduces the *Tractatus* and *Grammatica* to 32 octavo pages, but adds 153 new examples. It is based on the text of the 1699 edition.

(ii) An edition of the *Tractatus* alone, Königsberg, 1721, is listed by Alston (1965). 8° (4), 44 *pp.*

Zachrisson, (1917) *p* 70, says he used 'the 3rd edition, (Strassburg 1672)'; this is presumably the same as the Hamburg edition. He also used 'a late edition of 1775' (a misprint for 1765?).

12 Notes on the text

The facsimile text used in this edition is that of the 6th edition, 1765; it is virtually identical with that of the folio 5th edition, 1699, which was the last that Wallis himself supervised. What differences there are mostly result from misprints, or the use of different spellings – for example, *hee* (5th), *he* (6th), *doe* (5th), *do* (6th). Where these are significant they have been noted on the appropriate pages, together with the differences to be found in earlier editions. Substantial additions were made in both the 4th and the 5th editions, but a considerable part of these were in Chapters xiv and xv which are not included in this edition.

Where references in the textual notes are followed simply by edition numbers (for example, *p* xxvi. 25 pondo: 2nd–6th) this indicates that the section of the text concerned appears only in those particular editions. For the most part, corrections noted in the Errata of earlier editions are not reprinted here.

IOHANNES WALLIS D·D

GEOMETRIAE PROF· SAVILIANVS OXONIAE

REGALIS SOCIETATIS LONDINI SODALIS.

[74]

IOANNIS WALLISII GRAMMATICA LINGVAE ANGLICANAE.

CVI PRAEFIGITVR,

DE LOQVELA; SIVE DE SONO-RVM OMNIVM LOQVELARIVM FORMATIONE: TRACTATVS GRAMMATICO-PHYSICVS.

EDITIO SEXTA.

ACCESSIT EPISTOLA AD THO-MAM BEVERLEY; DE MVTIS SVRDISQVE INFORMANDIS.

LONDINI,

EXCVDEBAT GVIL. BOWYER.
PROSTANT APVD A. MILLAR.
MDCCLXV.

AUCTORIS AD EDIT. V.
PRAEFATIO.

———

Cum morem obtinuiffe videam, in operis veftibulo lectorem alloquendi; quaedam etiam et mihi praefanda judico, ut et Sufcepti operis Rationes, et quid hac in re praeftiterim, paucis oftendam; ipfiusque linguae Anglicanae originem et progreffus tradam.

Lingua illa quam tradimus Anglicana, quaeque nunc dierum non per Angliam modo fed et in Scotia ufurpatur, non eft vetufta illa lingua Britannica qua primi olim Britones ufi fuerunt, neque ulla quidem ipfius propago, fed alia prorfus aliunde advecta.

Lingua Anglicana.

Obtinuit fiquidem apud nos olim lingua vetufta admodum atque eleganter venufta; nobis quidem cum finitimis Galliae incolis communis. Sive enim haec Infula cum Gallia olim fuerit ifthmo conjuncta; feu potius mari disjuncta femper, et non nifi propter viciniam loci commercio fruens: five etiam nos ab illis, feu illi a nobis primitus acceperint incolas; aut etiam utrobique cognatae forfan coloniae, a Phoenicibus puta, aut Trojanis, aut aliunde deductae, fedes hic pofuerint; certe eadem olim utrisque lingua, iidem

Antiqua lingua Britannica.

24 hic: 5th–6th

Author's preface to the fifth edition

As it appears to be the custom to address the reader at the beginning of a book, I think I should say a few words by way of preface; my purpose being to explain briefly why I undertook this work, and what my contribution has been to this field of study, and also to describe the origin and development of the English language.[1]

The English language to be described here is now spoken all over England and in Scotland also, but it is not the same as the old British language spoken by the earliest Britons, nor is it in any way derived from that language. It is entirely different and has come from a different place.

THE ANCIENT BRITISH LANGUAGE

Formerly our language was an elegant and graceful one of ancient origin, which was also spoken by the inhabitants of neighbouring Gaul. This island may originally have been joined to Gaul by an isthmus, or, assuming it has always been separated by the sea, it may have had dealings with Gaul just because of its nearness; the inhabitants of our island may have originally come from Gaul or theirs from Britain, or perhaps related colonies sent by the Phoenicians or the Trojans, or from elsewhere,[2] settled in both these areas. Whatever their origin they certainly had a common language and

---

[1] Wallis's survey of the origin and development of the English language is based on the sources mentioned later in the Preface (*p* 83 *ff*), and as he admits (*pp* 81, 85) the evidence they provide contains a large element of guesswork and fable. In spite of this there is much in it of value; Lehnert (1936, §56), while emphasising its contribution to the discovery of a suitable methodology (i) for etymological research; (ii) for the study of the relationships of pre-historic peoples by means of their languages; (iii) for the examination of the influence of foreign languages on the development of a mother tongue, criticises Wallis for losing sight of the importance of 'der inneren Entwicklung der Sprache im Laufe der Zeit' (the internal evolution of the language in the course of time). Similar surveys of the English language are given by Gil (1621), Wilkins (1668) and Cooper (1685) who includes much of Wallis's material; Greenwood (1711) translates the whole of Wallis's Preface, and inserts in addition a number of excerpts from Wilkins and from Hickes (1689).

[2] It was popular to try to trace a connection with Troy; *cf* Pharamond (see *p* 87), who was said to have been a descendant of Priam.

iidèm mores fuerunt.   Et quidem, quantum
ego judico, *Gallis* et *Wallis*, hoc eft, Galliae
feu Franciae, et Walliae feu Cambro-Bri-
tanniae populis communis eft denominatio :
Nam literarum *G* et *W* frequentiffima eft
commutatio ; et quidem *Walliam*, quam nos
Wales appellamus, ipfi Galli *Gales* vocant ;
ipfosque *Gallos* Germani *Walfhen* appellant ;
certe, qui *Walli* et *Wallones* nunc dicuntur,
Gallos effe in confeffo eft ; nempe Artefiae
partiumque adjacentium incolas, ut et incolas Longobardiae, hoc eft, Galliae Cifal-
pinae ; et *Gafcoigne*, item *Vafconia* dicitur :
Sic Gallorum *guerre, garant, gard, gardien,
garderobe, guife, guile, gage, guichet, guimblet, guerdon (regard), Guillaum, gaigner,
gaftor, guetter*, etc. idem fignificant ac Anglorum *Warre, warrant, ward, warden,
wardrobe, wife, wile, wager, wicket, wimble,
re-ward, William, to winne, to waft, to
wait*, etc. Sic *Juglandes* alibi in Anglia
French-nuts (nuces Gallicas) alibi eodem
fenfu *Wall-nuts* (hoc eft *Walfh-nuts*) appellamus.   *Galatae* item, feu *Gallo-graeci*, linguam fuam fecum ex Gallia deportaffe dicuntur ; et (referente Strabone) bilingues
erant, fua fimul et Graecanica lingua uten-
tes.   *Gallovidia* etiam in Scotia ejusmodi
nominis originem forfan obtinuit.

                              Erat

---

4 denominatio: 4th has *dominatio* (misprint)
16 *(regard)*: 5th–6th
17 *gastor*: misprint for *gaster* of 1st–5th

customs. It is my belief that the *Galli* and *Walli*,[3] that is the people of Gaul (or France) and of Wales (or Cambro-Britain) have the same name. It is very common for the letters *g* and *w* to be interchanged;[4] the French name for *Wallia* (which we call Wales) is *Gales*, and the Germans call the French *Walshen*. It is a well known fact that the people now called *Walli* and *Wallones* are French, that is to say the inhabitants of Artois and the adjoining areas, and also those of Lombardy (Gallia Cisalpina).[5] Another name for Gascoigne is Vasconia.[6] And the French words: *guerre, garant, gard, gardien, garderobe, guise, guile, gage, guichet, guimblet, guerdon (regard), Guillaum, gaigner, gaster, guetter*, etc correspond in meaning to English *warre, warrant, ward, warden, wardrobe, wife, wile, wager, wicket, wimble, re-ward, William, to winne, to wast, to wait*, etc.[7] In some parts of England what are called *juglandes* in Latin are known as *French nuts (nuces Gallicas)*, while in other parts they are called *Wall-nuts* (that is, Walsh-nuts) with the same meaning.[8] The Galatians[9] (or Gallo-Greeks) too are said to have taken their language with them from Gaul. According to Strabo they were bilingual, speaking Greek as well as their own language. Galloway in Scotland may also have originally got its name in this way.[10]

[3] *Walli* comes from the Germanic *$wal\chi o$-z (*cf* OE *wealh*) meaning a foreigner, and was especially applied by the Germanic tribes to the Celts and Latins. *Galli*, the Latin name for the inhabitants of what is now France, was no doubt derived from a Celtic word.
[4] The North French dialect had *w* in many words where *g(u)* appeared in other French dialects. There is a regular correspondence between Germanic roots beginning with *w* and French roots beginning with *g*. *Walshen* and *Walloon* are both from the same root as *Walli* (see note 3).
[5] The inhabitants of Lombardy were descended from the *Langobardi*, a Germanic tribe who invaded Italy and settled in the north, mixing with the previous inhabitants, who were Celtic. It is not clear if Wallis is suggesting that they were actually called *Wallones* in his time; his main point is that they were French-speaking, like the *Walloons* of Artois.
[6] The former province of Gascony in the south-west of France took its name from a Spanish tribe, the *Vascones*.
[7] See note 4.
[8] Derived from Germanic *$wal\chi o$-z (see note 3). It signified the nut of the Roman countries (Gaul and Italy) as opposed to the hazel, which was native to Germanic lands.
[9] The Galatians were a Celtic people who settled in Central Asia Minor, after crossing the Hellespont in 278 BC. According to St Jerome they were still speaking a Celtic language when he visited them in the late fourth century AD. Strabo refers to them twice (XII.556; II.130).
[10] The Roman name for Galloway, *Gallovidia*, was a Latinisation of Welsh *Gallwyddel*, meaning literally *foreign Gauls*.

AUCTORIS PRAEFATIO.   xi

Erat autem prifca ifthaec Gallis et Britannis communis lingua, ultra omnium hiftoriarum memoriam antiqua; ut non nifi ex conjecturis, aut dubiae faltem fidei Hiftoricis, ipfius five linguae five etiam populi origines repetendae fint: et fortaffe (ficut et aliae Matrices linguae) ab ipfa confufione Babylonica ortum duxit. Magnam certe cum linguis Orientalibus affinitatem retinet; non modo in vocum originibus, ut notant D. *Johannes Davies* paffim in *Dictionario* fuo *Cambro-Britannico*, et *Samuel Bochartus* in fua *Geographia Sacra*; qui ipfum *Britanniae* nomen Arabicae vel Punicae originis effe putat, nempe Βρεϊανικλω dici quafi ברת אנך *barat anach*, hoc eft, *agrum* feu terram *ftanni et plumbi*, Infulasque Bretannicas (a Poenis dictas) easdem effe contendit quas Graeci κασιτεριδας (eodem fignificatu) appellarunt: Sed etiam in Syntaxeos ratione, quae *Praefixis*, *Affixis*, et varia *Statûs* permutatione peragitur (ut enim habent Hebraei ftatum Abfolutum et ftatum Regiminis, fic Cambro-Britanni *Status*, ut loquuntur, *Primarium*, *Mollem*, *Liquidum*, et *Afpiratum*, prout varietas conftructionis poftulaverit); ut liquet in linguae Cambro-Britannicae Grammaticis a *Johanne Davifio*, et a *Johanne Davide Rhefo*, latine editis: addo etiam,

Magnam habet cum Orientalibus affinitatem.

RELATIONSHIP WITH ORIENTAL LANGUAGES

This ancient language, spoken by the Gauls and the Britons, existed before any historical records were kept. The origins both of the language and people can only be a matter of guesswork, if one disallows the evidence of certain historians who are, to say the least, of doubtful reliability. Perhaps (like other mother tongues)[11] it actually dates back to the confusion of Babel. It undoubtedly still has a close affinity to Oriental languages in two respects:

First, in the derivation of its vocabulary: Dr John Davies[12] constantly remarks on this in his Welsh dictionary, as does Samuel Bochart in his *Sacred Geography*.[13] Bochart thinks that the very name *Britannia* is of Arabic or Punic origin and that Βρετανικήν is an imitation of בדת אנך *barat-anach*, which means field (or *land*) *of tin and lead*; he maintains that the *Bretannic islands* (as he says they were called by the Carthaginians) are the same as those which the Greeks called κασσιτερίδας, with the same meaning.[14]

Secondly, in the structure of the syntax, which has prefixes and affixes and various changes of *state*. For example the Hebrews have an *absolute state* and a *construct state*, and the Welsh, similarly have *states* called *primary*, *soft*, *liquid* and *aspirate* which they use according to the requirements of different constructions.[15] This can easily be seen in the grammars of Welsh (published in Latin) by John Davies and John David Rhys.[16] Another reminder of oriental cus-

---

[11] J.-J. Scaliger (see note 23) gave the name *matrices linguae* (mother tongues) to families of languages which he regarded as originating in a single language.

[12] Dr John Davies (*c* 1567–1644), Rector of Mallwyd and one of the greatest of Welsh scholars. Wallis is referring to his Double Dictionary: Welsh-Latin, Latin-Welsh, published in 1632 (facsimile edition, Scolar Press, 1968).

[13] Samuel Bochart (1599–1667) published his *Geographia Sacra* in 1646.

[14] The origin of the name *Britain* is still obscure. The earliest Hellenic visitor, Pytheas, in *c* 300 BC gave it the name Πρεταννικαὶ νῆσοι, and this may be cognate to Irish *cruithin* (= Picts). The Greek name κασσιτερίδες (from κασσίτερος = tin) is now thought to refer to the Scilly Isles rather than to Cornwall.

[15] See, for example, Wiliam (1960), *pp* 11–13; Weingreen (1948).

[16] John Davies – see note 12. His Welsh grammar was published in 1621, entitled *Antiquae Linguae Britannicae . . . Rudimenta* (facsimile edition, Scolar Press, 1968). John David Rhys (1534–1609?) published his grammar of Welsh in 1592 – *Cambrobrytannicae Cymraecaeve linguae institutiones et rudimenta*. It has little merit as a work of scholarship; Welsh is forced into the mould of Latin too rigidly.

etiam, Perſonarum denominationes, adjunctis nempe Patris, Avi, aliorumque forſan
majorum nominibus, morem Orientalem
ſapere; nam v. g. *Johannes David Rheſus*,
vel in eorum dialecto *Sión ap Dafyd ap
Rhys*, idem eſt ac *Johannes, filius Davidis,
filii Rheſi*: Et quamvis nunc dierum habeant quidem, ad Anglorum imitationem,
familiarum nomina; ſunt tamen ea plerumque mere Patronymica; ſunt enim *Price,
Powel, Bowel, Bowen, Pugh, Parry, Penry,
Prichard, Probert, Proger*, etc. nihil aliud
quam *Ap Rhys, Ap Howel, Ap Owen, Ap
Pugh, Ap Harry, Ap Henry, Ap Richard,
Ap Robert, Ap Roger*, etc. Et *Jones, Jenkin,
Davyes*, etc. ſunt mere patronymica; *Gryffith,
Morgan, Howel, Teudor, Lluellin, Lloyd*, etc.
ſunt majorum nomina, omiſſa tamen voce *ap*
(hoc eſt, *mab* filius): et ſimiliter de aliis
plerisque apud eos nominibus judicandum
eſt. Verum his de rebus non eſt prolixe
nobis differendum. Qui plura cupit, con-
ſulat *Pontici Virunnii* Hiſtoriam Britannicam; *Giraldi Cambrenſis* Itinerarium et
Deſcriptionem Cambriae; et Annotationes
D. *Davidis Powel* in duos illos auctores ab
ipſo Latine editos: item tractatus duos phi-
lologicos D. *Johannis Daviſii*, quorum alter ipſius Dictionario, alter ejusdem Grammaticae

10–17 Of these names *Bowel, Probert, Proger,* (*Ap Robert, Ap Roger*), *Lluellin,
Lloyd* first appear in 4th
14 *Pugh*: misprint for *Hugh* of 1st–5th
16 *Gryffith*: 1st and 2nd have *Griffin*

toms is the Welsh habit of identifying people by adding the names of their father, grandfather and perhaps of other ancestors. For example John David Rhys, or in their dialect, *Siôn ap Dafyd ap Rhys*, is equivalent to John, son of David, son of Rhys. And although nowadays they have family names, which they have copied from English, most of them are simply patronymics. For example, *Price, Powel, Bowel, Bowen, Pugh, Parry, Penry, Prichard, Probert, Proger, etc* are in fact *Ap Rhys, Ap Howel, Ap Owen, Ap Hugh, Ap Harry, Ap Henry, Ap Richard, Ap Robert, Ap Roger*, etc, and *Jones, Jenkin, Davies,* etc are also patronymics. *Gryffith, Morgan, Howell, Teudor, Lluellin, Lloyd*, etc are names of ancestors with the omission of the word *ap*, that is, *mab* (son), and this applies to many other names that they use. But I must not spend too much time on this topic. Anyone who wishes to pursue the matter should consult the following works:[17] *History of Britain* by Ponticus Virunnius; *Itinerary and description of Wales* by Giraldus Cambrensis, and the notes of Dr David Powel on these two authors whose works he published in Latin; two philological treatises by Dr John Davies, one of which is prefaced to his Dictionary, and the other to his Grammar;

---

[17] *Ludovicus Ponticus Virunius (d* 1520). His *Britannica Historia* was published in London in 1585 in an edition which included *Itinerarium Cambriae* and *Cambriae Descriptio* – works by Giraldus Cambrensis (1146? – 1223), with notes by David Powel. *Dr John Davies* – see note 12. *Dr John David Rhys* – see note 16; Humphrey Prichard wrote a preface to the grammar. *Humphrey Lloyd* (1527–1568): *Commentarioli Descriptionis Britannicae Fragmentum*, Cologne, 1572. *William Camden* (1551–1623); *Britannia* was published in 1586. *Samuel Bochart* – see note 13, *James Ussher* (1581–1656), Archbishop of Armagh: *Britannicarum Ecclesiarum Antiquitates*, Dublin, 1639. *Richard Verstegan* (1565–1620). His real name was Richard Rowlands, but he took his grandfather's name; *Restitution of decayed intelligence in antiquities concerning the English nation* was published in Antwerp in 1605. *Henry Lloyd*: Wallis is probably referring to David Powel's *The historie of Cambria*, written in the Brytish language translated into English by H. Lloyd, corrected, augmented, and continued . . . by D. Powel. 1584. *Edward Brerewood* (1565?–1613): *Enquiries touching the diversity of languages and religions* (1614). Brerewood was an antiquary and a mathematician, and the first professor of anatomy at Gresham College, London.

AUCTORIS PRAEFATIO. xiii

maticae praefigitur; fimilesque tractatus
duos D. *Johannis Davidis Rhefi* Grammaticae praefixos (fuum ipfius unum Cam-
brice fcriptum, alterum *Humphredi Prichard*
Latine): *Humphredi Lloyd* Defcriptionem
Britanniae. Item Guil. Camdeni Britanniam; *Samuelis Bocharti* Geographiam fa-
cram (part. ii. lib. I. cap. 39. 41, 42.) Item
Jacobi Ufferii, Armachani, Antiquitates
Britannicas; *Richardi Verftegan* Antiquitates Angliae reftitutas, Anglice editas;
Henrici Lloyd Hiftoriam Cambriae Chro-
nologicam a *Davide Powel* Anglice editam;
Brerewoodi antiquas Inquifitiones, Anglice
item editas; aliosque confimilis fubjecti
fcriptores: apud quos multa reconditioris
cognitionis monumenta reperiuntur. Et
quamvis Fabulae fortaffe vetuftiffimis nonnunquam fcriptis immifceantur, prout in
antiquiffimi temporis hiftoriis plurimis fieri
confuevit, multum tamen fubeffe veri non
dubito.

Verum primaeva haec utriusque Gentis
lingua utrobique magna ex parte evanuit.
Quod ad Galliam attinet; poftquam ea in
Romanorum poteftatem devenerat, conati
funt Romani Latinae linguae ufum intro-
ducere, ideoque edicta omnia aliaque fcripta
publica Latino idiomate ediderunt; adeoque,

Quomodo defuevit in Gallia; et praefentis Gallicanae origo.

---

3 Grammaticae praefixos: 1st has praefixas (misprint); 1st–4th insert *ipsius*
after *Grammaticae*
20 plurimis: 1st–4th have *omnibus*

two similar treatises prefaced to the grammar of Dr John David Rhys (one written in Welsh by himself, and the other in Latin by Humphrey Prichard); *Description of Britain* by Humphrey Lloyd; *Britannia* by William Camden; *Sacred Geography* by Samuel Bochart (Part 2, Book 1, Chapters 39, 41, 42); *British antiquities* by James Ussher of Armagh; *Restitution of the Antiquities of England* by Richard Verstegan, published in English; *Chronological History* of Wales by Henry Lloyd published in English by David Powel; *Ancient enquiries* by Brerewood, also published in English; and other writers on this subject. In these works one may find many out of the way facts recorded; and although the oldest written records tend to contain much that is pure fable, as was quite normal in most histories of very early times, they undoubtedly have a great deal of truth in them as well.

HOW IT FELL INTO DISUSE IN FRANCE AND THE ORIGIN
OF THE PRESENT FRENCH LANGUAGE
However, this language, which was originally spoken by both peoples, almost entirely disappeared in both countries. After Gaul came into their hands, the Romans tried to introduce the Latin language; with this in view they published all edicts and other public documents in Latin. Consequently the old Gallic language gradually

xiv AUCTORIS PRAEFATIO.

que, ut in Hifpania vetus lingua Canta-
br ca, ita et in Gallia prifca Gallorum lin-
qua paulatim defuevit, quafi fimul cum populo fubjugata; ejusque loco rudis, ut fit,
Latinifmus utcunque fucceffit, et *Romance*
vel *Romanfhe*, hoc eft lingua *Romana*, feu
Romanica, vel *Romanenfis*, dicebatur: re-
tentis tamen aliquot vocabulis ex antiqua
lingua. Quum autem *Franci* feu *Francones*
Germaniae populus, fub *Faramondo* duce,
ex Franconia in Galliam devenerunt, fuam
etiam fecum linguam attulerunt; ejusdem
quidem originis cum Germanica, noftraque
Anglicana, neque ab his admodum diver-
fam; quae etiam aliquandiu ab illis retenta
fuit et lingua *Francica* dicebatur; usque
dum, ipfis Gallis tandem cum Francis his in
unum quafi populum coalefcentibus, Franci
etiam rudem illum Latinifmum edidicerunt:
admifcuerunt tamen proculdubio ex fua
lingua voces non paucas: verum et fuam
Syntaxeos rationem retinuerunt (quam
etiam moderni Graeci, magna ex parte,
imitantur, neglecta puritate veteris linguae
Graecae; ut Itali, purioris Latinifmi);
quae eadem quidem eft cum Teutonica, fed
tam a Romana quam a veteri Gallicana
prorfus aliena, adeo ut nec a Romanis recepta nec ab antiquis Gallis tranfmiffa cenferi

22–25 (quam etiam . . . Latinismi): 5th–6th
28 prorsus: 1st has *prosus* (misprint)

fell into disuse, like the old Cantabrian language in Spain, conquered, as it were, along with the people.[18] It was replaced, as one
might expect, by a crude form of Latin, which was called *Romance*,
or *Romanshe*,[19] that is, the Roman, or Romanic language, though a
few words from the old language remained. However when the
Franks or *Franconians*, a German people, came into Gaul from
Franconia under Faramondus,[20] they brought their own language
with them, which came from the same stock as German and our own
English language, and was very little different from them. For a time
they continued to use this language, which was known as the Frankish language, until eventually the Gauls and the Franks became to
all intents and purposes one people, and the Franks learnt the same
crude form of Latin. They undoubtedly introduced a good many
words from their own language into it, and kept their own syntactic
structure. (The modern Greeks have mostly adopted this structure
and abandoned the pure form of the ancient Greek language, just
as the Italians have disregarded the purer forms of Latin.)[21] This was
the same as the Teutonic syntax, but so far different from the Roman
and the old Gallic syntax, that it is impossible to believe that it came
from the Romans or was passed on by the ancient Gauls. (It seems

[18] The Cantabrians were virtually wiped out by the Romans between 26 and 19 BC.
They inhabited an area on the north coast of Spain. Some (*eg* J.-J. Scaliger – see note 23)
have used 'Cantabrian' meaning Basque, and this is no doubt the language Wallis
refers to here.
[19] The area of the Old Roman Empire was called *Romania* in the Middle Ages, and the
language *Romancium*.
[20] The Franks under Clovis conquered Gaul in 481 AD, except for Burgundy and Pro-
vence. Pharamond (or Faramond) is a shadowy figure. According to Michaud's *Biographie Universelle*, Vol 33, he may have been the leader of the Franks in early invasions
of Gaul, and old chronicles put his death in either 420 or 428 AD. Other references to
him are very brief and suggest that he was legendary.
[21] He is presumably thinking particularly of the loss of inflexions, and the consequent
changes in word order.

AUCTORIS PRAEFATIO. XV

ſeri poſſit (quod etiam de ejusmodi ſyntaxeos
ratione apud Italos et Hiſpanos dicendum
videtur, eam Longobardos, Gothos, Van-
dalosque ex Germania illuc attuliſſe): atque hinc defluxit hodierna lingua Gallica;
quae tamen, ut ipſe populus, denominationem a *Francis* adhuc retinet. Adeoque
priſca illa Gallorum lingua per totam fere
Galliam penitus obruta eſt, in ſola nunc
Aremorica ſuperſtes, ubi lingua *Aremori-*
cana appellatur.

Parem etiam fortunam in Britannia ſortita
eſt. Pura ſiquidem manſit haec priſca apud
illos lingua usque ad Romanorum tempora:
Poſtquam autem *Julius Caeſar,* aliique poſt
illum, Imperium Romanum huc usque ex-
tenderunt, quanquam propter longiorem a
Roma diſtantiam et minorem Romanorum
huc confluentium numerum, minorem inde
ſubierit mutationem antiquitus recepta
lingua, quam apud Gallos, Hiſpanos, Longobardos, etc. utpote viciniores populos, con-
tigerat; multa tamen Latina vocabula ad-
miſit Lingua Britannica, quae adhuc reti-
nentur, ſed ita transformata et mutata ut
nativas linguae Britannicae leges et ſyntaxin
omnino ſubierint, neque inſignem aliquam
ipſius mutationem praeſtiterint: nec dubito e contra quin et Romani, ſive ex Britannia

Quomodo
deſuevit in
Anglia.

---

3 eam Longobardos: 1st has *eam nempe Longobardos*
20 subierit: 1st has *subiit*

likely that this applies also to the syntactic structure of Italian and Spanish, namely that it was brought in by the Lombards, Goths and Vandals from Germany.) This is how the modern French language came into being, but like the people it still takes its name from the Franks. The ancient language of the Gauls was completely lost almost everywhere in France, and survives now only in Brittany, where it is called the Breton language.

HOW IT FELL INTO DISUSE IN ENGLAND

It met with a similar fate in Britain. Up to the time of the Romans the ancient British language remained pure. Then Julius Caesar and others after him extended Roman rule to this area. Since it was further away from Rome, and fewer Romans found their way there, the native language was not changed by these influences to the degree that it was among the Gauls, Spaniards, Lombards, etc who were nearer Rome. However it borrowed many Latin words, which we still have, though they completely changed their form so as to fit in with the native rules and syntax of the British language, and did not cause any significant change in it. There is no doubt that the Romans, in their turn, borrowed British words, from Britain or from

tannia five ex Gallia, verba Britannica re-
portaverint (quorum non pauca apud *Camb-
denum, Bochartum,* aliosque collecta videmus). Poftea, vero, quum *Anglo-Saxones,*
Germaniae item populus (fi faltem Germaniae fines, quod aliqui faciunt, eo usque ex-
tendere liceat ut Danos etiam et Norwegios
comprehendant) in Britanniam pervenerunt, eodem circiter tempore quo Franci in
Galliam, et poft diuturna bella rerum po-
titi funt, Britannos, cum fua lingua Britannica, expulerunt; qui tamen montanas Cambriae feu Walliae regiones, adhuc obtinent *Cambri* et *Walli* dicti, fuamque linguam retinent; ut et Cornubienfes aliquot in extremis *Cornubiae* five *Cornwalliae*
partibus, linguamque *Cornubicam* appellant : fed et *Hiberni* (quo nec Romani, quod
fciam, nec Saxones olim pervenerunt), ut
et Infulares atque Monticolae in Scotia
(*Iflanders* et *Highlanders* vulgo dicti), quorum lingua ab *Hibernica* parum differt,
linguam adhuc retinent Cambro-Britannicae
affinem, quae et olim omnino eadem fortaffis erat, quamvis nunc dierum a Cambrica magis aliquanto differat quam vel
Cornubica, vel Aremoricana, vix autem
magis quam hodierna Germanica ab Anglicana. *Scaliger* tamen (de linguis Europae)

et

2–4 (quorum . . . videmus): 4th–6th
11–12 Britannica: 1st has *Britannia* (misprint)

Gaul (a good number of these, I see, have been collected by Camden, Bochart, and other writers).[22] Later on the Anglo-Saxons, who were also a German people (if the boundaries of Germany are extended, as they are by some people, to include the Danes and Norwegians) came to Britain at about the same time as the Franks came to Gaul. After long wars they gained control of it and drove out the Britons, together with their British language. These Britons, who now in-inhabit the mountainous regions of Cambria, or Wales, and are called Cambrians, or Welsh, still have a language of their own, like the Cornish in the distant parts of Cornubia, or Cornwall, some of whom retain a language which they call Cornish. The Irish (whose country as far as I know, was not entered either by the Romans or the Saxons) and the inhabitants of the islands and mountain regions of Scotland (commonly called *Islanders* and *Highlanders*), whose language is very similar to Irish, still speak a language which is related to Welsh, and perhaps at one time it was exactly the same. Now however it is less like Welsh than Cornish and Breton are, but the difference is scarcely more than that between present-day German and English. Scaliger (*On the languages of Europe*)[23] and, following

---

[22] For words of Celtic origin in Latin see Palmer, 1954, *p* 52 *ff*.
[23] J.-J. (1540–1609). *Diatriba de Europaeorum Linguis*, posthumously published in *Opuscula varia* (1610). See also Arens (1955), *p* 59 *ff*.

et eum fecuti *Merula* (in ipfius Cofmographia) aliique, manifefto errore, linguam *Hibernicam* pro *Matrice* diftincta reputant, nullamque cum *Britannica* cognationem habere fentiunt; at rem fecus effe et *Camdenus* antehac obfervavit, et res ipfa loquitur. An autem cum lingua *Cantabrica* Hifpaniae affinitatem ullam fortiatur, fateor me penitus ignorare, nec impraefentiarum vacat penitius inquirere, et potius contrarium fentio; in paucis faltem illis quae apud *Merulam* extant linguae Cantabricae fpeciminibus, nulla quidem linguae Cambricae veftigia notare poffum: fieri tamen poteft ut Hiberni nonnullas voces Cantabricas retineant, fi faltem *Hiberni* ab *Iberis*, ut creditur, defcenderint; habent certe Hiberni voces non paucas quae Britannicam originem non fapiunt, at unde habuerint nefcio. Verum *Cambriae* appellatio, quanquam quoad fonum *Cantabriae* videatur non abfimilis, majorem forte cum *Cimbris* vel *Cimmeris* (Cimbricae Cherfonefi incolis) quam cum Cantabris, cognationem fortiri poffit; nam Cambro-Britannus lingua fua *Cymro* (feu *Cumro*) dicitur, et a *Gomero* (uno ex Japheti pofteris) denominationem olim accepiffe poffe creditur. Sed et Gallos etiam *Cimbros* vel *Cimeros*

b   antiquitus

---

7 An autem cum lingua: 1st omits *cum*

[92]

him, Merula (in his *Cosmography*)[24] and others, quite wrongly believe that the Irish language was a distinct mother-tongue with no relationship to British. But Camden has already observed that this is not so, and the facts speak for themselves. As to whether the Cantabrian[25] language of Spain is related in any way I admit to my ignorance, and I have no time to investigate it more fully at present; I am inclined to think that it is not; at least, in the few examples of the Cantabrian language which survive in Merula's work, I can find no traces of Welsh. It is possible, however, that the Irish still have some Cantabrian words, if the Irish are descended from the *Iberi*,[26] as some think. They certainly have some words which do not suggest a British origin, but where they came from I do not know. The name Cambria,[27] though it resembles Cantabria in sound, may perhaps be more closely connected with the *Cimbri* or *Cimmerii* (inhabitants of the Cimbric Chersonese) than with the Cantabri. For a Welshman is called in his own language *Cymro* (or *Cumro*), and the name may have originally come from *Gomer*[28] (one of the descendants of Japhet). But Camden has shown that the Gauls were also called

[24] Published in Leiden, 1605.
[25] See note 18.
[26] *Iberia* and *Hibernia* are not in fact etymologically connected.
[27] *Cambria* derived from Welsh *Cymru*. The Cimbric Chersonese correspond to north Jutland, but there is no etymological connection between Cimbric and Cambria or Cantabria.
[28] Gomer appears in Genesis x.2 as one of the sons of Japheth; his descendants were identified with the Cimmerians.

xviii   AUCTORIS PRAEFATIO.

antiquitus dictos fuiffe, Camdenus oftendit.

Quod autem in Gallia factum diximus, nempe quod Galli, poft Francorum adventum, fuam tamen linguam (non quidem primigeniam, fed quae ipfius loco fuccefferat) tandem quafi poftliminio (mutato tamen nomine) reduxerint, ideo quidem quod in unum cum Francis populum coaluerint: hoc in Anglia neutiquam obtinuit. Nam Britanni, quanquam mille mala paffi, Religioni tamen fuae (Chriftianifmo fcilicet) et patriis ritibus addictiffimi, nunquam fuftinuerunt ejusmodi cum Saxonibus (tunc quidem Ethnicis) confortium aut coalitionem, fed infenfiffima odia per multa fecula coluerunt, quae quidem vixdum penitus depofuere.

Lingua Anglo-Saxonica.

Anglo-Saxones autem, antiquas, ut dictum eft, Britonum fedes nacti, partem illam quam obtinuerunt Britanniae, *Angliam* dixerunt; eamque quam fecum attulerunt linguam *Anglicam*; quam nunc *Saxonicam* vel *Anglo-Saxonicam* vulgo dicimus, ut ab hodierna Anglicana diftinguamus. Erat autem illa Anglo-Saxonum lingua, antiquae Teutonicae propago (nifi antiquae *Gothicae* feu *Geticae* potius dixeris, unde forfan ipfa *Teutonica* duxerit originem), ut et Francica illa in Galliam

27–29 (nisi . . . originem): 5th–6th

Cimbri or *Cimeri* at one time.

I said earlier that after the arrival of the Franks the Gauls eventually got their own language back (not the original one, but the one that followed it), as it were recovering their ancient heritage (though with a different name), because they and the Franks became one people. The situation was different in England. The Britons, although they suffered great persecution, were devoted to their religion (Christianity) and to their ancestral rites, and so never contracted any alliance or coalition of that sort with the Saxons (who were then heathens), but cherished an intense hatred of them for many generations, and have scarcely given it up entirely even now.

THE ANGLO-SAXON LANGUAGE

The Anglo-Saxons, as I have related, got control of what had been the demesne of the Britons and called the part of Britain that they occupied *England*, and the language which they brought with them *English*. We generally call it *Saxon* or *Anglo-Saxon* now, to distinguish it from modern English. The Anglo-Saxon language is descended from Old Teutonic, like the Frankish language which was introduced into Gaul, and also like modern German, Dutch, Danish,

AUCTORIS PRAEFATIO.   xix

Galliam advecta, et hodierna Germanica, Belgica, Danica, Suevica, Boruſſica, aliaeque affines linguae. Et fere pura manſit in Anglia, ſeu impermixta, usque ad *Normannorum* tempora; niſi quod voces aliquot Cambricas admiſerit, ut et Cambrica vice verſa ex hac nonnullas. Quamvis enim *Dani* interim hic pedem poſuerint, nulla tamen inde linguae inſignis immutatio ſecuta eſt, nam et eorum lingua vel plane eadem erat vel ſaltem maxime affinis.

Quum vero *Guilielmus* Normanniae dux, *Conqueſtor* dictus, Normannos ſuos huc advexerat; Angliam nactus, Anglicanae linguae mutationem aggreſſus eſt, Gallicanam inducere ſatagens, qua ipſe in Normannia uſus erat. Quamvis enim *Normanni,* five *Northmanni,* dum antea *Norwegiae* populus fuerant, eadem olim lingua uſi fuerunt qua et Anglo-Saxones (populus olim vicinus) ea nempe quae tunc in Anglia obtinuit; poſt eorum tamen in *Neuſtriam (Normanniam* deinceps dictam) adventum, nativa ſua lingua Gallicanam (nempe, Romanicam, ſeu Franco-Gallicam) permutarunt, quam etiam Conqueſtor ſecum nunc in Angliam inducere voluit; et propterea Diplomata et edicta publica, ut et res juridicas, lingua Neuſtrica ſeu Gallicana peragi curavit.

(marginal note) Quouſque Normanni linguam Anglicanam mutaverint.

b 2   Non

---

9 insignis: 2nd–6th
16 satagens: 1st has *cupiens*
27 inducere: 1st–4th have *apportare*; Diplomata: 1st has *Diplomata omnia*

Swedish, Prussian[29] and other related languages. It survived in a virtually pure and unadulterated form in England right up to Norman times, apart from borrowing some Welsh words, just as some Anglo-Saxon words were borrowed by Welsh. For although the Danes invaded the country during this period, there was no change in the language, because Danish, though not exactly the same as Anglo-Saxon, was very closely related to it.

TO WHAT EXTENT THE NORMANS CHANGED
THE ENGLISH LANGUAGE

When William of Normandy, called the Conqueror, brought his Normans here and occupied England, he attempted to change the English language and to introduce French, which he himself had used in Normandy. The Normans, or Northmen, while they lived in Norway spoke the same language as the Anglo-Saxons (once their neighbours there), that is to say the language then current in England. However, after their arrival in Neustria[30] (later called Normandy) they exchanged their native language for French (that is Romanic, or Franco-Gallic) and the Conqueror now wished to bring this language with him to England. Because of this he gave instructions that all official documents and public proclamations, and all judicial transactions, should be in Neustrian, or French. But

---

[29] Old Prussian, or Borussian, belongs to the Baltic sub-division of the Indo-European family (together with Lithuanian and Lettish), which has much in common with the Slavic branch and is often called Balto-Slavic. The other languages Wallis mentions are all Germanic.

[30] Originally the western kingdom of the Franks of the Merovingian dynasty, dating from the death of Clovis in 511 A D. Later the name referred simply to the area of Normandy.

XX   AUCTORIS PRAEFATIO.

Non autem quod aggreſſus erat, eſt aſſe-
cutus; quippe quod Normannorum qui
huc advenerant, ſi ad Anglos quibus im-
miſcebantur comparentur, exiguus erat numerus, qui ideo ſuam citius amiſerunt linguam quam Anglicanam immutare potuerint. Quamvis autem, hac de cauſa, prius
recepta lingua Anglica permanſerit; illud
ſaltem inde inſecutum eſt, ut multa vocabula Gallica, ſed Latinae ut plurimum originis (nam quae Galli retinent Germanicae
originis, a Francis illuc deducta, quanquam
Gallis forſan nobiscum nunc communia, nobis tamen quam illis potius nativa cenſenda
ſunt: et quae ex priſca ſua lingua retinuerunt, ipſis nunc cum Cambris communia,
nos etiam ex antiqua Britannica retinuiſſe,
vel a Cambris potius quam a Gallis ac-
cepiſſe cenſendum eſt), in linguam Anglicanam irrepſerint, multaque Anglicana
ſenſim deſueverint. Nec quidem temere
contigiſſe puto, quod Animalia viva, nominibus Germanicae originis vocemus, quorum
tamen Carnem in cibum paratam, originis
Gallicae nominibus appellamus; puta, bo-
vem, vaccam, vitulum, ovem, porcum,
aprum, feram, etc. *an ox, a cow, a calf, a
ſheep, a hog, a boar, a deer,* etc. ſed
carnem bubulam, vitulinam, ovinam, por-
cinam,

---

6 potuerint: 1st–4th have *possent*
8 Anglica: 1st has *Anglicana*
21–xxi.10 Nec quidem . . . sunt adepti: 4th–6th

he failed in his purpose because the number of Normans who came here was small compared with the number of English people with whom they mixed, and they lost their own language before they could bring about any change in English. So the English language, which had become established here, persisted, though many French words, mostly of Latin origin, gradually became current in English, and many English words in due course dropped out of use. (I say 'mostly of Latin origin' firstly because words of German origin which were brought in by the Franks and incorporated into French, though they may now be common to English and French, are better regarded as native to us than to them; secondly, because words which the French inherited from their ancient language, and which they now have in common with the Welsh, are better regarded as having come to us from the Ancient Britons or the Welsh, than from the French.) It is no accident, in my opinion, that we call living animals by names of German origin, whereas we use French names for their meat when prepared as food. For instance we say: *an ox, a cow, a calf, a sheep, a hog, a boar, a deer*, etc, but *beef, veal, mutton,*

cinam, aprugnam, ferinam ; *beef, veal, mutton, pork, brawn, venifon,* etc. Sed hinc id
ortum putaverim, quod Normanni milites
pafcuis, caulis, haris, locisque quibus vivo-
rum animalium cura agebatur, parcius fe
immifcuerint (quae itaque antiqua nomina
retinuerunt); quam macellis, culinis, men-
fis, epulis, ubi vel parabantur vel habe-
bantur cibi, qui itaque nova nomina ab illis
funt adepti.

Ex eo autem tempore admifta fuit exotica-
rum vocum farrago fatis fuperque nume-
rofa : Non, quod lingua Anglicana ex fe
fterilis fit et verborum inops, eft enim et
verborum et elegantiarum fatis abunde
plena, et (fi libet) ad luxuriem copiofa, nec
quicquam deeft quin ex propria fupellectili
acutiffimos fenfus valeamus fignanter exprimere et ἐμφαῖικῶς· ut vel ex unius *Spenferi*
poematis abunde liquet, cujus phrafis terfa
fatis et eleganter compta, et copiae plena,
cafta tamen et exotico ornatu minus adul-
terata : Sed partim quod, propter varia
cum exteris commercia, et frequentia praefertim in Regiis familiis connubia, aegre
potuerit evitari; partim etiam quod nimia
innovandi affectatio (hoc faltem fupremo
feculo) inordinata prurigine multos irrita-
verit peregrinas voces praeter neceffitatem
                    b 3   conquirendi,

pork, brawn, venison, etc. I think this arose from the fact that the Norman soldiers had little to do with pastures, sheepfolds, hencoops, and places in which living animals were looked after (so that these animals kept their old names); whereas they were more familiar with meat markets, kitchens, dining-tables, and banquets where food was prepared or eaten, and (because of this) the foods acquired new names.[31]

Since that time a hotch-potch of foreign words, far more than we need, has been introduced. This is not because of any sterility or poverty of vocabulary in English, which has a plentiful supply of words and choice phrases – almost (one might say) a superfluity of them; we can express clearly and forcefully the most precise shades of meaning by using our own resources. From Spenser's poems alone one can appreciate this; his phrases are terse and elegantly shaped, exuberant but pure, and unadulterated by foreign ornamentation.[32] The real reasons for the influx of foreign words were partly the various transactions we had with foreign countries and the frequent intermarriages, especially of royal families, which made it almost inevitable; and partly also an excessive craving for innovation (at least in this last generation). This has caused many people to be obsessed with a search for foreign words, not because we need them, but simply because they think that it is impossible to say any-

[31] *Cf* Sir Walter Scott, *Ivanhoe,* Chapter 1. This is a frequently quoted example; in fact both sets of words existed alongside one another without any differentiation for some time but, as in many instances, the French forms eventually replaced the others in the meanings more commonly required in higher society.
[32] The complaint against the introduction of foreign words occurs in a number of writers on English, for example Mulcaster (1582), Bullokar (1586), Gil (1619). Chaucer in particular was criticised for introducing too many French words.

conquirendi, qui nihil vel eleganter vel
emphatice dici posse exiftimant quod non
infolitum quiddam aut peregrinum fonum
fapiat.

Hodierna lingua Anglicana. Atque hisce partim misturis, partim longiori
temporis tractu, qui etiam in aliis linguis
infignem mutationem praeftare folet, factum
eft, ut lingua illa Anglo-Saxonica in prae-
fentem linguam Anglicanam fenfim mutata
fuerit.

Et Scotica. Neque Anglia fola conclufa eft haec lingua,
fed Angliae fines egreffa praecipuas etiam
Scotiae partes occupavit. Quod eo praefertim tempore factum puto, cum Normanni Angliam invaferunt : nam Anglorum Regia familia, et ex nobilibus non
pauci, praeter alios etiam ex plebe, Anglia
pulfi in Scotiam recepti, linguam fuam fecum portarunt, quae continuis fubinde com-
merciis confirmata eo usque invaluit, ut eadem nunc fit Anglorum et Scotorum lingua : nifi potius dicendum videatur, culti-
orem hanc Scotiae partem et Angliae
proximam eosdem cum Anglia incolas nac-
tam effe, ex Saxonibus oriundos, et fuiffe
olim Regni *Nordanhumbrorum* partem :
nam Scoti Montani *(Highlanders* dicti) hos
(qui vocantur *Lowlanders)* non minus quam
Anglos, *Saffons* (hoc eft, *Saxones)* appellant :

thing elegantly or emphatically unless it has an unusual or foreign flavour about it.

THE ENGLISH LANGUAGE TODAY

So, as a result of this kind of borrowing, and partly too just through time passing, which causes significant changes in other languages as well, the Anglo-Saxon language has slowly changed into the present English language.

This language is not confined to England, but has crossed the borders and established itself in the principal areas of Scotland; I think it did this chiefly at the time of the Norman invasion of England. The Royal Family of England, together with many of the nobles and some of the common people were driven out of England into Scotland, and took their language with them. Later it was strengthened by regular intercourse and the language of the English and Scots is now one and the same.[33] Another possible explanation is that this part of Scotland, which was more civilised and nearest to England, had the same inhabitants as England – descended from the Saxons, and was originally part of the kingdom of Northumbria. The Scottish mountain dwellers (called *Highlanders*) apply the term Sassons (that is, Saxons) just as much to these so-called *Lowlanders* as they do to the English, whereas they originally called themselves

[33] The best account of the early Scottish language is still to be found in the historical introduction to J. A. H. Murray (1873).

lant: fe vero *Gael* et *Gaiothel* dixerunt
olim. At Montani illi Scoti, et Infulani
(variarum adjacentium infularum incolae),
qui magnam quidem, fed incultiorem, Scotiae partem occupant, ad Septentrionalem
et Occidentalem Scotiae partem pofiti, anti-
quam linguam Britannicam, feu potius
Hibernicam, magna ex parte, etiamnum
retinent: funt enim *Pictorum* (hoc eft, anti-
quiffimorum Britonum, jugum Romanum
dedignantium, in montofas hasce et afper-
rimas regiones pulforum) reliquiae, admiftae
Scotis (a *Scythis* forfan, aut *Gothis*, olim
oriundis) ex Hibernia huc advectis: nam et
Hiberniae incolae olim dicebantur *Scoti*.

Eft igitur illa quam trado *lingua Anglicana*, antiquae Teutonicae propago, ficut
et hodierna Germanica, Belgica, Danica,
aliaeque affines; et quidem pari modo ab
his differt, quo et ipfae inter fe.

Hujusce autem linguae Grammaticam infti-   Operis fuf-
tutionem ideo aggreffus fum, quod ipfius   cepti ratio,
cognitionem videam ab exteris non paucis
maxime defideratam: quo poffint varia illa
et maximi momenti fcripta intelligere, quae
apud nos noftro extant idiomate. Multi
nempe funt, praefertim ex Theologis exteris, qui *Theologiam Practicam*, prout a
noftris tradi confuevit, fummopere cupiunt
       b 4   intueri;

8 magna ex parte: 5th–6th
14–15 nam . . . *Scoti*: 5th–6th

Gael and *Gaiothel*. The Highland Scots and the Islanders (inhabitants of the various nearby islands) who occupy a large but less civilised part of Scotland in the North and West still speak the old British, or rather Irish, language. They are survivors of the Picts (the earliest Britons, who scorned Roman dominion and were driven into these mountainous and rugged areas),[34] and of the Scots (perhaps descended from the Scythians or Goths)[35] who came here from Ireland (the inhabitants of Ireland were formerly called Scots).

So this English language which I am describing is a branch of Old Teutonic, like modern German, Dutch, Danish and other related languages; all of them differ from each other in much the same degree.

MY REASON FOR UNDERTAKING THIS WORK

I have undertaken to write a grammar of this language because there is clearly a great demand for it from foreigners, who want to be able to understand the various important works which are written in our tongue.[36] For instance there are many people, particularly foreign theologians, whose great ambition is to study *Practical Theology*, as it is normally taught in our tradition. It is well known

[34] Recent books dealing with the origin and history of this intriguing people are: *The Problem of the Picts*, ed F. T. Wainwright (1955), and *The Picts*, by Isobel Henderson, 1967.

[35] Another example of Wallis's etymological speculations (*cf* notes 26–27).

[36] Wallis wrote in Latin for the benefit of foreigners; *cf* P. Greaves, *Grammatica Anglicana* (1594), and Alexander Gil, *Logonomia Anglica* (1619) before him, and Christopher Cooper, *Grammatica Linguae Anglicanae* (1685) after him. Cooper's was the last English grammar to be written in Latin.

xxiv   AUCTORIS PRAEFATIO.

intueri; qua in re Concionatores noftros, faventibus Divini numinis aufpiciis, profectus non vulgares fecifle in confeflo eft; partim quidem quoniam minor fuerit neceffitas de rebus Controverfis ad populum verba faciendi, quam ubi Pontificii Reformatis paffim immifcentur; et partim etiam quod multi ex populo Anglicano ferio pii, fincero cordis affectu pietatis ἐνέργειαν amplexi, et (pro more populi) δυσεβέςεροι, feveriorem Religionis praxin et intelligere defideraverint et exercere, unde et ejusmodi Concionatorum avidi auditores fuerint qui Theologiae praxin efficacius tradiderunt, eorumque fcripta diligentius evolvere confueverint. Sed et praeterea, non Theologica tantum, verum etiam omnigenae literaturae fcripta, paffim exftant Anglicano idiomate edita: adeo ut fine faftu dicere liceat, vix quicquam folidioris eruditionis effe, quod non fit nunc dierum etiam in ipfa lingua Anglicana faltem mediocriter traditum; et multa quidem quotidie fcripta prodeunt defideratiffima.

Cum autem ea quae jam dicta funt hujusce linguae defiderium apud multos faciant, conqueruntur tamen exteri non raro, linguae noftrae difficultatem tantam effe ut illam non facile affequi valeant; fed et ex noftra-

tibus

---

10 severiorem: 1st has *intimiorem*

that in this field our public teachers, with God's help, have had out-standing successes. The reason is partly that they have not had to spend so much time instructing the people on controversial matters as is required in places where there is a higher proportion of Papists to Protestants; and partly because many English people who are genuinely religious, and engage in active religious work with a sincere purpose and (according to their custom) with great piety, have been eager to understand and pursue a stricter practice of religion; so they have eagerly listened to the more effective of our public teachers of practical theology, and have always been accus-tomed to read their works with great diligence. But it is not only theological works; all kinds of literature are widely available in English editions, and, without boasting, it can be said that there is scarcely any worthwhile body of knowledge which has not been re-corded today, adequately at least, in the English language. Every day many very highly sought after books appear.

For these reasons many people want to learn our language, but foreigners often complain that it is so difficult that they cannot easily acquire it. Even some of our own countrymen, surprising

AUCTORIS PRAEFATIO.

tibus aliqui, quod tamen mirandum eft, nefcio quam perplexam fomniant et intriᵥ catiorem linguae noftrae rationem, ut aegre poffit Grammaticae leges fubire; adeoque tam qui difcere quam qui docere volunt, confufe plerumque rem aggrediuntur, unde et taedii multum et moleftiae confequi ne- ceffe eft. Cui ego malo ut remedium fer- rem, hoc quicquid eft operis ultro fufcepi, ut linguam in fe facillimam brevibus prae- ceptis traderem, unde et exteri facilius il- lam addifcere valeant, et noftrates veram nativae fuae linguae rationem penitius per- fpiciant.

Non ignoro alios ante me hoc aliquando aggreffos effe, et aliquid etiam non contem- nendum praeftitiffe, nempe Doctorem *Gill* Latine, *Benjaminum Johnfon* Anglice, et nuper non male *Henricum Hexham* Belgice (quem tamen mihi non prius videre con- tigit quam totum opus confummaveram, et quidem ultimae paginae, editionis primae, fub prelo erant). At nemo eorum, quan- tum ego exiftimo, illa infiftit via quae huic negotio maxime eft accommodata: omnes enim ad Latinae linguae normam hanc noftram Anglicanam nimium exigentes (quo etiam errore laborant fere omnes in aliis modernis linguis tradendis) multa inutilia
                                                                                         praecepta

22 editionis primae: 5th–6th

though it may seem, have the foolish notion that the structure of our language is somehow complex and over-involved, and scarcely obeys any grammatical laws. Would-be learners and would-be teachers usually approach it in such a muddled way that the inevitable result is a great deal of boredom and difficulty. My purpose in taking it upon myself to write this book is to remedy this unfortunate situation. I aim to describe the language, which is very simple in essence, in brief rules, so that it will be easier for foreigners to learn, and English people will get a better insight into the true structure of their native tongue.

I am well aware that others before me have made the attempt at one time or another, and have produced worth-while contributions – for example Dr Gill in Latin, Benjamin Jonson in English and recently a valuable work by Henry Hexham in Dutch (though as it happened I did not see this last mentioned book until I had completed all my work – in fact until the last pages of the 1st edition were in the press).[37] None of them, however, in my opinion, used the method which is best suited to the task. They all forced English too rigidly into the mould of Latin (a mistake which nearly everyone makes in descriptions of other modern languages too), giving many useless rules about the cases, genders and declensions of nouns, the

---

[37] *Gil* – see note 36. *Ben Jonson:* The English Grammar, London, 1640, published posthumously. *Henry Hexham:* his grammar appeared with his English-Nether Dutch dictionary, Rotterdam, 1647–8.

xxvi AUCTORIS PRAEFATIO.

praecepta de Nominum Casibus, Generibus, et Declinationibus, atque Verborum Temporibus, Modis, et Conjugationibus, de Nominum item et Verborum Regimine, aliisque similibus tradiderunt, quae a lingua nostra sunt prorsus aliena, adeoque confusionem potius et obscuritatem pariunt, quam explicationi inserviunt.

Tractandi methodus.

Et propterea nova prorsus methodo incedendum esse mihi visum est, quam non tam usitata Latinae linguae, quam peculiaris linguae nostrae ratio suadet (quam, post haec primum edita, imitati videntur Gallorum aliqui in sua *Grammaire Universelle*; quae Latine post edita, *Grammatica Universalis* dicitur; methodo meae multum conformis): tota nempe Nominis Syntaxi Praepositionum fere auxilio praestita, et Verborum Conjugatione facili Auxiliarium ope peracta, illud levissimo negotio peragitur, quod in aliis linguis ingentem solet afferre molestiam.

Sunt quidem et apud Latinos nonnulla, tam Substantiva quam Adjectiva, quae *Aptota* sunt et plane Indeclinabilia, ut *pondo, nihil, instar, sat* (substantive positum), *frugi, nequam, praesto*, etc. quae tamen, ad aliorum imitationem, Genera et Casus habere finguntur, licet, per Casus omnes omniaque Genera,

5 a lingua nostra: 1st–4th have *linguae nostrae*
12–17 (quam, post haec . . . conformis): 5th–6th
25 pondo: 2nd–6th
28 finguntur: 1st–4th have *supponuntur*

tenses, moods and conjugations of verbs, the government of nouns and verbs, and other things of that kind, which have no bearing on our language, and which confuse and obscure matters instead of elucidating them.

MY OWN PROCEDURE

For this reason I decided to employ a completely new method, which has its basis not, as is customary, in the structure of the Latin language but in the characteristic structure of our own. (Some Frenchmen seem to have imitated this method, since its first publication, in their *Grammaire Universelle*,[38] which in a subsequent Latin edition is entitled *Grammatica Universalis*, and closely follows my own method.) The whole syntax of the noun depends almost entirely on the use of prepositions, and the conjugation of verbs is easily managed with the help of auxiliaries, so that what usually causes a great deal of difficulty in other languages, gives us no trouble at all.

In Latin there are some substantives and adjectives which have no cases and are wholly indeclinable, for instance *pondo*, *nihil*, *instar*, *sat* (used as a substantive), *frugi*, *nequam*, *praesto*, etc, though it is assumed, on the analogy of the others, that they have genders and cases, in all of which they remain completely invariable

---

[38] The Port-Royal Grammar appeared in 1660; it may be this that Wallis is referring to here, because the sentence in parentheses was first introduced in the 5th edition (1699). See Introduction *p* 32 *f*.

Genera, invariata prorfus maneant: at vero, fi eorum Subftantiva omnia Aptota effent, et Adjectiva plane indeclinabilia; certo certius de *Cafibus* et *Generibus* Nominum omnino altum fuiffet filentium, et magna fimul eorum pars, quae de Nominum Syntaxi jam neceffario traduntur, nufquam confpiceretur. Atque idem etiam de variis verborum *Modis* et *Temporibus* formandis plane eveniret, fi omnia utriusque vocis Tempora ejusmodi folum circumlocutionibus exprimenda effent, quales in quibusdam Paffivae vocis Temporibus confpiciuntur. Apud nos igitur, ubi res omnino fecus fe habet quam apud Latinos, cur hujusmodi *Cafuum, Generum, Modorum, Temporumque*. fictam et ineptam plane congeriem introducamus citra omnem neceffitatem, aut in ipfa lingua fundamentum, nulla ratio fuadet.

Recepta tamen apud Latinos artis vocabula, quanquam linguae noftrae non usquequaque accommodata, retinenda cenfui; partim quod fignificationis jam notae fint, partim etiam quod nollem praeter neceffitatem quidpiam innovare. Ut autem taedium quantum fieri poteft evitetur, fuccincta phrafi ufus fum, et ea quae minoris momenti et κϱλιϰώτερα videri

in form. But if none of the Latin substantives had cases and the adjectives were indeclinable, nothing would have been said about cases and genders of nouns at all, and much of the existing description of the syntax of the noun would be entirely unnecessary. The same thing, clearly, would also apply if, in forming the various moods and tenses of Latin verbs, all the tenses in both voices were expressed only by circumlocutions of the kind that are used in certain tenses of the passive voice.[39] So in our language, where the situation is quite different from that in Latin, there is no reason at all for introducing a collection of cases, genders, moods and tenses which are artificial and wholly inappropriate, and for which there is no need and no basis in the language itself.

Nevertheless I thought I had better keep the Latin terminology normally used in this Art, even though it is not entirely suited to our language; I do this partly because the meaning of it is well known, and partly also through an unwillingness to make any unnecessary innovations.[40] However I have kept my phraseology concise, to avoid making it tedious as far as this is possible, and have marked

---

[39] Tenses formed with *esse* and the past participle.
[40] See Introduction *p* 29.

xxviii   AUCTORIS PRAEFATIO.

deri poffint, diftincto charactere fecernenda curavi.

De Pronun-
ciatione et
Sonorum
formatura.

Pronunciationem, five Literarum Sonum quod attinet, conatus fum eodem modo explicare quo in aliis linguis fieri folet; collatis fcilicet fimilibus aliarum linguarum fonis cum noftris; ut, cum *e* Anglicum eodem fono efferri dico, quo Gallorum *é* mafculimum; aliaque fimilia.

Quoniam vero nonnunquam contingat, ut hoc modo ignotum per ignotius explicare videar, cum alii fortaffe non magis intelligant fonum Gallicum quam Anglicanum; neque tamen aptior modus occurrere foleat in hujusmodi fcriptis, quo, fine viva voce, literarum foni explicentur; nova etiam et hic via incedendum effe cenfui: ideoque variam literarum formationem ore aliisque loquelae inftrumentis peractam tradidi; unde non minus accurate debiti foni indicari poffe videantur, quam fi viva voce proferantur.

Hoc autem fufius aliquanto, et peculiari Tractatu praefixo, tradere mallem, quam ipfi Grammatices Syftemati immifcere, partim quod non magis ad linguam Anglicanam fpectare videatur quam ad quamvis aliam; partim etiam quod omnino novum fit, nec ab aliis, quod fciam, ante me, tentatum:

8 masculimum: misprint for *masculinum* of 1st–5th
9 aliaque similia: 5th–6th
20 indicari: 1st has *indigitari*
21 proferantur: *proferre* is used throughout the 5th and 6th editions where *efferre* was used in earlier editions, with one or two exceptions
29 ante me: 5th–6th

off in a different type those sections which may seem less important and more controversial.[41]

PRONUNCIATION AND THE FORMATION OF THE SOUNDS

As regards pronunciation, or the sounds of letters, I have tried to deal with it in the same way as is usual in other languages. That is, I have compared our own sounds with similar sounds in other languages;[42] for instance, I say that English *e* is pronounced in the same way as French *masculine e*, and so on.

However, I realise that I may sometimes seem to be explaining one unfamiliar thing by using another which, if anything, is less familiar (inasmuch as some people may be no better acquainted with the French sound than the English one). For this reason, since I have found no other suitable method in books like this for describing the sounds letters have (other than by actually pronouncing them) it seemed necessary to introduce a new method here also. I have therefore described the various articulations of the letters as formed by the mouth and other organs of speech. In this way I hope that the sounds in question may be indicated just as accurately as if they were being pronounced.

I prefer to go into this in some detail in a special introductory treatise, instead of including it with the grammatical system; partly because it seems to have no greater relevance to English than to any other language, and partly also because it is completely new, and has not, to my knowledge, been attempted by anyone else.[43,44]

---

[41] In editions up to the 4th (1674) this distinction in type is made only in the Grammar, and not in the *Tractatus de Loquela*. In the 5th and 6th editions it is made in both.

[42] Any description of pronunciation depends for its accuracy on the keenness of the observer's ear, and on whether the sounds were pronounced by a native speaker. There are a number of examples of Wallis failing to hear or to know about differences; for instance in the *Tractatus* (*p* 183) he identifies Spanish and Welsh *ll*, and later (*p* 207) he identifies French *huit* and English *whit*. See the notes on these passages.

[43] Introduction *pp* 39–40.

[44] The separation of the *Tractatus de Loquela* (as a general phonetic treatise rather than an account of the sounds of a particular language) is an excellent idea, but in fact Wallis often seems to allow the English sounds to influence his system unduly (see Introduction *pp* 47–8). Holder (1669) gives perhaps the best general phonetic description of his day (see Introduction *pp* 42, 44, 56).

AUCTORIS PRAEFATIO.   XXIX

tum: Quamvis enim quarundam literarum
formatura fparfim apud nonnullos tradita
confpiciatur, nefcio tamen an quispiam (me
prior) totam loquelae rationem conjunctim
et Syftematice tradiderit. Dum autem hoc
aggredior, novam me praeter aliorum methodum, literarum diftributionem inducere,
lector non mirabitur.

Eam vero quam hic trado Sonorum Forma-   _{Muti} *L*۪
tionem (anno 1653 primo editam) poftquam   _{quelam}
    _{edocti.}
attentius perpenderam; non modo hinc ex
noftratibus nonnullos, ad fonos praefertim
aliquot literarum, feu haefitantes, feu balbu-
tientes, docuerim clare atque expedite illos
eloqui; atque exteros aliquot de fonis quibusdam ut difficillimis aut (fibi faltem)
impoffibilibus conqueftos, docuerim extem-
plo eosdem facile et absque ulla moleftia
proferre (monftrato tantum, quo organorum pofitu, proferri debeant foni; aut cor-
rigi, quam five organorum vitio five prava
confuetudine contraxerant, haefitantia): Sed
duos etiam (eo quod furdi fuerint) plane
Mutos, Loqui docui et nulla non vocabula
(five ex noftris, five quae exteri ut omnium
difficillima propofuerint) diftincte proferre;
fed et (quod huc tamen non fpectat) animi
fui fenfa aut verbis eloqui aut fcripto con-
fignare, atque ab aliis fcripta legere et intelligere.

3 (me prior): 5th–6th
6 novam me praeter: 1st has *novam me, praeter*
9–xxx.4 Eam vero . . . vel maxime: 4th–6th

For although some sporadic descriptions of the articulation of certain letters are to be seen, I am not aware that anyone before this has described the whole structure of speech systematically in one place. It will not surprise readers to find that, in the course of this description, I introduce a new classification of the letters, which is not included in the methods hitherto used.

TEACHING THE DUMB TO SPEAK[45]

After I had pondered on this treatise on the *Formation of Sounds* (first published in 1653) more deeply, I used it to teach some of our own countrymen to pronounce clearly and readily the sounds of certain letters on which they had previously stammered or stuttered, and I also taught a number of foreigners to produce, on the spot, sounds which they had complained were very difficult and even, for them at least, impossible. They did this easily and without any effort (once they had been shown the correct position of the articulators for these sounds; or how to correct the stammer, which they had acquired as a result of defective speech organs or a bad habit). I even succeeded in teaching two men who were totally dumb (because of their deafness) to speak, and to pronounce words clearly (both words from our own language, and also some which foreigners suggested as particularly difficult). In addition (though this is not strictly to the point here) I taught them either to express their thoughts in speech or to write them down, and to read and under-

[45] Introduction *p* 11 *ff*. The whole of this section appeared first in the 4th edition, 1674.

telligere. Nec dubito idem in quovis alio
me praeftiturum (modo fani cerebri fit, et
cui loquelae organa non fint vitiata aut
prave formata) utut furdus fit vel maxime.

*De Etymo-
logia.*

Tandem, fub calcem operis, adjunxi de
Etymologia tractationem breviusculam; qua
vocum cognatarum invicem tam Conve-
nientiam quam Difcrepantiam breviter ad-
notavi, et fimul praecipuarum apud nos
fervilium Terminationum ufum; atque voces
exoticas in linguam noftram inferendi morem; denique et frequentem apud nos
ὀνομαϳοποιἲαν, feu vocum, ipfo fui fono varias
rerum fignificatarum affectiones indican-
dium, formationem infinuavi; non quidem
ejusmodi voces omnes recenfendo, fed ejusmodi faltem aliquot monftrando, qua-
lium ingentem quilibet numerum obfervare
poterit.

Si quis autem, ex noftratibus praefertim,
hoc totum quicquid eft operis penitus
omitti poffe credat, neque rem magnam
effe dicat vernaculam linguam callere, ejusque minutias obfervare: hoc folum regero;
Multa effe quae, quamvis cognita non
magnam mereantur laudem, eadem tamen
ignorata, non leve poffunt dedecus im-
primere.

                        Atque

---

24 regero: 1st has *replico*

stand what other people had written. I am confident that I could do the same for anyone else, however deaf (provided that they were sane and their vocal organs were not damaged or badly formed).

ON ETYMOLOGY

At the end of the work I have added a short[46] account of Etymology, in which I have described similarities and differences between cognate words; the use of the main derivative endings in our language; the method of introducing foreign words into it; and finally the frequent occurrence of onomatopoeia in English – that is, the formation of words which indicate by their actual sound the different characters of the things they signify; I have not listed all words of this kind, but have presented some, at any rate, out of the vast number which can be heard.

If anyone, particularly any of my own countrymen, believes that he can safely disregard all that is contained in this book, and thinks it a matter of little importance that he should get to know his native language and observe its subtleties, I will only say this to him; there are many things the knowledge of which gives us no special claim to praise, but ignorance of these very things may be the cause of great shame to us.

---

[46] The chapter *De Etymologia* when first published was quite short, but by the 5th edition (1699) it had been expanded more than any other section, so Wallis's description of it as *breviusculam* becomes quite inappropriate. For a summary of this chapter see *pp* 28–29 of the Introduction.

AUCTORIS PRAEFATIO. xxxi

Atque haec fere funt (faltem fi id quod de Mutis dictum eſt excipias) quae Lecto-rem monueram in Editione Prima Anno 1653, Oxoniae. In Secunda, ibidem, 1664, adjeci nonnulla, nec tamen multa. Quam fecuta eſt Hamburgi Tertia, 1671. In Quarta 1674, auctiora multa funt; prae-fertim Capitibus xiv et xv. Quaeque ad calcem ibi fequitur *Praxis Grammatica,* tum primum prodiit. Quinta haec, quam praecedentes, eſt adhuc auctior.

1–11 This final paragraph changes with each edition:

1st: Atque haec sunt quae Lectorem, Praefationis nomine, monendum esse duxi.

2nd: Atque haec sunt quae Lectorem, Praefationis nomine, duodecim abhinc annis monendum esse duxi. Nec est quod iam addam, praeterquam in Secunda hac Editione nonnulla, nec tamen multa, auctiora prodire.

3rd: As 2nd, except that *duodecim* is replaced by *novendecim*, and *Secunda* by *Tertia.*

4th: As 6th, except as follows:

    1–2 (saltem excipias): 5th–6th

    7   Quarta 1674: 4th has *Quarta hac*

    8   Quaeque ad calcem ibi sequitur: 4th has *Quae autem ad calcem sequitur*

    10   tum primum prodiit: 4th has *nunc primum prodit*; Quinta . . . auctior: 5th–6th

5th: As 6th

This (with the exception of the section on the deaf-mutes) is virtually the same preface as appeared in the 1st edition, published in Oxford in 1653. In the 2nd edition, also published in Oxford, in 1664 I made some additions, though not extensive ones. Then followed the 3rd edition, published in Hamburg in 1671.[47] In the 4th edition (1674) there are a large number of additions, especially to Chapters XIV and XV. The *Praxis Grammatica* which is added at the end first appeared in the 4th edition. This 5th edition is even larger than its predecessors.

[47] The 3rd edition is in fact dated 1672.

INDEX.

———

c   SECT.

Index

INTRODUCTORY TREATISE

On speech; or the true sound of all the letters and their formation in the mouth and the other vocal organs

ENGLISH GRAMMAR

xxxiv

INDEX.

INDEX.

PRAXIS GRAMMATICA.

PRAXIS GRAMMATICA

Note: Chapter xiv and xv and the *Praxis Grammatica* are omitted from this edition; see
Preface *p* v.

TRACTATUS PROOEMIALIS

DE LOQUELA,

SIVE LITERARUM OMNIUM FORMA-

TIONE ET GENUINO SONO.

SECT. I.

De Loquela in genere, ejusque affectibus.

Ex conjunctis Vocibus Sententias, ex conjunctis Syllabis Voces, et ex conjunctis Literis Syllabas, fieri; Sententias item in Voces, Voces in Syllabas, easque tandem in Literas, resolvi; notius est quam ut dictu opus sit. Cum autem in Literis terminetur analysis, seu vocum resolutio, tanquam in primis Elementis non ulterius resolvendis (quare et ϛοιχεῖα Graecis dicuntur): Litera dicenda est *Sonus in voce simplex seu incompositus, in simpliciores indivisibilis.* Et peculiari plerumque charactere designatur.

Litera, quid.

Sin malit aliquis non Sonum ipsum simplicem, sed Characterem soni simplicis indicem, Literam appellare, fruatur, per me licet, arbi-

B   trio

INTRODUCTORY TREATISE
ON SPEECH:
OR THE FORMATION AND THE TRUE SOUND
OF ALL THE LETTERS

Section 1
On speech in general and its characteristics[1]

It is common knowledge that words joined together make sentences, syllables joined together make words, and letters joined together make syllables, and equally that sentences are divided into words, words into syllables, and finally syllables into letters.[2] Since the analysis, or segmentation of words, ends with letters, as it were with primary elements which cannot be further segmented (this is why the Greeks called them στοιχεῖα) the letter must be defined as *a sound within the word which is simple or uncompounded and which cannot be split up into simpler components.*[3] It is usually represented by a special symbol. If anyone prefers to apply the term *letter* to the symbol representing the simple sound rather than to the sound itself,

---

[1] *Affectus:* cf Greek πάθη or παθήματα, signifying the *properties* a thing has, as opposed to its *essence* (Greek οὐσία; Latin *substantia* – see Plato, *Euthyphro* 11a; Arist. *Met.* 1022b). This usage was extended to the characteristic properties of different parts of speech – number, case, gender etc, and here to the properties of the spoken word.
[2] Introduction *p* 20.
[3] Introduction *pp* 62–3.

[129]

2 DE SONORUM FORMATIONE.

trio fuo: ego hac ex parte, nullam movebo litem. Fateor enim Graecorum γράμμα a *fcribendo*, et Latinorum Literam vel a *lineando* (ut Scaligero videtur) vel potius (ut ipfa Linea) a *linendo* dici: ut illud fignificet vox utraque quod chartae infcriptum eft vel *illitum*. Nec video cur per geminum *tt* fcribi debeat littera, nifi cum carminis ratio poftulat ut prima fyllaba (quae fit natura brevis) facienda fit longa, ut in *Relligio, Relliquiae*, et fimilibus.

Unde dicatur.

Quod fi occurrat aliquando Character aliquis fonum exprimens non omnino fimplicem, fed ex duobus pluribusve conflatum, et in totidem refolubilem; non tam *Litera* dicendus eft Character ifte, quam *literarum aliquot abbreviatura*, five in unam notam contractio, tot revera literas in fe continens quot funt fimpliciores illi foni ex quibus conflatur poteftas ejus. Hoc in Latinorum *&, x,* Graecorum ξ, ψ, ς, Hebraeorum צ, aliisque aliquot, notiffimum eft: conflantur enim ex *et, cs, xs, πς, στ,* צד.

E contra vero, Sonus fimplex, quamvis pluribus fortaffe Characteribus defcribatur, pro unica litera cenfendus eft. Sunt enim *th, ph,* non minus quam θ, φ, *f,* literae fimplices.

Inftrumenta loquelae, eorumque ufus.

Literas proferendi, et univerfam quidem loquelam perficiendi, inftrumenta funt praecipua, Pulmo et Larynx, cum adjacente Afpera Arteria; item Lingua, Nares, Labia, variaeque oris partes.

Ex

---

7 *illitum:* 1st–4th have *oblitum*
7–11 Nec video ... fimilibus: 5th–6th
23 The Hebrew symbols appear in the reverse order in 1st–5th

he is free to do so as far as I am concerned – I shall not raise any objection to it. In fact the Greek word γράμμα comes from a root signifying writing; and Latin *litera* either comes from *lineare*, to make a straight line (Scaliger's opinion), or like *linea* itself from *linere*, to bedaub, both words signifying something which is written or marked on a piece of paper. (I see no reason for writing *littera*, with a double *t*, except where poetic metre requires that the first syllable (which is short by nature)[4] should be made long, as is the case in *relligio*, *relliquiae* and similar words.)

However, sometimes a symbol is used which does not indicate a wholly simple sound, but a combination of two or more sounds which can be distinguished as separate parts; in this case it must not be called a *letter*, but an *abbreviation of several letters*, or a contraction of them into one sign, which contains within itself the same number of true letters as the simple sounds which make up its pronunciation. Very familiar examples of this type are Latin ℰ, *x*, Greek ξ, ψ, ς, Hebrew צ, and some other symbols: they are made up of *et*, *cs*, κς, πς, στ, צצ, respectively.

Conversely a simple sound, although it may be written with several symbols, should be regarded as only one letter. *Th*, *ph* are simple letters just as much as θ, φ, *f*.[5]

THE ORGANS OF SPEECH AND THEIR USE

The chief organs concerned in pronouncing the letters and producing all forms of speech are the lungs and the larynx, and the adjoining windpipe; also the tongue, the nose, the lips and the various parts of the mouth.[6] The breath, or indrawn air, is breathed out of

[4] Wallis is wrong; there is no example of the first syllable of *littera* being short, whichever spelling is used.
[5] Wallis does not regard English *sh*, or French *j* in *je*, as simple sounds; see Section 4, *pp* 201, 203. For his interpretation of φ and θ see note 62, *p* 173.
[6] Although he does not, in so many words, distinguish two different types of vocal organs, Wallis seems to be suggesting a twofold division (similar to that of Madsen, Montanus, Holder and Amman) into a *material* group and a *formative* group, the former being modified by the latter: (i) lungs, larynx, trachea (the sources of breath and voice); (ii) tongue, nostrils, lips, and the various parts of the mouth. See also note 12, *p* 135.

DE SONORUM FORMATIONE. 3

Ex Pulmone per Afperam Arteriam ef-
flatur fpiritus, five infpiratus aër, qui
quafi vocis five loquelae materiam fub-
miniftrat. Ex hujus enim varia collifi-
one Sonorum oritur varietas, tam quoad
Tonos, quam quoad Articulationem.
Haec autem diverfificatio non ab ipfo
Pulmone, fed aliunde, provenit; ut mox
dicetur. Nulla enim alia a Pulmone Sonorum
provenit Sonorum variatio, nifi quatenus debilitas,
majori minorive violentia fpiritum ex- unde.
trudit; unde vox evadit (caeteris paribus) magis minusve fortis et fonora.
Illud enim praeftat in loquela Pulmo,
quod in Muficorum organis pneumaticis
Folles.

Tonorum varietas, quoad Gravitatem Tonorum
fcilicet et Acumen, partim ex Trachea, acumen,
five Arteria Afpera, ortum habet : nam, unde.
ut tubus, fic Trachea, longior et ftrictior
fonum efficit magis Acutum, brevior autem et magis dilatata Graviorem (Unde, faltem ex parte, oritur Tonorum varietas in diverforum hominum vocibus,
aut quidem ejusdem hominis in variis ae-
tatibus) : Sed praecipue ex Larynge, feu
nodo gutturis : Prout enim Laryngis rimula magis minusve aperitur; ita et
vocis tonus magis Gravis eft aut Acutus.
Eftque haec totius modulationis Mufi-
cae fedes.

B 2 Ex

---

15 pneumaticis: 5th–6th
24–25 diversorum hominum . . . eiusdem hominis: 1st has *diversarum personarum*
. . . *eiusdem personae*

the lungs through the windpipe and, so to speak, supplies the raw material for voice or speech. For it is from the various interruptions which it encounters that we get the various sounds, differing in their tones[7] and their articulation. This differentiation does not take place in the lungs but elsewhere, as I shall soon explain. The only variation in sounds for which the lungs are responsible results from the different degrees of breath force which, *ceteris paribus*, cause the voice to have greater or less strength and sonority as it escapes. The lungs have the same function in speech as the bellows have in the musicians' wind-operated organs.

The difference in the tones[7] of the voice, from low to high, has its origin partly in the *trachea* or windpipe. The *trachea*[8] behaves like a tube; the longer and narrower it is, the higher the sound it emits, and the shorter and broader it is the lower the sound. (This is the cause, at least in part, of the difference of tones in the voices of different people, or in the same person's voice at different ages.) However it is the larynx, or knot of the throat, which is mainly responsible for tone variation; as the slit inside the larynx is widened or narrowed, so the tone becomes lower or higher respectively. All melody in music has its starting point here.

---

[7] That is, their pitch.
[8] See Introduction *p* 41 *ff*.

4   DE SONORUM FORMATIONE.

Sufurrus ab aperta loquela, quomodo differat.

Ex eadem etiam fede petenda eft ratio diverfitatis, mollioris *Sufurri*, ab aperta Loquela. Nam, fi inter loquendum tremula fiat Laryngis et Tracheae concuffio (nempe propter tenfionem) fit aperta Loquela; fin minus, fit Sufurrus *(Whifpering,* vulgo dicimus) laxiori nempe Trachea et minus tenfa.

In quibus Literis fentiatur.

Non funt autem Literae omnes hujusce diverfitatis capaces; fed eae folummodo quas Vocales, Semi-vocales et Semi-mutas infra dicimus (et quae ex Semi-mutis ortum ducunt): Nam quae fimpliciter Mutae funt *p, t, c* (vel *k*), earumque afpiratae, concuffionem illam nunquam admittunt; nec differt earum fonus in aperta Loquela, ab eo quem in Sufurro habent.

Raucedinis caufa.

Ad eandem etiam fedem referenda eft Raucedo, catarrhi faepe comes, Laryngis illam et Tracheae concuffionem impediens.

Vocis Articulatio, ubi fiat.

Vocum Articulatio, five diverfarum Literarum formatio, tunc incipit, poftquam Spiritus extra Laryngem pervenit: Et, Naribus, Ore, Lingua, Labiis, fere tota perficitur.

Literarum divifio in Vocales et Confonas.

Literarum autem aliae Vocales, aliae Confonae, dici folent.

SECT.

11–12 infra dicimus: 1st–2nd have *deinceps dicemus*
   14 *p, t, c*: 1st has *b, t, c* (misprint)
   19 comes: 4th has *omnes* (misprint)
   20 impediens: 1st–3rd have *impedientis*

Here also lies the explanation for the difference between a soft whisper and full speech. If, while we are speaking, there is a tremulous vibration of the larynx and the trachea (caused by tension) the result is full speech; otherwise it is what we customarily call whispering, in which the trachea is slacker and not so tensed. Not all letters have this potentiality for two forms, but only those which I shall later call *vowels*, *half-vowels*, and *half-mutes* (and letters derived from *half-mutes*).[9] The simple mutes, *p*, *t*, *c* (or *k*) and their aspirate forms,[9] are never accompanied by this vibration; their sound is the same in full speech as it is in whispering.[10]

The hoarseness which often accompanies catarrh originates in the same place, hindering this vibration of the larynx and the trachea.[11]

The articulation of words, or formation of the different letters, begins when the breath has passed through the larynx; the nose, the mouth, the tongue and the lips are responsible for almost all articulations.[12]

Some of the letters are traditionally called vowels, and others consonants.[13]

[9] *ie* the derivative forms, see *p* 163.

[10] Wallis implies that the half-mutes [b d g] and their aspirate forms [v w z ð ɣ j] may be whispered without becoming mutes, so that voice is not the main feature which distinguishes half-mutes from mutes (see Introduction *p* 52 *ff*). Modern phonetic definitions of whisper specify that the vocal cords are approximated, not fully open. In 'whispered' speech in the *popular* sense the voiceless consonants (Wallis's *mutes*) are not *technically* whispered, because the vocal cords are wide open during their production, as they are in normal speech; only the segments that are normally voiced have the technical whisper position (see Abercrombie, 1967, *p* 28).

[11] *Cf* Holder (1669 *p* 113), Cooper (1685, Jones *pp* 2–3), Amman (1700a *p* 29). Amman gives fever and shouting as causes of hoarseness, and explains it as due to an excess of mucus from the glands, which deprives the cartilages of their elasticity. Petrus Montanus, 1635, on the other hand, attributes it to dryness of the throat (Bk II, *p* 36 *f*). In the first three editions of the *Tractatus* the text here reads '. . . Tracheae concussionem impedientis' instead of '. . . impediens'. This would make the catarrh itself the factor hindering vibration of the larynx, not the hoarseness accompanying it.

[12] Wallis does not mention the uvula at this point. Holder includes both nose and uvula in his *material* group (*cf* note 6 above), as opposed to the *formal* group which includes tongue, palate, gums, teeth and lips. Amman, however, puts the uvula with his *articulatory* group – tongue, jaws, teeth, lips – and confines the *material* group to voice and breath.

[13] Introduction *pp* 42–3.

DE SONORUM FORMATIONE. 5

SECT. II.

De Vocalibus.

Vocalium numerus, apud diverſas gen- Vocalium
tes (ſaltem ſi Characteres ſpectemus) Diſtributioet
Numerus.
omnino idem non eſt. Plures autem
audiri Vocalium ſonos, quam ſunt Characteres vulgo adhibiti, apud omnes fere
in confeſſo eſt. Ego illas omnes in tres
omnino claſſes diſtinguendas eſſe judico;
Gutturales, Palatinas, et Labiales; prout
in Gutture, Palato, aut Labiis formantur.

> Quibus reſpondent totidem Arabum Voca-
> les; *phatha, keſra, damma;* iisdem ſedibus
> formatae: Hebraeorum item tres literae
> **׳ ׳ א** quas Matres lectionis vocant; atque
> olim omnium vocalium inſtar, ante inventa
> puncta vocalia, fuiſſe creditur.

Si vero pro numero Sermonum vocalium,
qui nunc dierum audiuntur, Vocalium
numerus (ut par eſt) cenſeatur, omnino
novem eſſe, dicendum erit: tres in Gutture, tres in Palato, et in Labiis totidem; pro triplici nimirum, in ſingulis
ſedibus, oris apertura, Majori, Mediocri,
Minori.

B 3 Guttu-

---

13 The Hebrew symbols appear in a different order in 1st–5th
16 sermonum: 1st–5th have *sonorum*

Section 2
Vowels

THE NUMBER AND DISTRIBUTION OF THE VOWELS

The number of vowels in different languages, that is if we judge by the written symbols, varies considerably. But it would be generally agreed that it is possible to hear more vowel sounds than the number of symbols commonly provided for them.[14] I think that all these vowels should be classified into a total of three groups: *gutturals*, *palatals* and *labials*, according to whether they are formed in the throat,[15] in the palate or at the lips. The Arabic vowels fit into this pattern; *phatha*, *kesra*, *damma* are formed in these three places,[16] and so are the Hebrew letters א ו י, which they call *matres lectionis*. Originally these are believed to have stood for all the vowels, before vowel points were invented. If, as seems reasonable, we reckon the number of the vowels from the number of vowel sounds which can be heard today, we must say that there are no more than nine: three in the throat, three in the palate and three at the lips – corresponding to the three degrees of aperture of the mouth at each point – wide, medium and narrow.[17]

---

[14] In Chapter I of the Grammar Wallis starts from the symbol, not the sound. For an account of early classifications of vowels see Introduction, Section 7(b).

[15] *Guttur* (throat) appears to signify what is now called the *pharynx* – stretching from the larynx to the faucal pillars; the guttural vowels are said to be produced 'at the top of the throat (*guttur*) or between the back of the tongue and the back of the palate'. Wilkins opposed *guttural* to *lingual*, describing the guttural as made *in the throat*, without any movement of the tongue or lips (though in his table of articulations he gives the root of the tongue as articulator). Cooper's *guttural u* is said to be entirely formed in the throat by the vibrating larynx.

Fauces – Wallis apparently means the passage between the upper and lower jaws, from the back of the tongue to the lips (*pp* 139, 141, 143). It is therefore virtually a synonym of *os*, mouth (see text *pp* 136, 140, 144), but is translated here 'mouth cavity'.

Palatum signifies the roof of the mouth from the uvula to the teeth. Wallis does not distinguish the soft palate from the hard palate specifically, though *posterior pars palati* seems to be equivalent to the soft palate, and *medium palati* or *anterior pars palati* to the hard palate and teeth ridge combined.

[16] The vowels in classical Arabic vary in their phonetic realisation according to their environment, but can be contrasted as open unrounded (fathah), close unrounded (kasrah) and close rounded (dammah), so they do roughly correspond to Wallis's division into guttural, palatal and labial. This applies also to the vowels of classical Hebrew (see *p* 45).

[17] See Introduction, *p* 46 *ff*. The mouth aperture may be varied either by moving the jaw, or by changing the lip or tongue position while keeping the jaw still, or by both together (at least in the case of the palatal vowels – p 143). The back of the tongue is highest in the gutturals and the middle highest in the palatals. Wilkins makes the *tongue* shape and position the sole relevant factor in determining his lingual vowels. Other seventeenth-century writers usually just talk of aperture without any attempt to distinguish between tongue and jaw movement. See also note 25 below.

6   DE SONORUM FORMATIONE.

Gutturales. Gutturales in fummo Gutture formantur, feu pofteriori linguae et palati parte, aëre moderate compreffo.

á, ŏ, aperta. Et quidem, fi apertura Majori, feu pleno
rictu, fpiritus exeat; formatur Germa-
norum *â*, vel noftrum *ō* apertum.

Neque Germani folum, fed et Galli, aliique
non pauci, eodem fono fuum *a* plerumque
proferunt.   Angli fonum illum correptum,
per *ŏ* breve; productum vero, plerumque
per *au*, vel *aw*, rarius per *â* exprimunt.
Nam, in *fâll, folly; hâll, haul, holly; câll,
collar; laws, loffe; caufe, coft; aw'd, odd;
faw'd, fod;* aliisque fimilibus; idem prorfus
Vocalium fonus auditur in primis fyllabis,
nifi quod illic producatur, hic corripiatur.
Atque hinc eft quod Hebraei fuum *camets
longum*, et *camets breve* feu *camets chatuph*,
(hoc eft, noftrum *â* apertum, et *ŏ* breve)
eodem charactere fcribunt.   Nam eorum
כָּל et כָּל non aliter differunt quam noftrum
câll et *coll*.

e foemini-
num. Eodem loci, fed apertura faucium Mediocri, formatur Gallorum *e* foemininum;
fono nempe obfcuro.   Non aliter ipfius
formatio differt a formatione praecedentis *â* aperti, quam quod magis contra-
hantur fauces, minus autem quam in
formatione Vocalis fequentis.

Hunc

---

6 vel noftrum *ō* apertum: 1st–4th have *vel ŏ apertum*
12 *hâll, haul, holly*: 5th–6th
17–22 Atque hinc . . . *câll* et *coll*: 5th–6th
    21 כָּל et כָּל non aliter differunt: 5th has כָּל et כָּל feu כָּל non aliter differunt

THE GUTTURALS

The gutturals are formed at the top of the throat, or between the back of the tongue and the back of the palate, with a moderate compression of the air.[18]

Open â and open ŏ.[19, 20] If the breath escapes through a wide aperture, that is, with the mouth fully open, German open *â* or our open *ŏ* is formed. Not only the Germans, but the French also and many others pronounce their *a* like this normally. The English represent the short variety of this sound with a short *ŏ* and the long variety with *au* or *aw*, or less often with *a*. In *fâll, folly; hâll, haul, holly; câll, collar; laws, losse; cause, cost; aw'd, odd; saw'd, sod* and other similar words the vowel sound in the first syllable of each word is exactly the same, except that in the first of each group it is long, and in the last, short. This is why the Hebrews write their *long camets* and *short camets* or *camets chatuph* (which correspond to our open *â* and short *ŏ*) with the same symbol. For the difference between their כָל and כָּל or כָּל־ is the same as that between our *call* and *coll.*[21]

Feminine e. At the same place, but with a medium aperture of the mouth cavity,[15] French *feminine e*[22] is formed, having an obscure type of sound. The only difference in its formation from that of the preceding vowel, open *â*, is that the mouth cavity is more constricted, though not so much as it is in the next vowel. *Feminine e* hardly

---

[18] This is the distinguishing mark of the vowels, and is opposed to *spiritus arcte compressus* (breath narrowly compressed) which is a feature of the *derivative* or *open* consonants. Compare the modern terms *open approximation* (vowels and semi-vowels) and *close approximation* (fricatives); see Abercrombie, 1967 *p* 45.

[19] Introduction *p* 48.

[20] This vowel is marked *ŏ* in editions up to the 4th, but the 5th has *ō* and the 6th *ō* and *ô*. Wallis provides for a long and a short version of it, and clearly thinks of *â* as referring to the long, and *ŏ* to the short, partly through the influence of the orthography: *fâll, fŏlly*. So it is better to follow the 4th edition and keep *ŏ*. The corresponding vowel today is classed as rounded, but the rounding may be non-existent in the case of the short vowel, in *folly, holly* etc. None of the sixteenth or seventeenth-century writers put it with the labial vowels – see Dobson (1968, *p* 578), Lehnert (1936, §§ 99, 148).

[21] For an account of the Hebrew vowels see Weingreen (1948, *pp* 4 and 12). The point here is simply that the basic symbol is unchanged and the difference indicated by a diacritic mark.

[22] Introduction p 49.

DE SONORUM FORMATIONE. 7

Hunc fonum Angli vix ufpiam agnofcunt: nifi cum vocalis *e* brevis immediate praecedat literam *r* (atque hoc quidem non tam quia debeat fic efferri, fed quia vix commode poffit aliter; licet enim, fi citra moleftiam fieri poffit, etiam illic fono vivido, hoc eft, mafculo, efferre); ut, *vertue*, virtus; *liberty*, libertas; &c.

Ibidem etiam, fed *Minori* adhuc faucium apertura fonatur *ò* vel *ū* obfcurum: Differt a Gallorum *e* foeminino, non aliter quam quod, ore minus aperto, labia propius accedant. *ò, ǔ, obfcura.*

Eundem fonum fere proferunt Galli in poftrema fyllaba vocum *ferviteur, facrificateur*, etc. Angli plerumque exprimunt per *ǔ* breve, in *turn*, verto; *burn*, uro; *dull*, fegnis, obtufus; *cut*, feco; etc. Nonnunquam *o* et *ou* negligentius pronuntiantes eodem fono proferunt, ut in *còme*, venio; *sòme*, aliquis; *dòne*, actum; *còmpany*, confortium; *country*, rus; *couple*, par; *còvet*, concupifco; *lòve*, amo; aliisque aliquot; quae alio tamen fono rectius proferri deberent. Cambro-Britanni ubique per *y* fcribunt; nifi quod hanc literam in ultimis fyllabis plerumque ut *i* proferant.

Vocales Palatinae in Palato formantur; aëre fcilicet inter palati et linguae medium moderate compreffo: Dum nempe *Palatinae.*

B 4   concavum

---

4 commode: 5th–6th
7 *vertue*, virtus; *liberty*, libertas; etc: 1st–5th have *vertue*, virtus; *liberall*, liberalis; *liberty*, libertas; etc
10 *ū* obscurum: 1st–4th have *ǔ*
20–23 The grave accents on *còme* etc do not appear in 1st–4th

exists at all in English, except where a *short e* immediately precedes the letter *r*; as in *vertue, liberall, liberty*, etc. (Even here, there is no compulsion to pronounce it like this, but it is virtually impossible to pronounce it properly in any other way: if one could do so without difficulty there is nothing against pronouncing it here with the bright or *masculine* sound.)

Obscure ò, ŭ. In the same place again, with a narrow opening of the mouth cavity, *obscure ò*, or *obscure ŭ* is formed. The difference from French *feminine e* lies only in the fact that the mouth is not opened so wide, so that the lips are closer together. The French sound in the last syllable of the words: *serviteur, sacrificateur*, etc is almost the same as this. In English it is usually represented by a short *u*, as in *turn, burn, dull, cut*, etc. Sometimes people carelessly pronounce *o* and *ou* with this sound, as in *còme, sòme, dòne, còmpany, country, couple, còvet, lòve* and some other words, but these should really be pronounced with a different sound.[23] The Welsh always represent the sound with *y*,[24] except that in final syllables, they normally pronounce *y* with the sound of *i*.

THE PALATALS
The palatal vowels are formed in the palate, the air being moderately compressed between the middle of the tongue and the middle of the

[23] From the Grammar (*p* 259) it is clear that Wallis thought these words should be pronounced with the short *o apertum*; Lehnert (1936, §§ 100, 107) attributes this to an undue concern about the orthography, and infers from the passage in the Grammar that Wallis did not mean it to apply to the native words *come, done, some, sonne* (son), *love, dove*, in spite of his statement here to the contrary.
[24] See Wiliam (1960).

8   DE SONORUM FORMATIONE.

concavum palati, elevato linguae medio,
minus redditur, quam in gutturalibus
proferendis.   Suntque hae in triplici
gradu, prout concavum magis minusve
contrahitur.

Quae quidem diverſitas duobus modis fieri
poteſt: vel fauces contrahendo, manente
lingua in eodem ſitu; vel faucibus in eodem
ſitu manentibus, linguae medium altius et
ad interiores palati partes elevando: utrovis enim modo fiat, vel etiam ſi utroque,
perinde eſt.

á exile. Majori apertura formatur Anglorum *a*,
hoc eſt, *á* exile.   Quale auditur in vocibus, *bat*, veſpertilio; *bate*, diſcordia;
pal, palla Epiſcopalis; *pale*, palidus;
Sam (Samuelis contractio); *ſame*, idem;
lamb, agnus; *lame*, claudus; *dam*, mater
(brutorum); *dame*, domina; *bar*, vectis;
bare, nudus; *ban*, exſecror; *bane*, per-
nicies; etc.

Differt hic ſonus a Germanorum *á* pingui
ſeu aperto; eo quod Angli linguae medium
elevent, adeoque in aërem in Palato comprimant; Germani vero linguae medium
deprimant, adeoque aërem comprimant in
Gutture. Galli fere ſonum illum proferunt
ubi *e* praecedit literam *m* vel *n*, in eadem
ſyllaba, ut *entendement*, etc. Cambro-Britanni, hoc ſono ſolent ſuum *a* pronunciare:
Italique ſuum.

Ibidem

10 interiores: 1st–5th have *anteriores* (the correct reading)
24 adeoque in aërem in Palato: 1st–5th have *adeoque aërem in Palato* (the
    correct reading)
28 ubi *e* praecedit: 4th has *ubi praecedit* (misprint)
31 Italique suum: 5th–6th

palate. The arch of the palate is made smaller[25] than it is in pronouncing the gutturals, by raising the middle of the tongue. These
vowels are divided into three classes, according to the relative size
of the arch of the palate. However the differences between them can
be produced in two ways – either by narrowing the mouth cavity,
while keeping the tongue in the same place; or by raising the middle
of the tongue higher and towards the front of the palate, without
altering the mouth cavity. It makes no difference whether you use
one method or the other, or even both methods.

Thin á. A wide aperture produces English *a*, that is *thin á* as in
the words *bat*, *bate*; *pal* [=pall], *pale*; *Sam* (contraction of Samuel),
same; *lamb*, *lame*; *dam* (of animals), *dame*; *bar*, *bare*; *ban*, *bane* etc.
This sound is different from German *fat* or open *â*: the English raise
the middle of the tongue, compressing the air in the palate, while
the Germans lower the middle of the tongue compressing the air in
the throat.[26] It is practically the same sound as the French use, when
e precedes the letter *m* or *n* in the same syllable, as in *entendement*
etc. The Welsh normally use it to pronounce their *a* and so do the
Italians.

---

[25] Dobson (*p* 226) incorrectly translates *minus redditur* as 'resounds less'. See notes
15 (fauces) and 17 above. Dobson (*p* 227) also comments that no sixteenth or seventeenth-
century writers recognised the significance of tongue height as the only means of
differentiating certain sounds; he regards Wallis's description as referring only to the
degree of opening of the mouth. But Wallis shows here that he was aware that the tongue
can operate independently to achieve the same effect. *Pace* Dobson, the degree of opening
of the mouth does not necessarily correspond to the relative height of the tongue, though
it may do so, as Wallis points out.
[26] Wallis is specifying the position of the highest point of the tongue – when the back is
high the middle is low, and vice versa. He appears to have been the first English writer
to record a palatal pronunciation for *thin a*. Lehnert (§§ 93 and 120) particularly criticises
the comparisons that Wallis makes with French *entendement*, and with Welsh and
Italian *a*. Thurot (1881–3, II.431–2) records a low back vowel in the French word by
the seventeenth century, except in northern dialect, and the Welsh sound varies according to its environment (Cooper, ed Jones, *p* 15*). See also Introduction *p* 60 *f* for the
effect of this vowel on preceding consonants.

DE SONORUM FORMATIONE. 9

Ibidem item, fed Mediocri oris apertu- *é* mafculi-
ra, formatur Gallorum *é* mafculinum: num.
Quo modo Angli, Itali, Hifpani, aliique
hanc literam proferre folent; vivido et
acuto fono. Eft enim fonus medius inter vocalem praecedentem, et eam quae
mox fequetur.

Hunc fonum Angli non modo per *e*, fed et
(ubi producitur) non raro per *ea*, et aliquando per *ei*, exprimunt. Ut, *the* (articulus); *there*, ibi; *thefe*, hi; *fell*, vendo; *feal*,
figillum; *tell*, nuncio, numero; *teal*, quer-
quedula; *fteal*, furari; *fet*, fifto; *feat*, fella;
beft, optimus; *beaft*, beftia; *red*, rubicun-
dus; *read*, lego; *receive*, recipio; *deceive*,
decipio; etc. Quanquam revera voces per
ea fcriptae rectius pronunciarentur, fi, praeter fonum ipfius *e* producti, etiam fonus
Anglici *a* (raptiffime pronunciati) adjunge-
retur; prout olim pronunciatas fuiffe veri-
fimile eft, atque in aliquibus locis, praefertim feptentrionalibus, etiamnum pronunciantur. Quae vero per *ei* fcribuntur, rectius
item per conjunctum utriusque literae fonum
proferri poffent.

Ibidem etiam, fed Minori adhuc oris a- *ee, ĭ,* exile.
pertura, formatur *ĭ* exile; Gallis, Hif-
panis, Italis; et plerisque aliis familiare.

Hunc fonum, quoties correptus eft, Angli
per *ĭ* breve exprimunt; quum vero producitur,

---

3 Quo modo: 1st has *Quo sono*
12 numero: 2nd–6th
27 *ĭ* exile: 1st–4th have *i* exile

[144]

Masculine é. The same place of articulation, but a medium aperture gives French *masculine é*. The English, Italians, Spanish and others pronounce this letter as the French do – with a bright and sharp sound, midway between the previous vowel and the one which follows. In English, we represent this sound not only with *e* but also with *ea* when the long variety is required, and sometimes with *ei*. For instance: *the, there, these, sell, seal, tell, teal, steal, set, seat, best, beast, red, read, receive, deceive*, etc. However a more correct pronunciation of words written with *ea* would really involve adding English *a* (rapidly pronounced) to a *long e*; this was probably how they used to be pronounced, and in some places, especially in the north, this is still so. Similarly a more correct pronunciation of words written with *ei* would involve joining up the sounds of both these letters.[27]

Thin ee, i. The same place again, with a narrow aperture produces *thin i* which is a sound that is familiar to the French, Spanish and Italians and most other people too. The English use short *i* to represent the short variety of this sound; the long variety is mostly

[27] Although Wallis is professedly not concerned in this treatise with specific languages, he often relates the sound in question to the orthography of the languages he knew. The reference here to the variant pronunciations of *ea* and *ei* is not strictly relevant, but he is always conscious of his underlying purpose – to provide a guide to English pronunciation. He is often concerned to show a connection between the pronunciation and the spelling, at least historically or through dialects. In the Grammar (*p* 263) Wallis states categorically that the *ea* spelling 'is nowadays pronounced like long *e* (*masculine e*) omitting the sound of *a* completely.' Gil (1619) provides evidence that in northern dialects *ea* was a diphthong.

IO   DE SONORUM FORMATIONE.

citur, fcribunt ut plurimum per *ee,* non raro tamen per *ie,* vel etiam per *ea.* Ut, *fit,*
fedeo; *fee't,* id video; *fit,* idoneus; *feet,* pe-
des; *fill,* impleo; *feel,* tactu fentio; *field,*
ager; *ftill,* femper, quietus; *fteel,* chalybs;
ill, malus; *eel,* anguilla; *in,* in; *inn,* hofpi-
tium; *fin,* peccatum; *feen,* vifum; *friend,*
amicus; *fiend,* cacodaemon; *near,* prope;
dear, charus; *hear,* audio; etc. Quanquam
revera, eorum quae per *ea* fcribuntur, nonnulla etiam (et quidem melius) fcribuntur
per *ee,* alia potius per *é* mafculum proferuntur, adjuncto etiam fi libet exilis *á* fono
raptiffime pronunciati. Cambro-Britanni
fonum hunc, non modo per *i,* et (in ultima
fyllaba) per *y,* fed et per *u* fcribunt, quam
literam hoc fono femper efferunt, adeoque
diphthongos *au eu* omnino ut *ai ei* pronunciant.

Labiales. Vocales Labiales, in ipfis Labiis (in ro-
tundam formam) collectis formantur;
aëre ibidem moderate compreffo. Suntque hae etiam in triplici gradu, feu dif-
ferentia.

ó rotundum. Majori labiorum apertura formatur *ó* rotundum; quo fono plerique proferunt
Graecorum *ω.*

Hoc fono Galli plerumque proferunt fuum
au. Angli ita fere femper proferunt *o*
productum, vel etiam *oa* (ipfo *a* nimirum,
nunc dierum, quafi evanefcente; de quo
idem hic judicium ferendum eft, ac fupra
de

17 efferunt: 4th has *efferuntur* (misprint)
21 formam) collectis: 1st–5th have *formam collectis)*

written as *ee*, but quite often *ie* or even *ea* is used, as in *sit*; *see't*;
fit; *feet*; *fill*; *feel*; *field*; *still*; *steel*; *ill*; *eel*; *in*; *inne*[28]; *sin*; *seen*;
friend; *fiend*; *near*; *dear*; *hear*, etc. In point of fact some of the words
written with *ea* are also written with *ee* (a better spelling); others are
pronounced with *masculine e*, with or without a rapidly pronounced
thin a. The Welsh write this sound either with *i* (or *y* in final syllables)
or with *u*, which always has this pronunciation; so the Welsh diphthongs *au*, *eu* sound exactly like *ai*, *ei*.

LABIALS

The *labial* vowels are formed at the lips (by bringing them together
in a rounded shape), moderately compressing the air between them.
These vowels too fall into three classes, or distinct groups.

Round ô.[29] A wide lip aperture produces *round ô*. Most people
pronounce Greek ω in this way, and it is the usual pronunciation
of French *au*. English *long o* nearly always has this sound, and even
oa may have it (the *a* is disappearing nowadays, and the same
applies here as applied to *ea* above). Examples are: *one, none,*

---

[28] Whereas Wallis is supported by contemporary evidence in making the vowel in *friend*
a *thin i*, Lehnert (§§ 86–87) is unhappy about the pairing of *inne* with *in*, with its sugges-
tion that the former had a long *i*. But not all of the examples that Wallis gives are in
pairs (for example, *near, dear, hear*), so it is possible that both words are meant to
exemplify the short vowel, and Lehnert's assumption of a dialectal pronunciation of
inne, from south-west England, is not necessary.
[29] The classification of this vowel as having the widest aperture goes against other
evidence of the time (see Lehnert, § 122; Dobson (1968), *p* 240); for the diphthongal
pronunciation of *oa* see note 27 above on *ea*.

DE SONORUM FORMATIONE. 11

de *ea*) : Ut, *one*, unus; *none*, nullus; *whole*,
totus; *hole*, foramen; *coal*, carbo; *boat*,
cymba; *oat*, avena; *thofe*, illi; *chofe*, elegi;
etc. At ubi *o* breve eſt, ut plurimum per
ŏ apertum (de quo ſupra) rarius per *ó* rotundum pronunciatur.

In labiis item, apertura Mediocri forma- *o, u* pingue.
tur Germanorum *ú* pingue: quo ſono
etiam Hiſpani, Itali, aliique non pauci
utuntur,

Galli per *ou :* Cambro-Britanni per *w :*
Angli plerumque per *oo* (rarius per *u* vel
ou) exprimunt; ut, *foot*, pes; *ſhoot* (arcu
vel bombarda) projicio; *full*, plenus; *fool*,
ſtultus; *pull*, vello; *pool*, piſcina; *good*, bonus; *ſtood*, ſteti; *wood*, lignum; *woo'd*, pro-
catus ſum; *mood*, modus; *mourn*, lamentor;
courſe, curſus; *ſource*, ſcaturigo; *could*, poſſem; *would*, vellem; *ſhould*, deberem; etc.
At, *do*, ago; *go*, eo; *move*, moveo; et ſiqua
ſunt ſimilia; reċtius per *ó* rotundum, quam
per *ú* pingue, efferuntur.

Ibidem etiam, ſed Minori adhuc apertu- *u*-exile.
ra, formatur *ú* exile ; Anglis ſimul et
Gallis notiſſimum.

Hoc ſono Angli ſuum *u* longum ubique
proferunt (nonnunquam etiam *eu* et *ew*
quae tamen reċtius pronunciantur retento
etiam ſono *e* maſculi): Ut, *muſe*, muſa; *tune*,
modu-

2 *hole*, foramen : 4th–6th
20 *move*, moveo : 4th–6th

whole, *hole*, *coal*, *boat*, *oat*, *those*, *chose*, etc. But where *o* is short it usually has the sound of *open ŏ* (see above) and *round ô* is not so commonly used.

Oo, fat û.[30] A medium aperture of the lips is used for German *fat û*. The Spanish and Italians have this sound, and so do many other people. The French use *ou* to represent it, the Welsh *w* and the English usually *oo* (or less often *u* or *ou*); as in *foot*; *shoot*; *full*; *fool*; *pull*; *pool*; *good*; *stood*; *wood*; *woo'd*; *mood*; *mourn*; *course*; *source*; *could*; *would*; *should*, etc. But *do*; *go*; *move* and other similar words are better pronounced with *round ô*, than with *fat û*.

Thin ú.[31] A narrow aperture at the same place of articulation produces *thin ú*; this is a very familiar sound to the English and French. In English *long u* always represents this sound (and sometimes *eu* and *ew* do also,[32] though a more correct pronunciation of these contains the sound of *masculine e* as well as *u*); for example, *muse*; *tune*; *lute*; *dure*; *mute*; *new*; *brew*; *knew*; *view*; *lieu*, etc.

---

[30] See Introduction *pp* 48 and 49. For a lengthy discussion of the distribution of the long and short versions of *fat u* in Wallis's examples see Lehnert, §§ 128–9. *Full/fool*; *pull/pool*; and *wood/woo'd* are clearly stated to be examples of long/short respectively by Wallis (1678, *p* 17).

[31] Introduction *pp* 45–9.

[32] See *p* 265 and Introduction *pp* 48–9.

12   DE SONORUM FORMATIONE.

modulatio; *lute*, barbitum; *dure*, duro;
mute, mutus; *new*, novus; *brew*, misceo (ce-
revisiam coquo); *knew*, novi; *view*, aspicio;
lieu, vice; etc. Hunc sonum extranei fere
assequentur, si diphthongum *iu* conentur
pronunciare; nempe *ĭ* exile literae *u* vel *w*
praeponentes (ut in Hispanorum *ciudad*,
civitas). Non tamen idem est omnino sonus,
quamvis ad illum proxime accedat; est enim
iu sonus compositus, at Anglorum et Gallorum *ú* sonus simplex. Cambro-Britanni
hunc fere sonum utcunque per *iw, yw, uw*,
describunt: ut in *lliw*, color, *llyw*, guber-
naculum navis; *Duw*, Deus; aliisque innumeris.

Hos ego novem sonos vocales esse agnos-
co; nec scio plures (Anglorum enim *ĭ*
latum, sonum esse simplicem, haud exis-
timo; ut post dicetur).

Vocalium
Numerus,
quo pacto
augeri possit.

Non nego tamen, in qualibet vocalium sede,
ubi ego tres tantum gradus aperturae pro-
posui, fieri posse, ut plures fortasse, vel nunc
dierum alicubi, vel saltem posteris aliquando seculis, observentur; adeoque posse sonos quosdam intermedios efferri (qualis forsan est Gallorum *e* neutrum, inter vocales
Palatinas *á* et *é*) : est enim aperturae men-
sura, instar quantitatis continuae, divisibilis
in infinitum. Ut enim, in ventis enume-
randis, olim quatuor, deinde duodecim, tandem triginta duo numerantur: Ita etiam,
cum Arabes, et forsan Hebraei antiquiores,
non

3 *view* . . . vice: 5th–6th

Foreigners will get very close to the sound if they try to pronounce the diphthong *iu*, putting in *thin ĭ* before *u* or *w* (as in Spanish *ciudad*). This is not quite the same sound, though very nearly so, because *iu* is a compound sound, while English and French *ú* is a simple one. The Welsh represent a sound very close to this variously by *iw*, *yw*, *uw*; as in *lliw* (colour), *llyw* (a ship's rudder), *Duw* (God) and many other words.

HOW THE NUMBER OF VOWELS MAY BE INCREASED

These are the nine vowel sounds which I recognise, and I know of no others (English *broad î* is not, in my opinion, a simple sound, as I shall show later). But I readily concede that at each of the places of articulation used for vowels, where I have postulated only three degrees of aperture, it is possible that more may be discovered in some part of the world, in our own time or at some time in the future.[33] So it would be possible to produce sounds in between the ones I have postulated (including, perhaps, the French *neutral e*, which lies between the palatal vowels *á* and *é*), because the total aperture, being a continuum, can be infinitely divided. The number of the winds was at one time said to be four, later twelve, and eventually thirty-two; similarly Arabic, and perhaps Ancient Hebrew,

---

[33] Introduction *p* 45 *ff*; *cf* Wilkins (1668), *p* 365.

DE SONORUM FORMATIONE. 13

non nifi tres vocales (hoc eft, in fingulis fedibus unam) habuerint, noftro autem feculo in fingulis fedibus, faltem tres manifefte
diftinguendas obfervemus; quid impedit,
quin pofteri etiam hisce intermedias quotli-
bet interponant?

Sunt autem hae vocales omnes tam pro- Syllabarum
longitudo
et brevitas,
unde.
duationis quam contraationis capaces
(unde fyllabarum *longarum brevium*que
difcrimen oritur).
Licet quaedam rarius producantur (ut *ū*
obfcurum et *e* foemininum); aliae rarius corripiantur (ut *ô* rotundum, et *ú*
exile, faltem apud nos. Sed et confonae
etiam produationis capaces funt (illae
praecipue quae ad vocalium naturam
propius accedunt): praeter *p, t, k* (vel
c durum), quae abfolute Mutae funt;
nec ullum per fe fonum edunt, fed folummodo fonum (five praecedentem, five
fubfequentem) modificant.

SECT. III.

De Confonantibus.

Confonas item in tres claffes diftribui- Confonarum
diftributio.
mus, non fecus ac vocales, Labiales, Pa-
latinas, et Gutturales; prout labiis, palato, aut gutture formantur: Nempe
dum

11 *ū* obfcurum: 1st–4th have *ŭ*
14 faltem apud nos: 1st–5th have *faltem apud nos*)

had only three vowels (one at each place of articulation), whereas nowadays we see that at least three vowels must be clearly distinguished at each place of articulation. There is nothing to prevent our descendants inserting even more vowels between these.

THE ORIGIN OF THE LENGTH AND SHORTNESS OF SYLLABLES

All of the vowels can be lengthened or shortened (this accounts for the difference between long and short syllables).[34] Some are rarely lengthened (for example, *obscure ú* and *feminine e*); others are rarely shortened (for example, *round ô* and *thin ú*) at any rate in English.[35] Consonants can be lengthened too (particularly the ones which are most vowel-like) except for *p, t, k* (or *hard c*); these are total *mutes*, which simply modify preceding or following sounds, and have no sound of their own.[36]

Section 3
Consonants

I divide consonants, like vowels, into three classes – *labials, palatals* and *gutturals* – according to whether they are formed by the lips, the palate, or the throat; the breath from the lungs being either com-

---

[34] Wallis attributes syllable length entirely to the length of the vowel (see *p* 63 *ff* and Abercrombie, 1961).

[35] Wallis's assumption throughout this section has been that there is no quality difference between the long and short vowels. This is stated specifically of *â apertum* (*p* 139). Wilkins (*p* 364) takes the same view. Relatively small quality differences are often not recorded, especially when they correlate with another factor such as duration; *cf* the vowel system of RP English today, where either length or quality may be made the primary distinguishing factor (Jones (1967), § 510 *ff*).

[36] Wallis excludes the possibility of long *p, t, k* on the grounds that they have no sound of their own. Amman criticised Wallis's failure to mention the explosion phase of the mutes (see *p* 55), and it appears that Wallis was not aware of the importance of the period of closure; this may vary considerably in length according to the position of the consonant in the syllable, and also (in English) according to the length of the preceding vowel. Final voiceless stops after a short vowel tend to be longer than they are after a long vowel, and arresting stops tend to be longer than releasing ones; this length is marked by the length of the closure, which is of course perceived on release, though not itself audible (see E. A. Meyer, *Englische Lautdauer* (1903), quoted by Jespersen, *M.E.G.* I.§ 16.33–4; D. Jones (1967), § 371).

14   DE SONORUM FORMATIONE.

dum spiritus, ex pulmonibus emissus, his in sedibus vel Intercipitur, vel saltem fortius Comprimitur.

Spiritus directio triplex.

Notandum autem est insuper, triplicem observari posse spiritus Directionem. Dirigitur nempe vel 1. totus ad fauces; per labia scilicet egressum appetens; vel 2. ad nares fere totus dirigitur, inde exitum quaerens; vel denique 3. quasi aequaliter inter fauces naresque dividitur. Hujus autem Directionis diversitatem, ex varia Uvulae positione, totam provenire credo.

Consonae Primitivae seu clausae.

Cum vero spiritus singulis hisce tribus Modis emissus, possit etiam in singulis illis tribus sedibus penitus Intercipi; Novem diversae Consonantes hinc originem sortiuntur, quas Primitivas sive Clausas appellare libet: Si vero non penitus Intercipiatur spiritus hisce sedibus, sed solummodo arctius Comprimatur, viam nempe (aegre licet) exeundi inveniens; pro vario compressionis modo, varii adhuc alii consonarum soni efficiuntur, quas consonas Derivativas sive apertas appellabimus.

Mutae.

Si Spiritus per fauces ad labia directus, occlusis Labiis intercipiatur; formatur

P.

litera *P*; Graecorum π; Hebraeorum פ dagessatum.

Arabes

---

29 Hebraeorum פ dagessatum: 1st–5th have *Hebraeorum Pe dagessatum*

pletely stopped, or at any rate strongly compressed, at these places of articulation.

TRIPLE DIRECTION OF THE BREATH

It is important to notice too, that one can distinguish three different directions of the breath: (i) entirely directed into the mouth cavity to escape through the lips; (ii) almost entirely directed into the nose, to escape through the nostrils there; (iii) divided equally between the mouth cavity and the nose. I think this difference in direction is entirely due to a difference in the position of the *uvula*.[37]

THE PRIMITIVE OR CLOSED CONSONANTS

The breath, when it is expelled in any one of these three ways, can be completely stopped in any one of the three different places of articulation. This gives us nine different consonants, which we may call *primitive* or *closed* consonants. But instead of being completely stopped in these places, it may simply be narrowly compressed,[38] but still find a way of escaping (though not easily). As a result of this type of compression we get a different group of consonant sounds, which I shall call *derivative* or *open* consonants.

MUTES

P. If the breath is directed through the mouth cavity to the lips and is then stopped by a closure of the lips, the letter *p* is formed – Greek π, Hebrew ‫פ‬ with *dagesh*. The Arabs do not have this letter

[37] This is Wallis's only mention of the uvula; he should strictly say 'soft palate', as more than just the uvula is involved in the valvular action. The soft palate had been described by Fallopius (1523–1562) – *palatum molle et pendulum*. Among seventeenth-century writers only Amman goes into any detail about the uvula. He says it is a soft and glandular piece of flesh, suspended from a movable membrane in the centre of the palate arch (*p* 38), and mentions its valve action, with the membrane, in shutting off the nose. Unlike Holder, Wallis does not give any place in his description to nasalised vowels and consonants, though in fact his divided air-stream would result in nasalised segments (see *p* 53).

[38] Compare the stricture for vowels – *aere moderate compresso* (note 18, *p* 139).

DE SONORUM FORMATIONE. 15

Arabes hanc literam non agnofcunt (fed ipfius loco fubftituunt vel *Be* vel *Phe*); Perfae tamen agnofcunt, qui praeter Arabum *Phe* habent et fuum *Pe*, quod a *Be* tribus fubfcriptis punctis diftinguitur.

Si vero ad Labia non perveniat, fed in Palato penitus intercipiatur (admoto nempe linguae extremo ad palati partem anteriorem, feu, quod idem eft, fuperiorum dentium radices) formatur confona *T*; Graecorum τ; Hebraeorum ט, vel ת dageffatum; Arabum *Te* (vel etiam *Ta*). **T.**

Si vero ne huc quidem pertingat, fed fummo Gutture intercipiatur (admota linguae parte pofteriori ad pofteriorem palati partem) formatur *K* vel *C* durum); hoc eft, Graecorum χ; Hebraeorum כ dageffatum, et ק; Arabum *Ceph*, et *Kaph*. Atque hoc fono Cambro-Britanni fuum *C* femper proferunt. **C.**

Has autem tres Confonas abfolute Mutas dicimus; nullum enim per fe fonum edunt, aut quidem edere poffunt, fpiritu nufpiam in liberum aërem exeunte; nam ad nares non pervenit, per fauces non exit.

Si Spiritus, inter nares et fauces aequaliter divifus, occlufis labiis intercipiatur; formatur confona *B*; Graecorum **Semi-mutae. B.**
Ϛ;

---

4 *Phe:* 1st has *Be*
17 *K* vel *C* durum): 4th–5th have *K*, (*vel C durum;*)

(in its place they put *Be* or *Phe*); the Persians recognise it, however – as well as the Arabic *Phe* they have *Pe*, which is distinguished from *Be* by writing three dots below it.

T. If the breath does not reach the lips, but is stopped in the palate the consonant *t* is formed – Greek *τ*, Hebrew ט or ת with *dagesh*, Arabic *Te*, or *Ta*.[39] (The passage is blocked by the tip of the tongue being pressed against the front part of the palate, or the roots of the upper teeth, which comes to the same thing.)

C. If the breath does not even reach this point, but is stopped at the top of the throat (by the back of the tongue pressing on the back of the palate) *k* or *hard c* is formed – Greek *κ*, Hebrew כ with *dagesh* and ק, Arabic *Ceph* and *Kaph*.[40] The Welsh always pronounce their *c* like this.

We call these three consonants *total mutes*; they have no sound of their own, and cannot have one, because the breath can find no way through to the outside air.[41] It does not reach the nose, and does not escape through the mouth cavity.

HALF-MUTES

B. If the direction of the breath is divided equally between nose and mouth cavity, and is stopped by the lips being closed, the consonant *b* is formed – Greek *β*, Hebrew ב with *dagesh* and Arabic *Be*.

[39] Wallis's description is of an apico-alveolar or apico-dental articulation – the tip of the tongue makes a closure at the base of the upper teeth. He does not distinguish dental from alveolar in his description; *cf* Holder and Cooper (see *p* 54 *f*). The two Hebrew and the two Arabic letters in the classical languages have the same primary articulation, but are distinguished from each other by their *secondary* articulation; see Abercrombie (1967), *pp* 61–2.
[40] Here the two Hebrew and the two Arabic letters have different *primary* articulations; Hebrew and Arabic Ceph are velar, whereas Hebrew ק and Arabic Kaph are uvular. Wallis's failure to distinguish them suggests that his knowledge of the sounds was largely a literary one. Petrus Montanus (1635) distinguished a uvular place of articulation between laryngeal and velar (Montanus, Appendix, *p* 160, Vos, *p* 212), but his work was very little known (Vos, *p* 7) and there is nothing to show that Wallis was aware of it.
[41] Introduction *p* 53.

16 DE SONORUM FORMATIONE.

Ϛ; Hebraeorum ב dageſſatum; Arabum *Be.*

D. Si, in Palato, formatur *D*; Graecorum *δ*; Hebraeorum ד dageſſatum; Arabum *Dal* (ut et *Da* et *Dad).*

G. Sin intercipiatur in Gutture (nempe inter posteriorem linguae et palati partem), formatur *G*; Graecorum *γ*; Hebraeorum ג dageſſatum; Arabum (non *Gjim,* quamvis ea ſit affinis litera, ſed) *Gain.* Cambro-Britanni ſic ſemper proferunt ſuum *g.*

Atque has ego Semi-mutas appello; exiguum enim ſonum in naribus efficiunt, qui per ſe quidem audiri poteſt nullo alterius literae ſono accedente.

Semi-vocales. Si vero Spiritus totus (vel ipſius, ſi ita placet, pars praecipua) ad nares dirigatur (aërem in oris concavo manentem ſolummodo in tranſitu concutiens); ob-

M. turatis tantum Labiis formatur *M*; Graecorum *μ*; Hebraeorum מ; Arabum *Mim.*

N. Sin obturatio in anteriori Palato fiat, formatur *N*; Graecorum *ν*; Hebraeorum et Arabum *Nun.*

Si autem in Gutture (hoc eſt, in poſteriori palati parte) fit obturatio, formatur ſonus ille, quem exprimunt Graeci per *γ* ante *κ, γ, χ, ξ.*

Latini

---

16 alterius: 1st has *ulterius*
25 formatur: 4th has *formatut* (misprint)

D. If it is stopped at the palate, *d* is formed – Greek δ, Hebrew ד with *dagesh*, Arabic *Dal* (also *Da* and *Dad*).[42]

G. If it is stopped in the throat (that is, between the back of the tongue and the back of the palate) *g* is formed – Greek γ, Hebrew ג with *dagesh*, Arabic *Gain*[43] (not *Gjim* though this is related to it). In Welsh, *g* always has this sound.

I call these consonants *half-mutes*, because they produce a small sound in the nose,[44] which can be heard by itself, without the sound of any other letter.

HALF-VOWELS

M. If the whole of the breath, or the major part of it,[45] is directed into the nose (striking the air which is left in the mouth cavity only in passing) and the lips are closed, the letter *m* is formed – Greek μ, Hebrew מ and Arabic *Mim*.

N. If the closure takes place in the front of the palate, not at the lips, *n* is formed – Greek ν, Hebrew and Arabic *Nun*.

If the closure is in the throat (that is, the back of the palate) we get the sound which the Greeks represent by putting γ before κ, γ, χ, ξ. In Latin it was sometimes represented by *g* in earlier

[42] Arabic *Da* and *Dad* are related in the same way as *Te* and *Ta* (see note 39 above).
[43] Classical Arabic had no *voiced* velar or uvular stop. *Gain* was a voiced velar or uvular fricative and should appear under Wallis's *gh*; on *p* 189 Wallis says that *gh* has no Arabic equivalent, but he correctly supposes that Hebrew Ghimel with *raphe* should be classed there. Gjim was the affricate [dʒ] (see *p* 201).
[44] Introduction *p* 52 *ff*.
[45] Presumably some of the air is envisaged as entering the mouth cavity, but not escaping through it until after the release of the nasal consonant.

Latini vero olim aliquando per *g*, ut *Agchi-
ſes, agceps, aggulus,* etc. (teſtibus Priſciano et
Varrone) : at nunc (ſicut et aliae nunc dierum
gentes) per *n* ante ejusmodi conſonas (praeſertim in eadem ſyllaba) puta *k, q, x,* item
c, g, ch, duro (hoc eſt, genuino) ſono prolatas. Alius enim auditur ſonus literae
n in vocibus *thin,* dilutum; *ſin,* peccatum ;
in, in: alius in *thing,* res; *think,* cogito;
ſing, cano; *ſingle,* ſimplex; *ſink,* ſubſido; *ink,*
atramentum; *lynx,* etc. Item in *hand,* manus; *band,* ligamentum; *ran,* currebam:
aliter ſonatur *n,* quam in *hang,* pendeo;
bank, collis; *rank,* ſeries; etc. Imo in iis-
dem vocibus, prout variae dividuntur ſyllabae, alius atque alius erit iſtius literae ſonus: aliter ſonabitur *n* in *lon-ger, ſtron-ger,
an-ger, drink-er, in-gruo, con-gruo:* aliter
vero in *long-er, ſtrong-er, ang-er, drink-er,
ing-ruo, cong-ruo.* Item, dum dicunt alii,
in-quam, tan-quam, nun-quam, etc. alios au-
diemus ita loquentes acſi ſcriberetur *inq-
wam, tanq-wam, nunq-wam;* vel *ink-wam,
tank-wam, nunc-wam.* In prioribus ubique,
dum *n* ſonatur, extremitas linguae anteriorem palati partem prope ſuperiorum dentium radices ferit; in poſterioribus, eadem
linguae extremitas potius ad inferiorum
dentium radices deflectit, poſterior vero
linguae pars ad palati partem poſteriorem
elevatur, ſonumque illic intercipit: eodem
nempe modo in ore formatur quo *G,* at illam ſpiritus directionem ſortitur quam habet *N.* Eſtque hic, ni fallor, ſonus ille quo
C   multi

15 variae: 1st–5th have *varie*
18 *an-ger, drink-er, in-gruo:* 1st–5th have *an-ger, drin-ker, in-gruo* (the correct
reading)
26 superiorum: 4th has *superiorem* (misprint)

times, as in *Agchises*, *agceps*, *aggulus*, etc (according to Priscian and Varro); nowadays (in Latin and in other languages) it is represented by *n* before consonants of that kind, especially if it occurs in the same syllable – I mean before *k*, *q*, *x*, and also before *c*, *g*, *ch*, when they have their hard, or true, sound. For there is a difference between the sound of the letter *n* in the words *thin*, *sin*, *in*, and that in *thing*, *think*, *sing*, *single*, *sink*, *ink*, *lynx*, etc. Similarly in *hand*, *band*, *ran* the *n* is not the same as it is in *hang*, *bank*, *rank*, etc. Moreover even in one and the same word the sound of this letter will vary, according to the syllable division: *n* in *lon-ger*, *stron-ger*, *an-ger*, *drin-ker*, *in-gruo*, *con-gruo* will not be the same as it is in *long-er*, *strong-er*, *ang-er*, *drink-er*, *ing-ruo*, *cong-ruo*.[46] And whereas some say *in-quam*, *tan-quam*, *nun-quam*, etc we hear others saying them as if they were written *inq-wam*, *tanq-wam*, *nunq-wam*, or *ink-wam*, *tank-wam*, *nunc-wam*. In the former of each of these two groups the pronunciation of *n* always involves the tip of the tongue striking the front of the palate, near the roots of the upper teeth; whereas in the latter the tip of the tongue is normally moved down to the roots of the lower teeth, and the back of the tongue is raised up to the back of the palate, blocking the sound at this point. That is to say, it has the same articulation in the mouth as *g*, but the direction of the breath is the same as for *n*. Unless I am mistaken this is the sound

---

[46] For guttural *n* see Introduction *p* 56. It is unlikely that Wallis is suggesting in this passage that anyone pronounced *n* as [n] in *longer*, *stronger*, *anger*, *drinker*. His point is that *if* a syllable division occurred after the nasal, the letter would be pronounced [n], but in fact the division is made after the stop. In the RP accent of English today only the unstressed prefixes *un-*, *in-*, *en-* allow a choice of either an alveolar or a velar nasal before a velar stop, as in *uncommon*, *ingressive*, *encourage* (Jones (1962), § 653).

18   DE SONORUM FORMATIONE.

multi vellent Hebraeorum ע pronunciari; dum per *ng, ngh, gn, nghn,* etc. proferendum docent: innuunt nempe fonum quendam qui nec literae *n,* neque literae *g,* perfecte refpondeat, fed quiddam habeat quafi cum utraque commune. Eundem etiam fonum nefcio an Hifpani proferant quoties literam *ñ* fuperne notatam ponunt; et Galli fuum *gn.*

Has ego tres confonas, Semi-vocales appello; majorem quippe fonum fortiuntur quam quas Semi-mutas nuper diximus.

Fiunt autem hae novem (quas jam recenfui) confonae, fpiritu prorfus intercepto, ne nempe per os omnino exeat: quas igitur Claufas diximus.

Confonae Derivativae, five Apertae; vel Afpiratae; tam Subtiliores quam Pinguiores.

Eadem vero manente formatura, fi Spiritus, arcte compreffus, exitum (aegre licet) inveniat, formantur Confonae quas Apertas dicimus; illarum nempe omnium a quibus derivantur (Semi-vocalibus exceptis) Afpirationes: Subtiliores quidam feu Tenuiores, fi per rimulam oblongam; Craffiores vero feu Pinguiores, fi per rotundum quafi foramen, fpiritus exeat. Referuntur autem ad easdem claffes cum Claufis feu Primitivis quibus funt affines.

Semi-vocalibus vero, quas diximus, nullas literas *Afpiratas* fubjungo; non quod, fi illas pronunciaturo fpiritus erumpat, nullus audi-

---

8 *ñ:* 1st has *n,* 4th has *ñ*
   et Galli suum *gn:* 5th–6th

which many people are attributing to Hebrew ע when they use *ng*, *ngh*, *gn*, *nghn*, etc to suggest its pronunciation. They are indicating a sound which does not exactly correspond either to *n* or to *g*, but which has something in common with both of these letters. It may be the same as the sound which the Spanish represent by writing the letter *n* with a mark above it – *ñ*;[47] and the French by writing *gn*.

I call these three consonants *half-vowels* because they have a stronger sound than the ones I have just called *half-mutes*.

These nine consonants (described above) are formed by stopping the breath from going out through the mouth; I have therefore called them *closed* consonants.

DERIVATIVE OR OPEN CONSONANTS, OR ASPIRATES,
THIN AND FAT

If, keeping the same place of articulation, one compresses the breath but allows it to escape, though not easily, what I call the *open consonants* are formed, that is, the *aspirate* forms of all the sounds from which they are derived (excluding the *half-vowels*): they are *thin* or *slender* if the breath passes through a long slit, and *thick* or *fat* if it goes through a rounded hole. They can be divided into the same classes as the *closed* or *primitive* consonants to which they are related. I have not assigned any aspirate letters to what I have called the half-vowels[48]; there would certainly be sounds if one allowed the breath to escape in pronouncing these consonants, but these

---

[47] Spanish palatal *ñ* (and in the 5th edition French *gn*) are cited as possibly representing guttural [ŋ] presumably because they were clearly different from Wallis's 'palatal' *n*, and the only other place of articulation open to him was guttural. He had the same problem with Spanish palatal *ll* (see note 74, *p* 183). Lodwick was the first to identify palatal *n* correctly in England (1686), though French grammarians had described it much earlier (Ramus, 1559, 1562).

[48] Open, or derivative, versions of the half-vowels [m, n, ŋ] would be nasalised fricatives or semivowels in modern terminology – [β̃, z̃, ɣ̃]. In Wallis's terms, they would differ from the derivative versions of [b d g] only in the *amount* of air passing into the nose, which would be greater in the half-vowels (see Introduction *p* 53 *ff*).

DE SONORUM FORMATIONE. 19

audiretur fonus; fed quod fonus qui fic effi-
citur, nondum (quod fciam) in literarum
cenfu locum obtinuerit: vel enim boum
mugitum, vel gemitum humanum refert;
illum nempe fi in Labiis, hunc praefertim
fi in Palato vel Gutture, fiat.

Literam *P* pronunciaturo, fi fpiritus e- *Labiales.*
rumpat, fit ipfius Afpiratio *F*, vel *Ph*; *F.*
Graecorum *φ*; Arabum *Phe*; Hebraeorum *Phe* raphatum; Cambro-Britanno-
rum *ff*.

Nec multum refert utrum per rimulam, an
per rotundum foramen exeat: Quamvis
enim eo modo fubtilior, hoc pinguior, fonus
audiatur; tantillum tamen eft utriusque
difcrimen, ut nefcio an ullibi pro diftinctis
literis habeantur.

Literam *B* pronunciaturo, fi fpiritus per *v.*
rimulam exeat, formatur Anglorum *V*
confonans; Hebraeorum *Bheth* raphatum.

Hifpani eodem fono etiam *b* non raro efferunt, literas *b* et *v* promifcue ufurpantes.
Cambro-Britanni hunc fonum per *f* defig-
nant (fonum autem praecedentem per *ff*).
Anglo-faxones vel fonum hunc non habe-
bant, vel per *f* fcribebant, nam *v* confonam
non agnofcunt, variaque paffim per *f* fcribebant (ut et poft illos Angli per aliquot
C 2   fecula)

---

10 *Phe* raphatum: 1st has *Pe raphatum*

sounds are not yet represented in any alphabet as far as I know. They resemble the lowing of oxen if formed at the lips, or human groans if formed in the palate or throat.

LABIALS

F. If one prepares to say the letter *p* but allows the breath to escape, the corresponding aspirate letter is formed – *f* or *ph*, Greek *φ*, Arabic *Phe*, Hebrew *Phe* with *raphe*, Welsh *ff*.[49] It makes very little difference whether the breath comes out through a slit or through a round hole; admittedly the former will produce a *thinner* sound and the latter a *fatter* one, but the difference is so slight, that I doubt whether they are considered anywhere to be distinct letters.

V. If one prepares to say the letter *b* but allows the breath to escape through a slit, this produces the English consonant *v*, and Hebrew *Bheth* with *raphe*. The Spanish often pronounce their *b* like this,[50] and make no distinction between the letters *b* and *v*. The Welsh use *f* to indicate the sound (and *ff* for the previous sound). The Anglo-Saxons either did not have this sound, or, if they did have it, they wrote it with *f*, because they had no symbol for the consonant *v*;[51] a number of words which we now write with *v*, they wrote with *f* (as the English did after them for some generations)

[49] See Introduction *p* 54 *ff* for the analysis of *f* and *v* as labials. Dobson criticises Wallis for saying that *f* could be produced *per foramen* as well as *per rimulam*, describing this as 'an incompetent blunder'. He goes on to criticise Wallis's 'failure to recognise voiceless [ʍ]'. If, as one may assume, the round aperture (*foramen*) described for this *f* has the same articulation as that later described for *w* (cheeks drawn in and mouth rounded) it would correspond to the articulation of [ʍ]. Therefore it can be said that Wallis *describes* [ʍ] though he does not associate it with [w]. The fact that he regards it as a form of *f* signifies only that he was not aware of [f] and [ʍ] being used in contrast to each other in any language. He interprets the initial sound in the word *which* as a compound of *h* and *w*. Auditorily [f] and [φ] are quite similar to [ʍ] if taken in isolation.
[50] Spanish *b* when intervocalic is a bilabial fricative or approximant [β] (for the term *approximant* see Abercrombie, 1967, 50). Its apparent articulation resembles [v] more than [w], because there is no protrusion of the lips; Wallis regards [β] as an alternative form of *v* (see Introduction *p* 54).
[51] In Old English the symbol *f* was pronounced [v] when intervocalic.

20   **DE SONORUM FORMATIONE.**

fecula) quae nunc per *v*, non minus quam
quae nunc per *f* fcribuntur; ut *gif, heofon*,
etc. quae nunc *give, heaven*, etc. fcribuntur.
Arabes et Perfae hunc fonum non habent:
Turcae tamen fic proferunt fonum *Vaw*;
ut et non pauci *Vaw* Hebraeorum (quod a-
lii potius ut Arabum *Waw*, feu *W*, rectius
proferri putant). Atque hoc fono Aeolicum
Digamma *F*, pronunciatum fuiffe non dubito; cum enim antea habuerint Graeci
characterem φ, non opus erat ut eidem fono
exprimendo novum characterem *F* excogi-
tarent. Quid quod, et Prifcianus agnofcit
Latinorum *F* ita fuiffe olim pronunciatum;
eodem nempe fono quo poftea *V* confona
prolata fuit, adeoque tandem literam *f* ad
fonum φ, feu *ph*, tranfiiffe.

Si vero fpiritus per foramen rotundum
exeat (genis nempe contractis, et ore rotundato) formatur Anglorum *W*; Arabum *Waw*. Quo fono et Hebraeorum
Vau pronunciandum effe multi fentiunt.

w.   Germanorum *W* apud plerosque fic proferri puto; apud alios tamen, ni fallor, fonum
exhibet compofitum ex hoc et praecedente,
illum nempe huic praeponendo; nempe
quod illi per *Wa*, Angli per *Vwa* fcriberent.
Non multum differt hic fonus ab Anglorum
oo, Gallorum *ou*, Germanorum *ú* pingui,
rapidiffime pronunciatis: adeoque a quibusdam pro vocali fuit habita, cum tamen
                                                    revera

5 sonum *Vaw*: 1st–2nd have *suum Vaw*
20 rotundato) formatur: 1st has *rotundato formatur* (misprint)
23–24 apud plerosque . . . tamen: 5th–6th
27 quod illi per *Wa*: 1st–4th have *quod Germani per Wa*
28 1st has bracket after *scriberent* (misprint)
31 rapidissime: 1st has *raptissime*; 4th has rapissime (misprint)

as well as the ones which we still write with *f* today; for example, they wrote *gif, heofon*, etc which are now spelt *give, heaven*, etc. This sound does not exist in Arabic or Persian, but it is the sound of Turkish *Vaw*, and some assign it to Hebrew *Vaw* also (others think this should be pronounced like Arabic *Waw*, or *w*).[52] I am convinced that Aeolic digamma (*F*) had this sound:[53] the Greeks already had a symbol φ and so had no need to introduce a new symbol *F* to express the same sound. Moreover Priscian attests that Latin *F* was once pronounced like this (that is, with the sound which the consonant *v* later acquired), but eventually changed to the sound φ or *ph*.[54]

W. If the breath escapes through a round hole (produced by drawing in the cheeks and rounding the mouth) the result is English *w* and Arabic *Waw*. Many believe that Hebrew *Vau* should also be pronounced like this. I think it is also the usual sound of German *w*, but if I am not mistaken, German *w* is sometimes a compound of this sound and the previous one, the previous one coming first; that is to say, in English we would write *vwa* where they write *wa*.[55] The sound closely resembles English *oo*, French *ou* and German *fat û*, when they are pronounced quickly, and for this reason some people have treated it as a vowel, though it is really a consonant, but very

---

[52] Classical Hebrew *Vau* had the value [w] not [v].

[53] It disappeared from the Attic/Ionic dialects quite early, though its former presence is often indicated by prosodic irregularities or the substitution of alternative letters for it. Digamma had the sound [w], but its symbol *F* has sometimes led to confusion with the sound [f]. Its voiceless counterpart [ʍ] existed in some Greek dialects (see note 54 below). Wallis is wrong in suggesting that digamma had the sound [v]. Priscian notes that in Latin it is often replaced by v (for example in *Argivum, ovum, bovis* – Priscian i.iv. 23; vi.xiii.69); but Latin *V*, until at least the first century A D, represented not fricative [v] but a semivowel, either labio-dental [ʋ] or bilabial [w] (see also Introduction *p* 57 *f*; Sturtevant (1940), §§ 72–78 and 148–155; Allen (1965), *pp* 40–42; Allen (1968) *p* 45 *ff*).

[54] Wallis is wrong in attributing the sound [f] to classical Greek φ which (like θ and χ) represented an aspirated stop – [ph]. There is no evidence for the fricative pronunciation before the first century A D, when it occurs, at least in Italy, in popular speech. From then on the fricative pronunciation spread, though the standard pronunciation was still taught as an aspirated stop right up to the ninth century (Sturtevant (1940), §§ 90–92; Allen (1968), *pp* 16–27). Priscian (i.iv.12) holds that the symbol F was originally used in Latin to represent the sound of Aeolic digamma (see note 53 above), and that PH was at that time used to represent the sound [f] in Latin; later, he says, the symbol V was introduced to represent the sound of digamma, and F then replaced PH as the symbol for [f]. Sturtevant (1940, § 149), sums up the sequence of events as follows: 'The earliest Italian alphabets took over from the Greeks the letter F . . . and also the digraph FH, by which some of the Greeks wrote their voiceless digamma [ʍ]. The Italians however, having no such sound as [ʍ], employed the digraph to represent their [f]. At an early date the Romans simplified the digraph to F and gave up the use of F in its Greek value of [w].' The sound of voiceless digamma – [ʍ] – is auditorily similar to [f] (see note 49 above) and the nearest sound classical Greek had to it.

[55] *Cf* Jones (1962), § 806.

revera confona fit, quanquam ipfi vocali admodum fit affinis. Cambro-Britanni tam
vocalem illam quam hanc confonam eodem
charactere *w* fcribunt; nempe, cum accentu fuperne notatur, vocalis eft, et producto
fono effertur; alibi faepe pro confonante
habetur correpto fono prolata: ut *gw'ydd*
(diffyllabum), anfer; *gw'ydd* (monofylla-
bum), arbufta: fic *gw'yr*, curvus; *gw'yr*,
viri. In vocibus Latinis quoties hic fonus
literis *f, q, g*, fubjungitur, ut in *fuadeo,
quando, lingua*, etc. a plerisque pro vocali
habitus eft; et quidem ab illis fortaffe qui
in Anglorum *wade, perfwade, fway*, etc.
confonam agnofcerent: utrobique tamen
idem omnino fonus eft. Sed et in diphthongis,
au, eu, ou, rite pronuntiatis, vocalis quae dicitur fubjunctiva, non alia eft quam haec
confona: qua de re videatur tractatus ille
quem *de Bivocalibus* edidit acutiffimus *Gatakerus* noftras.

Quum vero idem Vir Clariffimus contendit
(ut et alii magni viri) eodem fono Latinorum
V confonam *femper* olim fuiffe pronunciatam (quomodo etiamnum alicubi gentium
pronunciatur): Ego quidem hactenus faltem affentio; illo nempe fono in multis faltem vocabulis fuiffe pronunciatam: At vero
an in omnibus ita fuerit pronunciata, non
aufim affirmare. Exiftimo potius utrumque
fonum, non modo nunc dierum, fed et olim
(non autem ab initio) eidem characteri af-
fixum fuiffe; quaedam nempe vocabula hoc,
quaedam illo fono, fuiffe prolata, fortaffe et

C 3   eadem

7–9 ut *gw 'ydd* . . . *gw 'ydd* . . . *gw 'yr* . . . *gw 'yr*: 4th–5th have ut *gw 'ydd* . . .
    gwy 'dd . . . *gw 'yr* . . . *gwy 'r* (which gives the contrast – *cf* 1st *g 'wydd* . . .
    gwy 'dd . . . *g 'wyr* . . . *gwy 'r*)
26 hactenus saltem assentio: 1st–4th have *aliquatenus assentio*
32 (non autem ab initio): 5th–6th

like the vowel. The Welsh write both the vowel and the consonant with the same symbol – *w*; when it has an accent above it, it is a vowel and has greater length; otherwise it is often regarded as a consonant, and has a shorter sound, as in *gw ˆydd* (dissyllable) – a goose, *gwy ˆdd* (monosyllable) – trees; *gw ˆyr*, crooked, *gwy ˆr* men. In Latin words where this sound comes after *s, q, g*, as in *suadeo, quando, lingua*, etc, it has mostly been regarded as a vowel,[56] perhaps even by those who would call it a consonant in English *wade, perswade, sway* etc. However in both languages the sound is exactly the same. In the diphthongs *au, eu, ou* also (when they are correctly pronounced) the so-called *subjoined* vowel is in fact this consonant. Our talented fellow-countryman Gataker has dealt with this question in his treatise *On Double Vowels*.[57]

This distinguished authority, in common with other important men, also contends that the Latin consonant *V* was *always* pronounced with this sound, as it still is in some countries today. I will accept that in a large number of words it had this sound, but I would not venture to say that it had it in *all* words. I am more inclined to think that it is a case of two sounds being represented by one and the same symbol, both in earlier times and now (though not from the very beginning), some words being pronounced with one sound and others with the other; sometimes, perhaps, the same

[56] For a discussion of the relation between *u* and *w* see Introduction *p* 58.
[57] Thomas Gataker (1574–1654) was a Puritan divine. Like Wallis he was a member of the Westminster Assembly of Divines (1643–53, see *p* 7), and his views on religious matters were similar. He was known as a careful scholar. He changed the spelling of his name (originally Gatacre), in order to avoid mispronunciation (*cf* Grammar *p* 243). His treatise *De Diphthongis . . . Dissertatio philologica* was published in 1646 (see D.N.B.). For the 'subjoined' vowel see note 92, *p* 199.

22   DE SONORUM FORMATIONE.

eadem nonnunquam vocabula variis in locis,
aut a variis hominibus, utroque fono promifcue prolata: Hoc praefertim argumento
ductus, quod videam Latina nomina per
confonam *V* fcripta, cum in Graecam linguam transferuntur, quandoque per ϐ, quandoque vero per ϗ, Graece fcribi; atque illud
quidem jam olim obtinuiffe: Nulla enim
mihi apparet ratio cur non (verbi gratia)
Latinorum *Flavius* Graece Φλαύιος (et quidem femper) fcriberetur, potius quam Φλά-
ϐιος (quod et de innumeris vocabulis dici poteft), nifi confona illa *V* propius accederet
ad fonum Aeolici Digamma: Praefertim,
cum illam *V* confonam in multis quidem vocabulis ab ipfo Digamma Aeolico ortum
duxiffe, fit in confeffo: Quis enim aliam cau-
fam affignat cur in Latinorum *video, vis, vefper,*
vinum, venter, veftis, vefcor, Venetus, etc. confpiciatur *V* confona (quae in Graecorum εἴδω,
ἦς, ἕαστερος, οἶνος, ἔνlερον, ἔϑης, ἐϑίω, Ενϐος, non
confpicitur), quam, quod foliti fuerint Aeo-
les fuum Digamma hujusmodi vocibus prae-
figere? Neque mirum videri debet, fi lingua Latina, quae tunc ipfis erat vernacula,
parem cum aliis linguis vernaculis fortem
obtinuerit; ut nempe ejusdem literae non
fit eadem ubique et conftans pronunciatio.
Fortaffe etiam et Hebraeorum *Vaw* non
erat idem ubique fonus, ideoque Graece
Δαϐιδ, potius quam Δαυιδ, legitur: Quod de
ע certum eft, Jud. xii. 6. Sed genuinum fonum Latinorum *V* confonae, eundem effe
puto cum noftro *W;* indeque factum effe,
quod

---

2 hominibus: 1st–4th have *personis*
8 quidem iam olim: 1st–4th have *quidem olim*
32–23.8 Sed genuinum . . . novitiae: 5th–6th

words could be pronounced with either of these sounds, in different areas or by different people. My chief reason for saying this is that Latin names containing the consonant *V* appear to be written, when transliterated into Greek, sometimes with β and sometimes with ου, and this was the case in ancient times too. I can see no reason why the Latin name *Flavius*, for example, should not be written (in *all* cases) as Φλαύιος in Greek, and not Φλάβιος (and this applies to countless other words), unless the consonant *V* was nearer to the sound of Aeolic *digamma*. Certainly in many words this consonant *V* is derived from Aeolic digamma. What other reason is given for the occurrence of *V* in Latin *video, vis, vesper, vinum, venter, vestis, vescor, Venetus*, etc (when it is absent in Greek εἴδω, ἴς, ἕσπερος, οἶνος, ἔντερον, ἔσθης, ἐσθίω, Ἔνετος) than the fact that the Aeolians used their *digamma* to begin these words?[58] There should be nothing surprising in the fact that in Latin (which was then the vernacular) as in other vernaculars, one particular letter did not always have the same pronunciation everywhere. Perhaps Hebrew *Vaw* also varied in its sound in different regions, and for that reason Greek has Δαβίδ rather than Δαυίδ.[59] This is certainly true of ש in Judges 12:6.[60] However,[61] I believe that the true sound of the Latin consonant *v* is the same as that of our *w*, and this is why in our older

---

[58] See Introduction *p* 57 *f*.
[59] See note 52.
[60] The *shibboleth* story has often been used to illustrate accent differences within the same language (Madsen, *p* 126; Wilkins, *pp* 369, 382; and more recently Abercrombie (1967), *p* 6).
[61] This section first appeared in the 5th edition (1699) and shows that Wallis had by then accepted *w* as the sound of Latin *V*.

quod in vocabulis Antiquis Latinorum *V*
confona tranfit in noftrum *W;* ut via *way,*
vinum *wine,* ventus *wind,* vado *wade,* venio
veni *wend went,* virtus *worth,* vulnus *woon*
wound, vallum *wall,* aliisque innumeris.
Antiquis inquam. Nam *vain* vanus, *vein*
vena, *vally* vallis, *vertue* virtus, atque his
fimilia, funt voces novitiae.

Literam *T* pronunciaturo, fi fpiritus pin- *Palatinae.*
guius exeat, et quafi per foramen; for-   *Th.*
matur Graecorum *θ*; Hebraeorum *Thau*
raphatum; Arabum *The:* hoc eft Anglorum *Th* in vocibus *thigh,* femur;
thin, tenuis; *thing,* res; *thought,* cogitatio; *throng,* caterva; etc.

Anglo-faxones olim fcribebant hac nota þ
quam *Spinam* vocabant. Cambro-Britanni
per *Th* femper fcribunt.

Si vero fubtilius exeat, et quafi per ri-   *s.*
mulam (elevata paulum ea linguae parte
quae extremitati proxima eft, ut fpiritus
in tenuiorem quafi laminam feu bracte-
am comprimatur, in formam nempe latiorem fed minus craffam) formatur
Graecorum *σ*; Hebraeorum *Samech* et
Sin; Arabum *Sin* et *Sad*; Latinorum et
Anglorum *ſ* vero (hoc eft, ftridulo et a-
cuto) fono pronunciatum.

C 4   Ut

vocabulary Latin *v* becomes *w* in English; as in *via*, way; *vinum*, wine; *ventus*, wind; *vado*, wade; *venio*, *veni*, wend, went; *virtus*, worth; *vulnus*, woon, wound; *vallum*, wall; many other examples exist. I say 'in our older vocabulary' because vain, *vanus*; vein, *vena*; valley, *vallis*; vertue, *virtus* and words like these are of recent introduction.

PALATALS

Th. If one prepares to pronounce the letter *t*, but allows the breath to escape in a broad stream through a round shaped hole, Greek θ is formed.[62] This is the same as Hebrew *Thau* with *raphe*, Arabic *The* and English *Th* in the words *thigh*, *thin*, *thing*, *thought*, *throng*, etc. The Anglo-Saxons used to write this sound with the symbol þ, which they called *Thorn*. The Welsh always write it as *th*.

S. However, if the breath escapes in a narrow stream and, as it were, through a slit (produced by raising the part of the tongue adjacent to the tip slightly, so that the breath is compressed into a kind of thin layer, or section, wider but not so thick) the result is Greek σ, Hebrew *Samech* and *Sin*, Arabic *Sin* and *Sad*[63] and the true sound[64] of Latin and English *s*, that is, a high pitched hiss, for

---

[62] Ancient Greek θ was an aspirated voiceless stop – [th] – like φ and χ (*cf* note 54, *p* 167), but later became the fricative which Wallis is describing here. He interprets *th* and *dh* as simple sounds, unlike *sh* (see *p* 202 and note 68, *p* 177). The analysis of *th dh* [θ ð] as *per foramen* and *s*, *z* as *per rimulam* is presumably based on the comparative distance between tongue and palate. In *th dh* the friction occurs between tongue tip and teeth, the blade being usually kept away from the teeth-ridge whereas for *s z* the blade is raised. Cooper uses this opposition of *per foramen* / *per rimulam* to distinguish *W* from *V* (like Wallis), but says *th dh* are produced *per rimulam*. However, for him *s z* are distinguished from them not by the shape of the aperture but by being formed with a different part of the tongue (Cooper ed Jones, *p* 24).
[63] Hebrew *Samech* and *Sin*, like Arabic *Sin* and *Sad*, have the same primary articulation, and are distinguished by different secondary articulations (see note 39, *p* 157).
[64] [s], not [z].

24   DE SONORUM FORMATIONE.

Ut in vocibus *yes*, ita (affirmandi particula); *this*, hic; *us*, nos; *thus*, fic; *hifs*, fibilo; *lefs*, minor; *fend*, mitto; *ftrong*, fortis; etc. Hoc etiam fono pronunciamus *c* mollius (nempe ante *e*, *i*, et *y*), ut in *grace*, gratia; *mercy*, mifericordia; *peace*, pax; *fince*, poftquam; *principal*, principalis; etc. Galli eodem fono proferunt *c* nonnunquam etiam ante alias vocales (at tunc plerumque caudam affigunt), ut ça, *adesdum*; garçon, *puer*; etc.

Dh. Literam *D* pronunciaturo, fi fpiritus erumpat modo pinguiori, et quafi per foramen, formatur Arabum *Dhal*; Hebraeorum *Daleth* raphatum; Hifpanorum *D* mollius, qualiter nempe proferri folet ea litera in medio et fine vocabulorum, ut *Majeftad*, *Trinidad*, etc.

Ð ð   Hunc fonum Angli eodem prorfus modo fcribunt quo fonum alium paulo fupra nominatum, nempe per *th*, ut in vocibus *thy*, *thine*, tuus; *this*, hoc; *though*, quamvis; etc. Anglo-Saxones olim fonum illum per þ, hunc vero per Ð, ð, fcripfiffe puto, prout ex eorum fcriptis liquet (quanquam et ipfi charaéteres illos non raro promifcue ufurpabant):

Sequentibus autem feculis Angli eundem charaéterem þ utrique fono adhibuerunt, qui paulatim degeneravit in charaéterem ɤ, qui in libris quamplurimis manu-fcriptis perpetuo confpicitur in iis vocabulis quae nunc per *th* fcribuntur: Atque hinc eft quod

---

23–26 hunc vero . . . usurpabant): 1st–4th read as follows – hunc vero per Ð scribebant, prout ex eorum scriptis liquet (quamquam et characteres illos nonnumquam confundebant)
27–28 eundem characterem: 4th has *eodem charactere* (misprint)
   30 quamplurimis: 4th has *quamplurimi* (misprint)

example in the words: *yes, this, us, thus, hiss, less, send, strong,* etc. It is also the softer sound of *c* (occurring before *e, i,* and *y*) as in *grace, mercy, peace, since, principal,* etc. The French sometimes pronounce *c* like this even before other vowels (but then they usually attach a *cedilla* to it) as in *ça,* come here!; *garçon,* boy, etc.

Dh. If one prepares to pronounce the letter *d,* but allows the breath to escape in a broad stream and through a round-shaped hole the result is Arabic *Dhal,* Hebrew *Daleth* with *raphe,* and Spanish *soft d,*[65] which is the pronunciation *d* has medially and finally in Spanish words, for example *Majestad, Trinidad,* etc. In English this sound is written in exactly the same way as the other sound which I described just now, that is with the letters *th,* as in the words *thy, thine, this, though,* etc. I believe the Anglo-Saxons used to write the first of these two sounds with the symbol þ, and the second with Ð, ð, and this can be seen in their books, though they quite often used the two symbols without any distinction between them.[66]

In later times the English used the symbol þ for both sounds, and it gradually became distorted into the symbol ꝺ, which constantly recurs in very many manuscript books, in words which are now written with *th.* This led to the old custom, still often observed, of

[65] Wallis analyses this correctly, unlike Spanish *ll* and *ñ,* because it corresponds with an English sound.
[66] In Old English and Middle English the symbols þ (thorn) and ð both occur representing dental fricatives, but it is not true to say that they consistently represent [θ] and [ð] respectively. In Anglian the dental fricative was [θ] in initial and final position and [ð] medially between voiced sounds, but both of these sounds were symbolised by ð. In other dialects þ was used for both sounds, or sometimes þ was used initially and ð elsewhere, purely for aesthetic reasons (Sweet, 1888, *pp* 138–9). Later one finds the two symbols used at random, as Wallis suggests (Sweet, loc cit, *p* 160). According to Smith (1568) *thorn* was used for both [θ] and [ð] but written on the line for [θ] and above it for [ð]. For an account of the occurrence of these sounds in English see Dobson (1968), *pp* 932–4, 936, 942–4.

DE SONORUM FORMATIONE. 25

quod mos olim invaluerit, qui etiam adhuc non raro retinetur, fcribendi yͤ, yͭ, yͧ, pro *the, that, thou,* etc. Cambro-Britanni fonum illum per *th*, hunc per *dd* perpetuo fcribunt; nifi quod aliqui melius fcribi poffe contendunt per *dh*, qui non tamen obtinuerunt ut mos olim receptus immutetur.

Nos autem (ut dictum eft) utrumque fonum promifcue fcribimus per *th*: Sed male quidem; cum neuter eorum fit fonus compofitus, fed plane fimplex, a fonis literarum *t* et *d* eodem fere modo deflectentes quo *f* et *v* a fonis literarum *p* et *b*. Fateor tamen qua ratione pro *f* fcribitur *ph*, eadem etiam *bh, th, dh,* fcribi poffe: ut nempe literarum afpiratarum Affinitas fimul et Deflexio ab iis a quibus oriuntur aliquatenus innuatur. Compofitum autem ex his literis genuinum fonum, omnino alium effe quam qui eft literarum afpiratarum, patet ex vocibus *Cobham, Chat-ham, Wit-ham, Mait-ham, Wad-ham, Wood-houfe, Shep-heard, Clap-ham, Mep-ham,* etc.ꞌ (Item in *Oc-ham, block-head, hog-heard, Cog-hil, houf-hold, dif-honour, mif-hap, dif-honeft, dif-hearten, Maf-ham, Cauf-ham, Wif-heart,* etc. alios omnino fonos audimus quam quos vulgo fcribimus per *ch, gh, fh*).

Utrumque autem fonum quem nos per *th* fcribimus, Galli, Belgae, aliique non pauci, vix aut ne vix proferunt; dum illum autem proferre conantur, Galli plerumque *t*, Belgae *d*, alii nonnunquam *s* fubftituunt. Neutiquam tamen eft difficile genuinos hosce
fonos

2 1st omits *scribendi*

writing yᵉ, yᵗ, yᵘ, for *the, that, thou*, etc.⁶⁷ The Welsh use *th* for the first sound, and *dd* for the second, though some maintain that *dh* would be a better way of writing it than *dd*; however they have not succeeded in getting the old established custom altered.

In English, as I said above, we write both sounds as *th*, not making any distinction. This is an unfortunate practice, because neither of them is a compound sound; they are both clearly simple sounds which bear almost the same relationship to the sounds of the letters *t* and *d*, as *f* and *v* do to the sounds of *p* and *b*. Admittedly on the same principle by which we write *ph* instead of *f*, we should be able to write *bh, th, dh*; this would suggest to some extent the likeness and the difference between aspirate letters and the letters from which they are derived. But the fact that the true sound of these letters when combined is quite different from that of the aspirate letters is clearly demonstrated in the words *Cob-ham, Chat-ham, Wit-ham, Mait-ham, Wad-ham, Wood-house, Shep-heard, Clap-ham, Mep-ham,* etc. And in the words *Oc-ham, block-head, hog-heard, Cog-hil, hous-hold, dis-honour, mis-hap, dis-honest, dis-hearten, Mas-ham, Caus-ham, Wis-heart*, etc the sounds you hear are entirely different from those that we normally write as *ch, gh, sh*.⁶⁸

Both of the sounds which we write as *th* are difficult, if not impossible, for the French, Dutch and many others to pronounce. The French usually substitute *t*, the Dutch *d* and others sometimes use *s*, but there should be no difficulty in pronouncing them properly if

---

⁶⁷ Mentioned earlier by Hart (1551). The use of *y* for þ arose because most printing offices had no symbol for *thorn*, so they used the nearest symbol available (*cf* note 87 below).
⁶⁸ Digraphs are retained to represent compound sounds made up of *b* + *h*, *t* + *h*, *d* + *h*, *p* + *h*, *c* + *h*, *g* + *h*, *s* + *h*, not to be confused with the simple sounds *th*, *ph*, *ch*, *gh*, and the sound *sh*, which Wallis analyses as *s* + *y* (see Introduction *p* 60). In present-day pronunciation the *h* sound has disappeared in most of the words which Wallis quotes. Jespersen (*M.E.G.*, I. § 2.614) notes that the diagraph *th* (= [θ]) was probably brought into English by French scribes; *ph* (= [f]) was a spelling adopted from the fourteenth century onwards for many learned words.

26 DE SONORUM FORMATIONE.

fonos proferre fiquis eorum formationem paulo attentius obfervet; nempe, omnibus eodem modo manentibus acfi prolaturus quis effet literas *t, d,* nifi quod fpiritus erumpere permittatur: caveatur autem ne, etiam non attendenti, affurgat aliquantulum linguae pars extremitati proxima, adeoque literas *S* et *Z* efficiat: ut enim *S* ad *t,* fic *Z* ad *d;* ut jam dicemus.

z. Si eandem literam *D* pronunciaturus, fpiritum fubtiliori forma et quafi per rimulam protrudat (elevata quidem in illum finem linguae parte extremitati proxima), formatur Latinorum *Z;* Graecorum ζ; Hebraeorum *Zain;* Arabum *Ze:* quem fonum etiam Angli per *Z* exprimunt.

Nonnunquam tamen Angli etiam literam *S* (ficut et Galli) eodem fono proferunt; praefertim ubi inter duas vocales ponitur, et in fine dictionis: ut in *pleasure,* voluptas; *ease,* otium; *laws,* leges; etc. Et, quod fere folenne eft, ubi ex Nomine per ſ durum in ultima fyllaba pronunciato, fit Verbum; hoc verbum per *s* molle (hoc eft, per *z)* pronunciatur: Sic *a houſe,* domus; *a louſe,* pediculus; *a mouſe,* mus; *a price,* pretium; *adviſe,* confilium; *cloſe,* contiguum; *braſs,* aes; *glaſs,* vitrum; *graſs,* gramen; *greaſe,* pinguedo; *a fleece,* vellus; per ſ durum: at *to houſe,* in domum recipere; *to louſe,* pediculos

4 quis: 5th–6th
22 otium: 1st has *quies*
24 fit: 1st–4th have *fiat*

the method of production is studied more carefully. The same articulation is used as for the letters *t* and *d*,[69] but the breath is allowed to escape. Care must be taken to avoid allowing the part of the tongue adjacent to the tip to rise slightly, without realising it, as this would result in the letters *s* and *z*. *S* bears the same relationship to *t* as *z* does to *d*, as I shall now show.

Z. If one prepares to pronounce the letter *d*, but allows the breath to escape in a narrow stream, as it were through a slit (made by raising the part of the tongue adjacent to the tip) the resulting sound is Latin *z*, Greek ζ, Hebrew *Zain*, Arabic *Ze*. In English we write this sound as *z*. Sometimes, however, the English (and the French) pronounce the letter *s* like this too, especially when it occurs between two vowels or at the end of a word, as in *pleasure, ease, laws*, etc. It is normal also, when a verb is formed from a noun which has *hard s* in the final syllable, for the verb to be pronounced with a *soft s* (that is with a *z*). For example *hard s* occurs in *a house*; *a louse*; *a mouse*; *a price*; *advise*; *close*; *brass*; *glass*; *grass*; *grease*; *a fleece*. But *to house*; *to louse*; *to mouse*; *to prise*; *to advise*; *to close*; *to braze*;

---

[69] In fact the tongue position for the English fricatives [θ ð] is dental, while *t d* are alveolar, but this distinction of place is not available in Wallis's scheme.

DE SONORUM FORMATIONE. 27

culos captare; *to mouse*, captare mures; *to prise*, aeftimare; *to advise*, confulere; *to close*, conjungere; *to braze*, obaerare; *to glaze*, vitro obducere; *to graze*, gramen de-cerpere; *to fleese*, deglubere; per *s* molle proferuntur.

Sed et eodem modo etiam aliae literae analo-gam alleviationem fortiuntur; nam ex nomi-nibus *wife*, uxor; *life*, vita; *ftrife*, lis; *half*, femiffis; *calf*, vitulus; *fafe*, falvus; *breath*, fpiritus; *cloth*, pannus; per fonos duriores prolatis: fiunt Verba *to wive*, uxorem quae-rere; *to live*, vivere; *to ftrive*, litigare; *to halve*, bifecare; *to calve*, vitulum parere; *to fave*, falvum reddere; *to breathe*, fpirare; *to clothe*, veftire.

Itali literam Z (praefertim geminatam) non raro fortius proferunt, ut Hebraeorum **צ** vel *tz;* atque eodem fono proferunt non pauci in vocibus Latinis *t* ante *i*, fequente etiam alia Vocali: Nempe *Piazza, Vene-tiae*, etc, efferuntur *Piatza, Venetziae*, etc.

Eidem literae *D*, vel (fi placet) literae *N*, fubjungere etiam licet duas alias lite-ras eadem fede, nempe in Palato, for-matas: *L* et *R*. Has autem literis *D* aut *N*, potius quam literae *T*, fubjun-go; propter laryngis concuffionem, et fpiritus ad nares emiffionem, quae his proferendis fiunt; quarum litera *T*, et quae ab ea defcendunt omnes, funt in-capaces.

Litera

4–5 1st–3rd have *glaze*, vitrum adaptare; *graze*, gramine pasci; *grease*, pinguedine oblinere. 4th–5th omit *glaze, graze, grease*
15 reddere: 4th has *redere* (misprint)
21 alia vocali: 1st has *alia consona* (misprint)

to glaze; to graze; to fleeze all have *soft s.*

There are other letters too which are subject to a softening of this kind: from the nouns *wife, life, strife, half, calf, safe, breath, cloth,* which have the harder sound, we get the verbs *to wive, to live, to strive, to halve, to calve, to save, to breathe, to clothe.*[70]

The Italians often pronounce the letter *z,* especially double *z,* with a stronger sound, like Hebrew ‫צ‬[71] or *tz.* Many people pronounce *t* before *i* like this in Latin words, when another vowel follows the *i; eg: Piazza, Venetiae,* etc are pronounced *Piatza, Venetziae,* etc.

L.R. Two other letters also can be connected with the letter *d* or, if you prefer, with the letter *n,* inasmuch as they have the same place of articulation – that is, the palate; these are *l* and *r.* They are more closely connected with *d* or *n* than with *t* because in pronouncing them the larynx vibrates and the breath enters the nose[72]; whereas the letter *t* and letters that derive from it never have these characteristics in their pronunciation.

---

[70] In Old English *s* represented [z] when medial between voiced sounds, but was voiceless elsewhere (*cf:* *th* – note 66). It was also voiced in the unstressed ending *es* from which the *e* later dropped out – hence *laws* [lɔːz] (Lehnert, § 177). *Pleasure* came from French *plaisir* which had [z]; the occurrence of [ʒ] in English is not attested before Miége (1688), who gives *usual, leisure, osier* as examples. Earlier writers recognised the sound only in French, and Wallis interprets it as *z + y. Ease* is also a loan word from French *aise,* which already had [z]. The contrast between substantive, or adjective, with [s] and verb with [z] arose because in Old English *s* was final in the former and medial in the latter. However *fleeze* (verb) is a pronunciation which Wallis has arrived at by analogy, as the word was a late formation from the noun, and retained the [s], as it still does. The alternation of [f/v] and [θ/ð] in *wife, wive; breath, breathe* etc originated in the same way as that of [s/z].

[71] The normal pronunciation of this is not certain; [ts] was one possible realisation of it.

[72] Introduction *p* 52 *ff.*

28   DE SONORUM FORMATIONE.

L. Litera *L* formatur, fi literas *D* vel *N*
prolaturus fpiritum a laetre (five altero,
five utroque) in buccam leviter emittat,
et per buccarum anfractus ad aperta labia, adjuncto etiam linguae tremore.
Eftque hujus literae apud omnes (ni fallor) gentes idem fonus : nempe ut Hebraeorum ל; Graecorum λ.

LL. Habent autem Cambro-Britanni alium etiam
fonum huic quidem affinem, fed fortiorem
(quem per *ll* fcribunt, ut a litera *l* diftin-
guant); fpiritu nempe multo fortius in buc-
cas extrufo : Unde fit fonus fpumofior, et
quafi ex θλ conflatus. Apud alias gentes
fonus ille (quantum fcio) non auditur, nifi
forte apud Hifpanos.

R. Litera *R* (quae canina dici confuevit)
formatur etiam in Palato : fi nempe extremitas linguae, literam *D* vel *N* pro-
nunciaturae, introrfum flexa fpiritum
exiturum forti quidem et frequenti con-
cuffione verberet : Ex quo conflictu tremulo, horridus ille fonus auditur. Eftque hujus literae fonus apud omnes i-
dem : Nempe ut Hebraeorum *Refh* ;
Graecorum ϱ.

Rh. Cambro-Britanni huic literae frequenter
fubjungunt *h;* eorumque *Rh* refpondet
Graecorum ῥ afpirato. Americanos ferunt,
                                    Novan-

---

2 laetre: misprint for *latere* of 1st–5th
15–16 nisi forte apud Hispanos: 4th–6th
22 tremulo: 5th–6th

L. The letter *l* is formed by preparing to pronounce *d* or *n* and then allowing the breath to escape at the sides, one or both, and without much force, on to the cheeks and along the curve of the cheeks to the open lips, with a simultaneous vibration of the tongue.[73] This letter, if I am not mistaken, has the same sound in all countries, that is to say, the sound of Hebrew ל and Greek λ. The Welsh have another sound of the same type, requiring greater force (they write it as *ll* to distinguish it from *l*). The breath is expelled into the cheeks much more forcibly and this results in a frothier sound, rather like the combination θλ. As far as I know this sound cannot be heard in any other language, except perhaps Spanish.[74]

R. The letter *r*, which has often been called the *dog letter*, is also formed in the palate. The tip of the tongue must be bent back from the position it takes for *d* or *n*, and must strike the breath stream, as it passes, forcibly and with rapidly repeated strokes. The rough sound of *r* is the result of this tremulous vibration. It is the same everywhere, for example Hebrew *Resh* and Greek ρ.[75] The Welsh often add *h* to this letter and their *rh* corresponds to the Greek aspirated ῥ.[76] The story goes that the Americans who live in New

---

[73] Wallis and Holder are alone in describing both a unilateral and a bilateral *l*; most other sixteenth- and seventeenth-century writers only describe the bilateral. Vibration of the tongue in *l* is also peculiar to Wallis's description. Ellis talks of a very slight vibration of the sides of the tongue (*E.E.P.*I.193) and this is probably all that is meant here. It may be significant that the word used here is *tremor*, whereas in describing *r* and the mechanism of voicing (*pp* 182, 134) Wallis uses a more forceful word (*concussio*). *Cf* Helmholtz's description: 'In pronouncing *l* the moving soft lateral edges of the tongue produce, not entire interruptions, but oscillations in the force of air.'

[74] Wallis cannot make Welsh *ll* the voiceless counterpart of *l* (see *p* 53 *ff*) as Wilkins does, so he distinguishes it by its stronger and noisier sound. The expression *quasi ex θλ conflatus* perhaps implies that he is not identifying it with the *articulation* of these two letters, but with their *auditory impression*. Welsh *ll* is often interpreted as [θl] today, because voiceless *l* is unfamiliar to most English speakers. Wallis's description of it as 'spumosior' (frothier) is very apt. Spanish *ll* represented a voiced palatal sound – [j] or [λ] – very different auditorily from Welsh *ll*; Wallis's tentative identification must be based on the orthographic identity. Hart (1569) also wrongly identifies these two sounds, and goes on to say that they are the same as English syllabic *l* in *beadle* etc!

[75] The name 'dog letter' dates from Roman times: *irritata canis quod rr quam plurima dicat* (Lucilius; *cf* Persius I.109). Wallis's description is of a trill, a type of *r* which is still in Italian and Spanish, but is now rare in English, except as a one-tap trill (see D. Jones (1962), § 750; Gimson, *pp* 202–3). In Wallis's time the trill was probably still widely used in an educated accent intervocalically, but fricative *r* was almost certainly common in other positions, even though it is not described by major sources (see Dobson (1968), *p* 946). For its effect on a preceding vowel see Introduction *p* 49.

[76] Welsh still has voiceless *r*; for Greek ῥ see Allen (1968), *p* 39 *ff*.

DE SONORUM FORMATIONE. 29

Novangliae conterminos (aut eorum faltem magnam partem) literas *L* et *R* pronunciare non poffe, fed ipforum loco *N* fubftituere; adeoque *Nobſtan* dicere pro *Lobſtar*.

Literam *K*, vel *C* durum, pronunciaturo, fi fpiritus fubtilius erumpat, et ftrictius compreffus, formatur Graecorum χ; Hebraeorum *Cheth*; Arabum *Cha* (recte pronunciata); et forte *Caph* raphatum, fed vix a Noftratibus: fonus nempe medius inter *C* et *H*. Gutturales. *Ch.*

Eftque hic fonus Germanis familiaris, ut et Cambro-Britannis; utrique per *ch* fcribunt. Apud Anglos penitus defuevit; noftrum enim *ch* alio longe fono profertur, ut poft dicetur.

Si vero pinguius exeat fpiritus, et minus compreffus (ob laxiorem linguae pofitionem et latiorem exitum), formatur Latinorum *H*; Hebraeorum et Arabum *He*; Graecorum fpiritus afpiratus. *H.*

Eftque hic fonus plerisque gentibus familiaris. Galli faepe fcribunt *h*, fed raro pronunciant. Non differt a fono prioris literae, nifi quod illic fpiritus fortiori conatu et per anguftiorem quafi rimulam exeat (ideoque Afpiratio duplex dici foleat); hic vero liberius et quafi per foramen latius.

Graeci,

9–10 et forte . . . Nostratibus: 2nd–6th

England, or at any rate a great many of them, cannot pronounce the letters *l* and *r*, but substitute *n* for them; so they say *Nobstan* instead of *Lobstar*.[77]

GUTTURALS

Ch.[78] If one prepares to pronounce the letter *k* or *hard c* and then allows the breath to escape in a narrow and closely constricted stream, the result is Greek χ, Hebrew *Cheth* and Arabic *Cha* (if properly pronounced), and perhaps also *Caph* with *raphe*, though our countrymen rarely pronounce it like this. It is a sound midway between *c* and *h*, familiar to the Germans and the Welsh who both write it with *ch*, but in English it has entirely dropped out; our *ch* has a very different sound, as I shall show later.

H. If the breath escapes in a broad stream and with less constriction (due to the more relaxed position of the tongue and the wider opening) the result is Latin *H*, Hebrew and Arabic *He*, and the Greek rough breathing.[79] This sound is a familiar one to people of most countries; the French often write *h* but rarely pronounce it. The only difference between this and the sound of the previous letter (*ch*), is that in that sound the breath is expelled more forcefully and through a narrow slit (this is why it is usually said to have double aspiration) whereas in this sound it has a freer passage,

---

[77] Wilkins (*p* 382) and many later writers also quote this story, but none of them give the original source of it. For this type of phenomenon in American Indian languages see Mattingly (1960), *pp* 90–1; Sapir (1949), *p* 44; Boas (1911), *pp* 12–13.
[78] See Introduction *p* 58.
[79] Introduction *pp* 58–60.

30   DE SONORUM FORMATIONE.

Graeci, quafi non effet litera (quoniam exiguus quidem fonus eft) *Afpirationem* dixerunt et (faltem nunc dierum) in literarum
directa linea non fcribunt, fed literae verti-
ci imponunt; verum olim in ipfa literarum
ferie vocalibus praeponebant (at confonae
ϱ, ni fallor, poftponebant); atque hinc eft
quod apud eos *H* eft centenarii numeri nota; quod enim nunc ἵκατον fcribitur, olim
fcribebant Ηϵκατον.

In aliis linguis nil video cur non pro confona habeatur: Non enim, quia ipfius fonus
ab aliquibus (praefertim Gallis) inter pronunciandum aliquando omittatur, ideo litera
cenfenda non eft; illud enim et multis literis eft commune, praefertim Hebraeorum
(aliorumque Orientalium) literis quiefcenti-
bus et *Ain* (ne opus fit Gallorum hac in re
nimiam licentiam attingere): Neque etiam
quod, apud Latinos Poetas, ipfius interven-
tio, vocalium elifionem non impediebat;
nam neque *M*, nec (olim) *S*, impedimento
erant quo minus ejusmodi contractio fieret.
Fateor tamen Latinos hac in re eousque
Graecorum aemulos fuiffe, ut merito du-
bium videri poffit num ipfi *h* pro litera habuiffe cenfendi fint necne; praefertim cum
Grammaticos reclamantes videam.

Gh. Literam γ (feu *G* durum) pronunciaturo,
fi fpiritus arctius compreffus per fubtili-
orem quafi rimulam exeat; formatur
fonus qui per *gh* exprimitur.

Hunc

8 numeri: 5th–6th
23 fieret: 1st–2nd have *fiat*

[186]

through a broader hole. The Greeks called it *a breathing*, as if to distinguish it from a letter (since it has very little sound), and, nowadays at any rate, they do not write it on the same line as the letters but put it above the letter. At one time, however, they wrote it before the vowels on the same line, (though, I think I am right in saying that they put it *after* the letter ρ). This is why they use *H* as the sign for the number 100; the word they now write as ἕκατον was originally written Ἑέκατον.

In other languages I can see no reason for not regarding this sound as a consonant. The fact that it is sometimes not pronounced, especially in French, is no reason for denying that it is a letter, because this is just as true of many other letters, especially the *quiescent* letters and *Ain* in Hebrew[80] and other Oriental languages (not to mention the very considerable licence allowed in this respect by the French). And the fact that in the Latin Poets the occurrence of *h* between vowels did not prevent elision taking place is no argument, because *m* did not prevent this kind of contraction either, nor in earlier times did *s*. However, the Romans, admittedly, imitated the Greeks very closely in this respect, so it is reasonable to reserve judgement as to whether they regarded *h* as a letter or not; especially as I see that the grammarians[81] strongly deny that they did.

Gh. If one prepares to pronounce the letter γ (or hard *g*) and allows the breath to escape through a thin slit, narrowly constricting it, the sound produced is the one written as *gh*.[82] I believe that

---

[80] The quiescent letters in classical Hebrew are *Aleph, He, Waw*, and *Yodh* – see Weingreen, *pp* 18–19. *Ain* has been described in various ways (see Introduction *p* 56) and always causes difficulty for foreign learners, who may fail to hear it at all; some Hebrew grammarians say that it is not necessary to pronounce it.

[81] For example, Priscian (see Introduction *p* 59).

[82] Introduction *p* 60.

DE SONORUM FORMATIONE. 31

Hunc fonum Anglos in vocibus *light*, lux; *night*, nox; *right*, rectum; *daughter*, filia; etc. olim protuliffe fentio: at nunc dierum, quamvis fcripturam retineant, fonum tamen fere penitus omittunt: Boreales tamen, praefertim Scoti, fere adhuc retinent, feu potius ipfius loco fonum *h* fubftituunt. Hiberni in ipforum *gh* hunc fonum exacte exhibent, ut in *logh*, lacus; etc. Differt a Germanorum *ch* ficut ipfum *g* a *c;* directione nempe fpiritus partim ad nares, quam nec *c* nec *ch* omnino patiuntur. Germani tamen easdem voces fere per *ch* fcribunt, quas Angli per *gh;* eorum enim 𝖓𝖆𝖈𝖍𝖙, 𝖗𝖊𝖈𝖍𝖙, 𝖑𝖎𝖊𝖈𝖍𝖙, 𝖋𝖊𝖈𝖍𝖙𝖊𝖓, 𝖙𝖔𝖈𝖍𝖙𝖊𝖗, refpondent noftris *night, right, light, fight, daughter;* aliaque funt fimilia non pauca. Latini, Graeci, Hebraei, et Arabes fonum hunc non agnofcunt, nifi forte Hebraeorum *Ghimel* raphatum fic proferri debeat. Perfae eo fono fuum *Ghaf* pronunciant, quod tribus fuperne punctis ab Arabum *Kef* diftinguitur.

Si vero liberius et quafi per latius foramen exeat fpiritus; formatur Anglorum *Y* confona; Germanorum *J* confona; Arabum *Ye;* quo fono etiam Hebraeorum *Jod* five *Yod* multi pronunciandum contendunt. Sono nempe vocalis *i* exilis raptiffime pronunciatae admodum affinis eft.

r.

Ideoque

20 proferri debeat: 1st has *efferri poffit*
27 five *Yod:* 5th–6th

this sound used to be pronounced in the English words *light*, *night*, *right*, *daughter*, etc, but nowadays, although the words are still written like this, the sound is almost always omitted. The Northerners, however, and especially the Scots, still have it, or rather they put the sound *h* in its place. Irish *gh* represents exactly the same sound, as in *logh* (lake), etc. The difference between this sound and German *ch* is the same as that between *g* and *c*; that is, the breath is directed partly into the nose, which is never the case with *c* or *ch*. But in writing, the Germans use *ch* in words where the English have *gh*; their *nacht*, *recht*, *liecht*, *fechten*, *tochter*, correspond to our *night*, *right*, *light*, *fight*, *daughter*, and there are many other similar examples. This sound does not occur in Latin, Greek, Hebrew, or Arabic, unless Hebrew *Ghimel* with *raphe* is to be pronounced in this way. The Persians pronounced their *Ghaf* like this, distinguishing it from Arabic *Kef* by writing three dots above it.

Y. If the breath escapes more freely and through a broader, rounded hole, it produces the English consonant *y*;[83] this corresponds to the German consonant *j* and Arabic *Ye*, and many people think that Hebrew *Jod*, or *Yod*, should also be pronounced like this. It is closely related to the sound of the vowel *thin i*, quickly

---

[83] This analysis of *y* as a guttural consonant is forced on Wallis, in spite of his analysis of *thin i* as a palatal, by his lack of another place of articulation – his ' palatal' consonants are in fact alveolar/dental (see also Introduction *p* 54 *f*).

32   DE SONORUM FORMATIONE.

Ideoque Diphthongi (ut vocantur) *ai, ei, oi ;*
vel *ay, ey, oy,* fere promifcue fcribuntur per
i et *y :* apud Anglos praefertim et Gallos.
Eft autem fonus ille, qui pro vocali fubjunctiva cenfetur, revera Confona; eodem
nempe prorfus modo fonabitur litera *y* in
faying, praying, etc. five ad priorem fyllabam (ubi pro vocali habebitur) five ad
pofteriorem (ubi habebitur pro confona)
referatur; nempe five fit *fay-ing, pray-ing,*
five *fa-ying, pra-ying.* Parem fcilicet affinitatem agnofcimus inter *oo* (feu *ú* pingue) et
w, quae eft inter *i* exile et *y.* De utrisque
videatur acutiffimus *Gatakerus* in tractatu
fupra citato.

Sed et alibi etiam *y* pro *i* non raro ponitur,
ubi fcilicet *i* vocalis eft (praefertim in dictionum fine): quo cafu non modo antiquiores
Anglo-Saxones, fed et per multa fecula qui
ipfis fuccefferunt Angli, literam *y,* quoties
pro vocali *i* poneretur, puncto fuperne pofito femper notabant, hoc modo *ẏ.*

Affinitatem autem maximam effe hujus literae cum *g* et *gh,* inde manifeftum eft,
quod ea quae nunc per *gh* fcribimus *light,*
might, thought, etc. in manufcriptis libris
faepiffime per *y* confonam fcripta legimus,
eodem nempe charactere quo *yet, yonder,*
etc.   Triplicem nempe habuerunt figuram;
unam ᵹ pro qua nunc fcribitur *th,* ut fupra
dictum eft; alteram ẏ, quae loco *i* vocalis
folebat pingi, et a priori non nifi puncto
fupra pofito diftinguebatur; et tertiam ȝ,
quam pro *y* confona perpetuo fcribebant,
quae

---

2 scribuntur: 4th omits (misprint)

pronounced. This is why the (so-called) diphthongs *ai, ei, oi*, or *ay, ey, oy* are written almost without any distinction with other *i* or *y*, especially in English and French. However, although this sound is regarded as a subjoined vowel it is really a consonant. The letter *y* will have exactly the same pronunciation in *saying, praying*, etc whether you assign it to the first syllable (when it will be regarded as a vowel), or to the second (when it will be regarded as a consonant); that is, whether it is *say-ing, pray-ing*, or *sa-ying, pra-ying*. This relationship between *thin i* and *y*, also holds good between *oo* (or *fat û*) and *w*. For information on both of these I refer you to the treatise by Gataker, mentioned above.[84]

Y is also often written for *i* when *i* is a vowel (particularly at the end of words). The ancient Anglo-Saxons and, for some generations, the English who followed them, used to mark the letter *y* in these cases where it was written in place of the vowel *i*, by putting a dot above it, *eg: ẏ*.[85]

It is obvious that this letter is very closely related to *g* and *gh* because the words *light, might, thought*, etc, which we now write with *gh*, very often appear in manuscript books written with the consonant *y*; that is to say, the same symbol which appears in *yet, yonder*, etc.[86] There were three similar shapes: (i) ꝥ, for which we now use *th* (as stated earlier); (ii) ẏ, which was used in place of the vowel *i*, and was only distinguished from (i) by the dot written above it; (iii) ȝ, which they always used for the consonant *y*, and is

---

[84] For Wallis's analysis of diphthongs see Introduction *p* 57.

[85] Purely an orthographical point. It recurs in the Grammar (*p* 223) where it is more relevant, *cf* note 27, *p* 145.

[86] In Middle English the symbol ȝ was used for [j] and [ɣ] and also for [ç] and [x] in the combination ȝt (in *light, thought* etc). Later this symbol dropped out of use, and normally *y* was written to symbolise [j], and *gh* for [ç] and [x], which resulted in the spellings *light* etc. (See Jespersen, *M.E.G.*, I. § 2.312).

DE SONORUM FORMATIONE. 33

quae etiam in illis vocibus (ut dictum est)
reperitur quae nunc per *gh* scribuntur:
Hunc autem characterem, prout tunc pingi
solebat, nescientes forsan posteriores libra-
rii, ipsius loco characterem literae *z* foedis-
simo errore substituerunt; unde monstra illa
vocabulorum **thouʒt, souʒt,** etc. pro *thought,*
sought, etc. seu potius pro *thouyt, souyt,*
etc. (prout tunc nempe per *y* consonam scri-
bi solebant) in impressis Chauceri alio̶rum-
que veterum poetarum libris conspiciuntur.
Longe melius doctissimus *Wheelocus* (linguarum Arabicae et Saxonicae apud Cantabri-
gienses olim Professor) ejusmodi voces per *h*
scribit, in Venerabilis *Bedae Historia Eccle-*
siastica, aliisque scriptis, Saxonice ab illo e-
ditis: ubi (cnihte, mihte, ðurh, etc.) passim
occurrunt, quae nunc *knight, might, through,*
etc. scribuntur. Addo etiam, ea ipsa vocabula non pauca quae nunc apud nos per *y*
scribuntur, a Saxonibus olim (atque etiamnum ut plurimum a Germanis) per *g* scripta reperiuntur; nostra enim *slay,* occido;
sayl, velum; *say,* inquam; *day,* dies; *rain,*
pluvia; aliaque innumera, partim apud Anglo-Saxones, partim a Germanis dicuntur
schlagen, segel, segen, sag, tag, regen, etc. Et
contra, multa quae nunc per *g* scribuntur,
fuerunt olim per *y* scripta; ut *agayn,* iterum; *agaynst,* contra; *given,* datum; etc.
olim *ayen, ayainst, yeoven,* etc. Et ab Anglo-Saxonum ʒenoʒ, ʒenoh, (satis) factum
est primo Anglorum *yenough,* postea *ynough*
D scriptum;

14 olim: 4th–6th
16 ab illo: 1st has *per illum*
17 cnihte, mihte, ðurh: 1st has cnihte, mighte, þurh; 2nd has nihte, mighte,
þurch
31 ayainst: 1st–5th have *ayenst*
31–34.2 Et ab Anglo-Saxonum . . . vel *enough:* 5th–6th

also found (see above) in words which are now writen with *gh*. Later scribes, perhaps because they were not acquainted with the symbol as it was originally written, substituted for it the symbol of the letter *z*,[87] which was a disastrous mistake; because of this, monstrosities such as *thouzt, souzt*, etc appeared in the printed editions of Chaucer and other early poets, instead of *thought, sought*, etc, or rather instead of *thouyt, souyt*, etc (they usually wrote this sound with the consonant *y* at that time). That great scholar Wheelock[88] (formerly Professor of the Arabic and Anglo-Saxon languages at Cambridge) found a much better solution, in writing words of this kind with *h*, for example in the Venerable Bede's *Ecclesiastical History* and other books which he edited in Anglo-Saxon. In these works *cnihte, mihte, ðurh*,[89] etc regularly occur where we would now write *knight, might, through*, etc. In addition, there are a large number of words which we now write with *y*, though it has been discovered that they were written with *g* by the Anglo-Saxons (and are written like this even today by the Germans, for the most part). Our *slay, sayl, say, day, rain*, and many other words appear (some in Anglo-Saxon, some in German) as *schlagen, segel, segen, sag, tag, regen*, etc. Conversely, many words which we now write with *g* were formerly written with *y* – as *again, against, given*, etc which were, at one time, *ayen, ayenst, yeoven*, etc; and Anglo-Saxon ʒenoʒ, ʒenoh became, at first, English *yenough*, and later, *ynough*, which can now be either *inough* or *enough*.

---

[87] The names Menzies, Mackenzie, Dalziel are examples of words in which *z* replaced ʒ (= [j]), owing to the fact that in Scotland the practice of writing ʒ continued longer than in England, and *z* was the nearest in shape of available printing types. This led to the pronunciation (especially in England) of [z] in these words.

[88] Abraham Wheelock (1593–1653), a linguist who specialised in oriental languages, notably Persian. He published an Anglo-Saxon translation of Bede in 1643, which is ascribed to Alfred, together with an edition and translation of *Chronologia Saxonica* (see D.N.B.).

[89] In Old English [ç], [x] and [h] were members of one phoneme, and were all represented by the symbol *h*.

34   DE SONORUM FORMATIONE.

ſcriptum; atque jam tandem promiſcue *i-nough*, vel *enough*.

Atque ita literarum ſonos ſimplices, quos ſcio, omnes enumeravi, eorumque formaturam tradidi, eosque in ſuas familias ſeu claſſes diſtribui. Quos omnes uno aſpectu ſic intueri licet.

Lite-

---

4 scio: 1st has *suo* (misprint)

I have now been through all the simple sounds of letters that I know, and have described their method of production, and assigned them to their families, or classes. The following table allows the whole classification to be seen at a glance.[90]

[90] Wallis's table of consonants is given in a slightly different form in the Introduction *p* 55.

Literarum omnium Synopſis.
Apertura

		majori.	media	minori.
Vocales	Gutturales	$\hat{a}$ ó } aperta.	e foemini-num.	ū ò } obſcu-rum.
	Palatinae	á exile.	é maſculi-num.	ee ĭ } exile.
	Labiales	ó rotundum.	oo ú } pin-gue.	ú exile.

Conſonae	Labiales	Muta	P	F	F	
		Semi-muta	B	V	W	
		Semi-vocalis	M	mugitus		
	Palatinae	Muta	T	S	Th	
		Semi-muta	D	Z	Dh	L R
		Semi-vocalis	N	gemitus		
	Gutturales	Muta	C	Ch	H	
		Semi-muta	G	Gh	Ϋ	
		Semi-vocalis	N̄	gemitus.		

Subtili-ores. Pingui-ores.

Aſpiratae

Table â ô aperta: 1st–4th have â ŏ; 5th has ó
ū obscurum: 1st–4th have ŭ
ú exile: 4th has û
L.R.: 1st–5th put these opposite *Semi-muta* and *Semi-vocalis* jointly

SYNOPSIS OF ALL THE LETTERS

		aperture		
		wide	medium	narrow
vowels	guttural	open â ŏ	feminine e	obscure { ŭ ò
	palatal	thin á	masculine é	thin { ee ĭ
	labial	round ô	fat { oo û	thin ú

consonants	labials	mute	P	F	F		
		half-mute	B	V	W		
		half-vowel	M	mooing			
	palatals	mute	T	S	Th		
		half-mute	D	Z	Dh	L	R
		half-vowel	N	groan			
	gutturals	mute	C	Ch	H		
		half-mute	G	Gh	Y		
		half-vowel	N̄	groan			

thin   fat
aspirates

36 DE SONORUM FORMATIONE.

S E C T. IIII.

De Sonis Compofitis.

Literae
Compofitae.

Reliqui foni omnes funt plane Compofi-
ti; quamvis eorum nonnulli pro fimpli-
cibus vulgo habeantur.

*ay, ey, oy,
aw, ew, ow.*

Diphthongi, quae vocantur, *ai, ei, oi, au,
eu, ou,* vel *ay, ey, oy, aw, ew, ow,* recte
pronunciatae, componuntur ex Vocalibus Praepofitivis, et Confonantibus *y* et
w, quae tamen pro Vocalibus Subjuncti-
vis vulgo habentur.

Nempe in *ai, au,* vel *ay, aw,* praeponitur *á*
exile: in *ei* vel *ey, e* foemininum; in *eu* vel
ew, é mafculinum: in *oi, ou,* vel *oy, ow,* praeponitur aliquando *ŏ* apertum (ut in Anglorum *bóy,* puer; *tóys,* nugae; *fóul,* anima;
bówl, poculum); aliquando *ò* obfcurum (ut
in Anglorum *bòil,* coquo; *tòil,* labor; *òil,*
oleum; *bòul,* globus; *òwl,* bubo; etc. quanquam non negem etiam horum nonnulla a
quibusdam per *o* apertum pronunciari.

Quod autem contendant aliqui Confonas *y,
w,* nihil differre a Vocalibus *ĭ, ú,* feu (ut
noftri fcribunt) *ee, oo,* raptim pronunciatis;
manifeftum effe errorem facile deprehen-
det, qui formationem vocum *yee* et *woo* cu-
riofius attenderit (praefertim fi eandem re-
pétat aliquoties); quippe obfervabit, a fono
Confonae

19 per *o* apertum pronunciari: 1st–5th have end bracket after *pronunciari* (the
correct reading)
20–37.4 Quod autem . . . non fit: 4th–6th

Section 4
Compound sounds[91]

The remaining sounds are clearly all compound ones, though some of them are commonly thought of as simple.

DIPHTHONGS

The sounds called diphthongs *ai, ei, oi, au, eu, ou,* or *ay, ey, oy, aw, ew, ow,* when correctly pronounced are made up of *preposed* vowels followed by the consonants *y* and *w*, though these consonants are commonly regarded as *subjoined* vowels.[92] So in *ai, au* or *ay, aw,* the first element is *thin a*; in *ei,* or *ey,* it is *feminine e*; in *eu* or *ew,* it is *masculine é*; in *oi, ou* or *oy, ow* the first element is sometimes *open ŏ* (as in English *bóy, tóys, sóul, bówl*) and sometimes *obscure ò* (as in English *bòil, tòil, òil, bòul, òwl,* etc though admittedly some people also pronounce these words with *open o*).[93] Some maintain that the consonants *y* and *w* are the same as the vowels *ĭ, û* or, as we write them in English, *ee, oo,* pronounced quickly. It is easy to see that this is not the case by studying the manner of production of the words *yee* and *woo* more carefully, and especially by repeating them both several times. You will find that the transition from the consonant sound to that of the following vowel involves a definite

---

[91] This section is rather a medley, containing Wallis's analysis of diphthongs, compound consonants, false diphthongs and finally features of speech that are not assignable to particular letters.

[92] Introduction *p* 56 *f*. The terms *praepositivus* and *subjunctivus* (Greek προτακτικός, ὑποτακτικός) were used by grammarians not only with reference to sounds but also to parts of speech and sentences. *Subjunctivus* had the connotation of 'subordinate', as well as just 'placed afterwards', and is used of the subjunctive mood (Priscian XVIII. x.79; VIII.xiii.68) as well as of the second half of diphthongs (id I.ix.50).

[93] In spite of his professed general phonetic approach in the *Tractatus* Wallis bases his description of diphthongs on English. His *ei, ey* diphthong refers to English *long i* (see note 95 below, and Grammar *p* 257 *f*).

DE SONORUM FORMATIONE. 37

Confonae ad fequentis Vocalis fonum non
tranfiri, nifi Organorum manifefto motu
(adeoque nova pofitione) interveniente, quod
in iterandis fonis *ee ee, oo oo,* non fit.

Has autem (vulgo dictas) Diphthongos in
variis linguis varias fortiri a genuino fono
deflexiones non ignoro; de quibus nunc a-
gendum non eft: poterunt autem illi omnes inter fonos a nobis traditos (ab iis quorum id intereft in fingulis linguis) reperiri,
adeoque ad fuos locos referri.

Anglorum *i* longum feu pingue, eft plane fonus compofitus ex *e* foeminino et *y*
confona; eftque idem omnino fonus cum
Graecorum *ει*.

i.

Anglorum *j* confona vel *g* molle, vel e-
tiam *dg*; componitur ex confonis *dy*.

j confona.
dj.

Nam eorum *jar*, difcordia; *joy*, gaudium;
gentle, generofus; *lodging*, habitatio, feu lo-
cus commorandi; etc. fonant *dyar*, *dyoy*,
dyentl, *lodying*, etc. Atque eodem fono profertur Arabum *Gjim* (quae litera quamvis
ab Hebraeorum *Ghimel* defcendat, non tamen ipfius fonum retinet) et Italorum *Gj*.

Gallorum *j* confona, vel *g* molle, componitur ex confonis *zy*.

zj.

Nam eorum *je* ego, *age* aetas, etc. funt *zye*,
a-zye, etc. Hunc fonum Perfae per fuum
zye fcribunt; quod tribus fuperne punctis
ab Arabum *ze* dignofcitur.

D 3

At

---

5 (vulgo dictas): 4th–6th
24 et Italorum *Gj*: 4th–6th

movement and a new posture of the vocal organs; this movement does not occur when one repeats the sounds *ee ee, oo oo*.

I realise that these, commonly so-called, diphthongs diverge from their natural sound[94] in different ways in different languages. This is not my concern here. Anyone who has an interest in diphthongs in a particular language can find them all among the sounds which I have described, and can assign them to their appropriate place.

Long î. English *long* or *fat î* is clearly a compound of *feminine e* and the consonant *y*; it is exactly the same sound as Greek ει.[95]

Dy. The English consonant *j* or *soft g*, or *dg*, is a compound of the consonants *dy*.[96] The English words *jar, joy, gentle, lodging*, etc are pronounced *dyar, dyoy, dyentl, lodying*, etc. Arabic *Gjim* has the same sound; although it is derived from Hebrew *Ghimel*, it does not keep the Hebrew sound; Italian *Gj* is also pronounced in this way.

Zy. The French consonant *j*, or *soft g*, is a compound of the consonants *zy*. Their words *je* (I), *age* (age) etc, are pronounced *zye, a-zye*. The Persians write this sound with their *zye*, and distinguish it from Arabic *ze* by writing three dots above it. But the German

---

[94] By 'natural sound' (*genuino sono*) Wallis appears to mean the *English* sounds he has just described (see note 93). For *yee, woo* see Introduction *p* 57.
[95] This vowel is often described as the long version of *ĭ* (Wallis's *thin i*) because of its historical relationship, its development into a diphthong being ignored (for example by Hodges 1644; see Dobson, *pp* 277–278 and 659 *ff*; Lehnert, §§ 110–111). The identification with Greek ει may derive from French grammarians, who frequently equated the pronunciation of ει with their *ei* or *ai*, in *peindre* etc (Lehnert, loc cit).
[96] See Introduction *p* 60.

38   DE SONORUM FORMATIONE.

At Germanorum *j* confona, eft fonus plane
fimplex; idem nempe cum Anglorum *y:* ut
fupra dictum eft.

fh, ch, fch,
fy.

Anglorum *fh*; Gallorum *ch*; Germanorum *fch*; Hebraeorum et Arabum *fhin*;
fonant *fy*.

Nam Gallorum *chambre*, camera; Anglorum *fháme*, et Germanorum *fham*, pudor;
fonant *fyámbre, fyáme, fyám*. Cambro-Britanni hunc fonum per *fi* fcribunt, cum nota
productionis in vocali fequente: ideoque
apud illos *Sión* (Johannes) eft vox monofyllaba; at *Síon* (Sionis mons) eft vox diffyllaba.

ty.

Anglorum *ch* vel *tch*, fonat *ty*.

Nam *orchard*, hortus; *riches*, divitiae; etc.
fonant *ort-yard, rit-yes*, etc. Hoc fono Itali
fuum *c* proferunt ante vocales *e* et *i*. Perfae huic fono exprimendo, praeter Arabum
alphabetum, affumunt fuum *che*, quod tribus inferne punctis ab Arabum *Gjim* diftin-
guunt. Si voci Anglicanae *yew*, taxus, figillatim praeponantur *d, t, f, z,* fiunt *dyew,*
tyew, fyew, zyew, hoc eft Anglorum *Jew,*
Judaeus; *chew*, maftico; *fhew*, oftendo: et
Gallorum *jeu*, lufus. Qui fyllabis *yan, yer,*
praepofuerit *f, z,* formabit Gallorum *chan-*
ger, hoc eft *fyan-zyer;* at fi praepofuerit
t, d, formabit Anglorum *changer*, hoc eft,
tyan-dyer.

Non

8 *sham*: 1st–5th have *scham*
9 *syâme*: 1st has *sháme* (misprint)

consonant *j* is clearly a simple sound, and the same as English *y*, as I explained earlier.

Sh. English *sh*, French *ch*, German *sch* and Hebrew and Arabic *shin* all have the sound of *sy*: French *chambre* (room), English *sháme*, and German *scham* have the sounds *syâmbre*, *syáme*, *syâm*. The Welsh write this sound as *si*, with a length mark on the following vowel; so with them Siôn (John) is a monosyllabic word, while Sîon (Mount Sion) is dissyllabic.

Ty. English *ch* or *tch* has the sound *ty*. *Orchard*, *riches*, etc are pronounced *ort-yard*, *rit-yes*, etc. This is the sound of Italian *c* before the vowels *e* and *i*. The Persians use their *che* to express this sound, which is not in the Arabic alphabet, and distinguish it from Arabic *Gjim* by putting three dots underneath it. If the English word *yew* is prefixed in turn by *d*, *t*, *s*, *z*, the result is *dyew*, *tyew*, *syew*, *zyew*, that is, English *Jew*, *chew*, *shew*, and French *jeu* (game). If *s*, *z* are put in front of the syllables *yan*, *yer*, the result is French *changer*, that is *syan-zyer*; but if *t*, *d* are put in front instead the result is English *changer*, that is *tyan-dyer*. I know that some people

DE SONORUM FORMATIONE. 39

Non ignoro, effe qui velint, in Anglorum
che et *ge* audiri fonum *ſ* (quaſi *changer* fo-
naretur *tſyandſyer*); verum egó, in *changer* non alios fonos audio quam *tyan-dyer*;
atque ad aliorum aures provoco, num non,
qui hos protulerit, Anglorum *changer* exacte pronunciaverit.
Germani fcribunt per *ſch*: Quibus *Tſchirn-
haus* profertur ut noſtrum *Churn-houſe*.

Latinorum (et aliarum fere gentium) *X*,   **X.**
et Graecorum *ξ*, componuntur ex *cſ, κσ.*

Hanc literam Hebraei, aliique Orientales,
non agnofcunt, fed ipſius loco literas ſimplices fcribunt ex quibus componitur: Quod
etiam non raro faciunt Germani; eorum
nempe *ochs* bos, *wachs* fera, *ſechs* fex, *ſechſt*
fextus, etc. funt Anglis *ox, wax, ſix, ſixth.*
Cambro-Britanni hunc fonum per *cſ* femper
fcribunt.

Latinorum *K* olim pro *Ca* ponebatur: **K.**
fcribebant enim promifcue *calendae* et
klendae; item *cariſſimus* et *kriſſimus*; etc.

Nunc apud plerafque gentes eundem plane
fonum ſimplicem obtinet quem Graecorum
κ (unde defluxit) aut Latinorum *C:* effetque
litera plane fuperflua ſi *C* genuinum fuum
fonum femper retineret; ideoque Cambro-
Britanni (quibus literae *c* fonus ubique con-
ſtans eſt) literam *k* non habent; ut nec alii
aliqui. Galli pro eo ponunt *q* vel *qu.*
D 4   Lati-

1–7 Non ignoro . . . pronunciaverit: 4th–6th
8–9 Germani . . . *Churn-house*: 5th–6th
16 sera: 1st–5th have *cera* (the correct reading)
22 item . . . *krissimus*; etc: 5th–6th
30 Galli . . . *q* vel *qu*: 5th–6th

think that the sound *s* is discernible in English *che* and *ge* (in which case *changer* would be pronounced *tsyandsyer*): however, I can only hear *changer* as *tyan-dyer* and I appeal to others to judge from their own hearing, whether people who pronounce these sounds are giving the English word *changer* its correct pronunciation. The Germans write the sound as *sch*.[97] They pronounce *Tschirnhaus* like our *Churn-house*.

X. *X* in Latin, and in most other languages, and *ξ* in Greek are compounded from *cs*, *κσ*. The Hebrews and other Orientals do not have this letter; in its place they write the simple letters of which it is composed. The Germans often do this too; their *ochs, wachs, sechs, sechst*, etc correspond to English *ox, wax, six, sixth*. The Welsh always write this sound as *cs*.

K. Latin *K* was formerly used instead of *Ca*; they wrote both *calendae* and *klendae* without distinction; and also *carissimus* and *krissimus*, etc.[98] In most countries *k* now has the same simple sound as Greek *κ*, from which it originated, or Latin *C*, and it would be entirely superfluous as a letter if *C* always had its true sound. This is why the Welsh, whose *c* always has the same sound, and some others do not have a letter *k*. The French use *q* or *qu* in its place.

---

[97] This must be a misprint for *tsch*.
[98] In early Latin three different symbols occur representing the sound [k]: (i) K, before the vowel A; (ii) C, before the vowels E and I; (iii) ϙ (Greek *koppa*) before the vowels O and U and the consonant V. Subsequently C replaced K except in a few words for which K was used as an abbreviation, including *Kalendae, Kaeso, Karus*. The invariable association of K with a following A led to the use in inscriptions of abbreviations such as KLENDAE or KRISSIMUS for *Kalendae, Karissimus* (see Quintilian, I.7.10; Terentius Scaurus, ed Keil, VII.14–15).

40   DE SONORUM FORMATIONE.

ᴓ Latinorum *Q* olim pro *Cu*, vel potius *Cw*, ſcriptum fuiſſe recte contendit *Gatakerus.*

At nunc dierum (ubi ſubjungitur litera *u*) plane idem ſonat ac *C* vel *K*, eſtque litera ſuperflua. Cambro-Britanni hanc literam non agnoſcunt; ſed pro *qu* ſemper ponunt *cw* vel *chw*. Et Anglo-Saxones ſcribebant Cꞅen (hoc eſt *Gwen*) quod nos *Queen* ſcribimus.

wh. Anglorum *wh* pronunciatur omnino ut *hw.*

Idem nempe ſonant Anglorum *whit* et Gallorum *huict*, ſed ſenſu longe diverſo. Anglo-Saxones olim literam *h* priori loco poſuerunt (qui autem factum ſit ut Angli poſtponant, plane neſcio): ſic pro eorum (hꞅaet, hꞅilc) dicunt Angli *what, which*: at Scoti etiam *quhat, quilk.*

Eſt autem obſervatu non indignum, conſonas *y* et *w* (licet non attendentibus, et inobſervatas) plerumque inter pronunciandum ſubjungi conſonis affinibus ante affines vocales.

Nempe *y* ſubjungitur ſaepe Gutturalibus conſonis *c, g*, ſequente vocali palatina: ſonantur enim *can* poſſum, *get* acquiro, *begin* incipio, etc. acſi ſcriberentur *cyan, byeg, begyin*: aegrius enim tranſire poteſt lingua ab his gutturalibus conſonis ad vocales palatinas formandas, quin quis, etiamſi nolit,
pronun-

8–10 Et Anglo-Saxones . . . scribimus: 4th–6th
28 *byeg*: 1st–5th have *gyet* (the correct reading)
29 aegrius: 1st–4th have *vix*
31 quin quis, etiamsi nolit: 1st–4th have *quin etiamsi nolit*

Q. Gataker[99] is right in stating that Latin *Q* was formerly written instead of *cu* or rather *cw*.[100] Nowadays, however (when it is followed by the letter *u*), it clearly has the same sound as *C* or *K* and so is a superfluous letter. The Welsh do not have it; instead of *qu* they always write *cw* or *chw*. The Anglo-Saxons wrote *Cpen* (that is *Cwen*) where we write *Queen*.

Wh. English *wh* is pronounced exactly like *hw*.[101] English *whit* and French *huict* have the same sound, though the meaning is quite different.[102] The Anglo-Saxons used to put the letter *h* first (I have no idea what caused the English to put it in second place), so where they have *hpaet*, *hpilc*, the English have *what*, *which*, and the Scots *quhat*,[103] *quilk*.

It is worth noticing that the consonants *y* and *w* are very frequently inserted between a consonant and a vowel when they have something in common with both (though this is not consciously done and passes unnoticed). For example, *y* is often put in after guttural consonants when a palatal vowel follows: *can* (am able), *get*, *begin*, etc are pronounced as if written *cyan*, *gyet*, *begyin*.[104] The reason for this is that it is extremely difficult for the tongue to move from

---

[99] See note 57, *p* 169.

[100] In early Latin inscriptions and manuscripts there is considerable vacillation between *q*, *cu* and *qu*.

[101] This interpretation is also given by Hart, Smith, Newton, Holder and Lodwick, but Wilkins and Cooper make it the voiceless equivalent of *w ie* [ʍ]. Both pronunciations still occur in Scottish accents of English. Wallis could have identified it with his *f per foramen* if he had thought it a simple sound (see note 49, *p* 165).

[102] Assuming that French *hui(c)t* began with the same sound in Wallis's time as it does today *ie* [ɥ], the only resemblance to English *wh* would be in the close lip rounding. In other respects the two sounds are quite different, French [ɥ] being voiced throughout and palatalised, whereas English [hw] starts voiceless and is velarised. For evidence as to the seventeenth-century pronunciation of *huict* see Thurot (1881–3, III.409).

[103] According to Sweet (1888, § 725) *qu* represents an 'exaggerated back element'. He identifies it with the final consonant in German *auch* – a labialised voiceless velar fricative [x].

[104] Introduction *p* 60 *f*.

pronunciabit *y* (fic, pro *can*, poffum, audies
Scotos ct Boreales Anglos, dicentes, *kan;*
Meridionales, *kyan:* et fic in aliis): At ante
alias vocales non item; ut in *câll*, voco; *gâll*,
fel; *go*, eo; *gun*, bombarda; *goofe*, anfer;
come, venio; etc.

W fubjungitur nonnunquam confonis labialibus *p*, *b*, praefertim ante *o* apertum, ut in
pot, olla; *boy*, puer; *boil*, coquo; etc. quae
fonantur acfi fcripta effent *pwot*, *bwoy*,
bwoile, etc. fed neque femper, neque ab omnibus fic efferuntur.

Latinorum *ae*, *oe*; Anglorum *ea*, *oa*, *ee*, *ae,oe,ea,ea,*
oo, et quandoque *ei*, *ie*, *ou*, *au*, item *th*, *ee,oo.*
ph (quibus fimiles apud alias gentes reperiuntur); quanquam duplicibus characteribus fcribantur, funt tamen (faltem
prout nunc dierum pronunciari folent)
foni fimplices: prout fuis in locis fupra
oftendimus.

Atque hactenus fonos literarum omnes, qui
ubique fere gentium occurrunt, tam fimplices quam compofitos, quantum mihi fufficere
videtur, expofui: et vix quidem ullos audiri
credo quin poffint ad explicatorum aliquos
reduci.

Notandum tamen eft, apud varias gentes nonnihil diverfitatis inter pronunciandum reperiri, quae non tam fingularum literarum, quam totius potius loquelae

---

1–3 (sic, pro *can* . . . sic in aliis): 5th–6th
  8 ante o apertum: 1st–4th have *aut o apertum* (misprint)

these guttural consonants to produce palatal vowels, without *y* being pronounced, however unintentionally, in between; so you will hear the word *can* (am able) pronounced as *kan* by Scots and Northern English and *kyan* by Southerners, and this is so in other words too. It does not happen before other vowels – for example, *câll, gâll, go, gun, goose, come*, etc. *W* is sometimes put in after the consonants *p, b*, especially before *open o*, as in *pot, boy, boile*, etc which are pronounced as if written *pwot, bwoy, bwoile*, etc – but this is not invariably so, and not everybody does it.[105]

Ae, oe, ea, oa, ee, oo. Latin *ae, oe*, English *ea, oa, ee, oo*,[106] and sometimes *ei, ie, ou, au*, also *th, ph* (and similar combinations in other languages), are simple sounds, at least as they are pronounced nowadays, even though they are each written with two symbols. This was made clear earlier, in the relevant sections.

I have now completed my description, in what seems to me sufficient detail, of all the sounds of the letters, both simple and compound, as they occur in almost all parts of the world. I doubt whether any others are to be heard which cannot be analysed into those I have dealt with.

It is worth noting, however, that differences in pronunciation occur in various languages which are not attributable so much to the individual letters, as to the whole style of speech of the com-

---

[105] Introduction *p* 61.
[106] *Cf: pp* 145, 147 (Section 2) under *masculine e* and *round o*, where *ea, oa* are said to be more correctly pronounced if both vowels are heard, and note 27, *p* 145.

42   DE SONORUM FORMATIONE.

quelae communis eſt affectio. Angli nempe totam pronunciationem quaſi promovent verſus anteriorem oris partem, et faucibus apertioribus loquuntur; unde et ſoni fiunt diſtinctiores. Germani potius retrahunt verſus poſteriorem oris partem et gutturis imum; unde fortius et magis ſtrenue pronunciant. Galli propius ad palatum omnia formant, et faucibus minus dilatatis; unde pronunciatio evadit minus diſtincta, et quaſi admiſto murmure confuſa. Item; Itali, et praeſertim Hiſpani, productiori tenore loquuntur; Galli magis properantur; Angli tenore medio. Galli (et Scoti eorum aemuli) periodorum et clauſularum poſtremas ſyllabas elevant ſeu acuunt; Angli deprimunt ſeu gravant; quae non tam ſingularum vocum, quam totius ſententiae tenoris eſt affectio. Aliaque hujusmodi etiam apud alias Gentes diſcrimina, cuilibet, prout ſe res offert, obſervanda, relinquo.

GRAMMA-

15–20 Galli (et Scoti . . . affectio: 5th–6th

munity.[107] For instance the English as it were push forward the whole
of their pronunciation into the front part of the mouth, speaking
with a wide mouth cavity, so that their sounds are more distinct.
The Germans, on the other hand, retract their pronunciation to the
back of the mouth and the bottom of the throat, so that they have a
stronger and more forceful pronunciation. The French articulate
all their sounds nearer the palate, and the mouth cavity is not so
wide; so their pronunciation is less distinct, muffled as it were by an
accompanying murmur. The Italians, and the Spaniards even more,
speak with a slow tempo, the French speak faster, and the English
are in between. The French, and the Scots equally, raise or sharpen
the pitch of the last syllables of sentences and clauses, while the
English lower or deepen it; this is a characteristic not of individual
words but of the sentence taken as a continuous whole. I leave it to
others to observe differences of this kind among other peoples, as
the opportunity presents itself.

[107] See Introduction *p* 62.

GRAMMATICA
LINGUAE ANGLICANAE.

CAP. I.

De Linguae Anglicanae pronunciatione.

SECT. I.

De Literis in genere, et primo de Confonantibus.

Sermonis Anglicani rudimenta traditurus, a Literis, earumque apud nos pronunciatione, exordium fumendum effe
duco. Ideoque ex generali qui praeceffit
De Loquela tractatu quaedam feligenda
funt, aliaque quae ad hanc linguam fpeciatim fpectant adjungenda.
Sunt apud nos Literarum characteres hi
qui fequuntur.

a. b. c. d. e. f. g. h. i, j. k. l. m. n. o.
p. q. r. f, s. t. u, v. w. x. y, z.

Confonarum pleraeque nihil difficultatis
habent quo minus a quibusvis prununcientur, cum eundem habeant apud nos
fonum, quem et alibi fere ubique gentium

GRAMMAR OF
THE ENGLISH LANGUAGE

CHAPTER I
The pronunciation of English

Section 1
The letters in general, and firstly the consonants

In setting out to describe the elements of English speech I think I ought to begin with the letters and their pronunciation. I shall introduce selections from the general treatise *On Speech* which precedes this section, and I shall add any other material which has particular reference to the English language. In English we have the following symbols for the letters: a b c d e f g h i j k l m n o p q r ʃ s t u v w x y z.[1] Most of the consonants present no difficulties in pronunciation, since they have the same sound in our language as they do almost everywhere else in the world: especially b d f h k l m n p q r z.

Note: This Section of the Grammar is concerned only with *English* sounds, and in describing these Wallis starts from the *written symbols*, not from the sounds themselves; he does not describe the articulations of all the letters, but only those which may be ambiguous in their sound values (see Introduction *p* 63).

[1] McKerrow (1910) sums up the conventions of early printers regarding the use of the symbols i.j. and u.v. as follows: 'The practice of the earliest printers, which they presumably took over from the scribes of their time and country, with regard to the letters under discussion was as follows:

(1) There was an upper-case letter approximating in shape in Gothic founts rather to the modern J than to I, but serving indifferently for either.

(2) An upper-case letter approximating in shape in Gothic founts to U, and serving for U and V.

(3) A lower-case i serving for both i and j.

(4) A lower-case j, used for the second of two i's in words like 'perij' and in Roman numerals as 'viij'.

(5) A lower-case u, serving for both u and v, but only used medially or finally.

(6) A lower-case v, serving for both u and v, but only used initially.'

In roman type there was more fluctuation; Italian printers often used u initially, but in northern Europe the above conventions were normal.

The systematic use of the symbols I.i.U.u. for vowels and J.j.V.v. for consonants is first found in printers of the late fifteenth century, but did not become firmly established until early in the seventeenth century. In Spain the distinction was made as early as 1492 in E. A. de Nebrija's *Gramática sobre la lengua castellana*, and in Italy the outstanding pioneer was G. G. Trissino (1478–1550), who also introduced other spelling reforms in the early sixteenth century. The reform gained weight when supported by Petrus Ramus (1515–1572) in whose Latin grammar (1559) i.j.u. and v were used in a modern manner throughout, and j and v were often called 'lettres Ramistes'. In England the modern usage was firmly established by 1637, when it was used in Proclamations, but it is noteworthy that until quite recently no distinction was made between I and J in entries in the British Museum Catalogue. See also Kukenheim (1932), *pp* 31–37.

44   DE PRONUNCIATIONE. C.I. S.I.

tium obtinent: praefertim *b, d, f, h, k, l, m, n, p, q, r, z.* De paucis tamen quaedam funt monenda.

C ante vocales *e, i, y,* (aut etiam Apoftrophum abfentis *e* non raro indicem) ubique mollius fonatur; ut litera *f,* genuino fono prolata: alibi femper durius, et fuo fono; nempe ut Graecorum *κ.*

Galli *c* mollius, quandoque per *ç* fcribunt, quem charaɛterem etiam apud nos non incommode adhiberi poffe fentio: eo tamen minor eft novi charaɛteris neceffitas, quia regula tradita nullam (quam fcio) patitur exceptionem; quoties enim *c* durum fonandum occurreret ante vocales *e, i, y,* perpetuo vel adjungitur vel fubftituitur *k;* ut in *keep,* fervo; *ſkin,* pellis; *ſkill,* fcientia; *publike, publick,* publicus; etc. (nam *publique* etc. eft potius fcriptio Gallica quam Anglicana; Galli vero ideo fubftituunt *qu,* quia literam *k* non habent).

Hinc eft quod a Latino *ſcio,* jam olim factum eft (dum Latinorum *c* fonum fuum fortem et genuinum retinebat) *ſkill* (fcientia, peritia) tranfeunte *c* in *k* (ne, fi *ſcil* fcriberetur, legeretur *ſil;* ut pro *ſcio,* jam *ſio* dicimus): at in *ſcience* (fcientia) quanquam ab eodem vocabulo Latino, et fenfu fere eodem, retinemus Latinorum *c* literam, quia jam mollius proferendam, ut *f.* Sic, in *publication* (publicatio) retinemus *c* literam (licet fortius proferendam, ut *k)* quoniam fequitur *a* litera: at vero (a *publico)* fi fcriberetur

22–45.22 Hinc est quod . . . atque hic *k*: 5th–6th

However a few of them need some comment.

C. When *c* occurs before the vowels *e i y* (or before an apostrophe which often signifies the omission of *e*) it always has a soft sound, like the letter *s* pronounced with its true sound. Elsewhere it is always hard, and has its own true sound, like Greek κ. The French sometimes write *soft c* with the symbol ç, and I think this symbol could well be used by us too. However the fact that the rule given above admits of no exceptions, so far as I know, means that there is less need of a new symbol; whenever the sound of *hard c* is required before the vowels *e i y* the symbol *c* is always replaced by *k*, or has *k* added to it; as in *keep*; *skin*; *skill*; *publike*; *publick*; etc (the spelling *publique* is French rather than English – the French use *qu* because they have no letter *k*).

² This is how we got our word *skill* from Latin *scio*, in which *c* retains its true, strong sound – *c* is replaced by *k* (if it were written *scil* it would be read as *sil*, just as we now say *sio* for *scio*). But in *science*, even though this is derived from the same Latin word and has very nearly the same meaning, we keep the Latin letter *c*, because it is pronounced with a soft sound, like *s*. In *publication* (Lat. *publicatio*) we keep the letter *c* (though with its stronger sound, like *k*) because it is followed by the letter *a*; but if one used the spelling *publice* (from Latin *publicus*) in English (changing the Latin

---

² Wallis added this long paragraph in the 5th edition (1699). Lehnert deduces from Wallis's omission of any mention of a cluster *kn* that he assumes the *k* to be pronounced. Cooper (1685) interprets *kn* as equivalent to *hn*, by which he appears to mean [n̥].

C. I. S. I. DE PRONUNCIATIONE. 45

beretur *publice* (tranfeunte terminatione
Latina in Anglorum *e*) legeretur *publife;*
quapropter vel pro *c* fubftituunt *k,* fcribuntque *publike* (quo retineatur fortior fonus literae *c);* vel eidem fufficiunt, fcribuntque
publick (ut alibi *Arithmetick, Mufick, Phy-
fick,* aliaque multa). Sic a *Cato,* felem dicimus *cat* (retento *c),* fed catulum, *a kitten*
(fubftituto *k,* quoniam ante vocalem *i).* Sic
candelam dicimus *a candle,* fed (accendere)
to kindle. At vero (a *computo,* feu *recomputo;* aut, quod ego malim, a *recenfeo)* male
fcribunt plurimi *to reckon* (per *ck),* cum
nulla ratio fuppetit cur, pro *c,* fubftituere-
tur *k,* ante vocalem *o.* Scribendum itaque
vel *recon* (quafi a *recognofco),* vel (fi *ck* retentum velimus) *recken* (quafi a *recenfeo,*
quod et olim factum puto): Quippe in nullo (quod memini) vocabulo Anglicano, occurrit *k* ante vocales *a, o, u;* nec *c* durius
proferendum ante *e, i, y.* Sed, illic femper
c; atque hic *k.*
Si vero *c* alibi forfan mollius fonare vellent
(puta in fine fyllabae, vel ante confonam,
aut vocales *a, o, u),* adjungunt *e* mutum,
quo fonus mollior indicetur: ut *chance,* cafus; *advancement,* promotio; *forceable
(forcible)* violentus; etc. Quod et poft *g*
factum eft, mollius proferendam ante *a, o,* et
u (ut in *George,* quo a *gorge* diftinguatur),
pro quo Itali fubjungunt *j;* ut in *gjudice,*
gjovene, et fimilibus.

S acuto

28–32 Quod et post *g* . . . et similibus: 5th–6th

termination into English *e*) it would be read as *publise*. Therefore *k* is substituted for *c* to give *publike*, with the stronger sound of letter *c*, or alternatively *k* is added to *c* giving *publick* (like Arithmetick, Musick, Physick and many other words). So for Latin *catus* we have *cat* (keeping the *c*), but for *catulus* we have *kitten* (substituting *k* before the vowel *i*). Similarly for *candela* we have *a candle*, but *accendere* becomes *to kindle*. On the other hand the word we get from *computo* or *recomputo*, or, as I prefer to think, from *recenseo*, is usually written *reckon* (with *ck*), which is wrong because there is no need to put *k* in place of *c* before the vowel *o*. It should either be written *recon*, as if derived from *recognosco*, or (if we want to keep *ck*) as *recken*, as if derived from *recenseo*, as I believe it once used to be written.[3] As far as I can recall, *k* never occurs in English words before the vowels *a, o, u*, nor does *c* occur with a hard pronunciation before *e, i, y*; in the former case it is always *c*, and in the latter *k*.

If *c* is to have the soft sound elsewhere (for example, at the end of a syllable, or before a consonant or the vowels *a, o, u*) *e mute* is put after it, and this shows that it has the soft sound; as in *chance*, *advancement*, *forceable* (*forcible*), etc. This also happens with *g* when it is to have the soft pronunciation before *a, o* and *u* (as in *George*, to distinguish it from *gorge*). The Italians add *j* instead of *e* as in *gjudice*, *gjovene* and similar words.

---

[3] English *cat* and *kitten* both come from Latin *catta*, not *catus* or *catulus*. *Kindle* is probably from O. Norse *kynda*, and *reckon* from O. English *(ge)recenian*.

46   DE PRONUNCIATIONE. C. I. S. I.

s.   *S* acuto et ſtridulo ſono profertur ubi genuinum ſuum ſonum obtinet : At ubi dictionem claudit, fere ſemper ; et ubi media inter duas vocales aut diphthongos occurrit, non raro, obſcurius ſeu mollius profertur ; ut *z.*

Hanc ego literam, quoties mollius proferenda eſt, breviori charactere non male ſcribi poſſe putaverim; ut *his,* ſuus; *advise,* conſulo: alibi longiori; ut *hiſſe,* ſibilo; *adviſe,* conſilium.

Quatuor monoſyllaba (nec enim plura memini) *s* finale durum habent; *yes,* ita (affirmandi particula); *this,* hoc; *thus,* ſic; *us,* nos. Nam qui ſcribunt *needles, coynes, lightnes,* etc. pro *needleſſe,* non neceſſarium; *coyneſſe,* delicatia; *lightneſſe,* levitas; etc. vel ſaltem pro *needleſs, coyneſs, lightneſs,* omnino errant: ex diſſyllabis enim faciunt monoſyllaba; ſunt enim *needles,* acus; *coynes,* monetae; *lightnes* (vel *lightneth)* fulgurat; monoſyllaba per *e* mutum. At qui ſcribunt *greenes, fínes,* etc. pro *greenneſſe,* viriditas; *fineneſſe,* accuratio, ſubtilitas, etc. adhuc errorem duplicant.

ſ.   *T* ante *i,* ſequente alia vocali, ſonatur ut *ſ* ſtridulum : Alibi ſuum ſonum retinet.

Illud potiſſimum in vocibus quae a Latinis deſcendunt, non tamen in ſolis illis, conſpicitur. Sic *nation,* natio; *potion,* potio; *meditation,*

---

10 alibi longiori: 1st–4th have *alibi semper longiori*

S. S, in its true pronunciation, has a high pitched sibilant sound. But when it occurs finally in a word it nearly always has an obscurer or softer sound, like *z*, and quite often too when it occurs between two vowels or diphthongs.[4] I think it could well be written with the short symbol when it has this softer sound, as in *his, advise*; elsewhere the long symbol could be used, as in *hiſſe, adviſe*.[5, 6] Four monosyllables (I can think of no more) end in *hard s*: *yes, this, thus, us*. Those who write *needles, coynes, lightnes*, etc, instead of *needlesse, coynesse, lightnesse*, etc, or at any rate instead of *needless, coyness, lightness*, are entirely wrong; they are turning dissyllables into monosyllables.[7] *Needles, coynes* [coins], *lightnes* (or *lightneth*), are monosyllables with *e mute*. Those who write *greenes, fines*, etc instead of *greennesse, finenesse*, etc are making two mistakes.[8]

T. T before *i*, when another vowel follows, is pronounced like *sibilant s*; elsewhere it keeps its own sound. This is most obvious in words derived from Latin, but occurs in other words too; examples are: *nation, potion, meditation, exspatiate*, etc. However, in *question*,

---

[4] For the occurrence of [s] and [z] see Dobson, *p* 927 *ff* and note 70, *p* 181.

[5] Modern *advice*.

[6] Almost all the spelling reformers use the symbol *z* for soft *s*, but Wallis's suggestions for changing the orthography are always conservative. Even this suggested use of long ſ is not followed up – his own use of it elsewhere is determined solely by the graphic conventions, and has no phonetic significance.

[7] Introduction *p* 61 *f*. The omission of the second *s* allows the final *s* to be interpreted as the noun plural or verb third person singular termination, voiced after the preceding *l* or *n*.

[8] Namely (i) as for *needles* etc and (ii) in omitting one of the *n*'s, and so shortening the medial consonant, which should be double.

C. I. S. I. DE PRONUNCIATIONE. 47

tation, meditatio; *exfpatiate*, exfpatior; etc.
fonantur *nafion, pofion, meditafion, exfpafiate*,
etc. At in *queftion*, quaeftio; *mixtion*, mixtio;
combuftion, combuftio; *fuftian*, goffypium;
et ficubi alias *t* fequatur literas *f* vel *x*, genuinum fuum fonum obtinet.

X fonatur ut *cf*, vel *ξ* Graecorum.   *x.*

Qua de re Gallos praefertim monendos vellem, qui folent fonum *c* fupprimere. Sed et
Hifpani mollius quam par eft eam literam
proferunt; fere ut noftrum *fh*. Sic Hifpanorum *Xeres* noftri pronunciant *fherry*.

W fonatur, ut *u* in vocibus Latinis *quan-*   *w.*
do, lingua, fuadeo, aliisque poft *g, q, f.*

Hanc literam nos pro confona femper re-
putamus; fono tamen non multum differt
(differt tamen) a Germanorum vocali *ú* pingui, raptiffime pronunciata. Praecedit, apud
nos, non modo quasvis vocales (fi faltem *u*
excipias) fed et confonam *r*. Subjungi-
tur confonis *f* et *th;* ut *want*, careo;
went, ibam; *winter*, hyems; *wont*, fo-
lebam; *wrath*, ira; *write*, fcribo; *wry*,
curvatus; *fwim*, no; *perfwade*, fuadeo;
thwart, perverfus; (at poft *g* et *q* potius
fubftituitur *u*, ut *acquaint*, affuefco; *an-*
guifh, angor, feu dolor acris, etc.) Sequitur
etiam vocales *a, e, o*, cum quibus quafi in
diphthongum coalefcit, eodem prorfus mo-
do quo *u*, ut *sòw*, fus; *sów*, fero; *faw*, vidi;
few,

11–12 fere ut . . . *sherry*: 5th–6th
17 (differt tamen): 4th–6th

mixtion, combustion, fustian and other words where *t* follows *s* or *x* it has its own true sound.[9]

X. X is pronounced like *cs* or Greek *ξ*. The French particularly need warning about this, because they usually leave out the *c*. The Spanish, too, pronounce this letter more softly than they should, rather like our *sh*; and English people pronounce Spanish *Xeres* as *sherry*.

W. W has the sound of the letter *u* in Latin *quando, lingua, suadeo*, and other words where it follows *g, q, s*. We always regard this letter as a consonant; in reality it is almost the same (though not quite) as the German vowel *fat û*, pronounced quickly. In our language it occurs before any vowel (except *u*) and also before *r*, and it can follow the consonants *s* and *th*,[10] for example, *want, went, winter, wont, wrath, write, wry, swim, perswade, thwart* (though after *g* and *q* its place is normally taken by *u*, as in *acquaint, anguish*, etc). It can also follow the vowels *a, e, o*, and may be said to form a diphthong with them, in exactly the same way as *u* does, as in *sow* (pig), *sow* (seed), *saw, few*, etc. *W* also occurs before the letter *h*,

[9] Introduction *p* 60; Lehnert, 1936, § 82.
[10] Introduction *pp* 56–7. Wallis's remarks about the position of *w* may simply refer to the written symbol, except where he talks of it being 'pronounced'. If so they would not necessarily imply that *w* was still being pronounced before *r*. McIntosh (1956), in discussing Dalgarno's statement that 'except for *s* no letter of one organ may naturally precede in the main syllable a letter formed by another organ', notes that Wallis wrote in his own copy of Dalgarno *bra, bla, wrath* as exceptions. This is not conclusive either; Hodges (1644), Price (1668) and Cooper (1685) all testify to the omission of the sound *w* in *wr*. Wallis's reference here to *saw* and *few* as containing diphthongs contradicts *Tractatus pp* 139 and 149 (*â apertum, u exile*), but this is made a possible alternative later in the Grammar (*pp* 263, 265).

48   DE PRONUNCIATIONE. C.I. S.I.

few, pauci; etc. Praecedit etiam literam
h, fed revera poſt illam fonatur; *when*,
quando; *what*, quid, etc. fonantur *hwen*,
hwat, etc.

y.   *Y* conſona, apud nos, fonatur ut Germanorum *j* conſona; ſono nempe quam
proxime accedente ad ſonum vocalis *ĭ*
raptiſſime prolatae.

Arabes *y* per ſuum *ye*, ſicut et *w* per ſuum
waw, exprimunt. Praecedit (in ſyllabae initio) ſolas vocales (praeſertim *a, e, o*); easque
ſequitur et cum illis quaſi diphthongeſcit,
eodem modo et ſono quo *i:* idem nempe
ſonant *ay, ey, oy*, ac *ai, ei, oi*; ſed in fine
dictionis frequentius per *y* ſcribuntur, in
medio ſaepius per *i*.
Sed et *y* nonnunquam vices ſuſtinet vocalis
i; praeſertim in dictionum fine. Nam promiſcue ſcribimus *mercy* miſericordia, *pity*
commiſeratio, etc. ac *mercie, pitie*, etc. In
medio dictionis rarius pro *i* occurrit, niſi in
vocibus quae a Graecis deſcendunt per υ
ſcriptis. Quoties autem pro vocali cenſenda eſt haec litera, ſuperne puncto notari
optaverim, hoc modo *ẏ*, ut a conſona *y* diſtinguatur; quod olim factum fuiſſe video;
ſaltem apud **Anglo-Saxones**, et (poſt eos)
antiquiores Anglos; ut in Manuſcriptis libris liquet.

v.   *V* conſona profertur apud nos eodem ſono quo apud Gallos, Hiſpanos, Italos,
aliosque:

10–11 (in syllabae initio): 4th–6th
  25 optaverim: 1st–4th have *vellem*
  26 olim factum: 1st–4th have *olim semper factum*
  27–29 saltem . . . libris liquet: 5th–6th

though it is actually pronounced after it: *when, what*, etc are pronounced *hwen, hwat*, etc.[11]

Y. The consonant *y* is pronounced in English like the German consonant *j*, that is with a sound very close to that of the vowel *i* pronounced quickly.[12] In Arabic *y* is represented by the letter *ye*, and *w* by *waw*. At the beginning of a syllable *y* only occurs before vowels (especially *a, e, o*); it also follows these vowels, forming diphthongs with them, in the same way as *i* does and with the same sound as *i*; that is to say *ay, ey, oy*, have the same sound as *ai, ei, oi*. But at the end of a word *y* is usually preferred, whereas *i* is commoner in the middle of a word.

Sometimes *y* is found instead of the vowel *i*, especially at the end of words;[13] we make no distinction between the forms *mercy, pity*, etc and *mercie, pitie*, etc. It rarely replaces *i* within a word, except in derivations from Greek where it represents an original *v*. I should prefer it to be written with a dot above it (*ẏ*) whenever it stands for a vowel, to distinguish it from the consonant; and I see that this was the custom of the Anglo-Saxons at any rate, and (after them) of the early English, as may be seen in their manuscript books.

V. We pronounce the consonant *V* like the French, Spanish, Italians and others, namely with a sound very like the letter *f*. *F* and

---

[11] See *p* 207, note 101.
[12] Introduction *pp* 56–7.
[13] *Cf p* 191 under *y*.

C. I. S. I. DE PRONUNCIATIONE. 49

aliosque: fono nempe ad literam *f* proxime accedente.

Differunt enim *F* et *V*, eodem modo quo *P* et *B*. Scribitur nunc dierum fere femper diverfo charactere *v*, ut ab *u* vocali diftinguatur. Praecedit apud nos folas vocales, et quidem omnes; non autem confonam *r* ut apud Gallos, nec *l* ut apud Belgas: fequitur non modo vocales, fed et confonas *l*, *r*, in ejusdem fyllabae parte pofteriori (fed fequente *e* muto, aut ipfius vice apoftrophò, ne vocalis cenferetur); ut *vain*, vanus; *vein*, vena; *virtue*, virtus; *více*, vitium; *voíce*, vox; *vulgar*, vulgaris; *have*, habeo; *leave*, linquo; *lĭve*, vivo; *lòve*, amo; *carve*, fculpo; *calves*, vituli; etc.

J confona durius apud nos fonatur quam apud plerosque alios; nempe ut *dy*.

Productiori charactere nunc dierum pingi folet, hoc modo, *j*; ut diftinguatur ab *i* vocali. Syllabam femper inchoat, et folis vocalibus immediate praeponitur: *James*, Jacobus; *Jeoffray*, Galfridus; *jolly*, jovialis; *jump*, falto. Nam fiquando fonus ille in fyllabarum fine pronunciandus occurrit, per *g* molle, aut etiam *dg* exprimitur, fequente tamen *e* muto ut mollior fonus literae *g* innuatur; ut *age*, aetas; *rage*, furor; *knowledge*, fcientia; etc.

E

G genu-

5 diverso charactere: 1st has *hoc charactere*
9–10 consonas *l, r*: 1st has consonas *l, v* (misprint)
12 censeretur: 1st has *censeatur*
    vein, vena: 1st omits
22–24 *James . . . jump*, salto: 5th–6th
    25 pronunciandus: 1st has *sonandus*

[224]

V differ from each other in the same way as *P* and *B*. This letter is nearly always written nowadays with a distinct symbol, *v*, to distinguish it from the vowel *u*.[14] In English it only occurs before vowels, and it may come before any vowel. It cannot occur before *r*, as it does in French, or before *l* as in Dutch. However it can follow vowels, and the consonants *l* and *r*, in the latter part of the same syllable (but always with *e mute* following it, or an apostrophe in place of *e mute*, to prevent it being taken for a vowel).[15] Examples of its use are: *vain, vein, virtue, vice, voice, vulgar, have, leave, live, love, carve, calves*, etc.

J. The consonant *j* has a harder sound in English than in most other languages, equivalent to *dy*. Nowadays it is usually written with a longer symbol to distinguish it from the vowel *i*.[16] It always occurs in initial position in the syllable, and only vowels can immediately follow it, as in *James, Jeoffray, jolly, jump*; if this sound is to be pronounced at the end of a syllable it is represented by *soft g* or *dg*, followed by *e mute*, to signify that it has the softer sound, as in *age, rage, knowledge*, etc.

[14] See note 1 to this section.
[15] Since the symbols *u* and *v* were not consistently used as vowel and consonant respectively before the late fifteenth century a real ambiguity was possible; for instance Shakespeare, Sonnet 129, line 11). See also note 1 to this section, and *cf: p* 247.
[16] Introduction *p* 56 *f* and note 1 to this section.

5O   DE PRONUNCIATIONE. C. I. S. I.

G.

G genuino fono prolatum fonat ut Graecorum γ : Sed ante vocales *e, i, y,* (aut
apoftrophum abfentis *e* indicem) plerumque, nec femper tamen, mollius effertur; eodem nempe fono quo *j* confona.

Quoties autem molliori fono proferendum
fit, optarem ego ut puncto fupra pofito notetur, hoc modo *g̣*, quo a *g* duro diftinguatur: quod exteris linguam noftram addif-
centibus maximo effet adjumento.
In vocibus *give,* dono; *forgĭve,* condono; *get,*
acquiro; *forget,* oblivifcor; *beget,* gigno;
geld, caftro; *begin,* incipio; *together,* fimul;
eorumque derivatis; genuinum fonum retinet: aliifque vocibus Germanicae originis.
Item in *anger,* ira; *hunger,* fames; *linger,*
moras necto; *eager,* acris; *vineger,* acetum;
fwagger, Thrafonice glorior; *ftagger,* ebri-
orum more vacillo; *dagger,* fica; et fiqua
alia quae per *gg* fcribuntur. Item in derivatis a *long,* longus; *ftrong,* fortis; *big,*
magnus; *beg,* mendico; *fing,* cano; *bring,*
affero; aliifque quorum primitiva in *g* duro
terminantur. In quibusdam fubjungitur *u*
vel *h* (ficut apud Gallos) ut fonus fortior literae *g* innuatur, ut *guift,* donum; *guíde,*
ductor; *guilt,* reatus; *guíle,* dolus; *guild,*
deauro; *leaguer,* caftra; *tongue,* lingua;
gueft, hofpes; *guefs,* conjecturam facio;
ghoft, fpiritus; *Guilbert, Guifford* (propriis
nominibus), aliifque forfan aliquot; in quibus

8 posito notetur: 1st has *posito semper notetur*
16 aliisque vocibus . . . originis: 5th–6th
20–21 et siqua alia quae per *gg*: 1st–5th have *siqua . . . per gger*
30 *guess*: 1st–5th have *ghesse*
31 *ghost*, spiritus: 2nd–6th

[226]

G. G when pronounced with its true sound is like Greek γ. But before the vowels *e, i, y* (or an apostrophe standing for an omitted *e*) it usually, though not always, has the soft sound, that is to say the same sound as the consonant *j*. I would prefer it to be written with a dot above it when it is to have this soft sound (*ġ*), to distinguish it from *hard g*. This would be of considerable help to foreigners learning our language.[17] In the words *give, forgive, get, forget, beget, geld, begin, together* and words derived from these, it keeps its true sound, as it does in other words of Germanic origin. It does so too in *hunger, linger, eager, vineger, swagger, stagger, dagger* and other words written with *gg*;[18] also in words derived from *long, strong, big, beg, sing, bring* and others whose basic forms end in *hard g*.[19] In some words *u* or *h* is inserted (as in French) to show that *g* has its stronger sound, as in *guift* (gift), *guîde, guilt, guîle, guild* (gild), *leaguer, tongue, guest, guess, ghost, Guilbert, Guifford* (proper names) and perhaps some other words. *U* is not pronounced in

---

[17] Wallis's suggestions for reforming the orthography are nearly all confined to adding a diacritic mark : *cf : ẏ* (*p* 223), *obscure ù* (*p* 269), *fat â* (*p* 237), *long î* (*p* 259), *round ô* (*p* 261), *thin ù* (*p* 261). Occasionally he suggests the use of a different symbol: *long s* (*p* 219), the *ou* diphthongs (*p* 269), obscure *u* (*p* 259).

[18] In the 1699 and earlier editions *-gger* appears instead of *-gg*. This would exclude words such as *ragged, rugged, sluggish*, as well as *suggest. Exaggerate* is another exception.

[19] This indicates that *long, strong, sing, bring* still had a velar nasal and stop in Wallis's pronunciation, like *tongue* a few lines further on. Cooper (1685, *p* 69) says that the final *g* of *sing* is silent.

C.I. S.I. DE PRONUNCIATIONE. 51

bus *u* nihil fonat, ut neque in *buy*, emo;
build, aedifico.

B nonnunquam reticetur; ut in *debt*, debi-
tum; *doubt*, dubito; etc.

B.

L faepe excidit; ut in *talk, walk, chalk, calk,*
balk, halk (halkin, halkins), falcon, Fulk,
yolk, malt, falt, fhalt, qualm, calm, pfalm,
fhalm, halm, balm, palm, halfer, falcer, Cal-
cot, Halfe, half, Ralf, could, would, fhould,
aliisque aliquot, quae faepe (nec femper tamen nec ab omnibus) proferuntur *tauk,*
wauk, chauk, cauk, hauk (haukin, haukins),
faucon, fowk, yo'ke, maut, faut, fha't, quawm,
caum, pfaum, fhaum, haum, bawm, paum,
haufer, faucer, Caucot, Haws, hauf, Rafe,
cou'd, wou'd, fhou'd, etc.

L.

?

SECT. II.

De Vocalibus.

Vocalium Chara&teres funt *a, e, i, o, u;*
et *y* pro *i.* Quae plerumque cum fyllabam claudunt, producuntur; fecus autem ut plurimum corripiuntur.

Et quidem, hac in re, videmur Hebraeos
imitari; quibus quoties fyllaba in vocali de-
finit, eft ea vocalis (plerumque) longa (nifi
accentu forte fublevetur); fin confonante
claudatur fyllaba, vocalis (ut plurimum)
bev s eft (faltem nifi intercedat accentus).

E 2   Atque

3–16 *B* nonnumquam . . . *wou'd, shou'd*, etc: 5th–6th
25–55.5 Et quidem, hac in re . . . factum observamus: 5th–6th
   12 after *cauk*, 5th has *bauk* (correct reading)
   26 bev s est: misprint for *brevis est* of 5th

these words, any more than it is in *buy, build.*[20]

B. *B*[21] is sometimes silent, as in *debt, doubt*, etc.

L. *L* is often omitted, as in *talk, walk, chalk, calk, balk, halk*
(*halkin, halkins*), *falcon, Fulk, yolk, malt, falt* [fault], *shalt, qualm,*
calm, psalm, shalm, halm, balm, palm, halser, salcer, Calcot, Halse,
half, Ralf, could, would, should, and some other words: these words
are often pronounced *tauk, wauk, chauk, cauk, bauk, hauk* (*haukin,*
haukins), *faucon, fowk, yo'ke, maut, faut, sha't, quawm, caum,*
psaum, shaum, haum, bawm, paum, hauser, saucer, Caucot, Haws,
hauf, Rafe, cou'd, wou'd, shou'd, etc. But this pronunciation is not
always used, nor is it used by everyone.

Section 2
The vowels

The symbols for the vowels are *a, e, i, o, u,* and *y* used in place of *i.*[22]
When they end a syllable they are usually long; otherwise they are
mostly short. In this respect we seem to be imitating Hebrew. When
a syllable in Hebrew ends in a vowel, this vowel is (usually) long,
unless it is strengthened by the accent; but if the syllable ends in a
consonant the vowel is (usually) short, at least if no accent occurs

---

[20] For the use of *gh* and *gu* to represent *hard g* see Jespersen (*M.E.G.*, I. § 2.313–314);
'gh', he says, 'was extensively used by Caxton, who had evidently become familiar
with that group of letters during his stay in the Netherlands (where *gh* was used for the
fricative *g*)'.

[21] From here to the end of the chapter was newly introduced in the 5th edition. In
earlier editions there was no mention of *b* or *l* in this section, so the only comment on the
omission of *l* occurred in respect of *walk* and *talk* in the following section (*p* 237). It
seems likely, from contemporary evidence, that the omission of *l* took place in Wallis's
day in much the same circumstances as it does today, that is, when it followed a back
vowel and was followed by a velar or a labial consonant – [k b m v f], and also in *could,*
should, would. Wallis's examples all fall into these categories, except for *malt, falt, shalt,*
halser, salcer, Halse. The last of these is a proper name; *pace* Dobson (1968, *p* 244 note 3)
Lehnert does recognise this (1936, § 98). In *falt, halser* and *salcer* (modern *fault, hawser,*
saucer) the *l* is etymological (Jespersen, M.E.G., I. § 10.48). *Shalt,* like *could, would,*
should normally appeared in an unstressed position, where, except in careful speech, a
weak form without the *l* is known to have occurred (Lehnert (1936), § 181). *Malt* is not
given in other contemporary sources without *l*; it may well have been a dialectal pronunciation, but common enough to be making its way into Wallis's 'pure and authentic
pronunciation'.

[22] These symbols are here related to the vowel sounds of Section 2 of the *Tractatus*. The
only vowel sound of English not mentioned in this section is *u pingue (fat u)*, a curious
omission because Wallis uses the words *full, pull* to exemplify it in the *Tractatus* (*p* 149).

52   DE PRONUNCIATIONE. C. I. S. II.

Atque haec videtur genuina linguae noftrae
ratio antiqua.

Verum, prout nunc dierum fe res habet,
plurima hic monenda veniunt.

Et primo quidem, Plurima vocabula quae
vel nunc definunt, vel definebant olim, in *e*
foeminino (quod jam degenerat in *e* mutum),
plurium erant fyllabarum quam nunc funt.
Ut *ta-ke, ma-ke, ó-ne, bo-ne, fto-ne, wil-le,*
diffyllaba fuerunt, quae nunc habentur pro
monofyllabis; adeoque vocalis prior fyllabam terminabat, eratque igitur cenfenda
longa. Atque hinc etiamnum obtinet (utut
jam pro monofyllabis habeantur) quod vocalis prima in *one, wile, mile, bare, ware,*
ftare, fare, fire, fore, etc. produci cenfeatur
propter *e* finale; quae in *on, wil, mil, bar,*
war, ftar, far, fir, for, etc. corripiuntur;
eo quod in illis fyllabam olim terminaverit;
in his, non item. Et quidem fi in his retinendum vellent illud *e* finale (quod et fieri
folebat) geminabant confonam (ut *wille,*
mille, barre, warre, ftarre, firre, etc.) nempe, quo fit quae primam fyllabam termina-
ret confona, aliaque quae fequentem incho-
aret. Pariterque facit Hebraeorum dages;
duplicando, poft vocalem brevem, fequentem confonam.

Monendum porro; Linguae Graecae ge-
nium, eum a Grammaticis cenferi, ut inter-
mediae confonae, quantum fieri poffit, ad
fequentem vocalem fint referendae; adeoque fi vel unica fit (ut in ϖαἰήϙ) vel duae
pluresve, modo tales fint ut fyllabam poffint
                                        incho-

on it. This seems to be a genuinely ancient rule of our language also.[23] However, to explain the situation today, a number of comments are necessary.

Firstly, most words which now end, or formerly ended, in *feminine e* (which is now in the process of turning into *mute e*) used to have more syllables than they do now. For instance *ta-ke*, *ma-ke*, *ô-ne*, *bo-ne*, *sto-ne*, *wil-le*, were dissyllables whereas now they are regarded as monosyllables; the first vowel used to end the syllable and so had to be regarded as long. This is why the first vowel in *one*, *wile*, *mile*, *bare*, *ware*, *stare*, *fare*, *fire*, *fore*, etc is still considered to be long nowadays, because of the final *e* (though these words are now treated as monosyllables); whereas the first vowels in *on*, *wil*, *mil*, *bar*, *war*, *star*, *far*, *fir*, *for*, etc are short. The reason is that, in the first set, the vowel used to end the syllable, and in the second it did not. However, if they wanted to keep final *e* in the second set, as they usually did, they doubled the consonant (as in *wille*, *mille*, *barre*, *warre*, *starre*, *firre*, etc), so that one consonant could close the first syllable, and the other could begin the second. This is also the function of Hebrew *dagesh*;[24] it doubles the consonant which follows a short vowel.

It is also worth noticing that, according to the grammarians, a characteristic of the Greek language is the attachment of intervocalic consonants to the following vowel, where possible; so whether there is only one (as in πατήρ) or two, or more, provided that they can begin a syllable (as in πα-τρός, ἄ-στρον, τέ-μνω)

---

[23] Introduction *p* 63 *ff*.
[24] Hebrew *dagesh* is used (i) to change a fricative symbol to a stop symbol (*dagesh lene*); (ii) to double a consonant (*dagesh forte*); see Weingreen, *p* 56 *ff*.

C. I. S. II. DE PRONUNCIATIONE. 53

inchoare (ut in ϖα-ʃρὸς, ἄ-ʂρον, τέ-μνω) ad fequentem fyllabam fpectare cenfeantur (faltem nifi compofitorum ratio, aut tale quidpiam, contrarium in paucis fuadeat): Eosque fecuti, idem docent Grammatici Latini
(ut in *u-xor, o-mnis, ma-gnus*, etc.) quoniam
x, mn, gn, vocem inchoare poffint (ut in
xanthus, mna, gnatus, etc.); adeoque fyllabam multo magis.

Verum in Cymbrorum feu Cambro-Britan-
norum lingua, feu antiquorum apud nos
Britonum, res plane contraria videtur : Ut
qui, pronunciando faltem (quidni igitur et
fcribendo ?) confonas intermedias ad praecedentem vocalem (quam fieri commode poteft) retrahunt. Quod, fi Cymbros, feu
Wallos, diftincte legentes audias attente, non
inficiaberis. Quos fi imitari dixerim prae-
fentes Anglos; non miraberis, ubi dicentes
audias *let-er, mat-er, gen-e-ral, Ox-on, mag-
nify, pub-like, Doct-or,* etc. (retracta confona
intermedia ad praecedentem vocalem): utut
Latine dicendum fit (fi Grammaticos audia-
mus) *li-tera, ma-teria, ge-ne-ra-lis, O-xonium, ma-gnus, pu-blicus, Do-ctor,* etc.

Quicquid igitur fit de difpertiendis fyllabis
in Lingua Graeca Latinave ; in Anglicana
faltem noftra (quae non tam ad Graecorum aut Latinorum normas exigenda eft,
quam ad loquentium fonos auribus percep-
tos) putaverim potius (aurium judicio) ita
difpefcendas fyllabas, ut nunc ad antece-
dentem, nunc ad confequentem vocalem
referatur confonans intermedia, prout prae-

E 3   cedens

20 *gen-e-ral:* 5th has *gen-er-al* (correct reading)

they are regarded as belonging to the following syllable unless, that is, the structure of the component elements, or something of that sort suggests the contrary, as it does in a few instances. Taking the Greeks as their model the Latin grammarians divide syllables on the same principle, as in *u-xor, o-mnis, ma-gnus*, etc because *x, mn, gn* can begin a word (as in *xanthus, mna, gnatus*, etc) and so, *a fortiori*, a syllable.[25]

But in the language of the Cymbrians (or Welsh) or of the Ancient Britons, the situation appears to be quite different. In speaking, at any rate, so presumably in writing as well they attach intervocalic consonants to the preceding vowel as far as they reasonably can.[26] You can confirm this if you listen carefully to the Cymbrians (or Welsh) when they are reading something aloud. And if I tell you that the English today imitate this practice, you will not be surprised to hear pronunciations like *let-er, mat-er, gen-er-al, Ox-on, mag-nify, pub-like, Doct-or*, etc (in which the medial consonant goes with the preceding vowel); even though in Latin (if we are to believe the grammarians) the pronunciation would be *li-tera, ma-teria, ge-ne-ra-lis, O-xonium, ma-gnus, pu-blicus, Do-ctor*, etc. So whatever may be the rule for dividing up syllables in Greek or Latin, I think that syllables in English (which is not to be judged according to the norms of Greek or Latin, but by the sounds that we hear speakers of English make) should, on the basis of what we hear, be divided so that the medial consonant is attached sometimes to the

[25] Introduction *p* 65.
[26] Introduction *p* 65.

cedens vocalis vel corripienda fit vel producenda; aut etiam, fi plures concurrant inter-
mediae confonae, fic diftribuantur ut fuafe-
rit loquendi ratio (quam par eft ut fcripto
imitemur). Sic, verbi gratia, in voce *later*,
fi correptam vellem priorem fyllabam, fcriptum putaverim *lat-er;* fi productam, *la-*
ter; (eodem quippe fenfu utrumque dicitur).
Sic *doc-tor*, *doc-trine*, fcribendum dixerim (fi
difpefcendae fint fyllabae) quia fic loquimur.
Sed mos aliter obtinet. Sic *ab-out*, *ab-ound*,
ab-ove, *ab-ide*, *with-in*, *with-out*, *in-ure*, *un-*
ufual, *un-eafy*, *in-able*, *un-able*, *ab-ufe*, *dif-*
ufe, *mif-ufe*.
Qui autem hoc vel non attendunt, vel non
admittunt; fed ad Graecorum aut Latinorum Grammaticorum normam diftributas
volunt fyllabas Anglicanas (quod a plerisque
factum videmus); neceffe habent (quo auribus aliquatenus faveatur) ut intermediam
confonam (ubi corripienda eft vocalis praecedens) non raro geminent; etiam refragan-
te originis ratione: Hinc eft quod *matter*,
letter, *vallew*, *forrain*, aliaque iftiusmodi
multa fcribimus; quae, fi originem fpecte-
mus, fcribenda potius effent *mat-er*, *let-er*,
val-ew, *for-ain*, a vocibus Latinis *materia*,
litera, *valor*, *foraneus*, etc. Item *written*,
bitten, *fhotten*, *hidden*, *ridden*, *fmitten*, pro
writ-en, *bit-en*, *fhot-en*, *hid-en*, *rid-en*, *fmit-en*,
a verbis *to write*, *to bite*, *to fhoot*, *to hide*, *to*
ride, *to fmite*. Sed res non tanti eft ut fi-
mus de difpefcendis fyllabis admodum folli-
citi. Id faltem infinuatum vellem; Regu-
lam

preceding and sometimes to the following vowel, according to whether the preceding vowel is short or long. If more than one medial consonant occurs these consonants should be divided up as the way of speaking them suggests – it is reasonable to follow this in writing them. So, for example, in the word *later*, if I wanted the first syllable to be short I would think of the written form as *lat-er*, but if I wanted it to be long, then *la-ter* (there is no difference of meaning between the two). I think we should write *doc-tor*, *doc-trine* (if it is necessary to divide up the syllables) because that is how we pronounce these words. But the custom is different. Similarly: *ab-out*, *ab-ound*, *ab-ove*, *ab-ide*, *with-in*, *with-out*, *in-ure*, *un-usual*, *un-easy*, *in-able*, *un-able*, *ab-use*, *dis-use*, *mis-use*.[26]

Some people do not realise this, or do not accept it, because they think English syllables should be divided according to the norms of the Greek or Latin grammarians – this is a common belief; so they are often compelled to double the medial consonant (when the preceding vowel needs to be short) in order to fit in to some extent with what they hear, even though this obscures the word's derivation. This explains the spellings: *matter*, *letter*, *vallew* [value], *forrain* [foreign], and many similar ones; if we paid attention to their derivation we would spell them rather as *mat-er*, *let-er*, *val-ew*, *for-ain* from Latin *materia*, *litera*, *valor*, *foraneus*, etc. So also *written*, *bitten*, *shotten*, *hidden*, *ridden*, *smitten*, instead of *writ-en*, *bit-en*, *shot-en*, *hid-en*, *rid-en*, *smit-en*, from the verbs *to write*, *to bite*, *to shoot*, *to hide*, *to ride*, *to smite*. However the question of syllable-division is not all-important and we should not be too concerned about it. I should just like one thing to be remembered: the rule that, when it ends a syllable, a vowel is long, but when a con-

---

[26] Introduction *p* 65 *f*.

C. I. S. II. DE PRONUNCIATIONE. 55

Iam de producenda vocali quae syllabam ter-
minat, sed corripienda quae consonante
clauditur; intelligendam esse, de syllabis sic
divisis ut loquendo (magis quam scribendo)
factum observamus.

A plerumque pronunciatur sono magis *A.*
exili quam apud alias plerasque gentes:
eodem fere modo quo Gallorum *e* se-
quente *n* in voce *entendement,* sed paulo
acutius et clarius; seu ut *a* Italorum.

Non autem ut Germanorum *â* pingue; quem
sonum nos plerumque exprimere solemus
per *au* vel *aw*, si producatur; aut per *ŏ*
breve si corripiatur.

Pauca tamen sunt in quibus *a* sono illo pingui efferri solet: nempe cum in fine dictionis *a* praecedit geminum *ll;* ut *âll*, omnes;
tâll, procerus; *hâll,* aula; *câll,* voco; *wâll,*
murus; *bâll,* pila; *fâll,* cado; etc. cum eorum derivatis et compositis; ut *âllthough,*
quamvis; *âllways,* semper; *âllmost,* fere;
tâllness, proceritas; *câlling,* vocatio; *wâll-
flower,* luteola; etc. Quo casu suaderem ego
ut accentu circumflexo superne notetur, ut
pinguior ille sonus innuatur. At *walk,* am-
bulo; *talk,* colloquor; etc. rectius per *a*
Anglicum efferuntur; quae tamen negligentius loquentibus sonantur *wau'k, tau'k.* etc.
quo sono Gallos imitamur qui pro *al* (ante
consonam) non raro substituunt *au;* et
Scoti etiam, ubi non sequitur consona.

E 4 *E* pro-

10 seu ut *a* Italorum: 4th–6th
29–30 (ante consonam): 4th–6th
30–31 et Scoti . . . consona: 4th–6th

sonant ends the syllable the preceding vowel is short. The rule should be applied to syllables divided on the basis of what is perceived in speech, rather than in writing.

A.[27] *A* is normally pronounced with a thinner sound than it has in most other languages – in very much the same way as *e* before *n* in the French word *entendement*, but a little more sharply and clearly;[28] or like Italian *a*. It is different from German *fat â*, which we usually represent with *au* or *aw*, if it is long, or with *short ŏ* if short. However there are a few words in which *a* is regularly pronounced with this *fat* sound, namely when *a* precedes double *ll* at the end of a word, as in *âll, tâll, hâll, câll, wâll, bâll, fâll*, etc and in words derived and compounded from these, like *âllthough, âllways, âllmost, tâllness, câlling, wâll-flower*, etc. I would recommend putting a circumflex accent above the vowel, in these cases, to signify the fat sound. *Walk, talk*, etc are better pronounced with English *a*, though careless speakers say *wau'k, tau'k*, etc[29] copying the French, who often substitute *au* for *al* (before a consonant). The Scots also do this even when no consonant follows.[30]

[27] The vowels are now described, starting from the letters used for *writing* them. Under *A* both *thin a* (*p* 143) and *fat a* (*p* 139) are dealt with.
[28] *Sharply* and *clearly* are auditory terms which often correlate with a fronter articulation. Compare the use in modern phonetics of the terms 'clear *l*' for palatalised *l* and 'dark *l*' for velarised *l*. Sometimes Wallis uses *clear* of a back vowel (*eg: open o* in *oi*, on *p* 265) when contrasting it with an *obscure* vowel. See note 26, *p* 143.
[29] This is another example of Wallis's habit of quoting an earlier pronunciation as 'more correct'; by the 5th edition (1699) he had obviously accepted these pronunciations as, at least, not incorrect (see *p* 229 and note 21; also Introduction *p* 21).
[30] The qualification 'before a consonant' and the mention of Scots are additions in the 5th edition. He is thinking of words such as *call, wall* in which the final [l] is absent in many Scottish accents.

56   DE PRONUNCIATIONE. C.I. S.II.

E.   *E* profertur ſono acuto claroque, ut Gallorum *é* maſculinum.

> Vix unquam profertur ſono obſcuro ut Gallorum *e* foemininum, niſi forte cum *e* breve praecedit literam *r*, ut in *vertue*, virtus; *ſtranger*, extraneus; etc. ubi non tam requiritur ſonus ille quam aegre evitatur; difficilius enim tranſit lingua ab *é* maſculino ad *r*.

E mutum.   At *E*, quotiescunque in fine dictionis ſimplex occurrit, omnino mutum eſt, nec quicquam (nunc dierum) ſonat: Ut in *make*, facio; *have*, habeo; etc.

> Praeterquam in Articulo demonſtrativo *the*, quod per *e* ſimplex ſcribitur (ut diſtinguatur a pronomine *thee*, te) et Nominibus aliquot Propriis, aliunde deductis, ut *Phoebe*, *Penelope*, etc. Vix enim alias ullibi pronunciatur *e* ſimplex in dictionum fine. Nam *he* ille, *ſhe* illa, *be* eſſe, *we* nos, *me* me, et ſiqua ſunt ſimilia, rectius ſcribenda putem (prout etiam pronunciantur) per *ee* geminum, *hee*, *ſhee*, *bee*, *wee*, *mee*; contra quam fieri ſolet. Quoties autem vox aliqua terminanda occurrit ejusmodi ſono; vel ſubjungitur aliud *e* mutum, ut *Phariſee* Phariſaeus; vel ſubjungitur *a*, ut in *ſea* mare, *flea* pulex, *plea* argumentatio judicialis, *pea* piſum, *yea* ita (affirmativa particula), nec, quod ſciam, in pluribus; vel denique ſubjungitur *y*, ut in *Marſhalſey*, *Winchelſey*, *Langley*, *Hendley*, et paucis forſan aliis nominibus propriis.
>
> Ori-

---

20 rectius scribenda putem: 1st–4th have *rectius scribuntur*
22–23 contra quam fieri solet: 5th–6th

E. E has a sharp and clear sound, like French *masculine e*. It scarcely ever has the obscure sound of French *feminine e*,[31] except perhaps where *short e* comes before the letter *r*, as in *vertue, stranger*, etc; in these examples it is not so much a question of *feminine e* being obligatory; the fact is that it is difficult to avoid, because the tongue finds the transition from *masculine e* to *r* quite difficult.

E MUTE[32]

However, whenever *e* occurs as a simple vowel at the end of a word, it is *mute* and is never pronounced nowadays, as in *make, have*, etc. Exceptions include the definite article *the*, which has the simple vowel *e* (to distinguish it from the pronoun *thee*) and also some proper nouns which are derived from other languages, like *Phoebe, Penelope*, etc. There is scarcely one example otherwise of the pronunciation of simple *e* at the end of a word. For in my opinion, it would be better to spell the words *he, she, be, we, me*, and others like these with *ee* (as they are pronounced) – *hee, shee, bee, wee, mee*, though this is not usually done. Whenever a word needs to have this sound at the end, it either has a second *e mute* added, as in *Pharisee*, or an *a*, as in *sea, flea, pea, yea* (but no other words); or *y* may be added as in *Marshalsey, Winchelsey, Langley, Hendley*, and perhaps a few other proper names.

---

[31] *Masculine e* is described on *p* 145 and *feminine e* on *p* 139 *f*.

[32] This long description of the origin of *mute e* and the occasions on which it is used is the fullest and most accurate up to Wallis's time. Most of his remarks are borne out by subsequent research, though not all the examples he gives represent words which had a final *e* (see Jespersen (*M.E.G.*), I. §§ 6.1–6.3, especially § 6.28).

[239]

DE PRONUNCIATIONE. C.I. S.II. 57

Originem vero hujus *e* muti, nequis miretur unde devenerit, hanc effe judico. Nempe, quod antiquitus pronunciatum fuerit, fed obfcuro fono, ficut Gallorum *e* foemininum: adeoque voces *take* accipio, *óne* unus, *wíne* vinum, etc. quae nunc funt monofyllabae, fuerint olim diffyllabae, *ta-ke*, *ó-ne*, *wí-ne*, etc. ideoque etiam vocalis prior fyllabam terminaverit, fueritque propterea longa. Sonus autem ille obfcurus, finalis *e*, fenfim evanuit, ufque adeo ut tandem prorfus negligeretur (quod et de Gallorum *e* foeminino faepiffime accidit); retenta tamen praecedentis vocalis quantitate, reliquisque omnibus literis eodem prorfus modo pronunciatis acfi etiam ipfum *e* pronunciandum foret. Sic *commandement* (quadrifyllabum) etiamnum dicitur; quia fuerat *comman-de*, trifyllabum (nuperrime enim factum eft, aetate noftra, quod *Commandment*, triffyllabum, dici coeperit, neque hoc ab omnibus; cum ante quadrifyllabum omnibus fuerit). Sed et, parentum noftrorum aetate, dicebant *Baptif-me*, *Chatechif-me*, *beas-tes*, *pries-tes*, *clothes*, aliaque iftiusmodi (quae a vetulis quibusdam etiamnum audiuntur): et in Pfalmis metricis (Pf. cxxvi. 1.) etiamnum habetur *mou-thes* diffyllabum. Sed et utrumque dici folitum, *babe*, *clemence*, *excellence*, *eminence*, etc. atque *ba-be*, *clemen-ce*, *excellen-ce*, *eminen-ce*, etc. quae tandem fcribi coeperunt, *baby*, *clemency*, *excellency*, *eminency*, etc. (ne fcilicet *e* finale periiffe putaretur). Sic *naught*, et *naughty* (quod olim erat *naugh-te).*

Ipfius orige.

13 After *accidit* and still within the brackets 1st–3rd have: *quod ipsi multoties celeriter loquendo prorsus omittunt quamvis eorum Grammatici nondum id iubeant*; the same comment, in slightly different words, appears 59.6–9 (so in all editions)
17–58.11 Sic *commandement . . . sepulcher*, etc: 5th–6th

THE ORIGIN OF E MUTE

I will explain how I think this *e mute* originated, in case anyone is curious about it. Originally it was pronounced, but it had an obscure sound like French *feminine e*, so that words such as *take, ône, wîne*, etc, which are now monosyllables, were once dissyllables – *ta-ke, ô-ne, wî-ne*, etc; and the first vowel, since it ended a syllable, was long. The obscure final *e* gradually disappeared, and in the end it was entirely disregarded (as is frequently the case with French *feminine e*) but the quantity of the preceding vowel remained long, and all the other letters kept the same sound as if the final *e* had still to be pronounced. Even today we say *commandement* (four syllables) because *comman-de* was originally three syllables (the pronunciation *commandment* with only three syllables became current only very recently, during my lifetime, and not everyone pronounces it in that way, whereas previously it was universally pronounced with four).[33] In our parents' time the people said *Baptis-me, Chatechis-me, beas-tes, pries-tes, clo-thes*, and so on – even today these pronunciations can be heard in some old people's speech.[34] In the Metrical Psalms (126.1) *mou-thes* still has two syllables. In some cases both pronunciations were used: as in *babe, clemence, excellence, eminence*, etc and *ba-be, clemen-ce, excellen-ce, eminen-ce*, etc, and people eventually began to write these words as *baby, clemency, excellency, eminency*, etc (to make it clear that the final *e* had not disappeared); *cf naught, naughty* (originally *naugh-te*). Today we still call a Moor a

---

[33] The quadrisyllabic pronunciation of *commandement* is said by Hart as early as 1569 to be either a spelling pronunciation or an imitation of French.
[34] No other sixteenth- or seventeenth-century writers record these pronunciations; if Wallis heard them at all they must have been spelling pronunciations.

58 C. I. S. II. DE PRONUNCIATIONE.

naughte). Sic etiamnum Maurum dicimus *a
blackamore* (hoc eft, *blac-ke-more)* retento
veftigio priftini *e:* quod (elifo *e* muto) potius effet *black-more.* Atque huc etiam
fpectat, quod *lucre, theatre, chambre, numbre, acre, Whitacre, Gatacre, eagre, vinegre,
fepulchre,* aliaque quae olim per *e* foemininum fcriberentur (quod jam in mutum tranf-
iit) nunc potius fcribantur *luker, theater,
chamber, number, aker, Whitaker, Gataker,
eager, vineger, fepulcher,* etc.
Atque hoc eo magis patet, quia ejusmodi *e*
mutum antiquitus videmus perpetuo annecti
vocabulis plurimis, ubi jam plerumque o-
mittitur, ut *darke* obfcurus, *marke* noto, *felfe*
propria perfona, *leafe* folium, *waite* exfpec-
to, aliisque innumeris, in quibus nulla patet
vel probabilis conjectura cur annecteretur,
nifi quod pronunciarentur *dar-ke, mar-ke,
fel-fe, lea-fe, wai-te,* etc. Nam ad producendam fyllabam (qui praecipuus nunc eft
ipfius *e* ufus) omnino inutile eft: vel enim
fyllaba non producitur, vel diphthongo illud fatis innuitur. Quid, quod et in vocibus
have habeo, *crave* peto, *lĭve* vivo, *lŏve* amo,
dŏve columba, etc. confona *v* confpicitur ante *e* finale mutum, quae tamen nufquam in-
venitur fyllabam claudere? Item in vocibus
force vis, *fpace* fpatium, *ftrange* extraneus,
rage iracundia, aliisque multis, ante *e* finale mutum, reperiuntur *c* et *g*, molliori fono prolata; nulla vero conjectura fuppetit
cur naturalem fuum fonum exuerent nifi
propter fonum fequentis *e.* Praefertim
cum

---

25 *lĭve* vivo, *lŏve* amo: 4th–6th
32 nulla vero conjectura: 1st has *nulla vero vel conjectura*

blackamore (that is, *blac-ke-more*), with a trace of the original *e*. If the *e mute* had dropped out, it would be *black-more*.[35] It is also relevant that *lucre, theatre, chambre, numbre, acre, Whitacre, Gatacre, eagre, vinegre, sepulchre*, and other words formerly written with *feminine e* (now mute) are more likely nowadays to be spelt *luker, theater, chamber, number, aker, Whitaker, Gataker, eager, vineger, sepulcher*, etc.[36]

This becomes even more obvious[37] when we see that this *e mute* was originally always a part of many words, in which it is now normal to omit it, such as *darke, marke, selfe, leafe, waite*, and countless others, where the only reasonable explanation for the *e mute* being there is that these words were pronounced *dar-ke, mar-ke, sel-fe, lea-fe, wai-te*, etc. The *e* here has no effect on the length of the syllable (which is the main purpose of *e* nowadays); either the syllable is short, or, if it is long, the length is sufficiently shown by the diphthong. Another indication is the fact that in the words *have, crave, live, love, dove*, etc the consonant *v* occurs before a final *e mute*, though it is never found in final position in a syllable. Similarly in the words *force, space, strange, rage*, and many others *c* and *g* appear before final *e mute* with their softer pronunciation. The only possible reason for this change from their natural sound, seems to be the *e* which follows them; this is made even more likely by the

---

[35] See Lehnert (1936, §§ 163–4).
[36] The *-er* spelling is normal in American English today in *theater, center* etc. For Gataker see *p* 169, note 57.
[37] This paragraph originally followed immediately after *e pronunciandum foret* on *p* 240 ('final *e* had still to be pronounced'), and so it is to this he is referring when he goes on: 'This becomes even more obvious . . .'.

C. I. S. II. DE PRONUNCIATIONE. 59

cum hujusmodi vocum magna copia ad nos
a Gallis devenerint, apud quos etiamnum
manet non modo eadem ſcriptura, ſed et
prolatio *e* finalis foeminini: Quamvis et
apud eos parcius nunc dierum quam olim
prolatum videatur; et quidem a celeriter
loquentibus ſaepiſſime ſupprimatur (licet
eorum Grammaticae nondum doceant ſup-
primendum); eaque prolatio, quae quotidie
parcior evadit, brevi fortaſſe tam apud illos, quam apud nos, penitus evanitura eſt.
Certiſſimum autem hujus rei indicium eſt ex
antiquis Poetis petendum; apud quos reperitur illud *e* promiſcue vel conſtituere vel
non conſtituere novam ſyllabam, prout ratio carminis poſtulaverit (quod et de Gallorum *e* foeminino aliquatenus verum eſt,
quod, etiam non ſuadente Grammatica, poë-
ſeos ratione ſaepe abjicitur): Unde colligi-
tur, ipſum olim pronunciatum quidem, quia
quandoque, ſed debilius, quia non ſemper,
ſyllabam conſtituat; nempe, ut fit nunc dierum in *heaven* coelum, *ever* ſemper, etc.
quae promiſcue vel pro monoſyllabis vel
pro diſſyllabis apud Poetas occurrunt, ultimo ſcilicet *e* vel prolato vel quaſi per Syncopen extrito prout carminis ratio poſtulaverit. Sic *nation, ſtation*, aliaque iſtiusmo-
di multa, nunc pro diſſyllabis, nunc pro
triſyllabis occurrunt, prout opus fuerit.

Quanquam vero nunc dierum non ſonetur Ejus uſus.
illud *e* mutum, non tamen prorſus otioſum
eſt. Nam, praeterquam quod indicio eſt
voces illas pluribus olim ſyllabis, quam nunc,

fuiſſe

7 supprimatur: 1st–4th have *supprimitur*
20 olim pronunciatum: 1st–3rd have *sonari*, 4th has *olim sonatum*
28–30 Sic *nation* . . . opus fuerit: 5th–6th

fact that a very large number of words of this kind have come to us from the French, who not only spell them as we do, but also pronounce the final *feminine e*. But even in French it seems to be pronounced less often now than it used to be; and it is very frequently left out when speaking quickly, though their grammars do not yet recommend this omission. So perhaps *e mute*, which is to be heard less often every day, will soon disappear entirely, both in French and in English.

The old poets give a very clear pointer towards this; in their works you will find that this *e* may or may not constitute an extra syllable, according to the demands of the metre. (This is partly true of French *feminine e* also; it is often left out to suit the metre, even when the grammar is against its omission.) One gathers from this that originally it was pronounced (because sometimes it constituted a syllable), but it must have been pronounced weakly (because it did not always constitute a syllable). We have examples today in *heaven*, *ever*, etc, which occur in the poets either as monosyllables or as dissyllables, without any distinction, the final *e* being either pronounced or elided by a kind of syncope, according to the demands of the metre. This applies also to the words *nation*, *station*, and many others of a similar kind, which occur as dissyllables or as trisyllables according to what is required.[38]

THE USE OF E MUTE

Although *e mute* is not sounded nowadays it is not completely superfluous. Apart from the fact that it indicates that certain words were originally pronounced with more syllables than they are now,

---

[38] For a summary of contemporary evidence for this pronunciation see Dobson, *p* 846 *ff*.

60   DE PRONUNCIATIONE. C.I. S. II.

fuiſſe pronunciatas; his tribus ſaltem uſibus adhuc inſervit. 1. Ut praecedentis vocalis quantitas conſervetur, quae ſi producta olim fuerit (vel nunc futura eſſet, ſi pronuncia-retur *e* finale) manet etiamnum productum quamvis illud *e* nunc ſit mutum: Ita voca-bula *bat* veſpertilio, *mat* teges, *hat* pileus, *fil* impleo, *mil* mola, *wil* voluntas, etc. corri-piuntur; at *bate* contentio, *mate* ſodalis, *hate* odi, *file* lima, *mile* milliare, *wile* ſtratage-ma, etc. producuntur; utraque tamen mo-noſyllaba. 2. Ut literarum *c, g*, et *th*, ſo-nus mollior innuatur, quae ſecus fortius pronunciandae forent: ut *húge* grande, *ſince* poſtquam, *breathe* ſpiro, *ſeethe* coquo, *wreathe*, torqueo, etc. quae ſi *e* deeſſet for-tius eſſent pronuncianda, ut *hug* amplector, *ſink* mergor, *breath* ſpiritus, *ſee'th* videt, etc. 3. Ut *v* conſona poſt vocalem, diſtinguatur ab *u* vocali, ut in *have* habeo, *crave* precor, *ſave* conſervo, etc. ne putentur ut *hau, crau, ſau*, pronuncianda: cum autem nunc die-rum *v* conſona ab *u* vocali, diſtincto charac-tere ſcribatur, fieri poteſt ut *e* mutum hoc in caſu poſthac aliquando omittatur.

Quando
redundat.

Quando autem nulla praedictarum ratio-num urget continuationem ipſius *e*, ab ac-curatioribus typographis nunc dierum omit-titur: niſi quod poſt *l*, et *r*, alii conſonae ſubjunctum, a pleriſque adhuc retineatur, ut in *candle* candela, *handle* tracto, *tittle* punctulum, *fiddle* fidicula, *wrangle* litigo, *poſſible* poſſibilis, *legible* legibilis, etc. in qui-bus nulli nunc inſervit uſui, adeoque non   incom-

---

1 fuisse pronunciatas: 1st has *pronunciari*
18 *sink* mergor: 4th–6th
29 et *r*: 5th–6th

it still serves at least three purposes: (i) It ensures that the quantity of the preceding vowel remains the same; if the vowel was formerly long (or if it would now be long, given that the final *e* were pronounced) it remains long today, even though the *e* is now silent. So the words *bat*, *mat*, *hat*, *fil* [fill], *mil* [mill], *wil* [will], etc are short, whereas *bate*, *mate*, *hate*, *fîle*, *mîle*, *wîle*, etc are long, though both sets are monosyllables.

(ii) It indicates the softer pronunciation of the letters *c*, *g*, and *th*; without it they would have to be given their stronger sound. For instance, *huge*, *since*, *breathe*, *seethe*, *wreathe*, etc without the *e* would be pronounced with the stronger sound like *hug*, *sink*, *breath*, *see'th*, etc.

(iii) It helps to distinguish the consonant *v*, when it follows a vowel, from the vowel *u*, as in *have*, *crave*, *save*, etc, and prevents anyone thinking they should be pronounced *hau*, *crau*, *sau*. However, since nowadays the consonant *v* is written with a different symbol from the vowel *u*, in future *e mute* may perhaps sometimes be omitted in cases of this sort.[39]

REDUNDANCY OF E MUTE

When none of the above reasons requires this *e* to be used, the more accurate printers leave it out nowadays. It is often left in after *l* and *r* when they follow another consonant, in *candle*, *handle*, *little*, *fiddle*, *wrangle*, *possible*, *legible*, etc though it serves no purpose now,

[39] See note 15, *p* 225.

incommode omitti poterit : At in *idle* otio-
fus, *trifle* nuga, *title* titulus, *fable* fabula,
table tabula, *able* potis, *noble* nobilis, etc.
potius retinendum videtur, ut praecedentis
vocalis productionem notet. Sic in *lucre*
lucrum, *acre* acra, ager; atque, olim, in
multis aliis, ut *theatre*, *vinegre*, etc. quae
nunc potius fcribuntur *theater*, *vineger*, etc.
Verum *child* puer, *wild* fylveftris, imman-
fuetus, *mild* mitis, et fimilia, rectius fine finali *e* fcribuntur; quamvis enim producatur
vocalis *i*, non poteft tamen illud ex appofito
e finali fatis infinuari; fi enim illud *e* non
modo apponeretur, fed et pronunciaretur,
non tamen *i* fed *l* clauderet priorem fyllabam, acfi fcriberentur *chil-de*, *wil-de*, *mil-de*,
quare et *i* nihilominus pro vocali brevi re-
putanda videretur, utpote quae fyllabam
non terminet; non autem *chi-lde*, *mi-lde*,
wi-lde, cum *ld* nunquam inchoent fyllabam : Atque idem dicendum eft de *mind*
mens, *find* invenio, *bind* ligo, etc. Verum in voce *Chrift* (quae apud nos producto fono proferri folet) productio vocalis ex
appofito *e* fatis innui poterit, acfi fcripta
fupponatur *Chri-fte ;* nam et ejusmodi divi-
fionem patitur analogia linguae Anglicanae, et in Χρι-ςὸς, unde defcendit, ejusmodi
agnofcitur fyllabarum divifio; fed hîc mos
aliter obtinuit ut *Chrift* fcribatur ; et quidem ipfius derivata, *Chriftian*, etc. pronunciantur per *ĭ* exile feu breve; quin et ipfum
Chrift apud Scotos.

Voca-

5–8 Sic in *lucre . . . vineger*, etc: 5th–6th
32–33 quin et ipsum *Christ* apud Scotos: 5th–6th

and could easily be left out. However in *îdle*, *trîfle*, *tîtle*, *fable*, *table*, *able*, *nôble*, etc it seems better to keep it, to show the length of the preceding vowel; and this applies also to *lucre*, *acre*, and originally applied to many other words such as *theatre*, *vinegre*, etc. But *chîld*, *wîld*, *mîld*, and similar words are better spelt without a final *e*; because although the vowel *î* is long, the addition of final *e* is not enough to indicate this. If the *e* were pronounced as well as being inserted, the previous syllable would not end in *i* but in *l*, as if the words were written *chil-de*, *wil-de*, *mil-de*; so it appears that the *i* would have to be regarded as short, as it would not be final in the syllable. *Chî-lde*, *mî-lde*, *wî-lde* are not possible divisions, because *-ld* never begins a syllable.[40] The same thing applies to *mînd*, *fînd*, *bînd*, etc, but in the word *Chrîst* (which is usually pronounced long in English) the addition of *e* is enough to show that the vowel is long, if we assume it to be written *Chrî-ste*; for the structure of the English language permits this kind of division, and the same syllable division is recognised in *Χρι-στός*, from which it is derived. However our custom is different, and we write *Christ*; in fact, words derived from it – *Christian*, etc – are pronounced with a *thin* or *short* *i*, as the word *Christ* itself is by the Scots.

---

[40] This argument would at first appear to apply also to *idle*, *title*, quoted above, because *tl*, *dl* never appear as syllable-initial releasing clusters in English, except as a variant pronunciation of *kl*, *gl*. This variant pronunciation was well illustrated by Robinson (1617), who exemplifies its use in such words as *claim*, *clean*, and *glory*; see Dobson (1947), *p* 58. However, they may occur as releasing clusters within polysyllabic words, such as *Atlantic* (Abercrombie (1967), *p* 77).

62   DE PRONUNCIATIONE. C. I. S. II.

Quando manet in medio. Vocabula per *e* mutum terminata, quamvis (five in derivatis, five in compofitis) incrementum finale adfcifcant, retinent tamen, fi opus eft, fuum *e* mutum, quod eodem nunc munere quo prius fungitur.

Vix autem ufpiam in medio dictionis reperitur *e* mutum quod non ab origine fuerat finale. Sic *miles* milliaria, *wiles* ftratagemata, *graves* fepulcra, *lives* vitae, *defiles* polluit, *believes* credit, *rarely* rare, *finely* accurate, *chargeable* fumptuofus, *changeable* mutabilis, *unchangeablenefs* immutabilitas, *likenefs* fimilitudo, *enducement* argumentum, *enforcement* coactio, *commencement* principium, comitia, *advancement* promotio, *improvement* melioratio, *candle-ftick* candelabrum, aliaque innumera, retinent *e* mutum; quia in *mile*, *wile*, *grave*, *life*, *defile*, *believe*, *rare*, *fine*, *charge*, *change*, *unchangeable*, *like*, *enduce*, *enforce*, *commence*, *advance*, *improve*, *candle*, etc. ejusmodi *e* mutum eisdem rationibus adfcriptum fuerat quae adhuc manent; ideo tamen in illis non fonatur, quia nec in his; utrobique tamen non dubito fuiffe aliquando pronunciatum, non minus quam in voce *commandement* mandatum, ubi adhuc pronunciari folet.

Quando fit fonorum. Siquando tamen voces per *e* mutum terminatae ejusmodi argumentum finale affumant, ut accidentalis literarum illigabilium neceffitas poftulaverit interventum vocalis, illud *e* quod prius mutum erat nunc fonabitur, vel (fiquis ita loqui malit) *e* fonans ipfius

fius

2 quamvis (sive: 1st–4th have *quamvis deinceps* (*sive*
29 argumentum: misprint for *augmentum* of 1st–5th

[250]

RETENTION MEDIALLY

Words which end in *e mute* retain it, if necessary, even when they acquire a final suffix, whether in a derivation or a compound form, and it fulfils the same function as before. You scarcely ever find *e mute* in the middle of a word, unless it was originally final. *Mîles, wîles, graves, lîves, defîles, believes, rarely, fînely, chargeable, changeable, unchangeableness, likeness, enducement, enforcement, commencement, advancement, improvement, candle-stick*, and many other words keep the *e mute*, because in *mîle, wîle, grave, lîfe, defîle, believe, rare, fîne, charge, change, unchangeable, lîke, enduce, enforce, commence, advance, improve, candle*, etc this *e mute* was written, and it is still required for the same reasons. It is not pronounced in the former group because it is not pronounced in the latter. However, no doubt at one time it was pronounced in both these groups, as it still is, usually, in the word *commandement*.[41]

WHEN PRONOUNCED

When words ending in *e mute* are followed by a termination, and the result is an inadmissible combination of letters, which demand a vowel between them, the *e* which was previously mute is pronounced, or to put it another way a 'sounding' *e* replaces it.[42] Most cases of

---

[41] *Cf: p* 241 and note 33.
[42] Lehnert remarks (§ 160) that in fact the vowel was *i* and not *e* in these endings and in *-eth*, and says that Wallis was mistaking the quality. However, Wallis may perhaps be concerned only with the spelling here and so be implying nothing about the pronunciation; he says that a 'sounding' *e* replaces the *mute e*, but he does not specifically identify it with *masculine* or *feminine e*.

C. I. S. II. DE PRONUNCIATIONE. 63

ſius loco interſeretur. Atque hoc praeſertim accidit in formando Nominum numero plurali, Adjeﬆivis poſſeſſivis, et in tertiis perſonis Verborum; ut in *churches* eccleſiae, *houſes* domicilia, *priſes* pretia, *boxes* pyxides, *víces* vitia, *rages* furit, *chooſes* eligit, etc. ubi non tam analogia flexionis, quam concurſus literarum illigabilium, ſonum illum poſtulat (vix poteſt enim ſonus finalis *s*, immediate ſequi conſonas *ſ, z, x, ſh*, vel etiam *c, g, ch*, mollius prolatas): Nam, ubi haec neceſſitas non poſtulat, *e* vel non apparet, vel ſaltem non ſonatur; ut in *hands* manus, *lands* terrae, *miles* milliaria, *tends* tendit, *makes* facit, etc. At in *tendeth, maketh*, etc. ſonatur *e*, non quod erat mutum, ſed quod eſt terminationis *eth*.

Quando terminatio, poſt *e* mutum aſſumpta, a vocali incipit, illud *e* plerumque prorſus evaneſcit, et conſona praecedens in eandem ſyllabam cum ſequente terminatione coaleſcit. Ideoque melius ſcribuntur *ha-ving* habens, *gĭ-ving* dans, *lo-veth* amat, *dan-ceth*, ſaltat, etc. quam *have-ing, give-ing, love-eth, dance-eth*, etc. Pertinent enim conſonae finales non proprie ad ſyllabam praecedentem, quamvis propter defeﬆum propriae vocalis ad illam neceſſario relegatae fuerunt (ut cum Graece μὲτ vel μετ’ per Acopen, vel Apoſtrophum, pro μέτα ſcribitur), ideoque, adveniente vocali nova, cum illa potius coaleſcit.

Quando eliditur.

Quod etiam apud Hebraeos (quos hac in re imitamur) perpetuo fit: ut in voce טוב *tobh* bonus,

---

9 vix potest: 1st–4th have *Non potest*
28 fuerunt: 1st has *fuerant*

this kind occur in the formation of the plural of nouns, in possessive adjectives and in the third person of verbs, for example *churches, houses, prîses, boxes, vîces, rages* (vb), *chooses*, etc. The *e* is required not so much to satisfy the demands of the inflexional pattern, as to separate letters which cannot occur together (it is virtually impossible to have a final *s* immediately after the consonants *s, z, x, sh*, or after *c, g, ch* when they have their softer sound). When no considerations of this kind apply, either the *e* does not occur at all, or, if it occurs, it is not pronounced: as in *hands, lands, mîles, tends, makes*, etc. In *tendeth, maketh*, etc the *e* is pronounced, but here it is part of the termination *eth* and not *e mute*.

WHEN ELIDED

When a termination which is added after *e mute* begins with a vowel, the *e mute* usually disappears completely, and the preceding consonant joins up with the following termination to form one syllable. The spellings *ha-ving, gi-ving, lo-veth, dan-ceth* are preferable to *have-ing, give-ing, love-eth, dance-eth* etc. The reason is that the final consonants do not really belong to the preceding syllable, although the loss of their own vowel[43] has forced them to attach themselves to it (just as when, in Greek, μέτ or μετ' is written instead of μετά by apocope or apostrophe); so when another vowel appears the consonant tends to join that in preference.

This is a regular feature of Hebrew too (which provides us with a model here); for instance in the word טוב, *tobh* (good) the consonant

---

[43] The vowel that has become *e mute*.

64 DE PRONUNCIATIONE. C.I.S.II.

bonus, confona ב propter defectum propriae vocalis vocali praecedenti fubjungitur, fed coacte quidem quum י *holem* fit vocalis longa, quae (etiam apud illos) deberet potius fyllabam claudere; ideoque in טובה *to-bha* bona, טובים *to-bhim* boni, ubi advenit nova vocalis, confona ב in unam cum illa coalefcit fyllabam, priorem vocalem deferens cui non fine quadam quafi violentia fuerat annexa; quod fi confona brevis fuiffet, quae fuapte natura confonam ad fe trahit, vocalis de novo adveniens poftularet vel praecedentis vocalis productionem (ut illa fyllabam clauderet), vel *Daghes* finali confonae infcribendum, ut, duplicata confona, non defit vel quae priorem claudat, vel quae novam inchoet fyllabam; prout ex illius linguae analogia fatis liquet.

Ubi autem (apud nos) vocalis ultimae fyllabae brevis eft, poteft ea fuapte natura confonam unam vel plures poft fe admittere, easque in fua fyllaba retinere, quantumvis alia accedat vocalis. Sic *long* longus, incremento accedente fit *long-er* vel *lon-ger*, longior; nam analogia linguae utrumvis patitur; at potior videtur haec fyllabarum divifio *long-er*, partim quia fonus literae *n* ita ab ufitato ipfius fono paulum deflectit, ut folet ante literas (recte pronunciatas) *c, g, k, x,* in eadem fyllaba; partim quia *g* fonum fortiorem nacta eft, ideoque *e* mutum poft fe non habuiffe credendum eft: fi enim radix fuiffe putetur *longe*, per *g* molle potius. prolata foret, ut in voce *ftrange* extraneus.

Sic

---

10 quod si consona brevis fuisset: 3rd edition only has *quod si vocalis brevis fuisset* which appears to be what the sense requires

בּ is attached to the preceding vowel, because it has no vowel of its own; but this happens only by force of circumstances, inasmuch as וֹ *holem* is a long vowel, and in Hebrew too should end the syllable. In טוֹבָה *to-bha* (fem sing), טוֹבִים *to-bhim* (masc pl), where a new vowel has appeared, the consonant בּ joins with it to form a syllable, leaving the previous vowel, to which it had been attached only of necessity. However if the vowel[44] had been short, thus quite naturally attracting the consonant to join it, the addition of a new vowel would require either that the first vowel be lengthened (so that it could close the syllable) or that *dagesh* be added to the final consonant; this would double the consonant so that there would be one to close the first syllable and another to begin the new syllable. The structure of the language makes this quite clear.

However, in English, when the vowel of a final syllable is short, it is not against its nature to be followed by one or more consonants and to retain them in its own syllable, even though another vowel follows them. *Long*, with a termination added, becomes *long-er* or *lon-ger*;[45] the structure of the language permits either. But the division of syllables represented by *long-er* seems preferable; partly because, instead of its normal sound, the letter *n* here has the variant form which is normal when it precedes the letters *c*, *g*, *k*, *x* (rightly pronounced)[46] in the same syllable; and partly because the *g* has its stronger sound,[47] and so the assumption must be that it has not been followed by an *e mute*. For if one assumed that the root was *longe*, *g* would have to be pronounced soft, as it is in the word *strange*. Similarly from *drinke*, or *drink* we get either *drin-ker*, as if

---

[44] There is apparently a mistake in the text of all editions except the 3rd. *Consona* (consonant) appears where it is clear from the argument that *vocalis* (vowel) is intended; *cf: p* 229. The translation here follows the 3rd edition.

[45] That is, CVCC-V or CVC-CV; see note 46, *p* 161.

[46] That is to say, with their hard sounds – [k] [g].

[47] Namely, [g].

Sic a *drinke* vel *drink* poto, fit *drin-ker* po-
tator, tanquam a *drin-ke*, vel *drin-ker*, ut ab
origine *drink;* fed pofterius videtur potius
eligendum, quia *n* ita profertur ut quando
k fequitur in eadem fyllaba. Sic, *barking*
latrans vel a *bar-ke* vel a *bark* duci poteft,
ut fit vel *bar-king* vel *bark-ing*. At *dan-ger*
periculum, *ftran-ger* extraneus, dicendum
eft; non *dang-er*, *ftrang-er*, propter molliorem fonum literae *g*. In *changeable* mutabilis, dici poteft vel *change-able* (quae videri poffit fcriptio potior, propter retentum *e*
mutum), vel etiam *chan-geable*, ut maneat *e*
folummodo ut index mollioris foni, fed
quoad alia quafi fyncopata habeatur; quod
fieri videtur in voce *George*, fi nempe pro
monofyllaba habeatur; quodque fit perpetuo apud Italos in vocibus a *gj* inchoatis,
fequente *a, o,* vel *u,* in eadem fyllaba. Atque hactenus de *e* muto diximus.

I vocalis, quoties brevis eft, fonatur plerumque (ut apud Gallos aliosque) exili
fono.

Ut in *bĭt* morfus, *wĭll* volo, *ftĭll* femper,
wĭn lucro, *pĭn* acicula, *sĭn* peccatum, *fĭll*
impleo.

At quoties longa eft, plerumque profertur ut Graecorum **ει**.

Ut *bíte* mordeo, *wíle* ftratagema; *ftíle* ftilus,
wíne vinum, *píne* tabe confumor, etc. eodem

F   fere

L

---

2 vel *drin-ker:* misprint for *vel drink-er* of 1st–5th

from *drin-ke*, or *drink-er*[48] as if from *drink*; the second of these seems the better, because the *n* is pronounced here as it is when *k* follows it in the same syllable. *Barking* can be derived from either *bar-ke* or *bark*, and can be divided either *bar-king*, or *bark-ing*; but the division *dan-ger*, *stran-ger*, must be preferred to *dang-er*, *strang-er* because the *g* is soft. In *changeable*, the spoken division can be either *change-able* (which may seem the better way of writing it, because of the fact that the *e mute* is retained), or *chan-geable*; the *e* is kept only to indicate the softer sound, but like other *mute e*'s is considered to have undergone syncope. This seems to apply in the word *George*, if it is to be regarded as a monosyllable; and it is normal in Italian words which begin with *gj* followed by *a*, *o*, or *u*, in the same syllable. This is all I have to say about *e mute*.

I. The vowel *i*, when short,[49] is usually pronounced with a thin sound (as it is in French and other languages); as in *bĭt*, *wĭll*, *stĭll*, *wĭn*, *pĭn*, *sĭn*, *fĭll*. But when it is long, it is usually pronounced like Greek ει,[50] in *bîte*, *wîle*, *stîle*, *wîne*, *pîne*, etc; that is, rather like

---

[48] The 6th edition has a misprint here – *drin-ker* for *drink-er*.

[49] *Written* short *i* as opposed to *written* long *i*; see *Tractatus p* 145.

[50] See *Tractatus p* 201, and note 95. For comments on the pronunciation of this vowel and the comparison with the vowel in French *main*, *pain* see Lehnert (§111) and Dobson (*pp* 234 and 659 *ff*).

fere modo, quo Gallorum *ai* in vocibus *main*
manus, *pain* panis, etc. nempe fonum habet
compofitum ex Gallorum *è* foeminino, et *i*
vel *y*. Hunc autem fonum fuaferim ego fic
femper pingi *î* fuprapofito Latinorum accentu circumflexo, ut a fono exiliori diftinguatur.

Si quando fonus *i* exilis occurrat producen-
dus, fcribitur plerumque non per *i*, fed per
ee vel *ie;* ut in *fteel* chalybs, *feen* vifum,
feel tactu fentio, *field* ager, *fhield* fcutum,
etc.

O.   *O* breve eodem modo pronunciatur quo
Germanorum *a*, vel *o* apertum feu pingue, nifi quod corripiatur.

Eundem fonum productum exprimunt Án-
gli per *au* vel *aw*, rarius per *á:* Idem enim
eft fonus primae vocalis in *mollify* emollio,
maul malleus; *fond* indulgens, *fawn* hinnulus; *folly* ftultitia, *fáll* cafus; etc. nifi quod
hic productus, illic correptus fit.

Non raro tamen (fed male) pro *ŏ* brevi, fonatur *ù* obfcurum, ore nempe minus aperto (in quo folo ab illo differt) ut cum *condi-*
tion conditio, *London* Londinum, *compafs*
circuitus, etc. negligentius efferuntur, acfi
fcripta effent *cundition, Lundun, cumpafs,*
etc. et fic fere proferri folent *còme* venio,
dòne factum, *sòme* aliquis, *sòn* filius, *lòve* a-
mo, *dòve* columba, et pauca forfan alia. Sonus hic, fi quando opus fit, notari poterit
vel aliquantulum mutato charactere literae *o*,
vel,

9 fcribitur plerumque: 1st–4th have *fcribitur illud plerumque*
29–30 *lòve* amo, *dòve* columba: 4th–6th

French *ai* in the words *main*, *pain*, etc, with a sound consisting of French *feminine e* and *i* or *y*. I would suggest that the symbol *î* always be used for this sound, namely that a Latin circumflex accent should be written above *i*, to distinguish it from the thinner sound. If the sound of *thin i* occurs in its long form it is usually written not with *i*, but with *ee* or *ie* as in *steel, seen, feel, field, shield*, etc.

O. Short *o* is pronounced exactly like German *a*, or like *open* or *fat o*, except that it is short.[51] The long version of this sound is represented in English by *au* or *aw*, or more rarely by *â*. So the first vowel in the words *mollify*, *maul* [hammer]; *fond*, *fawn*; *folly*, *fâll*, etc is the same in every case, except that in the first word of each pair it is short and in the second long. Short *ŏ* is often, wrongly, given the sound of obscure *ù*, which requires a smaller aperture of the mouth (this is the only difference), as when *condition*, *London*, *compass*, are carelessly pronounced as if written *cundition*, *Lundun*, *cumpass* etc; this is also the usual pronunciation of *còme*, *dòne*, *sòme*, *sòn*, *lòve*, *dòve*, and perhaps a few other words.[52] If it proved necessary, one could represent this sound either by changing the symbol for letter *o* slightly, or, failing a new symbol, by putting a

[51] *Tractatus p* 139 and note 20.
[52] *Tractatus p* 141 (*u obscurum*) and note 23.

vel, propter characterum defectum, accentu gravi supra posito, ò.

O longum profertur ore rotundo; ut Graecorum ω et Gallorum *au.*

Ut in vocibus *sóle* solus, solea, *chóse* elegit, *móre* magis, plus, etc. Distinctionis gratia accentu circumflexo superne notari potest.

U vocalis, quando corripitur, effertur **v.** sono obscuro.

Ut in *but* sed, *cut* seco, *bur* lappa, *burst* ruptus, *curst* maledictus, etc. Sonum hunc Galli proferunt in ultima syllaba vocis *serviteur.* Differt a Gallorum *e* foeminino, non aliter quam quod ore minus aperto efferatur. Discrimen hoc animadvertent Angli dum pronunciant voces Latinas *iter, itur; ter ter, turtur; cerdo, surdo; ternus, Turnus; terris, turris; refertum, furtum,* etc.

U longum effertur ut Gallorum *ú* exile.

Ut in *lúte* barbitum, *múte* mutus, *múse* musa, meditor, *cúre* cura, etc. Sono nempe quasi composito ex ĭ et *w.* Hunc a sono superiori distinguere licet vel punctulo, vel accentu acuto supra posito; sic *ŭ, ú.*

F 2   S E C T.

17–18 *ter ter . . . furtum:* 4th–6th
  24 acuto: 5th–6th

grave accent above it, *ò*.

Long *o* is pronounced with the mouth rounded, like Greek ω and French *au*; for example, in the words *sôle, chôse, môre*. A circumflex accent can be put over it to distinguish it.[53]

U. The vowel *u*, when short, has an obscure sound, as in *but, cut, bur, burst, curst* (adj).[54] This is the same as the sound which occurs in the last syllable of the French word *serviteur*. It differs from French *feminine e* only in having a smaller opening of the mouth. English people will perceive this difference if they say the Latin words *iter, itur*; *ter ter, turtur*; *cerdo, surdo*; *ternus, Turnus*; *terris, turris, refertum, furtum*, etc.

Long *u* is pronounced like French *thin ú*, as in *lúte, múte, múse, cúre*, etc with a sound resembling the combination of *ī* and *w*. It can be distinguished from the previous sound by putting a dot or an acute accent above it, *eg ù, ú*.[55]

---

[53] *Tractatus p* 147, and note 29.
[54] *Tractatus p* 141, and Introduction *p* 49.
[55] *Tractatus p* 149, and Introduction *p* 49.

SECT. III.

De Diphthongis.

ai, ay.   *Ai* vel *ay* fonum exprimit compofitum ex *á* Anglico (hoc eft, exili) correpto, et *y*.

Ut in voce *day* dies, *praife* laus, etc.

au, aw.   *Au* vel *aw*, recte pronunciatum, fonum exhiberet compofitum ex Anglorum *á* brevi, et *w*. Sed a plerisque nunc dierum effertur fimpliciter ut Germanorum *â* pingue : fono nempe literae *â* dilatato, et fono literae *w* prorfus fuppreffo.

Eodem nempe fono efferunt *áll* omnes, *aul*, *awl*, fubula; *cáll* voco, *caul*, *cawl*, omentum, vel etiam tiara muliebris; etc.

ea.   *Ea* effertur nunc dierum ut *é* longum : fono ipfius *a* penitus fuppreffo, et fono literae *e* producto.

Nempe illud folum praeftat *a*, ut fyllaba reputetur longa. Ita, *met* obviam factus, *meat* victus; *fet* fifto, federe facio, *feat* fella; etc. non fono differunt nifi quod vocalis illic correpta, hic producta intelligatur.

Ee

Section 3
The diphthongs[56]

Ai, or *ay*, represents a sound made up of a short English *á* (that is, *thin a*) and *y*; as in the words *day*, *praise* etc.

Au, or *aw*, if properly pronounced, would represent a sound made up of short English *á* and *w*. But many people nowadays pronounce it as a simple vowel, like German *fat â*, by lengthening the sound of the letter *â* and completely omitting the sound of *w*, as in the words *âll*; *aul*, *awl*; *câll*; *caul*, *cawl* [a membrane, or a woman's hat] etc.[57]

Ea is nowadays pronounced like long *é*,[58] omitting the sound of *a* completely and lengthening the sound of the letter *e*. The only function of the *a* is to show that the syllable is long, as in *met*, *meat*; *set*, *seat*; etc, where the only difference in pronunciation is that the vowel of the first of each pair is short and that of the second long.

---

[56] Here again Wallis's starting-point is the written symbols. The 'diphthongs' are really digraphs. Wallis does not include *oa* in this section, though he should do so to be consistent.
[57] *Tractatus p* 139.
[58] *Cf: Tractatus p* 145, and note 27.

Ee vel *ie* effertur ut Gallorum *i* (hoc est, *ee, ie.* *i* exile) productum.

Eundem nempe fonum quem fcribunt Galli *fin*, *vin*, fcriberent Angli *feen*, *veen*, vel forte *fien*, *vien*. Hoc modo fcribunt *fiend* cacodaemon, *feen* vifum, etc.

Ei vel *ey* fonatur per *é* clarum feu maf-*ei, ey.* culinum, et *y*; vel etiam fimpliciter per *é* clarum, fuppreffo fono *y*.

Ut in *receive* recipio, *feize* apprehendo, *de-ceit* dolus, etc. Nonnulli tamen plenius ef-ferunt, acfi per *ai* fcripta effent.

Eu, *ew*, *eau*, fonantur per *è* clarum et *w*. *eu, ew, eau.*

Ut in *neuter* neutralis, *few* pauci, *beauty* pulchritudo. Quidam tamen paulo acutius efferunt acfi fcriberentur *niewter*, *fiew*, *bieuty*, vel *niwter*, *fiw*, *biwty*; praefertim in vocibus *new* novus, *knew* fciebam, *fnew* ningebat. At prior pronunciatio rectior eft.

Oo fonatur ut Germanorum *û* pingue, *oo.* feu Gallorum *ou*.

Ut in vocibus *good* bonus, *ftood* ftabam, *root* radix, *foot* pes, *loofe* laxus, *loose* laxo, amit-to, etc.

Oi, *oy*, efferuntur per *o* apertum feu cla-*oi, oy.* rum fed correptum, et *y*.

F 3   Ut

13 è clarum: 1st has é clarum (the correct accentuation)
25 o apertum: 1st has ó, 4th has ô (*cf: p* 6.6)

Ee, or *ie* is pronounced like French long *i* (that is, *thin i*).[59] The sound which the French write as *fin, vin* would be written in English as *feen, veen*, or perhaps *fien, vien*. *Fiend* and *seen* are examples of this spelling.

Ei, or *ey*, represents the sound of *clear* or *masculine é* and *y*; or simply of *clear é*, without the *y*: as in *receive, seize, deceit*, etc. Some pronounce these words with a fuller sound, as if they were written with *ai*.[60]

Eu, ew, eau are made up of *clear é*[61] and *w*; as in *neuter, few, beauty*, though they are given a rather sharper pronunciation by some, as if they were written *niewter, fiew, bieuty* or *niwter, fiw, biwty*, [62] especially in the words *new, knew, snew* (past tense of snow). However, the first pronunciation is more correct.

Oo is pronounced like German *fat û*, or French *ou*; as in the words *good, stood, root, foot, loose* [adj]; *loose* [vb] etc.

Oi, oy are pronounced with *open* or *clear o*, in its short form, and

---

[59] *Tractatus p* 145 *f.*
[60] Presumably *thin a* and *y*; see Lehnert (1936), § 135; Dobson (1968), *p* 650.
[61] *Masculine e*; see *Tractatus p* 145, and Introduction *p* 49.
[62] That is, with *thin i* and *w*.

70 ĐE PRONUNCIATIONE. C. I. S. III.

Ut in *noise* ſtrepitus, *boys* pueri, *toys* nugae, *toyl* labor, *oil* oleum. Nonnulli tamen in quibusdam ſaltem vocabulis potius per *ò* vel *ù* obſcurum efferunt, ut *tòil, òil*, vel *tŭyl, ŭyl*.

ou, ow.

Ou et *ow* duplicem ſonum obtinent; alterum clariorem, alterum obſcuriorem. In quibusdam vocabulis effertur ſono clariori per *o* apertum, et *w*.

Ut in *ſóul* anima, *ſóuld* vendebam, venditum, *ſnów* nix, *knów* ſcio, *ſów* ſero, ſuo, *ówe* debeo, *bówl* poculum, etc. quo etiam ſono et *ó* ſimplex nonnunquam effertur, nempe ante *ld*, ut in *góld* aurum, *ſcóld* rixor, *hóld* teneo, *cóld* frigidus, *óld* ſenex, antiquus, etc. et ante *ll* in *póll* caput, *róll* volvo, *tóll* vectigal, etc. Sed et haec omnia ab aliis efferuntur ſimpliciter per *ó* rotundum, acſi ſcripta eſſent *ſóle, ſóld, ſnó*, etc.

In aliis vocabulis obſcuriori ſono efferuntur; ſono nempe compoſito ex *ò* vel *ù* obſcuris, et *w*.

Ut in *hòuſe* domus, *mòuſe* mus, *lòwſe* pediculus, *bòul* globulus, *òur* noſter, *òut* ex, *òwl* bubo, *tòwn* oppidum, *fòul* immundus, *fòwl* volucris, *bòw* flecto, *bòugh* ramus, *ſòw* ſus, etc.
At *would* vellem, *ſhould* deberem, *could* poſſem, *courſe* curſus, *court* aula, curia, et pauca forſan alia, quamvis (ut proxime praecedentia) per *òu* pronunciari debeant, vulgo

---

4 *tŭyl, ŭyl*: 1st–5th have *tŭyl, ŭyl*
9–10 venditum: 5th–6th
15 *róll* volvo: 4th–6th

y; as in *noise, boys, toys, toyl, oil.* However in some words at any rate people pronounce them with obscure *ò* or obscure *ù*;[63] for example, *tòil, òil* or *tŭyl, ŭyl.*

Ou and *ow* have two possible sounds, the one clearer and the other obscurer. In some words the clearer sound consisting of *open o* and *w* occurs; as in *sóul, sóuld* [sold], *snów, knów, sów, ówe, ból*, etc, and sometimes *ô* by itself has this sound, namely when it occurs before *ld*, as in *gôld, scôld, hôld, côld, ôld*, etc, and before *ll* in *pôll, rôll, tôll*, etc. But all of these words are pronounced by others with the simple sound of *round ô*, as if they were written *sôle, sôld, snô*, etc.

In certain other words *ou* and *ow* have the obscurer sound, composed of *obscure ŏ* or obscure *ù*, and *w*; as in *hòuse, mòuse, lòwse, bòul* [ball], *òur, òut, òwl, tòwn, fòul, fòwl, bòw* [bend], *bòugh, sòw* [pig], etc. But *would, should, could, course, court* and perhaps a few other words, which, like the ones just above, ought to be pronounced with

---

[63] The accent on *u obscurum* varies. In *Tractatus p* 140, the margin and text in editions up to and including the 5th have *ŭ*, except for the 3rd edition's *û*. As it represents a short sound *ŭ* or *ù* (not *û*) would seem to be correct.

C. I. S. III. DE PRONUNCIATIONE. 71

vulgo tamen negligentius efferri folent per *oo*.

Optandum eft, in exterorum gratiam, ut Typographi fonum illum clariorem ab hoc obfcuriori diftinguerent; quod fieri poteft, fi non diftinctis characteribus, faltem fi vel illum femper accentu acuto (vel, fi libet, circumflexo) notarent; vel hunc accentu gravi: Aut etiam fi illum per *ow*, hunc per *ou* femper fcriberent.

SECT. IIII.

De Confonis aliquot conjunctis.

Gh in vocum principio ut nudum *g* durum pronunciatur.

Gh,

Ut in *ghóft* fpiritus, *gheffe* conjecturam facio.

Alias vero nunc dierum fere prorfus omittitur; fyllabam tamen producendam innuit: A quibusdam tamen (praefertim Septentrionalibus) per molliorem faltem afpirationem *h* effertur.

Ut in *míght* poteftas, *líght* lux, *níght* nox, *ríght* rectus, *fight* vifus, *figh* fingultus, *weigh* pondero, *weight* pondus, *though* quamvis, *thóught* cogitatio, *wróught* operatus eft,

F 4 *bróught*

---

3 optandum est: 1st–5th have *optandum esset*
  in exterorum gratiam: 5th–6th

[268]

òu are generally carelessly pronounced with *oo*.

It would be a good thing if the clearer of these diphthongs were distinguished by the printer from the obscurer one, for the benefit of foreigners. This could be done either by using different symbols or, failing that, by marking the clearer sound with an acute accent, or a circumflex if preferred, and the obscurer one with a grave accent; alternatively the former could always be spelt *ow* and the latter *ou*.

Section 4
Some compound consonants[64]

Gh at the beginning of words is pronounced like simple hard *g*; as in *ghost*, *ghesse*.[65] In other positions it is almost always left unpronounced, but indicates that the syllable is long. However, there are some people, especially Northerners, who pronounce it as *h*, though the aspiration may be slight.[66] It appears in *mîght*, *lîght*, *nîght*, *rîght*, *sîght*, *sîgh*, *weigh*, *weight*, *though*, *thóught*, *wróught*,

---

[64] The relation to the *Tractatus* is as follows:

Grammar (symbol)	*Tractatus* (sound)
Gh	(i) g *durum* (hard g)
	(ii) h (Northern accent)
	(iii) f
	(iv) silent
Ch	(i) ty
	(ii) k
Sh	sy
Ph	f
Th	(i) th (θ)
	(ii) dh (δ)

[65] *Cf* Grammar, *p* 227, where it is spelt *guess*, and note 20, *p* 229.
[66] *Tractatus p* 189 and Introduction *p* 60.

72 DE PRONUNCIATIONE. C. I. S. IIII.

bróught attulit, *taught* docuit, *faught* quae-
fivit, *fraught* refertus, *nought* nihil, *naught*
malus, etc. In paucis vocabulis effertur plerumque per *ff;* nempe *cough* tuffis, *tróugh*
alveolus, *tough* tenax, *rough* afper, *laugh* ri-
deo, proferuntur *cöff, tröff, tuff, ruff, laff*
Inough (fingulare) fat multum, fonatur *inuff;*
at *inough* (plurale) fat multa, fonatur *enow*.

Ch.   *Ch* effertur ut Italorum *c* ante *e* et *i*; fono nempe compofito ex *ty.*

Excipe vocabula a Graecis et Hebraeis deducta (praefertim nomina propria, et ubi
fequitur confonans); haec enim durius, ut
per *c* vel *k* efferuntur. Dicimus tamen *Ra-*
chel, Cherub, Archbifhop, (cum paucis aliis)
admodum Anglorum.

Sh.   *Sh* effertur ut Gallorum *ch,* vel *fy.*
Ph.   *Ph* effertur ut *f:* ufurpatur vix alibi
quam in vocibus a Graecis per φ fcriptis.
Th.   *Th* duplicem admittit fonum; alterum
molliorem, affinem literae *D;* alterum
fortiorem, affinem literae *T.*
Molliorem habet in Pronominibus, Re-
lativis, et Conjunctionibus, omnibus.

Ut *thou* tu, *thee* te, *thy, thine,* tuus, *the, this,*
that, hic, ille, *thefe, thofe,* hi, illi, *they* illi,
them illos, *their* illorum, *there* illic, *thence*
inde, *thither* eo, *whither* quo, *either* five,
whether

1–3 *brought* attulit, *saught* quaesivit, *fraught* refertus, *nought* nihil, *naught* malus:
    5th–6th
4–5 *tróugh* alveolus: 2nd–6th
   6 *tröff:* 4th–6th
14–16 Dicimus tamen . . . Anglorum: 5th–6th

bróught, taught, saught [sought], *fraught, nought, naught* [bad], etc.
In a few words the normal pronunciation is like *ff*; *cough, tróugh,
tough, rough, laugh,* are pronounced *cŏff, trŏff, tuff, ruff, laff. Inough*
(singular) is pronounced *inuff*, but *inough* (plural) is pronounced
enow.[67]

Ch is pronounced like Italian *c* before *e* and *i*, that is with the sound
of *ty.* Exceptions to this occur in words derived from Greek or
Hebrew (especially proper names, and when it is followed by a consonant), where it has a harder sound like *c* or *k.* However, *Rachel,
Cherub, Archbishop* and a few others are pronounced in the English
way.

Sh is pronounced like French *ch*, or like *sy.*[68]

Ph is pronounced like *f*; it is almost entirely confined to words in
which the Greeks used ϕ.[69]

Th has two sounds, one softer and similar to that of the letter *d*,
the other stronger and like that of the letter *t.*[70] It always has the
softer sound when it occurs in pronouns, relatives and conjunctions,
as in *thou, thee, thy, thine, the, this, that, these, those, they, them,
their, there, thence, thither, whither, either, whether, neither, though,*

---

[67] This distinction between singular and plural of *inough* survived until the eighteenth
century.
[68] Introduction *p* 60.
[69] *Tractatus* note 54, *p* 167; *cf* note 68, *p* 177.
[70] *Tractatus p* 173 *ff.*

whether utrum, *neither* neque, *though, although*, quamvis.

In paucis item nominibus et verbis, praefertim in *ther* finitis.

Ut *father* pater, *mother* mater, *brother* frater, *leather* corium, *weather* tempeſtas, *feather* pluma, *neather* inferior; *ſmooth* levis,
ſeethe coquo, *wreathe* torqueo, *breathe* ſpiro, *bequeath* (teſtamento) lego, *clothe* veſtio.

Alibi fere ſemper fortiorem ſeu duriorem ſonum obtinet.

Ut in Praepoſitionibus *with* cum, *without*
ſine, *within* intra, *through* per: in verbis
think cogito, *thríve* creſco, diteſco, *thrów*
projicio, *thruſt* trudo, etc. *loveth* amat,
teacheth docet, *hath* habet, *doth* agit, etc.
in Subſtantivis *thóught* cogitatio, *thígh* femur, *thing* res, *throng* turba, *death* mors,
breath halitus, *clóth* pannus, *wrath* iracundia, *length* longitudo, *ſtrength* fortitudo, etc.
et Adjectivis *thick* craſſus, denſus, *thin* ra-
rus, dilutus, tenuis, etc.
Atque hactenus, quae ad puram et genui-
nam linguae Anglicanae pronunciationem
ſpectare videntur, ſatis prolixe tradidi. Sin-
gulas vero variorum locorum dialectos, aut
affectatas muliercularum ineptias, aliosve
barbariſmos, operae pretium non eſt ut tradam; ut neque negligentiores quorundam
ſonorum prolationes, ſive quae paſſim apud
vulgus,

8–9 *breathe* spiro, *clothe* vestio: 2nd–6th
10–11 seu duriorem: 5th–6th
19 *breath* halitus, *cloth* pannus: 2nd–6th

although. The softer sound occurs also in a few nouns and verbs, especially those ending in *-ther*; for example *father, mother, brother, leather, weather, feather, neather* [lower], *smooth, seethe, wreathe, breathe, bequeath, clothe*. Elsewhere it almost always has its stronger or harder sound, as in the prepositions *with, without, within,*[71] *through*, in the verbs *think, thrîve, thrów, thrust*, etc; *loveth, teacheth, hath, doth*, etc; in the substantives *thóught, thîgh, thing, throng, death, breath, clŏth, wrath, length, strength*, etc; and in the adjectives *thick, thin*, etc.

This completes my description of all that appears to relate to a pure and authentic pronunciation of the English language; I have made it no longer than necessary. There would be no profit in describing the individual dialects of the various parts of the country, the absurdities affected by flighty women, or other 'barbarisms' of that kind. Nor is it necessary to mention the careless pronunciations of certain sounds that one may hear, whether those that are wide-

---

[71] This pronunciation of *with, without, within* is still current in Scotland and the north of England, and in the case of *with* occurs in other English accents also, before voiceless consonants (D. Jones (1956), §§ 333–4; Gimson (1962), § 11.07). See also Jespersen, *M.E.G.*, I. § 6.53.

74 DE PRONUNCIATIONE. C. I. S. IIII.

vulgus, five quae etiam apud Aulicos, aut affectatò delicatulos obtinuerunt; haec enim ego omnia dedifcenda potius quam imitanda duco. Quamvis enim non exiftimem linguam noftram a Gallicanae linguae five elegantia five morbo penitus immunem effe, quin ut inter celeriter loquendum litera nonnunquam una aut altera vel omittatur vel negligentius proferatur: illud tamen (ubi mos obtinuit) patimur magis quam jubemus; & pro tolerando potius errore, quam laudanda praxi ducimus; adeoque fiquis accuratius loqui velit, id ei laudi potius quam vituperio cedet.

Si cui autem nimis hac in re prolixus videar; fciat ille me non hoc velle, ut quilibet extraneus, dum linguam noftram addifcere fatagit, fingulos minoris notae apices exacte calleat, aut fe difcendo fatiget: fufficiet enim ad laudabilem hac in re progreffum, ut felectiores quasdam magisque generales regulas, easque non adeo multas, obfervet: Caetera vel exercitatio docebit, vel fine magno incommodo ignorari poterunt. Atque idem etiam de fequentibus judicium ferendum eft, quoties ad minutiora defcendo.

C A P.

spread among the mass of the people, or those current also in court circles or with people who affect to be fastidious.[72] All these, in my opinion, should be unlearnt rather than imitated. For while I do not believe that our language can remain entirely immune from what may be called the graces or the faults of the French language,[73] which may lead to an occasional omission (in quick speech) or a careless pronunciation of one letter or the other, my attitude to this (where it has become customary) is one of passive acceptance rather than approval. In my opinion it is not something to be praised, but a mistake which must be tolerated; if people wish to speak more carefully, they should be encouraged and not reproved.

In case anyone thinks I have been unduly prolix, I should like it to be understood that I do not expect foreigners, wishing to learn our language, to have a close knowledge of the *minutiae* which appear in smaller print,[74] or to exhaust themselves in learning these details. They will make quite satisfactory progress if they observe some of the more select and general rules, and there are not so very many of these. The rest will either come with practice or can be ignored without any great loss. The same applies in the following sections also, whenever I descend into detail.

---

[72] Introduction *p* 66.
[73] French, as a faster spoken language (*Tractatus p* 211), is held to blame for unduly quick speech in English.
[74] See Author's Preface, *p* 115 and note 41.

C. II.   DE NOMINE SUBSTANTIVO.

C A P. II.

De Anglicanae Linguae ſtructura;
et primum de nomine Subſtantivo.

Hactenus de Pronunciatione egimus: ſe-   Anglicanae
linguae faci-
litas.
quitur ut de tota Anglicani ſermonis
ſtructura agatur. Haec autem lingua
quanquam a quibusdam extraneis difficil-
ior habita fuerit (ideo forſan quia vel
nullis, vel non bene ordinatis praeceptis
in diſcendo uſi fuerint); eſt tamen revera omnium, quas ſcio, linguarum fa-
cillima; et pauciſſimis regulis tota ipſius
fabrica tradi poterit.

Has autem dum traditurus ſum, nollem exſpectetis ut ſingula artis vocabula, quae
Grammaticae Anglicanae cum aliarum linguarum Grammaticis ſunt communia, ſigilla-
tim explicarem; ut Quid ſit *Nomen, Pronomen, Verbum, Participium,* etc. Quid *Subſtantivum, Adjectivum, Simplex, Compoſitum,
Primitivum, Derivativum, Activum, Paſſivum, Tranſitivum, Intranſitivum,* etc. Quid
*Genus, Caſus, Numerus, Perſona, Modus,
Tempus,* etc. aliaque ſimilia. Eſſet enim plane ſupervacaneus labor; cum nemo ſit, Latinae linguae non prorſus ignarus, qui iſt-
haec ignorare poſſit.
Neque tamen exſpectetis vellem, ut in hac
lingua noſtra omnia Latinorum linguae penitus

CHAPTER II

The structure of the English language;[75]
the substantives

THE SIMPLICITY OF ENGLISH

I have now completed my description of the pronunciation; next to be considered is the structure of the English language as a whole. Although some foreigners think it is quite a difficult language (perhaps because they had no rules to guide them in learning it, or if they had, they were badly set out), it is really the easiest language I know of, and the whole of its structure can be contained in a very small number of rules.

In setting out these rules do not expect me to explain each individual grammatical term; these terms are used in grammars of other languages as well as English; for example, *noun, pronoun, verb, participle*, etc; *substantive, adjective, simple, compound, primitive, derivative, active, passive, transitive, intransitive*, etc; *gender, case, number, person, mood, tense*, etc, and things of this kind. It would clearly be wasted labour to explain them, because they must be familiar to anyone having even the slightest acquaintance with the Latin language.[76]

Do not expect, either, that everything in our language will be exactly equivalent to something in Latin. English, in common with

---

[75] Presumably the title of this chapter – *The structure of the English language* – is a general heading to Chapters II–XIII, though it does not appear at all in Wallis's Index.
[76] See *p* 105, note 36 and Introduction *p* 29.

76 DE NOMINE SUBSTANTIVO. C. II.

nitut respondeant. Est enim tum in hac, tum in modernis fere omnibus, a Graecae Latinaeque linguae syntaxi immanis discrepantia (inde praesertim orta, quod Casuum diversitates haud agnoscamus). Quam rem dum pauci animadvertunt, in nostra pariter et aliis modernis linguis tradendis, plus intricati laboris suscipiunt quam opus est.

Genera, Casus, et Numeri.

Nomina Substantiva, apud nos, nullum vel Generum vel Casuum discrimen sortiuntur. Adeoque multum taedii, quod in linguis aliis, praesertim Graeca et Latina, his de rebus reperitur, prorsus abscinditur. Numerorum tamen discrimen agnoscimus in Substantivis, atque etiam in Verbis.

Sexuum discrimen si quando velimus exprimere, non fit illud variis nominum Generibus; Masculino puta, Foeminino, et Neutro; quae ne quidem apud Latinos sexus distinguunt: sunt enim *scortum, mancipium, amasium,* etc. Neutrius Generis, at Sexum vel Masculum vel Foemineum referunt; et contra, *gladius, vagina, arcus, sagitta,* aliaque innumera, quanquam neutrius Sexus sint, sunt tamen Generis vel masculini vel foeminini. Sed nos Sexus eodem plane modo quo Aetates (aliaque accidentia) distinguimus; distinctis vocabulis, vel adjunctis Adjectivis (sicut et Latini non raro faciunt); ut vir *a man,* mulier *a woman,* juvenis *a youth,*

---

8 opus est: 1st has *opus esset*

nearly all modern languages, differs enormously in syntax from Greek and Latin (the main reason being that in English we do not distinguish different cases). Few people recognise this when describing our language and other modern languages, and, consequently, the task is usually made more complicated than it need be.

GENDER, CASE AND NUMBER

Substantives[77] in English do not have different genders[78] or cases. This means that we escape much of the tedium which they give rise to in other languages, especially in Greek and Latin. However, we do have a difference of *number* in substantives, and in verbs. If we want to express a difference of sex we do not do it by the use of different genders in our nouns – masculine, feminine and neuter. In fact these genders do not distinguish the sexes even in Latin, because *scortum* [whore], *mancipium* [slave], *amasium* [lover], etc are neuter in gender but refer to persons of male or female sex; and conversely, *gladius* [sword], *vagina* [sheath], *arcus* [bow], *sagitta* [arrow], and many other objects which belong to neither sex, nevertheless have masculine or feminine gender. In English we distinguish the sexes in exactly the same way as we do ages (and other attributes), that is, either by using different words or by adding adjectives (this is often the case in Latin too). For instance, *a man, a woman; a youth, a*

[77] Introduction *p* 34.
[78] Introduction *pp* 30–31.

C. II. DE NOMINE SUBSTANTIVO. 77

youth, virgo *a maid,* puer *a boy,* puella *a girl:*
equus *a horfe,* equa *a mare,* equus caſtratus
a gelding, pullus *a côlt:* lepus mas *a male
hare,* lepus foemina *a female hare:* dama *a
deer,* dama mas *a buck,* dama foemina *a doe:*
cervus *a ſtag, a hart,* cerva *a hínd;* damu-
la, hinnulus, *a fawn:* anſer mas *a gander,*
anſer foemina *a gooſe,* anſerculus *a goſlin:*
caper *a he-goat,* capra *a ſhe-goat,* capella
a kid.

Subſtantiva ſingularia fiunt Pluralia ad- Numerus
dendo *s:* cui etiam aliquando praefigi- Pluralis.
tur *e,* quoties nempe neceſſitas pronunciandi illud poſtulat.

Neceſſitas autem pronunciandi hoc poſtulat
quoties immediate praecedunt *ſ, z, x, ſh;*
vel etiam *c, g, ch,* ſono molliori prolata.
Ut *a hand* manus, *a tree* arbor, *a houſe* domus, *a fox* vulpes, *a fiſh* piſcis, *a maze* la-
byrinthus, *a prince* princeps, *an age* aetas,
a tench tinca; pluraliter *hands, trees, houſes,
foxes, fiſhes, mazes, princes, ages, tenches.*
Eſtque haec ſola (nunc dierum) pluralis numeri regularis formatio.
At olim etiam per *en* vel *yn* formabant pluralia; quorum pauca admodum adhuc retinemus. Ut *an ox* bos, *a chick* pullus (avium),
pluraliter *oxen, chicken* (ſunt qui dicunt in
ſingulari *chicken,* et in plurali *chickens).*
Item a *fere* filix, pluraliter *fern* (verum nunc
plerumque *fern* utroque numero dicitur, ſed
et in plurali *ferns;* nam *fere* et *feres* prope

28–29 (sunt qui . . . *chickens*): 1st has (nam qui dicunt in singulari *chicken* et in plurali
chickens omnino errant)

maid; *a boy, a girl*; *a horse, a mare, a gelding, a colt*; *a male hare, a female hare*; *a deer, a buck, a doe*; *a stag, a hart, a hind, a fawn*; *a gander, a goose, a goslin*; *a he-goat, a she-goat, a kid*.

PLURAL NUMBER

Singular substantives are made plural by adding *s*; sometimes this is preceded by *e*, when the pronunciation makes it necessary, for example when *s* immediately follows *s, z, x, sh*, or *c, g, ch* when they have their softer sound. So, for instance, *a hand, a tree, a house, a fox, a fish, a maze, a prince, an age, a tench* have the plural forms *hands, trees, houses, foxes, fishes, mazes, princes, ages, tenches*. This is the only regular way (nowadays) of forming the plural number.[79] At one time, however, they formed plurals with *en* or *yn* as well, and we still have a few examples of this; *an ox, a chick* have the plural forms *oxen, chicken* (some say *chicken* for the singular and *chickens* for the plural). Similarly the plural of *fere* is *fern* – though nowadays *fern* is usually used for both numbers, with *ferns* as an alternative plural form; *fere* and *feres* are almost obsolete.[80]

---

[79] Introduction *p* 27. Wallis is the first to emphasise the unproductiveness of the *-en*, *-yn* plural formation.

[80] *Chicken* (OE *cicen*) was never the plural of *chick*, but once stood for singular and plural, like *sheep*. The same applies to *fern*. Greenwood (who usually follows Wallis) simply records the invariable form *fern* for singular and plural, and adds *kine* to *shoon*, *eyen* and *houses* as 'not to be imitated'. *Housen* also appears in Butler, Jonson and Wharton (1655), but all record it as an exceptional form. *Peas* is given by Gil for singular and plural. Butler records *peas* (sing), *peasen* (pl), or *pea* (sing) *peas* (pl). *Peasen* came to be regarded as archaic by the eighteenth century, and Greenwood omits it.

78 DE NOMINE SUBSTANTIVO. C. II.

pe obſoleta ſunt). Dicunt etiam nonnulli
(ſed rarius) *houſen, eyn, ſhoon*, etc. pro *houſes,
eyes, ſhoes*, etc. Dicunt nonnulli *a peaſe* pi-
ſum, pluraliter *peaſen;* at melius, ſingulari-
ter *a pea*, pluraliter *peas.*

Sunt etiam et alia quaedam hujus forma-
tionis veſtigia, ſed quae alio etiam nomine
ut plurimum ſunt irregularia; ut *a man*
(olim *manne)* homo, vir, *a woman* mulier,
pluraliter *men, women (wemen, weomen)*,
per ſyncopen pro *manen, womenen* (Saxonice olim dicebant *a man* homo, *a weaponmar*
vir, *a wyſman* vel *wombman* mulier). Sic *a
brother* frater, *a child* puer, pluraliter *brethren, children.* Item *a cow* vacca, pluraliter *keen* vel *kíne* (quaſi *cowin).* Sic et *ſwíne*
ſues (quaſi *ſowin) a* ſingulari *sòw* (at nunc
sòw* tantum de ſue foemina dicitur; *ſwínc*
vero in utroque numero, de utroque ſexu).
Sed et harum nonnulla retinent etiam formationem analogam; ut *brothers, cows,
ſows.*

Sunt et alia pauca irregularia; *a mouſe* mus,
a louſe pediculus, *a foot* pes, *a gooſe* anſer,
a tooth dens; pluraliter *míce, líce* (vel *meece,
leece), feet, geeſe, teeth:* et vix plura. *Sheep*
ovis, *hoſe* caliga, promiſcue dicuntur in u-
troque numero; ſicut etiam *ſwíne, chicken,
fearn, peas*, ut ſupra dictum eſt.

Finita in *f* plerumque alleviantur in plurali numero, ſubſtituendo *v;* ut *wífe* uxor,
lífe vita, *knífe* culter, *ſheaf* faſciculus, *ſhelf*
abacus, vel ſcamnum cui aliquid imponitur,
wolf lupus, *ſelf* propria perſona, *half* ſe-
miſſis,

---

11 womenen: misprint for *womanen* of 1st–5th
13 vel *wombman:* 5th–6th
21 analogam: 1st has *analogiam* (misprint)

Occasionally, though this is less common, you hear *housen, eyn, shoon*, etc instead of *houses, eyes, shoes*, etc. Some say *a pease* and, in the plural, *peasen*, but the singular form *a pea* with plural *peas* is preferable. There are some other survivals of this type of formation, but most of them are irregular for other reasons too, for example *a man* (formerly *manne*), *a woman* have the plural forms *men, women* (*wemen, weomen*) by a syncope of *manen, womanen*;[81] in Anglo-Saxon they used to say *a man* (Latin *homo*), *a weaponman* (Latin *vir*) and a *wyfman* or *wombman* (Latin *mulier*). Similarly from *a brother, a child* we get the plural forms *brethren, children*, and from *a cow* the plural *keen* or *kine* (as if from *cowin*), and *swine* (as if from *sowin*) from the singular *sow*[82] though *sow* is now only used of a female pig, whereas *swine* is used in singular and plural, and for either sex. However, some of these words also have a plural form by analogy from the regular formation, for example *brothers, cows, sows*.

There are a few other irregular forms too: *a mouse, a louse, a foot, a goose, a tooth*, have the plural *mice, lice* (or *meece, leece*),[83] *feet, geese, teeth*, but there are hardly any other examples. *Sheep, hose*, are used for both numbers indifferently, and so are *swine, chicken, fearn, peas*, as I said above. Words ending in *f* are mostly softened in the plural by substituting *v*; for example *wîfe, lîfe, knîfe, sheaf, shelf, wolf, self, half, calf*, etc which in the plural become *wîves*,

---

[81] The 6th edition's *womenen* is a misprint. Jonson and Butler also suggest that *men* developed from *manen*, and *women* from *womanen* by syncope. *Wombman* is a false derivation. The plurals *brethren, children* are not formed from *brother + en, child + en* as Wallis implies (see Wright and Wright, 1924, § 296).

[82] *Kine* and *keen* both derive from the Old English plural *cy*, not from *cowin, keen* being probably a development of Kent dialect. *Cows* is given in Cooper, Brightland and Greenwood; but in the first half of the seventeenth century *kine* was still normal, and is the only plural listed by Gil and Greaves. *Swine*, like *sheep, deer, chicken*, had no distinct plural form in Old English. In spite of these false derivations – not surprising in view of the comparative ignorance about Old English in Wallis's time – the attempt to show regularities underlying the language is valuable, and reflects Wallis's keen interest in philology.

[83] The forms *meece, leece* are given by Jonson also; Cooper records them as *barbara dialectus*. Like *keen* they are a development of the Kentish dialect.

C. II. DE NOMINE SUBSTANTIVO.

miſſis, *calf* vitulus, etc. pluraliter *wives,
lives, knives, ſheaves, ſhelves, wolves, ſelves,
halves, calves,* etc. Eademque alleviatio eſt
etiam in *ſ* et *th*, quamvis retento charactere, in *houſe* domus, *clōth* pannus, *path* ſe-
mita, etc. pluraliter *houſes, clóthes, pathes,*
etc.

C A P. III.

De Articulis.

Subſtantivis non raro praefigimus duos *Articuli.*
(quos vocant) Articulos, *A* et *The.*

Sunt autem revera nomina Adjeſtiva, et eodem plane modo uſurpantur quo reliqua
adjeſtiva. His reſpondent Gallorum articuli
un et *le;* Germanorum *ein* et *der.*

A (ſeu, ante vocales, *an)* eſt articulus *A, an.*
Numeralis; atque idem omnino ſignifi-
cat ac *one* unus, ſed minus emphatice.

Notat vocis generalis particulari cuidam (ſive ſpeciei, ſive individuo, ſaltem vago) ap-
plicationem (ut *patience is a virtue,* patien-
tia eſt virtus, vel quaedam virtus): Ideoque
ſoli numero ſingulari praefigitur (neceſſitate
materiae, non formae, ut et vox *unus.* Si
vero pluribus particularibus (ſive ſpeciebus
ſive individuis) vox generalior applicetur,
illud numero Plurali innuitur (eſtque hic
revera

---

22 non formae, ut et vox *unus*: misprint for *non formae) ut et vox unus* of 1st–5th

lĩves, knĩves, sheaves, shelves, wolves, selves, halves, calves, etc. The same softening occurs with *s* and *th* though the actual written symbol used is the same; for example *house, cloth, path* have the plural forms *houses, clothes, pathes*, etc.[84]

CHAPTER III
The articles[85]

We often prefix substantives with two (so-called) *articles – a* and *the*. They are really adjectives, and are used in exactly the same way as other adjectives; they correspond to the French articles *un* and *le* and the German *ein* and *der*.

A (or, before vowels, *an*) is the numeral article; it has precisely the same meaning as *one*, though it is less emphatic. It denotes the application of a generic word to some particular thing[86] – species or individual, so long as it is indefinite – for example *patience is a virtue*. It is therefore only prefixed to the singular number (not because of its form but because of its meaning, like the Latin word *unus*). If a generic term is applied to more than one particular, whether species or individual, we indicate it by using the plural number – this is really the only use the plural has; clearly *men* refers

---

[84] *Cf: Tractatus pp* 179, 181, and notes 66 and 70 (*pp* 175, 181).
[85] Introduction *p* 34 *ff*.
[86] Introduction *p* 35.

8o DE ARTICULIS. C. III.

revera folus numeri Pluralis ufus): fic *men*
homines, de individuis dici manifeſtum eſt:
et *virtues* virtutes, de virtutis vel ſpeciebus
vel individuis.

Tb* *The* eſt articulus Demonſtrativus, idemque ſignificat ac *that* illud, ſed minus
emphatice.

Notat Particularium unius pluriumve (quibus actu applicatur vox Generalis) Deter-
minationem. Sic [terram] dicimus *earth*
ubi ipſam ſpeciem, ſeu elementum terrae
deſignamus; at *the earth* ſi globum terre-
num (quod Individuum quoddam determi-
natum eſt) intelligamus. Attribuitur tam
numero Singulari quam Plurali; quia tam
de uno quam de pluribus individuis poſſu-
mus determinate loqui.

Neuter horum articulorum praefigitur vel
voci generali generaliter ſignificanti (utpote
cujus ſignificatio particularibus actu non
applicatur); vel nomini proprio (quod ex
ſe ſatis innuit et individuum et quidem de-
terminatum); vel etiam ubi aliud aliquod
adjectivum adeſt quod hos articulos virtualiter contineat (redundarent enim), ut vir *a*
man, vir unus *one man*, vir aliquis *ſome*
man, vir quilibet *any man*: mundus *the*
world, hic mundus *this world*: ubi *one*,
ſome, *any*, virtualiter includunt *a*; et *this*
etiam virtualiter includit *the*. Fluviorum
tamen et Montium nominibus Propriis, aliquando

25–26 vir *a man*: 5th–6th
30–81.3 Fluviorum . . . *the Alps:* 5th–6th

to individuals while *virtues* may refer either to various species of virtues or to individual virtues.

The is the demonstrative article, and means the same as *that*, though it is less emphatic. It denotes the delimitation of one or more particular things, when a generic term is applied to them. For instance we talk of *earth* when we mean the species or substance earth, but we say *the earth* if we mean the world, which is not only individual but delimited. It can be attached both to singular and to plural forms, because we can speak in a delimiting sense of one individual object or of more than one.

Neither of these articles is used either before a generic word with a generic application (that is, a word whose meaning is not actually applied to particular things), or before a proper name, which gives sufficient indication in itself that an individual, delimited object is involved; nor are they used where another adjective occurs which virtually contains these articles within itself (they would be superfluous in a case like this); as in *a man, one man, some man, any man, the world, this world*, where in effect *one, some, any* include *a*, and *this* includes *the*. However we sometimes put *the* before the proper

quando praefigimus *the;* ut Thamefis *the
Thames,* Danubius *the Danube,* Alpes *the
Alps.*

Peculiares funt phrafes *many a man, never
a man;* differunt enim ab his *many men, no
men,* ficut *every man* ab *all men:* priores e-
nim fignificant *multos homines, nullos homines, omnes homines,* figillatim five diftribu-
tive acceptos; pofteriores faltem conjunctim
feu collective acceptos. Nec hisce prorfus
abfimiles funt, ubi (poft *fuch* talis, et adverbia comparationis *as, fo,* tam, *too* nimis,
at vix alia) articulus *a* Subftantivo et fuo
Adjectivo praecedenti interponitur (qui folet alias utrique praeponi): ut *fuch a gift,
is too fmåll a reward, for fo great a labour,
and as great a benefit;* tale munus, eft nimis exigua merces pro tanto (tam magno)
labore, tantoque etiam beneficio).

C A P. IIII.

De Praepofitionibus.

Diverfitatem Cafuum (quos habent prae-   Praepofitio-
fertim Graeci et Latini) Anglicana Lin-   num ufus.
gua (ut dictum eft) neutiquam agnofcit:
Sed Praepofitionum auxilio rem omnem
illam praeftamus, quam Graeci et Latini, partim Praepofitionibus, partim Cafuum diverfitate perficiunt.

G   Ideoque

11 *such* talis, et: 4th–6th
15–16 *such a gift, is:* 4th–6th
17 tale munus, est: 4th–6th
24 praestamus: 1st has *praestant*

names of rivers and mountains, for example *the Thames, the Danube, the Alps*.

The phrases *many a man, never a man* are special cases, because they differ from *many men, no men*, in the same way as *every man* differs from *all men*; the former expressions refer to men regarded one at a time, distributively, while the latter refer to them all in a group, collectively. Not unlike these are cases where the article *a* (following *such*, and the adverbs of comparison *as*, *so*, *too*, but virtually no others) comes between the substantive and its preceding adjective,[87] whereas elsewhere it comes before both of them; for example *such a gift, is too small a reward, for so great a labour, and as great a benefit*.

CHAPTER IV
The prepositions[88]

THE USE OF PREPOSITIONS

The English language, as I have already said, does not have a variety of different cases as Greek and Latin, in particular, do. Instead we use prepositions to convey all the meanings which in Greek and Latin are expressed partly by different cases and partly by prepositions. For this reason I decided, contrary to the normal custom, to

[87] This does not apply to *such*, which Wallis added in the 4th edition.
[88] Introduction *pp* 30, 36, 37, 38.

82 DE PRAEPOSITIONIBUS. C. IIII.

Ideoque Praepofitionum doctrinam, dum de
nominibus Subftantivis ago (folis enim Subftantivis, aut Subftantive pofitis, praefiguntur, funtque horum quafi communis affectio), praeter aliorum methodum placuit in-
terferere. Paucarum enim harum vocula-
rum fignificatu cognito, tota fere Nominum
fyntaxis fimul intelligitur.

Praepofitio enim, Subftantivo quod regitur
praefixa, oftendit quem habeat illud refpec-
tum ad vocem illam (five verbum fit, five
nomen, aliave orationis pars) a qua regitur.
Praepofitiones enim ut plurimum Argu-
mentis (ut loquuntur) Logicis five Locis
Topicis innuendis inferviunt.

Vox Nomi-
nativa, et
Accufativa. Vox Subftantiva Verbo praefixa ut Latinorum cafus Nominativus (quam igitur
vocem Nominativum, diftinctionis ergô,
vocabimus); aut etiam Abfolute pofita
(ut loquuntur Latini); aut denique Verbo tranfitivo poftpofita ut Latinorum
cafus Accufativus (quam igitur vocem
Accufativam dicemus); nuda folet poni
fine praefixa Praepofitione.

Notandum autem eft, Subftantivum apud
nos Abfolute poni, non modo ut Latinorum
cafus Ablativus abfolute pofitus, qui nempe
a nullo regitur: Sed etiam ut eorum cafus
Nominativus abfolute pofitus, qui nempe
nulli verbo praeponitur; puta in librorum
titulis, ut cum poema Virgilianum infcribi-
tur

---

18 vocem Nominativum: misprint for *vocem Nominativam* of 1st–5th
23 nuda solet poni: 1st–4th have *nuda semper ponitur*

introduce the teaching of prepositions at this point, while I am dealing with substantives, inasmuch as prepositions are used only before substantives, or words acting as substantives, and are as it were a common property of them. When you have learnt the meanings of these few small words, you can immediately understand practically the whole syntax of nouns.

When a preposition is prefixed to a substantive governed by another word, it shows what relationship exists between the substantive and the word by which it is governed, whether it is a verb, a noun or another part of speech. For the main function of prepositions is to indicate logical connections, to use the current term, or local relationships.

NOMINATIVE WORDS AND ACCUSATIVE WORDS
Substantives which precede the verb, resembling the Latin nominative case (which we shall therefore call *nominative words*, to distinguish them), substantives occurring in an *absolute* construction (a Latin term), and substantives which follow a transitive verb, and resemble the Latin accusative case (which we shall call *accusative words*) are not, normally, preceded by prepositions. It is important to note that in English the substantive is said to be in an *absolute* construction, not only when it is not governed by any other word, like the Latin ablative absolute, but also when no verb follows it, like the Latin nominative absolute; this occurs in the titles of books – as when Virgil's poem is entitled *Aeneis* – and also where the

tur *Aeneis;* et ubi casus Nominativus quasi
suspenditur, alio nempe ante Verbum in-
terserto, ut *Alexander magnus, ille quidem
orbem vicit;* qualis constructio in Latina
lingua rarius occurrit, in Graeca Hellenisti-
ca saepius, in Hebraica sicut et nostra Anglicana saepissime.

Praepositio *Of* idem omnino innuit quod *of.*
Latinorum casus Genitivus, et eandem
cum illo significationis varietatem admittit, sive Substantivis, Adjectivis, aut
Verbis postponatur.

Ut Opera Aristotelis, *The Works of Aristotle.* Pro illo autem non raro ponitur Adjectivum Possessivum, de quo suo loco dicetur.

Sed et significat Objectum circa quod, ut
Latinorum *De;* ut et Materiam ex qua,
ut Latinorum *Ex.*

Ut, Tractatus de virtute. *A treatise of virtue*
(aut *concerning virtue);* Poculum ex auro,
A cup of gold.

Off separationem significat; ut aliquan- *Off, on.*
do Latinorum *abs, ex;* ut *abscindo, exuo:*
Cui opponitur *On,* continuationem in-
nuens (exuo *to put off,* induo *to put on):*
hinc *up-on* super.

G 2 *From*

nominative is, as it were, left hanging, another nominative word being inserted between it and the verb; for example *Alexander magnus, ille quidem orbem vicit.* This construction is not very often used in Latin; in Hellenistic Greek it occurs more frequently, and in Hebrew and our own language it is very common.

Of. The preposition *of* has exactly the same connotation as the Latin genitive case, and enjoys the same variety of meanings,[89] regardless of whether it occurs after substantives, adjectives or verbs; for example *The works of Aristotle.* It is often replaced here by the possessive adjective, which will be described in the appropriate section.

It also indicates the *object concerning which* like Latin *de*, or the *material from which* like Latin *ex*. For instance, *A treatise of virtue* (or *concerning virtue*); *a cup of gold.*

Off, on. Off indicates separation, as Latin *ab, ex* sometimes do, as in *abscindo, exuo.* The opposite to this is *on*, which implies connection (*exuo, to put off; induo, to put on*);[90] hence the word *up-on.*

---

[89] One could do with more examples here to show the full variety of meanings, and so throughout this chapter. Greenwood (1711) makes up for it with a multiplicity of examples.

[90] *Off* and *on* in the examples *to put off, to put on* (clothes) are not prepositions but parts of phrasal verbs, and better regarded as adverbs. *Cf* Wallis's final sentence in this chapter.

84   DE PRAEPOSITIONIBUS. C. IIII.

From. *From* innuit terminum a quo; ut Latinorum *Ab.*

To, unto. *To,* vel *unto,* innuit terminum ad quem, atque idem terminum Relationis; quae Latini partim per cafum Dativum, partim per praepofitionem *Ad* infinuant.

Notandum autem eft hanc praepofitionem nonnunquam tam inter loquendum quam fcribendum omitti; ut quum dicimus *like me* mihi fimilis, *give me* da mihi, *tell me* dic mihi, *near me* mihi propinquum, etc. ubi ponitur *me* elliptice pro *to me.*

Till, un-till. *Till, un-till,* Ufquedum. Tantum de tempore dicitur, faltem apud Anglos. Sed Scoti nonnunquam utuntur pro *to* et *unto.*

For. *For* innuit finem cui, vel pro quo: idemque valet quod Latinorum *pro,* et quod (nonnunquam) cafus Dativus.

Quod mihi (feu pro me) paratur, alteri datur; *What is prepared For me, is given To another.*

By. *By* innuit Latinorum *per;* ut et Ablativum caufae efficientis (tam principalis, quam inftrumentalis, et moralis), cui non raro praeponunt Latini praepofitionem *Ab:* Item *juxta* vel *praeter* (non modo

4 atque idem: misprint for *atque item* of 1st–5th
9 scribendum omitti: 1st has *scribendum aliquando omitti*
14–16 saltem . . . *to* et *unto:* 5th–6th

From. From signifies the point of departure, like Latin *ab*.

To, unto. To, or *unto* signifies the point aimed for and also a point of reference;[91] in Latin this is expressed partly by the dative, and partly by the preposition *ad*. Notice that this preposition is sometimes omitted both in speech and in writing, as when we say *like me, give me, tell me, near me*, etc, where *me* occurs elliptically instead of *to me*.[92]

Till, until. Till, un-till are only used of time, at any rate by the English; the Scots sometimes use them in place of *to* and *unto*.[93]

For. For indicates destination or purpose and is used where Latin uses *pro* and (sometimes) the dative case, for example *What is prepared for me, is given to another*.

By. By corresponds to Latin *per*, and also to the ablative of efficient cause (principal, instrumental and moral)[94] which is often preceded by the preposition *ab*. It also corresponds to *iuxta* or *praeter*, not only as signifying place but also exception.[95] In com-

---

[91] This may refer to its use in phrases such as *dear to, devoted to, helpful to* or in *give, bring, mention, suggest* etc *to*.

[92] Wallis does not formulate a rule to govern the omission or otherwise of *to* with the verbs such as *tell, give*, as he might easily have done: *cf* Cooper (1685), *p* 173.

[93] To indicate place relationships.

[94] The *principal* cause corresponds to the personal agent – *he was slain by his enemy*; the *instrumental* to the means – *by his enemies sword*; the *moral* cause is exemplified in *wounded by his own fear*.

[95] Place = *near to, beside*. Exception = the compound *beside(s)* meaning *except for*.

C. IIII. DE PRAEPOSITIONIBUS.   85

modo in fignificatione locali, fed et exceptiva).

Hoc in compofitione fit *be*.   Unde, *be-fide* juxta, praeter, (quafi, juxta latus); *be-neath*, *be-low*, infra (quafi, in humili); *be-fore*, ante; *be-hind* poft, a tergo; *be-yond* ultra; *be-hither (on this fide)* citra; *be-tween*, *be-twixt*, inter (faltem de duobus dicitur; at *among*, inter, non nifi de pluribus).
Ab hofte occifus eft per (juxta, prope) aquae fontem, fed primum fuo ipfius metu, deinde hoftis gladio vulneratus, *He was flain By his enemy, By (befide, near) a fpring Of water, but wóunded firft By his own fear, then By his enemies fword.*

With indicat Inftrumentum, ut Latino- *With.* rum Ablativus Inftrumenti: atque etiam concomitantiam, ut Latinorum *Cum.*

Gladio occifus, *flain with a fword;* mecum moratur, *he abideth with me.*

Through indicat Medium; et proprie *Through.* quidem medium Locale; fed et etiam medium Phyficum, et Morale.

Radii folis incredibili pernicitate tranfeunt, a coelo, per aërem, ad terram, calore et lumine praediti, quibus nos oblectat, et plantas vivificat, quas Deus nobis paravit, nobisque dedit, in ufum noftrum et ipfius gloriam.

G 3

3 Hoc in compofitione fit *be*: 5th–6th
24 pernicitate: 1st has *celeritate*

[296]

position *by* becomes *be*. Hence *be-side* (as it were, by the side of); *be-neath, be-low* (as it were, on a low level); *be-fore*; *be-hind*; *be-yond*; *be-hither* (on this side); *be-tween, be-twixt* – when used of two people; *among* is only used of more than two. *He was slain by his enemy, by (beside, near) a spring of water, but wounded first by his own fear, then by his enemies sword.*

With. With indicates the instrument, like the Latin ablative of instrument; it also shows accompaniment, like Latin *cum*; for example, *slain with a sword; he abideth with me.*

Through. Through indicates the medium; especially the spatial medium, but also the physical and moral medium. *The beams of the sun, with incredible speed, pass from heaven through the air to the earth, indued with light and heat, by (with, through) which it comforteth us, and quickeneth the plants, which God hath prepared for us, and given to us, for our use and his glory.*

86   DE PRAEPOSITIONIBUS. C. IIII.

riam. *The beams Of the fun, With incredible fpeed, paſs From heaven Through the air To the earth, indued With light and heat, By (with, through) which it comforteth us, and quickeneth the plants, which God hath prepared For us, and given To us, For our uſe and his glory.*

After, etc.   *After* poſt, *againſt* contra; *among, amongſt,* inter; *near, nigh,* prope; unde *next* (quaſi *nigh'ſt*) proxime; *under, below,* ſub, infra ; *over, above,* ſuper, ſupra.

In.   *In* reſpondet Latinorum praepoſitioni *in* cum Ablativo ; et ſignificat quaſi praeſentiam in loco.

Unde, *within,* intra, ζὺν τοῖς ἔσω.

Into.   *Into* reſpondet Latinorum praepoſitioni *in* cum caſu Accuſativo; et ſignificat quaſi motum in locum.

Out.   *Out* vel *out of* valet *ex.* Unde *with-out* extra, *ab-out* circa.

At, etc.   *At* (apud) indicat exiſtentiam in loco.

Pro quo in compoſitione ſaepe ponitur *a,* et (ante vocalem) *ab;* ut *a-bed* in lecto, *a-broad* foras (quaſi, in lato); *ab-ove (over)* ſupra; *a-low, a-fore, ab-aft* (pro *below, before, after*); *a-board* in navi (quaſi, ſuper tabulatum); *ab-out* circa (quaſi, in extremitatibus); *a-gain* iterum (quaſi, in lucro); *a-doing,* faciens, facturus, in faciendo; *a-dying,*

10–11 *under . . .* supra: 5th–6th
22 saepe: 1st–4th have *plerumque*
27 *ab-out*: 4th has *a-bout* (misprint)
28 *a-gain . . .* in lucro): 5th–6th

After etc. *After*; *against*; *among, amongst*; *near, nigh*; and, derived from this, *next* (as it were, nigh'st); *under, below*; *over, above*.[96]

In. *In* corresponds to the Latin preposition *in* with the ablative, and signifies (approximately) *presence in a place*. From it we get *within*.

Into corresponds to the Latin preposition *in* with the accusative case, and signifies (approximately) *movement to a place*.

Out. *Out* or *out of* is equivalent to *ex*. Hence *with-out, ab-out*.

At, etc. *At* signifies *existence in a place*. In compounds it is often replaced by *a*,[97] or (before a vowel) *ab*; for example: *a-bed*; *a-broad* (as it were, in a broad place); *ab-ove* (over); *a-low, a-fore, ab-aft* (instead of *below, before, after*); *a-board* (as it were, *above the floor*); *ab-out* (as it were, *at the extremities*); *a-gain* (as it were *in a state of gain*); *a-doing*; *a-dying*; *a-fraid, a-feard*; to *a-fright*; *at-length*,

---

[96] This is a curiously jumbled group with no explanation or examples. Again Greenwood (1711) is profuse in his illustrations.

[97] In fact this prefix *a* comes from a weakening of Old English *an* (on), except in *afraid*, *afeard*, *afright* where no preposition is involved.

C. IIII. DE PRAEPOSITIONIBUS. 87

ing, moriens, in moriendo; *a-fraid*, *a-feard*,
territus, in timore pofitus; *to a-fright*, terre-
facio; *at-length*, *at-laft*, tandem (quafi, ad
longitudinem, ad extremum); *at-left*, faltem (quafi, ad minimum); etc. Forfan et *a-
gainft*, contra (quafi, in victoria); *a-mong, a-
mongft*, inter (quafi, in miftura); hinc etiam
deduci poffunt.

Ward, verfus, femper poftponitur.   *Ward.*

Ut *to-ward*, erga, adverfus; *hither-ward*,
huc, huc-verfus; *up-ward*, furfum, fus-ver-
fum; *down-ward*, deorfum, de-verfum;
fore-ward, prorfum, antrorfum, prae-ver-
fum, anterius-verfum; *back-ward*, retror-
fum, retro-verfum; *heaven-ward*, *to-ward
heaven*, *to-heaven-ward*, coelum verfus.
Touching, *concerning*, (fpectans, attingens, *Touching,*
concernens) proprie funt Participia, at ufur- *etc.*
pantur faepe ut Praepofitiones: Sic *according to* confonans, *belonging to* attinens, aliaque forfan aliqua participia.

Praepofitiones non raro degenerant in
Adverbia: Sicut et Latinorum, fine fuis
cafibus pofitae.

G 4   C A P.

4 *at-lest*: 1st has *at-least* (*cf* Chapter XIII, note 136)
6 (quasi, in victoria): 5th–6th
7 (quasi, in mistura): 5th–6th

at-last (as it were, *at the length, at the last point*); *at-least* (as it were, *at the smallest degree*) etc. Perhaps *against* (as it were, *in a victorious state*), *among, amongst* (as it were, *in a mixture*) can also be derived from *at*.

Ward. Ward is always in second position; for example *to-ward*; *hither-ward*; *up-ward*; *down-ward*; *fore-ward*; *back-ward*; *heaven-ward*; *to-ward heaven*; *to-heaven-ward*.

Touching, etc. *Touching, concerning* are really participles, but they are often used as prepositions, like *according to, belonging to* and perhaps some other participles too.

Prepositions often become adverbs; this is so in Latin too, when they occur without being followed by the appropriate case.

CAP. V.

De Adjectivis.

Adjectiva, sine omni vel Casuum, vel Generum, vel etiam Numerorum discrimine, suis Substantivis adjunguntur: Eodem plane modo quo Adverbia Verbis aliisve orationis partibus. Et quidem plerumque immediate praefiguntur, si saltem sola veniunt nec suo (quod regunt) satellitio comitata.

Ut vir bonus *a good man*, bona mulier *a good woman*, res bona *a good thing*, pluraliter *good men, good women, good things*. Substantivum autem cum suo Adjectivo (sicut et vox rectrix quaecunque cum toto suo quantocunque satellitio) habetur quasi una vox composita: unde illud Aggregatum non raro aliud assumit Adjectivum (vel etiam aliam quamvis affectionem) eodem prorsus modo acsi esset una vox (atque hoc demum tertium, et sic deinceps). Ut vir *a man*, vir senex *an old-man*, senex prudens *a wise old-man*, senex valde prudens *a very-wise old-man*, tres prudentes senes *three wise old-men*. Ubi Substantivo *man* praefigitur articulus Adjectivus *a;* deinde eidem substantivo *man* praefigitur adjectivum *old*, et substantivo *old-man* articulus *an;* item Substantivo

stantivo

Note — marginalia: Adjectivorum usus.   Eorum sedes.

CHAPTER V
The adjectives

THE USE OF THE ADJECTIVES

Adjectives are linked to their substantives without showing any indication of case, gender, or even number, in precisely the same way as adverbs are linked to verbs and other parts of speech.

Their position. They are mostly put immediately before the substantive, if they are alone, and not accompanied by subordinate qualifiers which they govern;[98] for example, *a good man, a good woman, a good thing,* with the plural forms *good men, good women, good things.* The substantive and its adjective (like any governing word and the whole of its dependent phrase or phrases) are regarded as one compound word; so this aggregate is often accompanied by a further adjective, or even by some other qualifier, exactly as if it were only one word, and then this second aggregate may have a third adjective, and so on; for example *a man, an old-man, a wise old-man, a very wise old-man, three wise old-men.* In this example the substantive *man* has the article-adjective *a* prefixed to it; then the same substantive *man* has the adjective *old* prefixed to it, and the resulting substantive *old-man* is preceded by the article *an*; similarly the sub-

[98] Introduction *p* 38.

ſtantivo *old-man* Adjectivum *wiſe*, aut etiam
Adjectivum Adverbio modificatum *very-
wiſe*, et toti item huic aggregato Adjectivum *a* vel (pluraliter) *three*.

Ubi vero vel plura ſunt Adjectiva quaſi
collateraliter copulata, vel etiam unum
cum ſuo ſatellitio, plerumque poſtpo-
nuntur Subſtantivo.

Ut vir prudens pariter et fortis, *a man both
wiſe and valiant;* vir ſumme prudens, *a
man exceeding wiſe;* vir multis rebus peri-
tus, *a man ſkilful in many things:* Sed e-
tiam dicimus *A wiſe and valiant man, An
exceeding wiſe man, a ſkilful man in many
things.*

Duo tamen ſunt Adjectivorum genera, **a**
Subſtantivis immediate deſcendentia,
quae ſemper Subſtantivis ſuis praeponuntur.   Eademque omnium fere praepoſi-
tionum vices ſupplent.
Primum quidem Adjectivum Poſſeſſi-   Adjectiva
vum libet appellare.   Fit autem a quo-   Poſſeſſiva.
vis Subſtantivo (ſive ſingulari ſive plurali) addito *s* (aut *es,* ſi neceſſitas pronun-
ciationis poſtulaverit). Illud autem innuit quod praepoſitio *of,* quum Latinorum Genitivo Poſſidentis aut etiam Efficientis reſpondet.

Ut

stantive *old-man* is preceded by the adjective *wise* or by the adverbially modified adjective *very-wise*, and before the total aggregate comes the adjective *a*, or (in the plural) *three*.

When two or more adjectives of equal status are linked together, or one adjective occurs with a dependent phrase, they usually follow the substantive, as in *a man both wise and valiant*; *a man exceeding wise*; *a man skilful in many things*. But we also say *a wise and valiant man*; *an exceeding wise man*; *a skilful man in many things*.

However, there are two kinds of adjectives, immediately derived from substantives, which always come before their substantives. They can take the place of almost any preposition.

POSSESSIVE ADJECTIVES

The first of these may be called the *possessive adjective*. It is formed from any substantive, singular or plural, by the addition of *s* (or *es* if required by the pronunciation) and has the same meaning as the preposition *of*, when this corresponds to the Latin possessive or effective[99] genitive; as in *mans nature*, *the nature of man*; *mens*

---

[99] As in *Virgils poems* – written by Virgil.

Ut *mans nature, the nature of man,* natura humana vel hominis; *mens nature, the nature of men,* natura humana vel hominum; *Virgils poems, the poems of Virgil,* poemata Virgilii vel Virgiliana.

Atque idem omnino fit ubi fubftantivum aggregatum occurrit (hoc eft, fubftantivum primarium cum fuo quafi fatellitio), toti nempe aggregato poftponitur *s* poffeffivi formativum, *The King's Court,* Aula Regia vel Regis; *The King of England's Court,* Aula Regis Angliae (vel *the Court of the King, the Court of the King of England):* toti nempe illi aggregato *the King of England,* tanquam uni Subftantivo, poftponitur litera formativa *s.*

Neque id mirum cuiquam videri debeat, quod ex vocum aggregato formetur vox Derivativa; quippe illud in ipfa Latina lingua (ne alias memorem) faepe fit. Nempe a *trans-Alpes, cis-Alpes,* formantur *Tranfalpinus, Cifalpinus;* fimiliterque *fubterraneus, fupercoeleftis, ultramarinus, antemeridianus, poftmeridianus, antelucanus, antefignanus, intercolumnium, intertignium, intermuralis, internodium, intramuranus, extramuranus, extemporaneus, extraordinarius, aborigines, ingeniculus, praecordia, praeludium, fubdialis, fubjugis, fubjugare, fuburbia, fuburbanus, fummoenium, fummoenianus, fupplanto, fuperliminare, praeliminaris, circumforaneus,* aliaque multa, formantur ab his vocum aggregatis, *fub terra, fuper coelum, ultra mare, ante meridiem, poft meridiem, ante lucem,*
                                        ante

11–14 1st–4th have *Hispania* for *Anglia* and *Spain* for *England* in these lines
17–91.7 Neque id mirum cuiquam . . . *circum fora,* etc: 4th–6th

nature; the nature of men; Virgils poems, the poems of Virgil.

It is formed in exactly the same way from a 'substantive aggregate' – that is, the primary substantive together with its dependent phrases; in other words the *s* which forms the possessive follows the total aggregate: *The King's Court, The King of England's Court* (or *the Court of the King, the Court of the King of England*); the formative letter *s* follows the whole of the aggregate, *the King of England*, as if it were one substantive.[100]

No-one should find it surprising that derivative words are formed from an aggregate of this kind because it often happens in Latin, and in other languages. For instance from *trans-Alpes, cis-Alpes* are derived *Transalpinus, Cisalpinus; cf: subterraneus, supercoelestis, ultramarinus, antemeridianus, postmeridianus, antelucanus, antesignanus, intercolumnium, intertignium, intermuralis, internodium, intramuranus, extramuranus, extemporaneus, extraordinarius, aborigines, ingeniculus, praecordia, praeludium, subdialis, subjugis, subjugare, suburbia, suburbanus, summoenium, summoenianus, supplanto, superliminare, praeliminaris, circumforaneus,* and many other words, which are formed from an aggregation of the following: *sub terra, super coelum, ultra mare, ante meridiem, post meridiem, ante lucem, ante signa, inter columnas, inter tigna, inter muros, inter*

---

[100] Although the *s* is a remnant of the genitive case, the fixed position of the noun to which it is added dissociates it from the genitive's freedom of position in the sentence. Many grammarians (for example, Gil) retain the Latin case names and use them to refer to semantically and syntactically equivalent expressions, usually consisting of prepositional phrases (see Introduction *p* 24 *f*); the prepositions are thus regarded as 'signs' of the cases.

C. V. DE ADJECTIVIS. 91

ante figna, inter columnas, inter tigna, inter
muros, inter nodos, intra muros, extra muros,
ex tempore, extra ordinem, ab origine, in ge-
nua, prae corde, prae ludo, fub dio, fub ju-
go, fub jugum, fub urbe, fub moenibus, fub
planta, fuper limine, prae limine, circum fo-
ra, etc.

Si tamen Subftantivum Plurale exeat (ut
plerumque fit) 'in *s;* duo *s* (nempe formativum pluralis, et formativum poffeffivi) in unum coincidunt, feu potius prius (euphoniae gratia) eliditur : ut *the*
Lord's Houfe, the Houfe of Lords, Domus Dominorum, feu Magnatum; *the*
Common's Houfe, the Houfe of Commons,
Domus Communium : pro *the Lords's*
Houfe, the Commons's Houfe.

Quod idem etiam fieri non raro folet in numero Singulari, quoties nomen Proprium
exit in *s :* ut *Priamus Daughter, the Daugh-*
ter of Priamus, Priami filia; *Venus Temple,*
the Temple of Venus. Veneris templum: pro
Priamus's Daughter, Venus's Temple.
Sed et plena fcriptio retinetur (et quidem
nunc dierum frequentius quam olim); ut
King Charles's Court, Aula Regis Caroli ;
St. James's Park, Vivarium Sancti Jacobi,
feu, ad Sti Jacobi (aedes).
Qui autem arbitrantur illud *s,* loco vocis
his, adjunctum effe (priori fcilicet parte per
Aphaerefin abfciffa) ideoque Apoftrophi
notam

24–28 Sed et plena scriptio . . . Sti Jacobi (aedes): 4th–6th

nodos, intra muros, extra muros, ex tempore, extra ordinem, ab origine, in genua, prae corde, prae ludo, sub dio, sub jugo, sub jugum, sub urbe, sub moenibus, sub planta, super limine, prae limine, circum fora, etc.

However if a substantive ends in *s* in the plural, as it usually does, the two *s*'s (the plural formative and the possessive formative) join into one, or rather the first is elided, for reasons of euphony. For example, *the Lord's House, the House of Lords; the Common's House, the House of Commons*; instead of *the Lords's House, the Commons's House*. The same thing often happens in the singular as well, when a proper name ends in *s*: for example, *Priamus daughter, the daughter of Priamus; Venus temple, the temple of Venus*; instead of *Priamus's daughter, Venus's temple*.[101] The full form may also be kept, and is commoner now than it used to be; for example *King Charles's Court; St James's Park* or *at St James's*.

Some people believe that the *s* is added instead of the word *his* (which, they say, has lost its first part by *aphaeresis*), and that an apostrophe should always be inserted or at any rate understood,

---

[101] *Cf* the modern written forms: *Lords' house, Commons' house, Priamus' daughter, Venus' temple*; or *Lords's house, Priamus's daughter* etc.

92 DE ADJECTIVIS. C. V.

notam femper vel pingendam effe vel faltem fubintelligendam ; omnino errant.
Quamvis enim non negem quin Apoftrophi
nota commode nonnunquam affigi poffit, ut
ipfius literae *s* ufus diftinctius, ubi opus eft,
percipiatur; ita tamen femper fieri debere,
aut etiam ideo fieri quia vocem *his* innuat,
omnino nego. Adjungitur enim et Foemi-
narum nominibus Propriis, et Subftantivis
Pluralibus, ubi vox *his* fine foloecifmo locum habere non poteft: atque etiam in
poffeffivis *ours, yours, theirs, hers,* ubi vocem *his* innui nemo fomniaret: et quidem
ipfa vox *his,* ut et interrogativum *whofe,* nil
aliud funt quam *hee's, who's,* ubi *s* idem
omnino praeftat quod in aliis poffeffivis:
Scribitur autem *his* pro *hee's,* eodem errore
quo nonnunquam *bin* pro *been;* item *whofe*
pro *who's,* eodem errore quo *done, gone,
knowne, growne,* etc. pro *doen, goen, knowen,
growen,* vel *do'n, go'n, know'n, grow'n;* u-
trobique contra analogiam linguae ; fed ufu
defenditur.

Refpectiva. Alterum Adjectivorum (quod innuebа-
tur) genus eft, quod Adjectivum Refpec-
tivum (quoniam aptius non occurrit vo-
cabulum) appellare libet : Quo Refpec-
tus alii fere omnes (praeter eos qui adjectivo Poffeffivo innuuntur) innui folent : Qui tamen multo diftinctius, ubi
illud requiritur, per Praepofitiones ex-
primuntur. Eft autem nihil aliud quam
ipfa

22–23 sed usu defenditur: 5th–6th

but this is not true at all. Admittedly it helps sometimes to put in an apostrophe, to show the function of the *s*, when this is necessary. But I certainly do not agree that it should always be done, or that the reason for doing it is that it indicates the word *his*. For *s* is often used with women's proper names and with plural substantives, where it would be a solecism to replace it with *his*; and it is also used with the possessives: *ours, yours, theirs, hers*, where it could not by any stretch of the imagination stand for *his*. In fact the word *his* itself, and the interrogative *whose* are simply *hee's, who's*, with the *s* performing the same function as in other possessives. The spelling *his* instead of *hee's* results from the same mistake which accounts for the spelling *bin* instead of *been*; and *whose* for *who's* from the same mistake as *done, gone, knowne, growne*, etc written for *doen, goen, knowen, growen*, or *do'n, go'n, know'n, grow'n*; in each case the spelling contravenes the regular forms of the language but is sanctioned by usage.[102]

RESPECTIVE ADJECTIVES

There is another type of adjectives, as I said above, which one might call *respective adjectives* in the absence of a more suitable name. These are used to express nearly all relationships other than those expressed by the possessive adjective. These relationships can, if desired, be expressed much more clearly by using prepositions. The respective adjective is, in fact, simply a substantive used as an ad-

---

[102] *Hee's, who's, doen* etc: further examples of Wallis's search for basic regularities; see Wright and Wright, §§ 326, 410.

C. V.   DE ADJECTIVIS.   93

ipfa vox Subftantiva adjective pofita: et
quidem non raro fequenti voci per Hyphen conjungitur, quafi fieret vox compofita.

Sic *a fea-fifh, a fifh of the fea*, pifcis mari-
nus, vel maris (in mari, ex mari, ad mare
pertinens); *a river-fifh*, pifcis fluvialis; *a
wine-veffel, a veffel for wine*, vas vinarium,
feu vino deftinatum; *a Turkey-voyage, a voyage to Turkey*, navigatio Turcica feu in Tur-
ciam; *a fea-voyage, a voyage by fea*, iter
marinum, feu per mare; *home-made, made
at home*, domi factum, vel apud domum;
felf-love, φιλαυλία, fui amor; *felf-murder*, αὐτο-
χειρία, fui caedes; *man-flaughter, the flaugh-
ter of man*, homicidium, humana caedes,
caedes hominis; *a gold-ring, a ring of gold*,
annulus aureus, vel ex auro: et infinita
alia.
Neque folis Subftantivis, fed et Adjectivis,
Participiis, aliisve forfan orationis partibus,
hujusmodi Adjectiva Refpectiva adjiciuntur: ut *a fun-fhiny day*, dies ἡλιαυγής, folis
fplendore clarus; *a felf-tormenter*, vel *felf-
tormenting man*, heautontimorumenus, ἑαυτὸν
τιμωρήμενος.
Cum autem Adjectiva non nifi Subftantivis
adjungi foleant; Dicendum eft, vel illa hic
loci (ut alia etiam Adjectiva) iu Adverbia
degenerare; vel potius fupponenda funt
cum Subftantivis primo conflari, ut *fun-
fhine* folis fplendor, *felf-torment* αὐτο̕ιμωρία,
fui tormentum; et deinde ex his aggregatis

jective, and is often joined up with the following word by a hyphen, as if to form a compound word. For example, *a sea-fish, a fish of the sea*; *a river-fish*; *a wine-vessel, a vessel for wine*; *a Turkey-voyage, a voyage to Turkey*; *a sea-voyage, a voyage by sea*; *home-made, made at home*; *self-love*; *self-murder*; *man-slaughter, the slaughter of man*; *a gold-ring, a ring of gold* and very many others.

Respective adjectives of this kind may be joined not only to substantives, but also to adjectives, participles and perhaps other parts of speech: for example, *a sun-shiny day*; *a self-tormenter*, or *self-tormenting man*. Since adjectives are usually joined only to substantives, we must either say that respective adjectives change into adverbs in positions like this (as other adjectives are known to do), or we must assume that first of all they join up with the substantives, for example *sunshine, selftorment*, and the adjectives are then formed from these aggregates – *sunshiny, self-tormenting*.

94   DE ADJECTIVIS.   C. V.

gatis formari Adjectiva, *fun-fhin-y, felf-torment-ing.*

Si quis autem haec omnia pro Compofitis haberi contendat; ego non prorfus abnuo, modo talia compofita dicat effe qualia funt ὅςτις, ὥντινων, ἑκέτι, τοιγαρῦν, *etjam, quare, quamobrèm, quandoquidem, nihilominus, respublica, fenatusconfultum, hujusmodi,* etc. in quibus et voces ipfae et Syntaxis manet integra.

Materialia. Notandum autem eft, quod hujusmodi Adjectiva nonnulla, quoties Materiam fignificant (et Materialia igitur dici poffunt) terminationem *en* aliquando affumunt: ut *a gold-ring, a golden-ring,* annulus aureus; *a brafs-veffel, a brazen veffel,* vas aeneum; *a horn top, a hornen top,* trochus corneus: Sic *a leaden pipe,* tubus plumbeus; *a wooden beam,* trabs lignea; *woollen cloth,* pannus laneus; *linen cloth, flaxen cloth,* pannus lineus; *hempen cloth,* pannus cannabinus; *an earthen veffel,* vas fictile, vas terreum; et raro alia.

Sed nec haec Adjectiva Materialia tam strictam fubeunt legem quin aliquando poffint fuis fubftantivis poftponi: Ut nec alia Adjectiva (praeter duo jam enumerata genera) five primitiva fint, five a Subftantivis aut aliunde formata; quorum non pauca genera fuo loco recenfebuntur.

Adjectiva Subftantive pofita (hoc eft, o-miffo fuo Subftantivo) pro Subftantivis habentur: Et, Adverbialiter pofita, adverbiafcunt.   C A P.

---

8 *senatusconsultum*: 4th has *senatus, consultum* (misprint)
19–21 *woollen cloth* . . . cannabinus: 4th–6th

Someone may object that all these examples should be regarded as compound words; this I can accept, provided that they are regarded as compounds of the same type as ὅστις, ὧντινων, οὐκέτι, τοιγαροῦν, *etiam, quare, quamobrem, quandoquidem, nihilominus, respublica, senatusconsultum, huiusmodi,* etc in which the component words themselves and their syntax are unaffected by being joined together.[103]

MATERIAL ADJECTIVES

It is worth noticing that some adjectives of this kind, which signify a material, and so may be called material-adjectives, sometimes take the ending *en,* for example, *a gold ring, a golden ring*; *a brass-vessel, a brazen vessel*; *a horn top, a hornen top*; *cf: a leaden pipe*; *a wooden beam*; *woollen cloth*; *linen cloth, flaxen cloth*; *hempen cloth*; *an earthen vessel* and a few others. However, there is no strict rule in the case of these material-adjectives to preclude them from occasionally following their substantives, any more than other adjectives (except the two kinds just described), whether they are adjectives in origin, or formed from substantives or in some other way. A good many of these types of adjectives will be mentioned in the appropriate section.[104]

Adjectives which are used substantivally, their own substantive being omitted, are regarded as substantives. If they are used as adverbs, they assume the nature of adverbs.

[103] Wallis distinguishes the group of respective adjectives + noun from compound words, apparently on the grounds that compounds are usually understood to be more closely integrated, because he concedes that they may be called compounds provided that the two component parts retain their identity. The examples from Greek and Latin are compounds normally written as one word, but with the exact form and syntax of the originally separate words. They contrast with compounds such as *signifer, magnanimus* where the original words have lost their separate identity. *Cf* English *daisy* (day's eye). Wallis does not appear to be making the sort of distinction which exists between loose compounds and closer knit ones, usually marked by different stress (*'gold 'coin* as opposed to *'goldfish*).
[104] This refers to Chapter xiv (Etymology); see Introduction *p* 28.

CAP. VI.

De Comparationibus.

Nomina Adjectiva (ut apud Latinos) Gradus Comparationis. Comparationem fortiuntur; Gradus nempe adfcifcunt Comparativum et Superlativum.

Gradus Comparativus formatur a Pofitivo addendo *er*; Superlativus addendo *eft*.

Ut *fair* formofus, *fairer* formofior, *faireft* formofiffimus. Sed et uterque gradus per circumlocutionem formantur, ut apud Latinos; ut, *more fair*, *moft fair*, *very fair*, magis formofus, maxime formofus, valde formofus.

Tria quidem (et vix plura) formantur irregulariter. *Good*, bonus, *better*, *beft* (pro *bet'ft*); *Bad*, *ill*, malus, *worfe* (et *worfer*), *worft* (pro *wors'ft*); *Little*, parvus, *lefs* (et *leffer*) *left* (pro *les'ft*).

Multi pro *left* fcribunt *leaft* (ut diftinguatur a conjunctione *left*, ne, ut non), verum omnino contra analogiam Grammaticae. Mallem ego Adjectivum *left*, Conjunctionem *leaft* fcribere.

Ex quibusdam five Praepofitionibus five Adverbiis formantur (ut apud Latinos) Adjectiva Comparativa et Superlativa. Sic *Before*, *former*, *formeft* (et *firft*, quafi *for'ft*),

prae,

CHAPTER VI
Comparison

Adjectives are compared, as in Latin; that is to say, they have a comparative and a superlative.

The *comparative* degree is formed by adding *er* to the *positive* and the *superlative* by adding *est*; for example, *fair, fairer, fairest*. An alternative method of forming the degrees, also used in Latin, involves a circumlocution: *more fair, most fair, very fair*,[105] (Latin *magis formosus, maxime formosus, valde formosus*).

Three words, and that is about all, have irregular forms: *good, better, best* (for *bet'st*); *bad* (or *ill*), *worse* (and *worser*), *worst* (for *wors'st*); *little, less* (and *lesser*), *lest* (for *les'st*). Many people use the spelling *least* instead of *lest* (to distinguish it from the conjunction *lest*) but this is quite contrary to the regular grammatical formation. I would rather see the adjective written *lest* and the conjunction *least*.

Some comparative and superlative adjectives are formed from prepositions or adverbs, as they are in Latin; for example *before, former, formost* (and *first*, as it were, *for'st*); *ab-ove, over, overmost*

---

[105] Grammarians of this period do not distinguish *most fair* from *very fair* in meaning. The formations in *-er, -est* were less restricted in Wallis's time than they are now, but were never used with participles. Bullokar, Jonson and Cooper all mention their use with adverbs in *-ly* (for example, freelier, freeliest – Cooper (1685), *p* 134). Greenwood augments Wallis's account by including a list of exceptions which do not take *-er, -est* (that is, endings in *-al, -able, -ing, -ish, -est, -ous, -ant, -ent, -ible, -id, -som*, excluding *able* and *handsome*).

96   DE COMPARATIONIBUS. C. VI.

prae, prior, primus: *Ab-ove, over, overmoſt,*
vel *up, upper, upmoſt,* et *uppermoſt,* ſupra,
ſuperior, ſupremus: *Be-neath, neather, nea-*
thermoſt, infra, inferior, infimus: *Be-hind,*
hinder, hindmoſt, et *hindermoſt: Late, later,*
lateſt, la'ſt, poſt (ſero), poſterior, poſtre-
mus: *Much,* multum, et *many* (olim *moe)*
multi, faciunt *more, moſt,* quaſi *mo'r, mo'ſt.*

Ut alia Adjectiva, ita praeſertim Comparativa et Superlativa ſaepiſſime adver-
biaſcunt.

Ut *ill-done* male factum, *much leſs* multo
minus, *leſs pleaſant* minus volupe, *moſt*
learned maxime doctus.

CAP. VII.

De Pronominibus, ſeu Nominibus Perſonalibus.

Nomina quaedam Perſonalia, vulgo Pronomina dici ſolent; ideo quia alterius
Nominis quaſi vicem ſupplent.

Sunt quidam revera Nomina, ſed aliquan-
tum irregularia.

Pronomi-
num ſtatus
duplex.   Haec autem, tam ſingularia quam pluralia, duplici fere forma ſeu ſtatu occurrunt: alterum ego Rectum appello, alterum

---

18 Sunt quidam: misprint for *Sunt quidem* of 1st–5th

or *up, upper, upmost* and *uppermost; beneath, neather, neathermost; be-hind, hinder, hindmost* and *hindermost; late, later, latest, la'st; much* and *many* (originally *moe*),[106] *more, most* (as it were, *mo'r, mo'st*).

The comparatives and superlatives of adjectives are very frequently used as adverbs, even more than other adjectives; for example, *ill-done, much less, less pleasant, most learned.*

CHAPTER VII
The pronouns, or personal nouns[107]

There is a group of personal nouns that are commonly called *pronouns*, on the grounds that they can be said to take the place of another noun. They are, in fact, nouns, but have rather irregular forms.

THE TWO FORMS OF PRONOUNS
They occur, both in singular and plural, in two different forms or states; I call one of these *rect* and the other *oblique*.[108] They have

---

[106] Wallis is not correct in identifying *moe* with *many. Mo(e)* was originally an adverb (OE *ma*), while *more* (OE *mara*) was the adjective. However, the former was often used with a genitive plural, so that in Middle English *mo(e)* comes to be used as a plural and *more* as a singular. This distinction was already becoming obsolete by the end of the sixteenth century, though it is to be found in Bullokar (1586).

[107] Introduction *p* 36.

[108] Latin *rectus, obliquus* (see Priscian v.xiii.68 *ff*). The terminology *rectus casus* goes back to the Greek ὀρθὴ πτῶσις (upright case, or nominative); earlier πτῶσις had been used to signify cases other than the nominative, tenses of the verb other than the present, derived forms etc, in its sense of a 'decline' from a chosen basic form (Aristotle, *Interp.* 16b, *Poetics* 20.10 and Koller, 1958, *p* 34 *ff*); *Cf* Latin *declinatio*. Butler uses the terms *rect* and *oblique case* in describing the verb, as well as the noun.

C. VII. DE PRONOMINIBUS. 97

terum Obliquum. Habentque fua Adjectiva Poffeffiva, licet peculiari plerumque modo formata.

In ftatu recto ufurpantur quoties vel Abfolute ponuntur; vel Verbo praecedunt, ut
Latinorum cafus rectus: In ftatu vero obliquo, ubivis alias; quippe cum Verbo, Prae-
pofitioni, aliive voci rectrici poftponuntur.

Primam perfonam defignat in Recto Sin- *Pronomi-*
gulari *I* ego, in Obliquo *me*, cujus Pof- *num enu-*
feffivum *my*, *mîne*, meus; in Recto Plu- *meratio.*
rali *we* nos, in Obliquo *us*, cujus Poffef- *I.*
fivum *our*, *ours*, nofter.
Secundam perfonam defignat *thou* tu, in *Thou,*
obliquo *thee*, unde Poffeffivum *thy*, *thîne*,
tuus; Pluraliter (tam in recto quam obliquo) *ye*, *you*, vos, unde Poffeffivum
your, *yours*, vefter.
Tertiam perfonam, ubi de Maribus fit *Hee.*
fermo, *hee* ille, in obliquo *him* (pro *heem*),
unde Poffeffivum *his* (pro *hee's*): Sin
de Foeminis agatur, *fhee* illa, in obliquo *Shee.*
her, Poffeffivum *her*, *hers*: Si autem de
neutro fexu agatur, *it* illud (tam in ftatu *It.*
recto quam obliquo), unde Poffeffivum
its. In plurali (five de maribus, foeminis, aut neutris agatur) *they* illi, illae,
illa; in obliquo *them* (*theim*); Poffeffivum *their*, *theirs*, fuus.

H   Inter-

16 tuus: 5th–6th
20 (pro *heem*): 4th–6th
28 (*theim*): 4th–6th

their own possessive adjectives, though these are mostly formed in an unusual way. The rect state is used when they appear in absolute position or before a verb, like the Latin *rect* case. Elsewhere the oblique state is used, that is, when they follow a verb, or a preposition or another governing word.

LIST OF THE PRONOUNS

I. The first person singular in the rect form is *I*, in the oblique form *me*, and its possessive is *my*, *mine*. In the plural of the first person the rect form is *we*, the oblique *us*, and its possessive is *our*, *ours*.

Thou. The second person singular has the rect form *thou*, oblique form *thee*, and possessive *thy*, *thine*; in the plural the rect and oblique forms are *ye*, *you* and the possessive *your*, *yours*.[109]

Hee, shee, it. In the third person singular, when the reference is to a male the rect form is *hee*, the oblique *him* (for *heem*)[110] and the possessive *his* (for *hee's*); if the reference is to a female the rect form is *shee*, the oblique *her* and the possessive *her*, *hers*. But if the reference is to neither sex *it* is used for both rect and oblique forms, with possessive *its*. In the plural, whether the reference is to male, female or neither, the rect form is *they*, the oblique *them* (*theim*) and the possessive *their*, *theirs*.

[109] For the use of the second person, singular and plural, forms see Wright and Wright (1924), §§ 317–18.
[110] Note 102, *p* 311.

98   DE PRONOMINIBUS. C. VII.

Who.

Interrogativum, in utrovis numero, de Perſonis eſt, *who* quis, in obliquo *whom* ; De Rebus (tam in recto quam obliquo) *what* ; Poſſeſſivum *whoſe* (vel potius *who's*) cujus. Quod tamen de rebus rarius uſurpatur, ſed potius *whereof*.

Notandum autem Poſſeſſiva *my, thy, her, our, your, their,* tunc uſurpari quando Subſtantivis conjunguntur; ut, *this is my houſe,* haec eſt mea domus: at *mine, thine, hers, ours, yours, theirs,* ubi Subſtantivum ſubintelligitur; ut *this houſe is mine,* domus haec eſt mea: ſed et *mine, thine,* dicimus nonnunquam ubi Subſtantivum exprimitur, ſed ſolummodo ante Vocalem; ut *my arm* vel *mine arm,* brachium meum. Nonnulli etiam *hern, ourn, yourn, hisn,* dicunt, pro *hers, ours,* etc. ſed barbare, nec quiſquam (credo) ſic ſcribere ſolet.

Notandum item apud nos morem obtinuiſſe (ſicut apud Gallos aliosque nunc dierum) dum quis alium alloquitur, ſingularem licet, numerum tamen pluralem adhibendi; verum tunc *you* dicimus, non *ye.* Singulari vero numero ſiquis alium compellet, vel dedignantis illud eſſe ſolet, vel familiariter blandientis.

Haec

5 cujus: 5th–6th

[322]

Who. The interrogative pronoun, if it refers to persons, is *who*, in both numbers, with oblique form *whom*; if it refers to things the rect and oblique forms are both *what*.[111] The possessive is *whose*, or better *who's*: this is rarely used of things, being usually replaced by *whereof*.

Notice that the possessive forms *my, thy, her, our, your, their* are used before substantives; for example, *this is my house*; whereas *mine, thine, hers, ours, yours, theirs* are used when the substantive is left to be understood; for example, *this house is mine*. Occasionally we use *mine, thine* when the substantive is expressed, but only before a vowel – *my arm*, or *mine arm*. *Hern, ourn, yourn, his'n*[112] are also used in speech by some people for *hers, ours* etc, but they are not educated forms and I do not think anyone uses them in writing.

Notice also that it is customary in English (and also in contemporary French and other languages) to use the plural number, even when addressing only one person; but in this case we say *you* not *ye*. To use the singular in addressing someone usually implies disrespect or close familiarity.[113]

---

[111] This usage dates from the sixteenth century. Before then *what* was regularly used to refer to persons also.

[112] These forms are still to be found in dialects, especially in the south of England and in America.

[113] See Wright and Wright, § 317.

C. VII. DE PRONOMINIBUS. 99

Haec autem omnia Pronomina fimul confpicienda
proponit haec Synopfis.

		Pronomina Primitiva, in ftatu		Eorum Pof-feffiva.	
		Recto.	Obliquo.	Cum Sub-ftantivo.	Sine Sub-ftantivo.
Perf. 1.	Singularis.	*I*	*me*	*my*	*mine*
	Pluralis.	*We*	*us*	*our*	*ours*
Perf. 2.	Singularis.	*Thou*	*thee*	*thy*	*thine*
	Pluralis.	*Ye*	*you*	*your*	*yours*
Perf. 3.	Sing. Maf.	*He*	*him*	*his*	
	Sing. Foe.	*She*	*her*	*her*	*hers*
	Sing. Neu.	*It*		*its*	
	Pluralis.	*They*	*them*	*their*	*theirs*
Inter-rogati-vum.	Perfonarum.	*Who*	*whom*	*who's*	
	Rerum.	*What*		*whereof*	

H 2   Demon-

The following table gives a conspectus of all the pronouns:

			BASIC FORMS		POSSESSIVE FORMS	
			rect state	oblique state	with sub- stantive	without sub- stantive
1st person		singular	I	me	my	mîne
		plural	we	us	our	ours
2nd person		singular	thou	thee	thy	thine
		plural	ye	you	your	yours
3rd person	singular	masculine	he	him	his	
		feminine	she	her	her	hers
		neither	it		its	
	plural		they	them	their	theirs
interrogative		persons	who	whom	who's	
		things	what		whereof	

100   DE PRONOMINIBUS. C. VII.

This, that.   Demonſtrativa *this, that*, hic, ille ; pluraliter *theſe, thoſe*; Item *the ſame* idem ; et Relativum vel etiam Interrogativum *which* qui ; nulla ratione dicenda puto Pronomina, ſed plane nomina Adjeſtiva.

Non enim pro nomine Subſtantivo poni ſolent, ut nempe ipſius locum ſuppleant (quod in Pronominibus fieri debere ipſa Denominatio oſtendit): ſed Subſtantivis adjiciuntur, eodem plane modo quo alia quaelibet Adjeſtiva; ut *this man, that man, which man, the ſame man*, homo hic, ille, quis, idem. Si enim aliquando ſine ſuis ſubſtantivis occurrant, quod quidem non raro fit, ipſa tamen Subſtantiva ſubintelliguntur; prout in omnibus fere Adjeſtivis fieri ſolet. Dicimus enim Latine *unus, multi, omnes, a lii, doſti, indoſti*, etc. Anglice, *one, many, áll, others, the learned, the unlearned*, etc. omiſſis Subſtantivis: Nec tamen haec Adjeſtiva in Pronominum numerum accenſeri ſolent.

Which.   Relativum *which,* qui, uſurpatur etiam interrogative ; ut in aliis linguis fieri ſolet: et (de perſonis) *who* et *whom.*

Eſt autem nomen Adjeſtivum.
De his autem notandum eſt, dici non raro *hereof, thereof, whereof; hereby, thereby, whereby,* etc. pro *of this, of that, (of theſe, of thoſe,) of which; by this, by that, (by theſe, by thoſe,) by which,* etc.

Notandum

---

16 prout . . . fieri ſolet: 1st has *prout in aliis fere omnibus Adjeſtivis fieri ſolet*; 4th omits entirely
24 et (de personis) *who* et *whom*: 4th–6th

This, that. I would not apply the name pronoun either to the demonstratives, *this, that* (plural *these, those*), or to *the same*, or to the relative or interrogative *which*, for they are clearly adjectives. My reason for saying this is that they are not used to replace a noun, that is, as a substitute for it (which should be a characteristic of pronouns, as their name indicates).[114] Instead, they occur with substantives in exactly the same way as any other adjective; for example, *this man, that man, which man, the same man.* When they occur without a substantive (as they often do) the substantives are taken as understood; this is usual with nearly all adjectives. In Latin we say *unus, multi, omnes, alii, docti, indocti*, etc, and in English *one, many, all, others, the learned, the unlearned*, etc omitting the substantives; but these adjectives are not normally included among the pronouns.

Which. The relative *which* is also used as an interrogative, as it often is in other languages. When persons are referred to, *who* and *whom* are used. *Which* is also an adjective. Notice, in this connection, that *hereof, thereof, whereof; hereby, thereby, whereby*, etc are often used rather than *of this, of that* (*of these, of those*), *of which; by this, by that* (*by these by those*), *by which*, etc.

---

[114] Melanchthon, in his Latin Grammar (1525–6), is one of the few early grammarians who give reasons for this substitutory function: (i) it saves repeating the noun, (ii) it saves mentioning the noun (demonstratives).

C. VII. DE PRONOMINIBUS. 101

Notandum item vocem *what* (interrogative, *What.*
aut indefinite aſſumptam) aliquando Adjec-
tive poni; ſed non eodem ſenſu quo inter
Pronomina ſupra retulimus: Nam *what*
Pronomen ſignificat *quid* (Subſtantive ſum-
ptum); at *what* Adjectivum potius eſt *qualis; ut *what man*, qualis homo.
Pro Relativo *which*, non raro ponitur *that*.

Vox *own*, quae poſſeſſivis non raro ἐμφα|ι- *Own.*
κῶς ſubjungitur, eſt plane nomen Adjectivum, et valet Latinorum *Proprium*.

Sic *my own houſe, your own lands, Alexander's own ſword*, etc. [mea ipſius domus,
veſtri ipſorum fundi, Alexandri ipſius enſis,
etc.] ſunt ad verbum *mea propria domus,
veſtri proprii fundi, Alexandri proprius gladius*, etc.

Vox *ſelf*, pluraliter *ſelves*, quamvis etiam *Self.*
Pronomen a quibusdam cenſeatur (quo-
niam ut plurimum per Latinum *ipſe* redditur); eſt tamen plane nomen Subſtantivum, cui quidem vix aliquod apud
Latinos Subſtantivum reſpondet; proxime tamen accedit vox *perſona* vel *propria perſona*.

Ut *my ſelf, thy ſelf, our ſelves, your ſelves*,
etc. [ego ipſe, tu ipſe, nos ipſi, vos ipſi, etc.]
ad verbum *mea perſona, tua perſona, noſtrae
perſonae, veſtrae perſonae*, etc. Fateor tamen
H 3   *himſelf,*

8 pro Relativo . . . *that*: 4th–6th

What. Note too that the word *what* (with interrogative or indefinite meaning) is sometimes used as an adjective, but not with the meaning that it had when I mentioned it earlier among the pronouns. The pronoun *what* is equivalent to Latin *quid*, used in place of a substantive, whereas the adjective *what* corresponds more to Latin *qualis* (what sort of) as in *what man*.

That is often used instead of the relative *which*.

Own. The word *own*, often used emphatically with possessives, is clearly an adjective, and equivalent to Latin *proprium*; for example *my own house, your own lands, Alexanders own sword*, etc can be literally translated as *mea propria domus, vestri proprii fundi, Alexandri proprius gladius*, etc.

Self. The word *self*, plural *selves*, is included by some among the pronouns (because it is usually rendered by Latin *ipse*). However it is clearly a substantive, and has virtually no equivalent among Latin substantives. The nearest would be their word *persona* or *propria persona*; for example *my self, thy self, our selves, your selves*, etc would correspond literally to *mea persona, tua persona, nostrae personae, vestrae personae*, etc. Admittedly *himself, itself, them-*

himſelf, itſelf, themſelves, vulgo dici pro *his-
ſelf, its-ſelf, their-ſelves*; at (interpoſito *own*)
his own ſelf, its own ſelf, their own ſelves,
ipſius propria perſona, illorum propriae
perſonae. Eodem ſenſu apud Graecos Poetas occurrunt ἴς, β´, κράτος; ut βίη Ἡρακληΐη,
vel Ἡρακλέος βίη, Hercules ipſe, vel propria
Herculis perſona; *Hercule's ſelf, Hercules
himſelf, Hercule's own ſelf.* Sic iilud Pſalm.
xcix. 4. עֹז מֶלֶךְ *robur Regis juſtitiam amat,*
reddi non incommode poterit, *the Kings
ſelf* (vel *the Kings Majeſty*) *loveth right-
eouſneſs ;* Rex ipſe, Regia Majeſtas, Regis
perſona propria, juſtitiam amat.

C A P.   VIII.

De Verbo.

Verborum flexio ſeu conjugatio, quae
in reliquis linguis maximam ſortitur difficultatem, apud Anglos leviſſimo negotio peragitur.

Tempora. Nos duo tantum habemus Tempora in
quovis Verbo, Praeſens et Praeteritum
Imperfeſtum : Duo item Participia, Activum et Paſſivum, quae plane Adjeſtiva
ſunt, aliorumque Adjeſtivorum naturam
omnino obtinent. Quod ſupereſt, verborum aliquot auxiliarium adjumento fere
totum perficitur.

Praeſens

---

9 *Hercule's own self*: 1st has *Hercules's own self*

selves are commonly used instead of *his-self, its-self, their-selves* but we also get (by inserting *own*) *his own self, its own self, their own selves.*[115] The Greek poets use the words ἴς, βίη, κράτος in the same way, for example βίη Ἡρακληίη, or Ἡρακλέος βίη – *Hercule's self, Hercules himself, Hercule's own self.* Similarly Psalm 99, 4. עומלך (Latin *robur regis iustitiam amat*) can fairly be translated *the Kings self* (or *the Kings Majesty*) *loveth righteousness.*

CHAPTER VIII
The verb

The inflection or conjugation of verbs, which causes a great deal of difficulty in other languages, is very simple in English.

THE TENSES

Verbs have only two tenses – *present*, and *imperfect past*.[116] They also have two participles – active and passive – which are clearly adjectives, and exhibit exactly the same characteristics as other adjectives. Otherwise almost everything is expressed by using auxiliary verbs.

---

[115] *Myself* etc. See Wright and Wright, § 323, for an account of the historical development of these forms.
[116] Introduction *pp* 31, 37.

C. VIII.   DE VERBO.   103

Praefens eft ipfum thema; ut *burn* uro : <small>Praefens.</small>
Atque illud innuit quod jam cum loqui-
mur praefens eft.

Praeteritum Imperfectum themati regu- <small>Praeteritum Imperfec-</small>
lariter adjungit *ed*; ut *burned* urebam : <small>tum.</small>
Illud autem innuit quod illo quidem
tempore (de quo fit fermo) praefens erat,
feu (ut loquuntur) in fieri. Atque eadem
etiam vox eft Participium Paffivum re- <small>Participium Paffivum.</small>
gulariter formatum; ut *burned* uftus.

Praeteriti Imperfecti, et Participii Paffivi Anomaliae poft tradentur.

Participium Activum themati adjungit <small>Activum.</small>
ing; ut *burning* urens. Eademque vox
Subftantive pofita eft Nomen Verbale,
atque etiam Gerundiorum vices fupplet;
ut *in burning this* in urendo hoc, *in the
burning of this* in uftione hujus.

Verbo infinite pofito praefigi folet parti- <small>Infinitum.</small>
cula *to* (quae tamen nonnunquam omit-
titur; ut poft dicetur).

Ufurpatur autem poft alia (non pauca) verba, et Adjectiva; ut etiam ubi Subftantive
ponitur: omnino ut Latinorum modus infi-
nitivus.

Perfonarum et Numerorum diftinctio, <small>Perfona.</small>
per praefixa nomina Perfonalia (vel, in
H 4   tertia

17–18 *in the burning of this*: 1st–5th have *in burning of this*

The *present* is the same as the verb-stem; for example *burn*; it indicates what *is present* at the moment when we are speaking.

The *imperfect past* regularly has *ed* added to the stem; for example *burned*. It indicates what *was present* at the time which is spoken about, or what was *in fieri*[117] (to use the current term). This is also the regular form of the *passive participle*, that is, *burned*. Irregular forms of the imperfect past and the passive participle will be described later.[118]

The *active participle* is formed by adding *ing* to the stem – as in *burning*. When this word is used substantivally it is the verbal noun,[119] and also takes the place of the gerund; for example, *in burning this* (Latin *in urendo hoc*), *in burning of this* (Latin *in ustione huius*). The *infinitive* of the verb regularly has the particle *to* before it, though this is sometimes left out, as I shall show later. The infinitive is used after a good number of other verbs, and after adjectives, for instance when it is used substantivally; in this respect it is exactly like the Latin infinitive mood.

PERSON

The distinction of person and number is mostly shown by the personal nouns (in the third person other substantives may be used)

---

[117] 'in the course of taking place'.

[118] The forms *I am burning, I was burning* are used in a sense distinct from *I burn, I burnt* only from the seventeenth century onwards. Hume mentions them, and Cooper (1685, *p* 147) explains them as signifying *actum praesentem in actu* ('a present action in the course of taking place').

[119] The participle and the verbal noun are distinguished here by a syntactic criterion; the *-ing* form which they share is a result of the coalescence of what were two quite different forms in Old English (Wright and Wright, § 334).

tertia perfona, alia quaevis Subftantiva)
inftar Latinorum cafus Nominativi, maxime indigitatur; ut *I burn* uro, *they
burn* urunt.

In fecunda tamen perfona fingulari, utriusque Temporis, additur terminatio *eft*;
et in tertia fingulari, praefentis Temporis, terminatio *eth*, vel ipfius loco *s* (aut,
fi neceffitas pronunciandi poftulet, *es*).
Thou burneft, *he burneth* (vel *burns*), *thou
burned'ft*; uris, urit, urebas.

Dicimus autem (verbis auxiliaribus *will,
fhall*) *wilt, fhalt*, per Syncopen, pro *will'ft,
fhall'ft*: Item *haft, hath*, hoc eft, *ha'ft, ha'th*,
pro *hav'ft, hav'th* (ut et *had* pro *hav'd*).
Et in verbis auxiliaribus *will, fhall, may,
can*, terminatio *eth* prorfus omittitur.
Omittitur etiam utraque terminatio in Imperando; et, poft Conjunctiones *if* fi, *that*
ut, *though, although*, quamvis, *whether* u-
trum, et aliquando etiam poft alias aliquot
Conjunctiones et Adverbia; tunc fcilicet
ubi Latini modum Imperativum aut Sub-
junctivum adhiberent.
In Terminationibus *eft, eth, ed* (et *en*, de qua
poftea dicetur, ut et paffim alias), vocalis *e*,
fere ad placitum, per Syncopen tollitur (nifi
forfan afperitas pronunciandi aliquando impediat); ejusque defectus, ubi opus eft, Apoftrophi nota innuitur; ut *do'ft* pro *doeft*
agis; *do'th, doth*, pro *doeth* agit; *did'ft,
didft*, pro *diddeft* agebas; *plac'd* pro *placed*
locatus;

12 (verbis auxiliaribus: 1st–4th have (*a verbis auxiliaribus*
30–32 *do'st* pro *doest* . . . *diddest* agebas: 4th–6th

which are put before the verb, corresponding to the Latin nominative case; for example *I burn*, *they burn*.

However, in the second person singular of both tenses the termination *est* is added, and in the third person singular, present tense, the termination *eth*, or alternatively *s* (or *es* if the pronunciation requires it. *Thou burnest*, *he burneth* (or *burns*), *thou burned'st*. We also say (from the auxiliary verbs *will*, *shall*) *wilt*, *shalt*, by syncope,[120] for *will'st*, *shall'st*, and *hast*, *hath* (*ha'st*, *ha'th*) for *hav'st*, *hav'th* (and *had* for *hav'd*). In the auxiliary verbs *will*, *shall*, *may*, *can* the termination *eth* never occurs.

Both terminations are left out in commands, and after the conjunctions *if*, *that*, *although*, *whether*, and sometimes after other conjunctions and adverbs, namely where Latin would have the imperative or subjunctive mood.

The vowel *e* in the terminations *est*, *eth*, *ed* (and *en*, which I will talk about later, and in a number of other places) may be freely omitted by syncope, except perhaps where the resulting sound is harsh. The omission is indicated, when necessary, by an apostrophe: for example, *do'st* for *doest*; *do'th*, *doth* for *doeth*; *did'st*, *didst*, for

[120] No syncope is involved in *wilt*, *shalt*; they come from Middle English *wilt*, *schalt*. *Cf* note 102, *p* 311.

locatus; *burn'd, burnd.* pro *burned* uſtus; *know'n, known,* pro *knowen* notus.

CAP. IX.

De Verbis Auxiliaribus Mutilis.

Verbis infinitis (ſed omiſſa particula *to)* praeponuntur haec Verba Auxiliaria *do, will, ſhall, may, can,* cum eorum Praeteritis Imperfeᴄtis *did* (pro *doed), would, ſhould* (ab antiquis *wolle, ſholle), might* (olim *mought), could:* Item *muſt,* quod extra tempus praeſens vix reperitur.   Auxiliaria mutila.

> Sed et Verba *let* permitto, *bid* jubeo, *dare* audeo, *help* adjuvo, et fortaſſe alia nonnulla (quaſi eſſent verba Auxiliaria) praeponuntur etiam verbis infinitis, omiſſa nonnunquam particula *to.*
> Haec autem verba Auxiliaria, ideo Mutila nominanda cenſeo, quoniam ultra tempus Praeteritum Imperfeᴄtum non uſurpantur: Participia nempe non habent, nec verba Auxiliaria ſibi praefixa admittunt.
> Duo tamen, *do* ago, et *will* volo, quoniam, depoſita Auxiliarium natura, non raro ut verba Abſoluta occurrunt, integre formantur, nempe tam participia habent *(doing, do'n, willing, willed)* quam verba Auxiliaria admittunt; ubi ſcilicet ſunt verba Abſoluta, non autem ubi ſunt Auxiliaria.

Do

---

2 *know'n, known* . . . notus: 4th–6th
9 vix reperitur: 1st–4th have *non reperitur*
13–14 nonnunquam: 4th–6th

diddest; *plac'd* for *placed*; *burn'd*, *burnd* for *burned*; *know'n*, *known* for *knowen*.

CHAPTER IX
The defective auxiliary verbs

The following auxiliary verbs are used before infinitives (without the particle *to*): *do*, *will*, *shall*, *may*, *can* together with their imperfect past tenses *did* (for *doed*), *would*, *should* (from the old *wolle*, *sholle*), *might* (previously *mought*)[121] *could*. *Must* also occurs, though it is very rarely found except in the present tense.

The verbs *let*, *bid*, *dare*, *help* and perhaps some others are also used before infinitives (as if they were auxiliary verbs), sometimes with the omission of the particle *to*.

I think these auxiliary verbs should be called *defective*, because they are not used beyond the imperfect past – that is to say they have no participles and cannot be preceded by auxiliary verbs.

However two of them – *do* and *will* – often occur as independent verbs, losing their auxiliary character, and so have the complete range of forms: they have participles (doing, do'n, willing, willed) and can be preceded by auxiliaries, but only when they are independent verbs, and not when they are auxiliaries themselves.

---

[121] This form was common until the end of the seventeenth century, and still survives in some dialects (Wright and Wright, § 404 and Wright, 1896, *sv*).

106 DE VERBIS AUXILIARIBUS. C. IX.

Do. *Do* et *did* indicant emphatice tempus Praefens, et Praeteritum Imperfectum. Uro, urebam, *I burn, I burned,* vel (emphatice) *I do burn, I did burn.*

Shall, will. *Shall* et *will* indicant Futurum. Uret, *it shall burn, it will burn.*

Quoniam autem extraneis fatis eft cognitu difficile, quando hoc vel illud dicendum eft (non enim promifcue dicimus *shall* et *will*); neque tamen alii quos vidi ullas tradidere regulas quibus dirigantur: has ego tradere neceffarium duxi, quas qui obfervaverit hac in re non aberrabit.

Quomodo differunt. In primis perfonis *shall* fimpliciter praedicentis eft ; *will*, quafi promittentis aut minantis.
In fecundis et tertiis perfonis, *shall* promittentis eft aut minantis ; *will* fimpliciter praedicentis.

Uram, ures, uret; uremus, uretis, urent: *I shall burn, you will (thou wilt), he will; we shall, ye will, they will, burn;* nempe hoc futurum praedico: vel *I will, you shall (thou shalt), he shall; we will, ye shall, they shall, burn;* nempe, hoc futurum fpondeo, vel, faxo ut fit.

Would, should. *Would* et *should* illud indicant quod erat, vel effet, futurum : cum hoc tamen difcrimine ;

Do and *did* are used to express the present tense and imperfect past tense emphatically.[122] *I burn, I burned* or (emphatic) *I do burn, I did burn.*

Shall and *will* indicate the future: *it shall burn, it will burn.* It is difficult for foreigners to know when to use the first form and when the second (we do not use them both interchangeably), and no other description that I have seen has given any rules for guidance, so I thought I ought to give some;[123] if these rules are observed they will prevent any mistakes being made. In the first person *shall* simply indicates a prediction, whereas *will* is used for promising or threatening. In the second and third persons *shall* is used for promising or threatening, and *will* of a straightforward prediction. *I shall burn, you will (thou wilt), he will*; *we shall, ye will, they will, burn* all simply predict what will happen; whereas *I will, you shall (thou shalt), he shall, we will, ye shall, they shall, burn* are used for guarantees or pledges of what will happen.

Would and *should* signify what would have been or might be in the future, though with this difference: *would* implies intention or

[122] The emphatic use of *do* was comparatively new in Wallis's time – it appears to have been mentioned first by Gil. Wallis does not mention what is now the obligatory use of *do* in negative and interrogative constructions, though he gives examples (emphatic?) of them (*pp* 349, 353): *burn I . . .* or *do I burn? . . . it burned not, it did not burn.*

[123] *Shall* and *will* derive from Old English *sceal* and *wile* expressing respectively *obligation* and *wish or intention*. For some centuries there was no clear rule for their use to express the future. Wallis seems to have been the first to formulate this rule; the usage he describes has been prevalent in England (but not in Scotland, Ireland or America) until the present day, though the tendency now is for *will* to replace *shall* to indicate futurity in the first person. See Jespersen *M.E.G.*, iv, § 18.9.

C. IX. DE VERBIS AUXILIARIBUS. 107

crimine; *Would* voluntatem innuit feu agentis propenſionem; *ſhould* ſimpliciter futuritionem.

Urerem; urere debebam, deberem, vole-bam, vellem; *I ſhould, or would, burn.*

May et *can*, cum eorum Praeteritis Im- *May, can.* perfectis *might* et *could*, potentiam innu-unt : cum hoc tamen diſcrimine : *may* et *might* vel de Jure vel ſaltem de rei poſſibilitate dicuntur; at *can* et *could*, de viribus agentis.

Poſſum (ſive potis ſum) urere, *I can burn;* poteram vel poſſem (potis eram vel eſſem) urere, *I could burn;* poſſum urere (nempe poſſibilis eſt, aut licet), *I may burn;* pote-ram vel poſſem urere (poſſibile vel licitum erat vel eſſet), *I might burn.*

Muſt neceſſitatem innuit. Debeo, opor- *Muſt.* tet, neceſſe eſt, urere, *I muſt burn.*

Aliquando, ſed rarius, in praeterito dicitur *muſt* (quaſi ex *muſt'd* ſeu *muſt't* contractum). Sic, ſi de praeterito dicatur, *he muſt* (ſeu *muſt't) be burnt*, oportebat uri, ſeu neceſſe habuit ut ureretur.

C A P.

20–24 Aliquando . . . ut ureretur: 5th–6th

[340]

inclination on the part of the subject, while *should* simply indicates futurity:[124] *cf* Latin *urerem*; *urere debebam,* ·*deberem, volebam, vellem – I should, or would, burn.*

May and *can,* and their imperfect past tenses *might* and *could* indicate potentiality, but there is a difference between them: *may* and *might* are used to signify the permissibility or, at any rate, the possibility of something, whereas *can* and *could* refer to the ability of the doer. *I can burn* (I am capable of burning); *I could burn* (I was or would be capable of burning); *I may burn* (it is possible or permissible for me); *I might burn* (it was or would be possible or permissible for me).

Must indicates necessity: *I must burn* (Latin *debeo, oportet, necesse est, urere*). On some rare occasions *must* occurs as a past tense (as if contracted from *must'd,* or *must't*).[125] For instance in speaking about the past, *he must* (or *must't*) *be burnt* (it was necessary for him to be burnt).

---

[124] Although Wallis says that *should* 'simply indicates futurity' his Latin examples *urere debebam,* and *urere deberem* express obligations – *I ought to burn, I should burn* or *I ought to have burnt, I should have burnt. Debeo* is in fact given shortly afterwards as a Latin equivalent of *must,* indicating necessity.
[125] See Wright and Wright, § 405.

108   DE VERBIS AUXILIARIBUS. C. X.

CAP. X.

De Verbis Auxiliaribus Integris.

Auxiliaria *integra.* Alia duo verba auxiliaria, *have* et *am* (feu *be)*, praeponuntur Participiis Paffivis; eodem plane modo quo aliis quibusvis vel Adjectivis vel etiam Subftantivis.

> Eodem plane modo quo Gallorum *j'ay, je fuis;* aliaque ejusdem fignificationis in linguis aliis modernis; quibus haec noftra refpondent.
>
> Integra vero ideo appello, quoniam non modo duo tempora (praefens et imperfectum) fed et participia habent, et verba auxiliaria fibi praefixa admittunt (dummodo ipfa tamen adhuc maneant auxiliaria) non fecus ac alia quaevis Verba abfoluta.
>
> Auxiliaria tamen dico, quia non modo Praeteritorum perfectorum et plusquam perfectorum omnium, fed et totius vocis Paffivae vices fuftinent.

Have, had. *Have* (participio paffivo junctum) indicat Praeteritum Perfectum; illud nempe quod nunc eft praeteritum, feu (ut loquuntur) in facto effe : *Had,* praeteritum plufquam perfectum; illud nempe quod tunc

CHAPTER X

The complete auxiliary verbs

Two other auxiliary verbs, *have* and *am* (or *be*) are used before passive participles, in exactly the same way as they are before other adjectives or even before substantives. This English usage corresponds to French *j'ay, je suis* and to words with this meaning in other modern languages. I call them *complete* because in addition to having two tenses (present and imperfect) they have participles, and can be preceded by auxiliary verbs (as long as they themselves remain auxiliaries) like the independent verbs. However I classify them as auxiliaries because they are the means of forming not only the whole of the perfect and pluperfect past, but also the entire passive voice.

Have, when used with the passive participle, marks the *perfect* past, namely what is now past or, to put it another way, is in a state of having been completed. *Had* marks the *pluperfect past*, namely

tunc erat praeteritum (eo scilicet tempore de quo fit sermo).

Ussi *I have burned*, usseram *I had burned*, ussisse *to have burned*, καύσας *having burned*, loquutus *having spoken*. Sic *shall have, will have*, illud indicant quod erit praeteritum; quod Graeci fortasse per ipsorum paulo-post-futurum, vel mox-futurum exprimere possunt: Latini vero aegrius exprimunt nisi in verbis formae Passivae; ut loquutus ero *I shall have spoken*, loquutus essem *I should have spoken;* nam *I shall have burned, it will have burned*, difficilius Latine redditur, nisi forsan *ussero, usserit*, tantundem significare dicamus: At *I should have burned, I would have burned*, Latine dicimus, *ussissem, ussisse vellem.*

Am vel *be* sum (participio passivo junc-　*Am, be.* tum) totius vocis Passivae (ut loquuntur Latini) vices gerit.

Prout etiam in aliis nunc dierum linguis: et quidem ex parte in lingua etiam Latina.

Est autem hoc verbum satis anomalum; et duplicem quidem formam habet.

In Praesenti $\begin{cases} am, art, is, \text{pluraliter } are. \\ be, be'st, be, \text{pluraliter } be. \end{cases}$

In Praeterito imperfecto $\begin{cases} was, \quad wast, \quad was, \\ were, wert, were, \end{cases} \begin{cases} \text{plura-} \\ \text{liter} \\ were. \end{cases}$

Infi-

what was then past, at the time referred to. *I have burned, I had burned, to have burned, having burned, having spoken.* Similarly *shall have, will have* mark what will be past; the Greeks could perhaps express this with their *future shortly-to-be* or *future soon-to-be.*[126] In Latin it is scarcely used except in verbs with a passive form, for example *loquutus ero – I shall have spoken, loquutus essem – I should have spoken. I shall have burned, it will have burned* are more difficult to put into Latin, unless we may say that *ussero, usserit* have this meaning. *I should have burned, I would have burned* are, in Latin *ussissem, ussisse vellem.*

Am or *be*, used with the passive participle, supplies the whole of the passive voice, to use the Latin terminology, as it does in other modern languages, and to some extent in Latin too. It is an irregular verb and has two separate forms:

present $\begin{cases} am, art, is, \text{plural } are \\ be, be'st, be, \text{plural } be \end{cases}$

imperfect
past $\begin{cases} was, wast, was \\ were, wert, were \end{cases}$ plural *were*

---

[126] Examples of this are πεποιήσομαι, τετύψομαι, but few Greek verbs had a special paradigm for the future-perfect; in most verbs it was formed by means of a periphrasis consisting of the perfect participle and the future tense of the verb εἶναι – *to be*. It was sometimes used in Attic Greek with the implication 'it is as good as done' (Priscian VIII.viii.38).

IIO   DE VERBIS AUXILIARIBUS. C. X.

Infinitum *to be.* Participium Activum *being;*
Paſſivum *been.*

Prior forma (tam in Praeſenti, quam in
Praeterito Imperfecto) illic plerumque
adhibetur, ubi Latini modum indicati-
vum ponerent; alibi fere ſemper ſecun-
da.

Uror, uſtus ſum, *I am burned;* ſi urar, ſi
uſtus ſim, *if I be burned;* urebar, uſtus e-
ram, *I was burned;* quamvis urerer, quamvis uſtus eſſem, *although I were burned;*
uſtus fui, *I have been burned;* uſtus fueram,
fuiſſem, *I had been burned;* urar, *I ſhall be
burned;* uſtus ero, *I ſhall have been burned;* uſtus eſſem, fuiſſem, *I ſhould be burned,
I ſhould have been burned;* uſtus eſto, *be
burned;* uri, *to be burned;* uſtus eſſe vel
fuiſſe, *to have been burned.*
Atque ad hanc formam nos omnem Modorum et Temporum varietatem, quae apud
Latinos conſpicitur, facile abſolvimus. Amo,
I love, I do love; amabam, *I loved, or did
love;* amavi, *I have loved;* amaveram, *I
had loved;* amabo, *I ſhall love, I will love;*
ama, *love thou;* amem, *I may love, I can
love;* amarem, *I might love, I could love, I
ſhould love, I would love;* amaverim, ama-
vero, *I ſhould have loved, I will have loved;*
amaviſſem, *I ſhould have loved, I would have
loved, I could have loved, I might have loved;*
amare, *to love;* amaviſſe, *to have loved;* a-
mandi, *of loving;* amando, *in loving;* aman-
dum,

19–111.6 Atque ad hanc formam . . . Participio Passivo: 5th–6th

infinitive: *to be*   active participle: *being*
passive participle: *been*

The first form, both in the present tense and the imperfect past, is used mostly where Latin would have the indicative mood; almost everywhere else the second form is used. For example, *I am burned*; *if I be burned*; *I was burned*; *although I were burned*; *I have been burned*; *I had been burned*; *I shall be burned*; *I shall have been burned*; *I should be burned*; *I should have been burned*; *be burned*; *to be burned*; *to have been burned*.

In this way we easily dispense with all the various moods and tenses which are found in Latin. *I love, I do love* (Latin present indicative),[127] *I loved* or *did love* (Latin imperfect indicative); *I have loved* (Latin perfect indicative); *I had loved* (Latin pluperfect indicative); *I shall love, I will love* (Latin future indicative); *love thou* (Latin present imperative); *I may love, I can love* (Latin present subjunctive); *I might love, I could love, I should love, I would love* (Latin imperfect subjunctive); *I should have loved, I will have loved* (Latin perfect subjunctive and future perfect indicative); *I should have loved, I would have loved, I could have loved, I might have loved* (Latin pluperfect subjunctive); *to love* (Latin present infinitive); *to have loved* (Latin perfect infinitive); *of loving* (Latin genitive of gerund); *in loving* (Latin ablative of gerund); *to love* (Latin accusa-

---

[127] Wallis gives, in each case, the Latin equivalent of the English auxiliary + principal verb. In translating it seemed best to give the tense and mood of each Latin form, rather than to repeat the Latin words; the voice is *active* except where *passive* is specified.

C. X.   DE VERBIS AUXILIARIBUS.   III

dum, *to love;* amatum, *to love;* amatu, *to be loved;* amans, *loving;* amaturus, *being to love;* amatus, *loved;* amandus, *being to be loved.* Et pariter in Paſſiva voce, mediantibus Auxiliari *am* ſeu *be,* et Participio Paſſivo.

C A P. XI.

De ſede Vocis Nominativae et Accuſativae, aliisque ad Verborum ſyntaxin ſpectantibus.

Interrogando et Imperando, vox Nominativa ſuo Verbo poſtponitur; (nempe Auxiliarium primo, ſi quod adſit; vel, ſi non adſit auxiliare, ipſi verbo Abſoluto) : Alibi plerumque (nec ſemper tamen) praeponitur.

Sedes vocis Nominativae.

Ubi autem Imperando dixi, etiam intelligendas vellem Permiſſiones, Conceſſiones, etc. quae a Latinis per modum Imperativum efferuntur.
Uro, uris, urit, *I burn, thou burneſt, he burneth,* etc. vel *I do burn,* etc. Uro? uris? urit? etc. *burn I? burneſt thou? burneth he?* etc. vel *do I burn? doſt thou burn? doth he burn?* etc. Uram, uras, urat, etc. vel *ure,* urito, etc. *burn I, burn thou, burn he,* etc.
Notandum autem quod ubi in ſecundis perſonis fit Imperium ſeu Conceſſio, vox nominativa ſaepiſſime omittitur; ut *ure, urite, burn;*

19 burnest thou?: 1st–3rd have *burnst thou?*

tive of gerund); *to love* (Latin supine in *-um*); *to be loved* (Latin supine in *-u*); *loving* (Latin present participle); *being to love* (Latin future participle); *loved* (Latin passive past participle); *being to be loved* (Latin gerundive). The same is true of the passive voice, in forming which the auxiliary *am, be* is used together with the passive participle.

CHAPTER XI

The position of the nominative word and the accusative word, and other matters relating to the syntax of verbs

POSITION OF THE NOMINATIVE WORD[128]

In questions and commands the nominative word comes after its verb – that is, after the first auxiliary, if there is one, or after the independent verb, if there is not. Otherwise it usually, but not always, comes before the verb. (When I said 'in commands' I meant it to apply also to *permissions, concessions,* etc which are expressed by the imperative mood in Latin.) For example, *I burn, thou burnest, he burneth,* etc or *I do burn,* etc. *Burn I? burnest thou? burneth he?* etc or *do I burn? dost thou burn? doth he burn?* etc. *Burn I! burn thou! burn he!* etc. Notice also that when the command

---

[128] *Cf: p* 291.

112 DE SEDE VOCIS NOMINATIVAE C. XI.

burn; pro *burn thou, burn ye:* In reliquis vero perfonis fit faepe circumlocutio per vocem *let* (permitte, fine), ut uram, urat; uramus, urant; *let me burn, let him burn; let us burn, let thêm burn;* hoc eft, ad verbum *fine me urere (permitte ut uram), fine eum urere,* etc. Quod ipfum quidem apud Latinos fit; nam cum *urat, uramus,* etc. (quae funt revera modi Subjunctivi) Imperative ufurpantur, ponuntur ellliptice, pro *efto ut urat, licet ut urat, licet urat, fine urat,* aut alia ejusmodi formula.

Nec mirum fit, me primam perfonam fingularem modi Imperativi recenfuiffe, quod pauci faciunt; nam qui hujusmodi formas Imperativas effe concefferit [Petat quoties velit, nunquam obtinebit; Petamus quoties velimus, nunquam obtinebimus, etc.] *Aſk he* (vel *let him aſk) as oft as he will, he ſhall never obtain;* etc. idem de hac, eadem ratione, concedere debet [Petam ego quoties velim, nunquam obtinebo] *Aſk I* (vel *let me aſk) as oft as I will, I ſhall never obtain.*

Eadem fere forma nonnunquam poftpofitio vocis Nominativae (poft Praeteritum Imperfectum, praefertim verborum auxiliarium) fupplet defectum conjugationis *if* fi. Si petiiffet, obtinuiffet; *had he aſked* (pro *if he had aſked), he had obtained.*

Sedes vocis Accufativae. Vox Accufativa Verbis Tranfitivis (nunc dierum) plerumque poftponitur; ut urit me, *he burneth me.*

At

---

3 ut uram, urat: 1st–5th have *ut uram, uras* (misprint)
27 conjugationis: 1st–5th have *conjunctionis*

or concession is in the second person, the nominative word is very often left out – *burn!* instead of *burn thou! burn ye!* In the other persons there is often a circumlocution using the word *let* (allow), as in *let me burn, let him burn, let us burn, let them burn,* which is literally equivalent to Latin *sine me urere (permitte ut uram), sine eum urere* etc. This type of circumlocution occurs in Latin too; when *urat, uramus* etc, which are really in the subjunctive mood, are used to express the imperative, they are used elliptically for *esto ut urat, licet ut urat, licet urat, sine urat,* or some formula of that kind.

The fact that I have listed a first person singular of the imperative mood should be no cause for surprise, though few others do it. If it is granted that the forms contained in *Ask he* (or *let him ask*) *as oft as he will, he shall never obtain* etc are imperatives, the same principle should permit *Ask I (or let me ask) as oft as I will, I shall never obtain.*[129]

In much the same way the nominative word is sometimes put after the verb (in the imperfect past, especially where the verb is an auxiliary) to make up for the omission of the conjunction *if*; for example *had he asked* (instead of *if he had asked*) *he had obtained.*

POSITION OF THE ACCUSATIVE WORD
The accusative word usually follows transitive verbs nowadays, for example, *he burneth me.* At one time it often preceded the verb, *he me burneth, me he burneth*; this is still a regular construction in

---

[129] For the use of *ask I* as an imperative see Jespersen, *M.E.G.*, v. § 24.13–15.

At olim folebat faepe praeponi, *he me burn-eth*, *me he burneth;* prout adhuc apud Germanos et Belgas ufu fit; et aliquando etiam apud Anglos, praefertim Poetas.

Adverbium negandi *not* (non) Verbo poftponitur (nempe auxiliari primo, fi quod adfit; aut, fi non adfit auxiliare, Verbo principali) : aliis tamen orationis partibus praefigi folet. Sedes particulae Negativae.

Non urebat, *it burned not, it did not burn;* non me, *not me;* me non-urebat, *it burned me not, it burned-not me, me it burned-not;* non-me urebat, *it burned not-me, me it burned not.*

Latinorum Participia Futuri temporis (in *rus* et *dus*) nos plerumque efferimus per Verbum Infinitum. Latinorum Participia in *rus* et *dus*.

Praefixo tamen (aut per Ellipfin omiffo) Adjectivo aptae fignificationis (vel aliquando Praepofitione) ut fiat circumlocutio. Moriturus *to dye*, vel *about to dye* (quafi, circiter ipfum mori), *ready to dye* (mori paratus), *like to dye* (morti vicinus, verifimiliter moriturus), *condemned to dye* (morti damnatus). Sic, occidendus, *to be killed, ready to be killed, like to be killed,* aut alia non abfimili forma.

Eft (ut loquuntur) tertii adjecti, innuitur praefixa voce *there,* et poftpofita voce No-

I mina-

German and Dutch and sometimes in English as well, especially in poetry.

POSITION OF THE NEGATIVE PARTICLE

The adverb of negation, *not*, follows the verb, – that is, the first auxiliary verb, if there is one; otherwise the principal verb. But it usually precedes other parts of speech; for example, *it burned not, it did not burn; not me; it burned me not, it burned-not me, me it burned-not; it burned not-me, me it burned not.*[130]

THE LATIN PARTICIPLES IN RUS AND DUS

In English we often use the infinitive where Latin uses its future participles (in *rus* and *dus*). But we put an adjective of suitable meaning before it (which may be omitted, by an ellipse) or sometimes a preposition, to give a circumlocution. Latin *moriturus* becomes *to dye*, or *about to dye* (as it were, *round about death*), *ready to dye, like to dye (in the neighbourhood of death, probably going to dye), condemned to dye.* Similarly for Latin *occidendus* we have *to be killed, ready to be killed, like to be killed*, or something similar.[131]

The use of Latin *est* of the 'added third' as it is called, is rendered by putting the word *there* before the verb and the nominative word

---

[130] The distinction made here by Wallis between *it burned me not, it burned-not me, me it burned-not* (Latin *me non-urebat*) and *it burned not-me, me it burned not* (Latin *non-me urebat*) is apparently one between a contrastive use of *me*, as opposed to *you, him* etc (second group), and a non-contrastive use (first group).

[131] *Cf* Buck (1933), *pp* 309–10: 'the earliest force (sc. of the Latin gerundive) was substantially that of a simple active and middle participle, as it appears in *oriundus* "rising" . . .; it was (later) used with the force of "that which is to do, to be done" '.

minativa. Ut Eſt (datur) calor in ſole, *there
is heat in the ſun:* Non ſunt (non dantur)
orbes ſolidi (nulli dantur orbes ſolidi) *there
are no ſolid orbs,* etc.

**Verba Im-
perſonalia.** Verba Imperſonalia proprie non habemus; ſed quae Latini Imperſonaliter efferunt, nos efferimus perſonaliter, praefixa voce Nominativa *it.*

Placet, juvat, oportet me, juſtum eſſe; *It
pleaſeth, it delighteth, it behoveth me, to be
juſt.* Ubi tamen ſiquis dicat [*juſtum eſſe*]
caſum eſſe Nominativum verbis *placet, juvat, oportet,* ideoque ipſa eſſe Perſonalia;
ego neutiquam inficias ibo. Conſtructio Anglicana ſic accipienda eſt, *To be juſt, it pleaſeth me* (juſtum eſſe, id mihi placet): Ubi
vel prior vox Nominativa (*to be juſt,* juſtum
eſſe) abſolute ponitur; vel poſterior *(it,* id)
redundat; ſaltem emphatica vel exegetica
fit reduplicatio.

C A P. XII.

De Verbis Anomalis.

Reſtat ut de Verborum aliquot Anomalia
pauca tradam. De quibus haec duo
primitus monenda ſunt.

1. Tota

9–17 In these lines 1st–4th have *virtuosum, vertuous* for *justum, just*

after it.[132] For Latin *est (datur) calor in sole* we say *there is heat in the sun*; and for *non sunt (non dantur) orbes solidi (nulli dantur orbes solidi)* we say *there are no solid orbs*, and so on.

IMPERSONAL VERBS

We have no true impersonal verbs. Instead we turn Latin impersonal constructions into personal ones, putting the nominative word *it* before the verb. For Latin *placet, iuvat, oportet me, iustum esse*, we say *it pleaseth, it delighteth, it behoveth me, to be just*. However if anyone claims that *iustum esse* is the nominative case which goes with the verbs *placet, iuvat, oportet*, and that they are therefore personal verbs, I shall not contradict him. The English construction should be interpreted as *to be just, it pleaseth me*, where either the first nominative word (*to be just*) is used in an absolute construction or the second one (*it*) is redundant. One would only use them both together for additional emphasis or explanation.

CHAPTER XII
The irregular verbs[133]

It remains for me to say something about the irregularity of certain verbs. Two points need making at the very beginning:

---

[132] See Jespersen, *M.E.G.*, VII. §§ 3.1–3.2, for this usage.
[133] Introduction *p* 37.

C. XII. DE VERBIS ANOMALIS. 115

1. Tota quae sequitur Anomalia non ni- Duo Prae-
si praeteriti Imperfecti temporis, et Par- monita.
ticipii Passivi formationem spectat.

Nam in ipsis quidem Verbis Irregularibus
nihil aliud irregulare est.

2. Tota illa quantacunque Anomalia,
Verba Exotica vix omnino attingit, sed
illa sola quae Nativa sunt.

Exotica vero illa appello quae a Latinis,
Gallicis, Italicis, Hispanicis, aut etiam Cam-
bro-Britannicis deduximus, quae quidem
multa sunt: Nativa vero illa voco quae ab
antiqua lingua Teutonica, seu Saxonica, o-
riginem ducunt; quae quidem omnia sunt
Monosyllaba (aut saltem a Monosyllabis deducta), et plerumque nobis cum Germanis,
Belgis, Danis, etc. communia sunt (levi saltem immutatione facta); quorum nempe sive Linguae sive Dialectus ejusdem cum nostra Anglicana sunt originis.

Anomalia prima, quae maxime generalis Anomaliae
est, ex celeritate pronunciandi originem Generales.
duxit: nempe (post syncopen vocalis *e*
in regulari terminatione *ed*), relicta consona *d* saepissime mutatur in *t*; quoties
scilicet pronunciatio sic evadit expeditior
(et quidem contractio potius dicenda videtur, quam Anomalia).

Nempe

(i) All the irregularities which follow concern only the formation of the imperfect past tense and the passive participle. There is nothing else irregular about these irregular verbs.

(ii) All the irregularities, whether small or great, are confined to words of native origin and hardly affect imported words at all. I mean by imported words those which we have got from Latin, French, Italian, Spanish, or even Welsh, and there are a great many of them. By native words I mean those which originally came from the ancient Teutonic or Saxon language; these are all monosyllabic (or, at any rate, derived from monosyllables) and we share most of them with the Germans, Dutch, Danes, etc (if slight changes of form are allowed for), whose languages or dialects, whichever they are, have the same origin as our English language.

GENERAL IRREGULARITIES

The first irregularity and the most general, arises from speed of utterance; if the vowel *e* in the regular termination *ed* is omitted by syncope, the *d* which remains very often changes into *t*, when this makes the pronunciation easier (I think it should be called a *contraction* rather than an irregularity). This usually happens after

Nempe poſt *c, ch, ſh, f, k, p, x,* et poſt conſonas *ſ, th,* durius pronunciatas, et aliquando poſt *l, m, n, r,* modo praecedat vocalis brevis: hae enim literae facilius poſt ſe recipiunt *t* quam *d.* Ut *plac't, ſnatch't, fiſh't, wak't, dwel't, ſmel't, burn't,* etc. pro *plac'd, ſnatch'd, fiſh'd, wak'd, dwell'd, ſmell'd, burn'd,* vel *placed, ſnatched, fiſhed, waked, dwelled, ſmelled, burned,* a verbis *to place* loco, *to ſnatch* rapio, *to fiſh* piſcor, *to wake* evigilo, *to dwell* habito, *to ſmell* olfacio, *to burn* uro.

Sed et vocalis longa praecedens non raro abbreviatur, vel in cognatam breviorem tranſit: quae et ipſa conducunt ad celeriorem pronunciationem. Sic *kept, ſlept, wept, crept, ſwept, lept,* a Verbis *to keep* ſervo, *to ſleep* dormio, *to weep* fleo, *to creep* repo, *to ſweep* verro, *to leap* ſalto.

At poſt conſonas *b, g, v, w, z,* atque *s, th,* mollius prolatas; et *l, m, n, r,* praecedente vocali longa, manet *d :* facilius enim coaleſcunt cum *d,* propter ſimilem ſpiritus ad nares directionem, quam cum *t.* Sic *liv'd, ſmil'd, raz'd, believ'd,* etc. a Verbis *to live* vivo, *to ſmile* ſubrideo, *to raze* deleo, *to believe* credo.

Niſi cum vocalis longa abbreviatur ante *l, m, n, r ;* et ubi *b, v,* in *p, f,* ſonusque mollior literarum *s, th,* in earundem ſonum duriorem tranſit. Ut *felt, delt, dremt, ment, left, bereft, beleft,* etc. a Verbis *to feel* tactu ſentio, *to deal* diſtribuo, *to dream* ſomnio, *to mean* intendo, *to leave* linquo, *to bereave* orbo, *to believe* credo.　　　　　　Ubi

---

5–12 1st–3rd omit *snatch't, snatch'd, snatched, to snatch* rapio: 1st–4th omit
　　burn't, burn'd, burned, to burn uro
　20 *b, g, v, w, z:* 1st omits *w*

c, ch, sh, f, k, p, x, after the consonants *s* and *th* when they have their harder sound, and sometimes after *l, m, n, r* if they are preceded by a short vowel; the reason is that these letters combine better with a following *t* than a *d*; for example, *plac't, snatch't, fish't, wak't, dwel't, smel't, burn't*, etc instead of *plac'd, snatch'd, fish'd, wak'd, dwell'd, smell'd, burn'd*, or *placed, snatched fished, waked, dwelled, smelled, burned*, from the verbs *to place, to snatch, to fish, to wake, to dwell, to smell, to burn*. It often happens, too, that where a long vowel precedes, it is shortened, or changes into a cognate short vowel; this also helps to speed up pronunciation; for example, *kept, slept, wept, crept, swept, lept* from the verbs *to keep, to sleep, to weep, to creep, to sweep, to leap*.

However, after the consonants *b, g, v, w, z*, and *s, th* with their softer sound, and after *l, m, n, r* when they are preceded by a long vowel, the *d* remains unchanged. This is because these sounds combine better with *d* than with *t*, inasmuch as they involve a similar direction of the breath stream, into the nose;[134] for example, *liv'd, smil'd, raz'd, believ'd*, etc from the verbs *to live, to smile, to raze, to believe*.

Exceptions to this are cases where a long vowel before *l, m, n, r* is shortened, and where *b, v* change to *p, f* and the softer sound of *s, th* changes to the harder one; for example *felt, delt, dremt, ment, left, bereft, beleft*, etc from the verbs *to feel, to deal, to dream, to mean, to leave, to bereave, to believe*.

---

[134] See *p* 155 and Introduction *p* 52 *f*.

C. XII. DE VERBIS ANOMALIS. 117

Ubi autem *d* vel *t* praecefſerat, litera addi-
titia *d* vel *t* (in hac contracta forma) cum *d*
vel *t* radicali in unam literam coaleſcunt.
Nempe ſi *t* radicalis eſſet, coeunt in *t;* ſin
d eſſet radicalis, tum vel *d* in *t* coeunt, prout haec vel illa litera promptius proferri
poſſit. Ut *read, led, ſpread, ſhed, dread,
ſhred, tread, bid, hid, chid, fed, bled, bred,
ſped, ſtrid, ſlid, rid,* etc. (ſeu potius *readd,
bidd,* etc. quaſi *read'd, bid'd,* etc.) a Verbis
to read lego, *to lead* duco, *to ſpread* expan-
do, *to ſhed* effundo, *to dread* revereor, *to
ſhred* minutim ſeco, *to tread* conculco, *to bid*
jubeo, *to hide* abſcondo, *to chide* objurgo,
to feed paſco, *to bleed* ſanguinem emitto, *to
breed* pario, educo, *to ſpeed* expedio, *to ſtride*
paſſum extendo, *to ſlide* labor, *to ride* equito.
Sic *caſt, hurt, coſt, burſt, eat, beat, ſweat, ſit,
quit, ſmit, writ, bit, hit, met, ſhot, cut, put,*
etc. (aut fortaſſe melius *eatt, bitt, hitt,* etc.
quaſi *eat't, bit't, hit't*) a Verbis *to caſt* projicio, *to hurt* laedo, *to coſt* conſto (de precio
dictum), *to burſt* rumpo, *to eat* edo, *to beat*
verbero, *to ſweat* ſudo, *to ſit* ſedeo, *to quit*
libero, *to ſmite* percutio, *to write* ſcribo, *to
bite* mordeo, *to hit* percutio, *to meet* occurro,
to ſhoot ex machina projicio, *to cut* ſeco, *to
put* pono. Item *lent, ſent, rent, girt,* etc. (pro
lend'd, ſend'd, etc. vel *lendt, ſendt,* etc.) a
verbis *to lend* mutuo do, *to ſend* mitto, *to
rend* lacero, *to gird* cingo.
Verba autem hanc Anomaliam ſeu contractionem paſſa, admittunt ut plurimum etiam
formam regularem, non minus eleganter
I 3   quam

---

5 tum vel *d* in *t*: misprint for *tum vel in d vel in t* of 1st–5th
19 *cut, put*: 5th–6th
28–29 *to cut* seco, *to put* pono: 5th–6th

When the verb ends in *d* or *t* in the first place, the additional *d* or *t* combines (in the contracted form) with the *d* or *t* of the root, to make one letter. That is to say, if the root letter is *t*, they become *t*, but if it is *d* they become either *d* or *t*, according to which letter gives the easier pronunciation; for example *read, led, spread, shed, dread, shred, tread, bid, hid, chid, fed, bled, bred, sped, strid, slid, rid,* etc (or better *readd, bidd,* etc as if from *read'd, bid'd,* etc) come from the verbs *to read, to lead, to spread, to shed, to dread, to shred, to tread, to bid, to hîde, to chîde, to feed, to bleed, to breed, to speed, to strîde, to slîde, to rîde.* Similarly *cast, hurt, cost, burst, eat, beat, sweat, sit, quit, smit, writ, bit, hit, met, shot, cut, put,* etc (perhaps better *eatt, bitt, hitt,* etc as if from *eat't, bit't, hit't,* etc) come from the verbs *to cast, to hurt, to cost, to burst, to eat, to beat, to sweat, to sit, to quit, to smîte, to wrîte, to bite, to hit, to meet, to shoot, to cut, to put.* And *lent, sent, rent, girt,* etc (for *lend'd, send'd,* etc or *lendt, sendt,* etc) come from the verbs *to lend, to send, to rend, to gird.*

Verbs which possess this irregular or contracted form mostly have a regular form as well which is no less acceptable than the

11̣8   DE VERBIS ANOMALIS. C. XII.

quam hanc contractam; ut *placed, fished, believed, bereaved, girded, burned,* etc. vel *plac'd, fish'd,* etc. Nisi fortaffis cacophonia nonnunquam impediat fyncopen paffa (ut *gird'd*); aut etiam (in Verbis frequentiffimi ufus) celeritas pronunciandi contractiorem formam in quibusdam ut plurimum fuadeat; unde *kept, wept,* fere femper dicimus; *keeped, weeped,* rarius.

Participia in *en.*

Anomalia fecunda etiam frequens eft, fed folummodo Participium Paffivum fpectat : Nempe Participium Paffivum olim faepiffime formabatur in *en :* Cujufmodi fatis multa adhuc retinemus, praefertim ubi Praeteritum Imperfectum infignem aliquam anomaliam patitur (atque haec quidem Altera Participii Formatio, potius quam Anomalia, non incommode dici poteft).

Ut *been, taken, given, slay'n, know'n,* etc. a Verbis *to be* effe, *to take* accipio, *to give* do, *to slay* occido, *to know* cognofco.
Et quidem nonnunquam poft Praeteriti Imperfecti et Participii Paffivi communem five contractionem five anomaliam, etiam haec Participii Paffivi peculiaris anomalia accedit. Scilicet tam *written, bitten, eaten, hidden, chidden, shotten, rotten, chosen, broken,* etc. quam *writ, bit, eat, beat, hid, chid, shot, rot, chose, broke,* etc. in Participio Paffivo (at non item in Praeterito Imperfecto) promifcue

2 *burned*: 4th–6th
27 *eaten, hidden*: 1st–5th have *eaten, beaten, hidden* (*cf : eat, beat, hid* in 118.29)

contracted one, for example, *placed, fished, believed, bereaved, girded, burned,* etc or *plac'd, fish'd,* etc. However sometimes syncope may result in an ugly sound, and prevent the use of this form (as *gird'd*); or, in the most frequently used verbs, speed of utterance may be a strong factor in support of the contracted form in some cases; for instance we rarely say *keeped, weeped,* but nearly always *kept, wept.*

PARTICIPLES IN EN
Another irregularity is also common, but applies only to the passive participle. At one time the commonest way of forming the passive participle was with *en,* and we still have quite a large number of these forms, especially where the imperfect past tense is subject to a marked irregularity – it may be best to regard this simply as an alternative way of forming the participle, rather than as an irregular form. For example, *been, taken, given, slay'n, know'n,* etc come from the verbs *to be, to take, to give, to slay, to know.*

Sometimes, where the imperfect past tense and the passive participle have the same contracted or irregular form, the passive participle has an irregular form of its own in addition. For instance the passive participle can have the form *written, bitten, eaten, beaten, hidden, chidden, shotten, rotten, chosen, broken,* etc just as much as *writ, bit, eat, beat, hid, chid, shot, rot, chose, broke,* etc, but this is not true of the imperfect past tense. These forms come from

C. XII. DE VERBIS ANOMALIS. 119

cue efferuntur; a Verbis *to write* scribo, *to bite* mordeo, *to eat* edo, *to beat* verbero, *to hide* abscondo, *to chide* objurgo, *to shoot* projicio, *to rot* putresco, *to choose* eligo, *to break* frango; aliaque ejusmodi multa.

Item promiscue formantur Participia *sow'n, shew'n, hew'n, mow'n, loaden, laden;* atque *sow'd, shew'd, hew'd, mow'd, loaded, laded;* a Verbis *to sow* sero, *to shew* ostendo, *to hew* dolo, *to mow* meto, *to load* vel *lade* onero; aliaque forsan aliquot similia.

Sunt et aliae Anomaliae non paucae, praesertim in Praeterito Imperfecto; sed quae magis speciales sunt, nec quidem adeo multae quam ut possint sigillatim recenseri. _{Anomaliae Speciales.}

Verba auxiliaria, eorumque anomaliam, supra tradidimus. Alia sequuntur, quae in suas classes distribuemus, praemissis illis quae utrobique eandem vocem retinent, adjunctis deinde aliis quae aliter in Praeterito Imperfecto, aliter in Participio Passivo efferuntur.

1. *Win* lucro, *spin* neo, *begin* incipio, *swim* no, *strike* percutio, *stick* haereo, *sing* cano, *sting* aculeis pungo, *fling* jacio, *ring* campanam pulso, *wring* torqueo, *spring* germino, *swing* pendulus agitor, *drink* bibo, *sink* mergor, *shrink* contrahor, *stink* foeteo, *hang* pendeo, *come* venio, *run* curro, *find* invenio, *bind* ligo, *grind* contero, *wind* convolvo;

I 4   tam

the verbs *to wrîte, to bîte, to eat, to beat, to hîde, to chîde, to shoot, to rot, to choose, to break*; many others exist, of a similar kind.

Similarly the verbs *to sow, to shew, to hew, to mow, to load, to lade,* have equally good participle forms – either *sow'n, shew'n, hew'n, mow'n, loaden, laden* or *sow'd, shew'd, hew'd, mow'd, loaded, laded.*

SPECIAL IRREGULARITIES
There are a number of other irregularities, especially in the imperfect past tense, but they are more special cases and are few enough to be listed individually.

I described the auxiliary verbs and their irregularities earlier. Now here are some other irregular words which I shall divide up into their different classes; I shall start off with those that have the same form in imperfect past and passive participle and then add others which have different forms:

(i) *win, spin, begin, swim, strike, stick, sing, sting, fling, ring, wring, spring, swing, drink, sink, shrink, stink, hang, come, run, fînd, bînd, grînd, wînd* have the following forms in imperfect past and

tam in Praeterito Imperfecto, quam in Participio Passivo, dant *wònne, ſpun, begun, ſwum, ſtruck, ſtuck, ſung, ſtung, flung, rung, wrung, ſprung, ſwung, drunk, ſunk, ſhrunk, ſtunk, hung, còme, run, found, bound, ground, wound:* Sed et eorum pleraque formantur etiam in Praeterito Imperfecto per *a*, ut *wan, began, ſang, rang, ſprang, drank, came, ran;* et quaedam alia, ſed rarius. Quaedam in Participio Paſſivo aſſumunt etiam *en*, ut *ſtricken (ſtrucken), drunken, bounden.* Sed et utrobique forma analoga fere in omnibus retinetur, ut *ſpinned, ſwimmed,* etc.

2. *Fight* pugno, *teach* doceo, *reach* extendo, *ſeek* quaero, *beſeech* oro, *catch* capio, *buy* emo, *bring* affero, *think* cogito, *work* operor; faciunt utrobique *fought, taught, raught, ſought, beſought, caught, bought, brought, thought, wrought.* Sed et ex his non pauca analogiam retinent, ut *teached, reached, beſeeched, catched, worked,* etc.

3. *Take* capio, *ſhake* quatio, *forſake* deſero, *wake (awake)* evigilo, *ſtand* (olim *ſtead)* ſto, *break* frango, *ſpeak* loquor, *bear* fero, pario, *ſhear* tondeo, *ſwear* juro, *tear* lacero, *wear* induo, tero, *weave* texo, *cleave* haereo, *cleave* (olim *clíve)* findo, *ſtrive* contendo, *thrive* diteſco, *drive* pello, *ſhine* ſplendeo, *ríſe (aríſe)* ſurgo, *ſmíte* percutio, *write* ſcribo, *bíde (abíde)* maneo, *ríde* equito, *chooſe (chúſe)* eligo, *tread* conculco, *get* acquiro, *beget* gigno, *forget* obliviſcor, *ſeethe* coquo; faciunt utrobique *took, ſhook, forſook, wóke, awóke, ſtood, bróke, ſpóke, bóre, ſhóre, ſwóre,*

---

8 *wan*: 5th–6th
11 *(strucken)*: 4th–6th
17 utrobique: 5th–6th
29 *(arise)*: 4th–6th

passive participle: *wònne, spun, begun, swum, struck, stuck, sung, stung, flung, rung, wrung, sprung, swung, drunk, sunk, shrunk, stunk, hung, còme, run, found, bound, ground, wound.* But many of them have an imperfect past in *a* also; for example, *wan, began, sang, rang, sprang, drank, came, ran,* and some others, but less commonly. Some also have *en* in the passive participle; for example, *stricken (strucken), drunken, bounden.* Both in the imperfect past and the passive participle a regular form is retained as well, in nearly all cases: as *spinned, swimmed,* etc.

(ii) *Fight, teach, reach, seek, beseech, catch, buy, bring, think, work,* have for their imperfect past and participle, *fought, taught, raught, sought, besought, caught, bought, brought, thought, wrought.* A number of these retain a regular form too, for example, *teached, reached, beseeched, catched, worked,* etc.

(iii) *Take, shake, forsake, wake (awake),* stand (originally *stead*), *break, speak, bear, shear, swear, tear, wear, weave, cleave* [= stick], cleave (originally *clîve*) [=*split*], *strîve, thrîve, drîve, shîne, rîse (arîse), smîte, wrîte, bîde (abîde), rîde, choose (chúse), tread, get, beget, forget, seethe,* have for their imperfect past and passive participle *took, shook, forsook, wôke, awôke, stood, brôke, spôke, bôre, shôre, swôre, tôre, wôre, wôve, clôve, strôve, thrôve, drôve, shône, rôse,*

C. XII. DE VERBIS ANOMALIS.

fwóre, tóre, wóre, wóve, clóve, ſtráve, thróve, dróve, ſhóne, róſe, aróſe, ſmóte, wróte, bóde, abóde, róde, chóſe, trod, got, begot, forgot, ſod. Sed et utrobique dicimus etiam *thrĭve, rĭſe, ſmit, writ, abid, rid.* In Praeterito Imperfeéto quaedam etiam formantur per *a ;* ut *brake, ſpake, bare, ſhare, ſware, tare, ware, clave, gat, begat, forgat,* et fortaſſe quaedam alia, ſed rarius. In Participio Paſſivo formantur eorum non pauca per *en ;* ut *taken, ſhaken, forſaken, bróken, ſpóken, bŏrn (bór'n), ſhór'n, ſwór'n, tór'n, wór'n, wóven, clóven, thriven, drĭven, rĭſen, ſmitten, written, ridden, chóſen, trodden, gotten, begotten, forgotten, ſodden.* Multa etiam utrobique retinent analogiam; ut *waked, awaked, beared, ſheared, weaved, cleaved, thríved, abíded, chooſed, ſeethed,* etc.

4. *Give* do, *bid* jubeo, *ſit* ſedeo, faciunt in Praeterito Imperfeéto *gave, bad, ſate :* In Participio Paſſivo *given, bidden, ſitten.* Sed et utrobique *bid, ſit.* Atque huc referenda ſunt multa ex prima et tertia claſſe, quae formant praeteritum imperfeétum etiam in *a.*

5. *Draw* traho, *know* ſcio, *ſnow* ningo, *grow* creſco, *throw* jacio, *blow* flo, *crow* cano (inſtar galli), *fly* volare, *ſlay* occido, *ſee* video, *lie* jaceo, faciunt Praeterita Imperfeéta *drew, knew, ſnew, grew, threw, blew, crew, ſlew, ſlew, ſaw, lay :* Participia Paſſiva per *en ; draw'n, know'n, ſnow'n, grow'n, throw'n, blow'n, crow'n, flyen (flow'n), ſlay'n, ſeen, ly'n (lay'n).* Sed et utrobique *draw'd, ſnow'd,*

---

5 *writ*: 4th–6th
8 *clave*: 4th–6th
10 non pauca per *en*: 1st has *non pauca etiam per en*

arôse, smôte, wrôte, bôde, abôde, rôde, chôse, trod, got, begot, forgot, sod. But we also say *thrĭve, rĭse, smit, writ, abid, rid,* for both parts. Some of these verbs also form their imperfect past tense with *a,* for example *brake, spake, bare, share, sware, tare, ware, clave, gat, begat, forgat,* and perhaps, less often, some others. Many of them form their passive participle in *en: taken, shaken, forsaken, brôken, spôken, bōrn (bôr'n), shôr'n, swôr'n, tôr'n, wôr'n, wôven, clôven, thriven, drĭven, rĭsen, smitten, written, ridden, chôsen, trodden, gotten, begotten, forgotten, sodden.* Many keep the regular form in both parts: *waked, awaked, beared, sheared, weaved, cleaved, thrîved, abîded, choosed, seethed,* etc.

(iv) *Give, bid, sit,* have imperfect pasts *gave, bad, sate* and passive participles *given, bidden, sitten. Bid, sit,* can also be used for both parts. Many of the verbs in the first and third classes, which have an alternative form of the imperfect past, in *a,* should be included in this section.

(v) *Draw, know, snow, grow, throw, blow, crow, fly, slay, see, lie,* have imperfect past forms *drew, knew, snew, grew, threw, blew, crew, flew, slew, saw, lay* and passive participles in *en: draw'n, know'n, snow'n, grow'n, throw'n, blow'n, crow'n, flyen (flow'n), slay'n, seen, ly'n, (lay'n).* One also gets, for both parts, *draw'd,*

122   DE VERBIS ANOMALIS. C. XII.

snow'd, throw'd, crow'd. At a *flee* fugio, fit
fledd; a *go* eo, fit *went* (ab Antiquo *wend*)
et participium *go'n.*

Suntque haec (quae memini) omnia linguae
Anglicanae Verba Anomala: Alia vel nulla
funt, vel certe pauciffima.

CAP. XIII.

De Adverbiis, Conjunctionibus, Praepofitionibus, et Interjectionibus.

Adverbia. Adverbia eandem fortiuntur naturam
apud nos, quam apud Latinos, aliasque
gentes: Nempe non Verbis tantum, fed
et aliis orationis partibus adjiciuntur.

Quorum praecipua fequuntur.
Adverbia Temporis; Quando *when*, nunc
now, tunc *then*, hodie *to-day*, cras *to-morow*,
heri *yefterday*, perpetuo *ever*, nunquam *never*, dum *while*, diu *long*, *a great while*, do-
nec *till*, *un-till*, dudum *fince*, *ago*, *long fince*,
long ago, antehac *here-to-fore*, pofthac *hereafter*, jamjam *allready.*
Numeri; Quoties *how-oft*, toties *fo oft*, fe-
mel *once*, bis *twice*, ter *thrice*, *three-times*,
quater *four times*, faepe, multoties, *oft, often,
often-times, many-times*, raro *feldom*, femper
all-ways (quafi omnibus vicibus, a Cambrica
voce *gwaith* vices: nifi forte Italorum hic
imitemur *tutte-via;* aut faltem Germanorum *all-weg*).

Ordinis;

---

1 1st has *blow'd* also, after *throw'd*
15 dum *while*: 4th–6th
16–17 *long since, long ago*: 4th–6th
20 *three-times*: 5th–6th
24–26 nisi forte . . . *all-weg*: 5th–6th

snow'd, throw'd, crow'd. But from *flee* we get *fledd*; from *go* we get *went* (from the old *wend*) and the participle *go'n*.

These are all the irregular verbs, as far as I can recall, that are found in the English language. If there are any others, they are very few in number.

CHAPTER XIII

Adverbs, conjunctions, prepositions and interjections[135]

ADVERBS
Adverbs have the same characteristics in English as in Latin and other languages; that is to say, they qualify not only verbs but other parts of speech as well. The following are the principal ones:

Adverbs of time: *when*; *now*; *then*; *to-day*; *to-morrow*; *yesterday*; *ever*; *never*; *while*; *long*; *a great while*; *till, untill*; *since*; *ago*; *long since*; *long ago*; *here-to-fore*; *hereafter*; *allready*.

Adverbs of number: *how-oft*; *so-oft*; *once*; *twice*; *thrice*; *three times*; *four times*; *oft*; *often*; *oftentimes*; *many-times*; *seldom*; *allways* (as it were, *by all turns* from the Welsh word *gwaith* – a turn; unless it is an imitation of Italian *tutte-via* or German *all-weg*).

[135] Introduction *p* 37 *f.*

C. XIII. DE ADVERBIIS, ETC.

Ordinis; Primo *firft*, deinde *afterward*, proxime *next*, fecundo *fecondly*, tertio *thirdly*, ultimo *laftly*, tandem *at laft*, *at length*, etc.

Loci; Ubi *where*, hic *here*, illic *there*, ubique *every-where*, nufquam *no-where*, ufpiam *any-where*, alicubi *fome-where*, alibi (alicubi alias) *elfe-where*, *fome-where-elfe*, intus *within*, foris *with-out*: Quo *whither*, huc *hither*, illuc *thither*, aliquo *fome-whither*, nullo *no-whither*, intro *in*, foras *out*: Quorfum *which way*, horfum *this way*, eorfum *that way*, nullorfum *no-way*, furfum *up-ward*, deorfum *downward*: Unde *whence (from whence)*, hinc *hence*, inde *thence*: Simul *together*, feorfum *a-funder*, *in-funder*, prope *near*, *hard-by*, longe *far-off*, *a great way off*.

Affirmandi; Etiam *yea*, *yes*, *I*; forte *perhaps*, *perchance*, *peradventure*, *it may be*.

Negandi; Non (abfolute pofitum) *no* (conjuncte pofitum), *not*.

Monftrandi; En *lo*, *behold*.

Similitudinis et Comparationis; Quam, quomodo, *how*; tam, fic, *fo*; ut *as*, quantum (quam multum) *how much*, magis *more*, minus *lefs*, maxime *moft*, minime *leaft*, valde *very*, *very much*, omnino *altogether*, *wholly*; ferme *almoft*, *well nigh*; folummodo *only*, *but*; potius *rather*, quam *than*, vix *fcàrce*, aegre *hardly*, bene *well*, male *ill*, mélius *better*, pejus *worfe*, optime *beft*, peffime *worft*, docte *learnedly*, fortiter *valiantly*, cito *quickly*, etc.

Reliqua

10–11 nullo *no-whither*: 5th–6th
12 eorsum *that way*: 4th–6th
13 nullorsum *no-way*: 5th–6th
17–18 *a great way off*: 5th–6th
27 *least*: 4th–5th have *lest* (*cf: p* 373, note 136)

Adverbs of order: *first*; *afterward*; *next*; *secondly*; *thirdly*; *lastly*; *at last*; *at length*, etc.

Adverbs of place: *where*; *here*; *there*; *every-where*; *no-where*; *any-where*; *some-where*; *else-where*; *some-where-else*; *with-in*; *with-out*; *whither*; *hither*; *thither*; *some-whither*; *no-whither*; *in*; *out*; *which way*; *this way*; *that way*; *no-way*; *up-ward*; *down-ward*; *whence (from whence)*; *hence*; *thence*; *together*; *a-sunder*; *in-sunder*; *near*; *hard by*; *far-off*; *a great way off*.

Adverbs of affirmation: *yea, yes, I*; *perhaps, perchance, peradventure, it may be*.

Adverbs of negation: *no* (absolute position); *not* (with other words).

Adverbs of demonstration: *lo, behold*.

Adverbs of likeness and comparison: *how*; *so*; *as*; *how much*; *more*; *less*; *most*; *least*;[136] *very*; *very much*; *altogether*; *wholly*; *almost*; *well-nigh*; *only*; *but*; *rather*; *than*; *scarce*; *hardly*; *well*; *ill*; *better*; *worse*; *best*; *worst*; *learnedly*; *valiantly*; *quickly*, etc.

[136] The 4th and 5th editions have the spelling *lest*; *cf* Wallis's earlier comments (*p* 317).

124   *DE ADVERBIIS, ETC. C. XIII.*

Reliqua fere Adverbia (et ex enumeratis
non pauca) funt vel Periphrafes; ut diu *a
long while*, jamdudum *a great while ago*
faepenumero *many times*, etc. Vel Praepofitiones aut Adjectiva Adverbiafcentia; ut
ante *before*, prope *near*, praeter *befide*, infra
under, *below*, etc. multum *much*, parum *little*,
magis *more*, etc. Vel denique a quibusvis
fere Adjectivis formantur, adjuncta terminatione *ly;* ut docte *learnedly*, fortiter *valiantly*, fubito (fubitaneè) *fuddenly*, tertio
thirdly, etc.

Conjuncti- Conjunctiones item eundem habent u-
ones.   fum, quem apud Latinos, aliosque.

Quarum hae funt praecipuae; Et *and*, quo-
que *allfo*, *likewife*, nec *nor*, *neither*, utrum
whether, five *or*, *either*, fed *but*, nam *for*,
quia *becaufe*, quare *why*, *wherefore*, ergo
therefore, fi *if*, tum *then*, quamvis *though*,
all-though, *not-with-ftanding*, tamen *yet*, ut
that, quod *that*, cum *feeing*, *fince that*,
when as, nifi *but*, *except*, *unlefs*, faltem *at-
left*, vel *even*.
Si quis tamen harum aliquot voces potius
Adverbia effe dicat; aut etiam ex Adverbiis aliquot ad Conjunctionum claffem re-
ferre malit: non tanti eft ut hac de re quis
contendat, cum, et apud Latinos, eadem non
raro vox nunc pro Adverbio, nunc pro
Conjunctione cenfenda eft. Neque aliquod
grave detrimentum pateremur, fi tam Adverbia quam Conjunctiones et Interjectio-
nes,

22 *but*: 4th–6th
30 Neque aliquod: 1st has *Neque forsan aliquod*

Nearly all other adverbs, and quite a lot of those already listed, are either periphrastic, for example, *a long while, a great while ago, many times,* etc, or are really prepositions or adjectives acting as adverbs: *before, near, beside, under, below, much, little, more,* etc., or are formed by adding *-ly* to almost any adjective, for example *learnedly, valiantly, suddenly, thirdly,* etc.

CONJUNCTIONS
Conjunctions too are used in the same way as in Latin and other languages. The following are the principal ones: *and; also; likewîse; nor; neither; whether; or; either; but; for; because; why; wherefore; therefore; if; then; though; all-though; not-with-standing; yet; that; seeing; since that; when as; but; except; unless; at-lest; even.*

It may be objected that some of these words are adverbs, or that some of those listed as adverbs should be put under conjunctions, but the point is not worth arguing, since in English and in Latin the same word is often to be interpreted as an adverb in one place and a conjunction in another. There would be no great harm in putting adverbs, conjunctions and interjections all in the same class.

C. XIII. DE ADVERBIIS, ETC.

nes, ad eandem claſſem redigerentur. Eſt
quidem nonnihil diſcriminis, ſed leviuſcu-
lum.

Praepoſitiones etiam eandem ſortiuntur Praepoſitio-
naturam, quam in aliis linguis : Sed nes.
frequentiori apud Anglos uſu occurrunt
quam apud Latinos, eo quod nos Caſu-
um diſcrimina non agnoſcamus.

Verum de hisce quicquid dicendum erat,
ſupra, ubi de Nomine Subſtantivo agebatur, tradidimus.

Interjeótiones non ita multas habemus. Interjeétio-
O, oh, ah, ſi, ha ha he, ſt, nobis ſunt nes.
cum Latinis communes. Heu *alas,* do-
lentis eſt : Vah *tuſh,* contemnentis: *Foh,*
foetorem abominantis. Vae *wo,* potius
nomen eſt.

There is a difference between them, but it is very small.

PREPOSITIONS
Prepositions also have the same characteristics as in other languages, but they are commoner in English than in Latin because we have no differences of case. I gave a full account of prepositions earlier, when I was talking about the noun.[137]

INTERJECTIONS
We have only a few interjections: *O*; *oh*; *ah*; *fi*; *ha ha he*; *st*, occur in English and Latin. *Alas* expresses grief; *tush* expresses contempt; *foh* disgust at an unpleasant smell. *Wo* [woe] is really a noun.

[137] Chapter IV.

BIBLIOGRAPHY

ABERCROMBIE, D. (1948) 'Forgotten phoneticians', *Studies in Phonetics and Linguistics*, O.U.P. (1965), *pp* 45–75

ABERCROMBIE, D. (1949) 'What is a letter?' *ibid*, *pp* 76–85

ABERCROMBIE, D. (1961) 'Syllable quantity and enclitics in English', *ibid*, *pp* 26–34

ABERCROMBIE, D. (1967) *The Elements of General Phonetics*, Edinburgh University Press

AELFRIC (tenth-eleventh century AD) *Aelfric's Grammatik und Glossar*, ed J. Zupitza, Berlin, 1880 (reprinted 1966)

ALLEN, W. S. (1965) *Vox Latina*, C.U.P.

ALLEN, W. S. (1968) *Vox Graeca*, C.U.P.

ALSTON, R. C. (1965) *A Bibliography of the English Language, from the invention of printing to the year 1800. Vol 1: English grammars written in English and in Latin by native speakers.* Leeds

AMMAN, J. C. (1700a) *Dissertatio de Loquela*. Amsterdam; translated by Charles Baker; Sampson Low, London, 1873

AMMAN, J. C. (1700b) *Letter to John Wallis* (contained in the preface to his *Dissertatio de Loquela* and in Baker's translation; see previous item)

ANDERSON, J. (1969) 'Syllabic or non-syllabic phonology', *Journal of Linguistics*, 5 (1969), *pp* 136–142

APOLLONIUS DYSCOLUS (second century AD) *Opera omnia*, ed R. Schneider and G. Uhlig, 1878–1910 (reprinted Leipzig, 1965)

ARENS, H. (1955) *Sprachwissenschaft*, Freiburg

ARNOLD, T. (1718) *Neue englische Grammatica*, Hanover

AUBREY, J. (1898) *Brief Lives* 1669–1696, ed A. Clark, Oxford, 1898; ed O. L. Dick, London, 1949; ed A. Powell, London, 1949

BAKER, H. G. (1938) *The contribution of John Wallis to the methods and materials of English grammar*; dissertation, John Hopkins University

BARWICK, P. (1724) *The Life of the Rev Dr John Barwick*, London

BELL, A. M. (1867) *Visible Speech; the Science of Universal Alphabetics*, London

BERG, J. W. VAN DEN (1968) 'Mechanism of the larynx and the laryngeal vibrations', *Manual of Phonetics*, ed Malmberg, *pp* 278–308, North Holland Publishing Company

BIOGRAPHIA BRITANNICA Vol VI, Part II, London, 1766 *sv Wallis, John*

BLOCH, B. and G. L. TRAGER (1942) *Outline of Linguistic Analysis*, Baltimore

BLOOMFIELD, L. (1935) *Language*, New York, 1933; London 1935

BOAS, F. (1911) *Introduction to the Handbook of American Indian languages*, University of Nebraska Press (reprint) 1966

BOLINGER, D. L. (1965) *Forms of English*, ed I. Abe and T. Kanekiyo, Tokyo

BONET, J. P. (1620) *Simplification of the Letters of the Alphabet and Method of teaching Deaf-Mutes to speak . . .* translated by H. N. Dixon, Harrogate, 1890

BRADLEY, H. (1904) *The Making of English*, London

BREWSTER, D. (1855) *Memoirs of Sir Isaac Newton*, Edinburgh (reprinted by Johnson Reprint Corporation, 1965)

BRIGHTLAND, J. (1711) *A grammar of the English tongue*, London; facsimile reprint, Scolar Press, 1967

BUCK, C. D. (1933) *Comparative Grammar of Greek and Latin*, University of Chicago Press

BULLOKAR, W. (1580) *Book at Large*, London

BULLOKAR, W. (1581) *A Short Introduction or guiding, to print, write and reade English speech*, 2nd ed London (1st ed 1580); ed B. Danielsson and R. C. Alston, University of Leeds, 1966

BULLOKAR, W. (1586) *Pamphlet for Grammar*, London

BULWER, J. (1644) *Chirologia*, London

BULWER, J. (1648) *Philocophus*, London

BURKERT, W. (1959) 'Stoicheion', *Philologus*, 103 (1959), 167–197

BUTLER, C. (1633) *The English Grammar*, Oxford (2nd edition, 1634); ed A. Eichler, Halle, 1910

CELY PAPERS (1475–88) *A Selection from the Correspondence of the Cely family*, edited for the Royal Historical Society by H. E. Malden, London, 1900

CHOMSKY, N. (1966) *Cartesian Linguistics*, Harper and Row

CHOMSKY, N. and M. HALLE (1968) *The Sound Pattern of English*, Harper and Row

COOPER, C. (1685) *Grammatica Linguae Anglicanae*, London; ed J. D. Jones, Halle, 1911; facsimile reprint, Scolar Press, 1968

COOPER, C. (1687) *The English Teacher*, London; ed B. Sundby, Lund Studies in English, xxii, 1953

DAINES, S. (1640) *Orthoepia Anglicana*, London; ed Rösler and Brotanek, Halle, 1908; facsimile reprint, Scolar Press, 1967

DALGARNO, G. (1661) *Ars Signorum*, London; ed T. Maitland, Edinburgh, 1834; see also FUNKE (1929); facsimile reprint, Scolar Press, 1968

DALGARNO, G. (1680) *Didascalocophus . . .; Double Consonants*, Oxford, ed T. Maitland, Edinburgh, 1834

DAVYS, J. (1737) *An Essay on the Art of Deciphering, in which is inserted a discourse of John Wallis*; London

DIELS, H. (1899) *Elementum*, Leipzig

DIGBY, K. (1644) *Of Bodies*, Paris

D.N.B. (1885–) *Dictionary of National Biography*, London

DINNEEN, F. P. (1967) *An introduction to general linguistics*, Holt, Rinehart

DIONYSIUS THRAX (second century BC) Τέχνη γραμματική, ed Uhlig, Leipzig, 1884; *Scholia*, ed Hilgard (Grammatici Graeci, I.3, Leipzig, 1901)

DIRINGER, D. (1958) *The Story of the Aleph Beth*, Lincolns-Prager (Publishers) Ltd, London

DISRAELI, I. (1814) *Quarrels of Authors*, London, III.90–119

DOBSON, E. J. (1947) 'Robert Robinson and his phonetic transcripts . . .', *Trans. Phil. Soc.*, 1947, 58

DOBSON, E. J. (1968) *English Pronunciation 1500–1700*, 2nd edition, 2 vols, O.U.P.

DODART, D. (1700–1707) 'Memoire sur les causes de la voix de l'homme, et de ses differents tons', *Memoires de l'Academie Royale des Sciences de Paris* (1700), p 244 *ff*; 'Memoire sur la voix et sur les tons' etc, *ibid* (1706), pp 136 *ff*, 388 *ff*; Supplement, *ibid* (1707), p 66 *ff*. (Summarised in *L'Histoire de l'Academie des Sciences* for the appropriate year)

DONATUS, AELIUS (fourth century A D) *Ars Grammatica*; ed Keil, Grammatici Latini, IV.355–402, Leipzig, 1857–80

ELLIOTT, R. V. W. (1954) 'Isaac Newton as a phonetician', *Mod. Lang. Rev.*, xlix.5–12

ELLIS, A. J. (*E.E.P.*) *On Early English Pronunciation*, London, 1869–89

FABRICIUS, H. *ab Aquapendente* (1687) *Opera omnia anatomica et physiologica*, Leipzig

FALLOPIUS, G. (1606) *Opera omnia*, Frankfurt

FERREIN, A. (1741) 'De la formation de la voix de l'homme', *Memoires de l'Academie Royale des Sciences de Paris* (1741), pp 409 *ff* and 430 *ff*. (Summarised in *L'Histoire de l'Academie des Sciences* (1741), p 51 *ff*)

FILLMORE, C. J. (1968) 'The case for case', *Universals in Linguistic Theory*, ed E. Bach and R. T. Harms; Holt, Rinehart and Winston, *pp* 1–88

FIRTH, J. R. (1946) 'The English School of Phonetics', *Papers in Linguistics*, 1934–51, O.U.P. (1957), *pp* 92–120

FOSTER, J. (1891) *Alumni Oxonienses, 1500–1714*, Oxford, 1891–2

FRY, D. B. (1964) 'The function of the syllable', *Phonetica* 17 (1964), *pp* 215–221

FUNKE, O. (1929) *Zum Weltsprachenproblem in England im 17 Jahrhundert – G. Dalgarno's Ars Signorum (1661) und J. Wilkins' Essay towards a Real Character and a Philosophical Language (1668)*, Heidelberg

FUNKE, O. (1941) *Die Frühzeit der englischen Grammatik*, Bern

GALEN (second century A D) *De usu partium corporis humani*, Teubner, 1907–9

GALEN (second century A D) *De placitis Hippocratis et Platonis*, ed I. Müller, Teubner, 1874

GATAKER, T. (1646) *De Diphthongis . . . Dissertatio Philologica*, London

GIL, A. (1619) *Logonomia Anglica*, London (second edition 1621); ed O. L. Jiriczek, Strasbourg, 1903; facsimile reprint, Scolar Press, 1968

GIMSON, A. C. (1962) *An Introduction to the Pronunciation of English*, Arnold

GREAVES, P. (1594) *Grammatica Anglicana*, Cambridge; ed O. Funke, Vienna, 1938; see also SCHEURWEGS AND VORLAT (1959)

GREENWOOD, J. (1711) *Essay towards a Practical English Grammar*, London; facsimile reprint, Scolar Press, 1968

GREENWOOD, J. (1737) *Royal English Grammar*, London

GREGORY, D. (1727) *Short life of Wallis*, Bodleian MS Smith 31, *ff* 58–59, printed in Collier's Dictionary, 2nd edition, London, 1727

HART, J. *John Hart's Works*, ed B. Danielsson, Stockholm, 1955:
    (1551) *The Opening of the Unreasonable Writing of our English Tongue*
    (1569) *An Orthographie*
    (1570) *A Methode or comfortable beginning for all unlearned*

HAUGEN, E. ed (1972) *First Grammatical Treatise*, Longman

HEARNE, T. (1725) *Works*, Vols I–III, Oxford

HEARNE, T. (1711) *Hearne's Collections*, ed C. E. Doble, Oxford, Vol III, 1889

HEFFNER, R.-M. S. (1949) *General Phonetics*, Wisconsin, 1949

HENDERSON, I. (1967) *The Picts*, Thames and Hudson

HEXHAM, H. (1647) *An English Grammar, appended to A Copious English and Nether-Duytch Dictionary*, Rotterdam

HICKES, G. (1689) *Institutiones Grammaticae Anglo-Saxonicae*, Oxford

HILL, A. A. (1958) *Introduction to Linguistic Structures*, Longmans

HOBBES, T. (1662) *Mr Hobbes considered in his loyalty, religion, reputation, and manners*, London

HOCKETT, C. F. (1955) *A Manual of Phonology*, Waverly Press, Baltimore

HODGES, R. (1643) *A Special Help to Orthographie*, London

HODGES, R. (1644) *The English Primrose*, London; ed H. Kauter, Heidelberg, 1930

HOLDER, W. (1668) 'An Experiment concerning Deafness', *Philos. Trans.* May, 1668

HOLDER, W. (1669) *The Elements of Speech*, London; facsimile reprint, Scolar Press, 1967

HOLDER, W. (1678) *A Supplement to the Philosophical Transactions of July 1670, with some Reflexions on Dr John Wallis, his letter there inserted*, London

HONIKMAN, B. (1964) 'Articulatory settings', in *In Honour of Daniel Jones*, Longmans

HORN, W. (1954) *Laut und Leben; Englische Lautgeschichte der neueren Zeit (1400–1950)*, bearbeitet von Martin Lehnert, Berlin

HUME, A. (1617) *Of the Orthographie and Congruitie of the Britan Tongue*, London; ed H. B. Wheatley, Early English Text Society, 1865

ICKELSAMER, V. (1534) *Teutsche Grammatica*, ed Kohler, Tübingen, 1881

IN HONOUR OF DANIEL JONES (1964) ed Abercrombie et al, Longmans

JACKSON, K. H. (1953) *Language and History in Early Britain*, Edinburgh U.P.

JEEP, L. (1893) *Zur Geschichte der Lehre von den Redeteilen bei den lateinischen Grammatikern*, Leipzig

JELLINEK, M. H. (1913) *Geschichte der neuhochdeutschen Grammatik von den Anfängen bis auf Adelung*, Heidelberg

JESPERSEN, O. (1922) *Language; its nature, development and origin.* Allen and Unwin

JESPERSEN, O. (*M.E.G.*) *A Modern English Grammar on Historical Principles*, 7 vols, Heidelberg, 1909–27

JOHNSON, R. (1706) *Grammatical Commentaries*, London

JONES, D. (1956) *The Pronunciation of English*, 4th edition, C.U.P.

JONES, D. (1962) *An Outline of English Phonetics*, 9th edition, Heffer

JONES, D. (1967) *The Phoneme*, 3rd edition, Heffer

JONES, J. (1701) *Practical Phonography*, London; ed E. Ekwall, Halle, 1907

JONSON, B. (1640) *English Grammar*, London

KIM, CHIN-W. (1965) 'On the autonomy of the tensity feature in stop classification', *Word*, 21.3 (1965), *pp* 339–59

KITTREDGE, G. L. *Some landmarks in the history of English Grammars* (no date)

KOLLER, H. (1958) 'Die Anfänge der griechischen Grammatik', *Glotta* 37 (1958), *pp* 5–40

KUKENHEIM, L. (1932) *Contributions à l'histoire de la grammaire italienne, espagnole, et française a l'époque de la Renaissance*, Amsterdam

KUKENHEIM, L. (1951) *Contributions à l'histoire de la grammaire grecque, latine, et hébraïque à l'époque de la Renaissance*, Leiden

KUKENHEIM, L. (1962) *Esquisse historique de la linguistique française*, Leiden

LADEFOGED, P. (1967) *Three Areas of Experimental Phonetics*, O.U.P.

LANCELOT, C. and A. ARNAULD (1660) *Grammaire générale et raisonée* (de Port-Royal), Paris; facsimile edition, Scolar Press, 1968)

LEDIARD, T. (1726) *Grammatica Anglicana Critica*, Hamburg

LEHISTE, I. (1964) *Acoustical characteristics of Selected English Consonants*, The Hague

LEHNERT, M. (1936) *Die Grammatik des englischen Sprachmeisters John Wallis (1616–1703)* (Sprache und Kultur der germanischen und romanischen Völker, Anglistische Reihe, Bd. xxi), Breslau

LEHNERT, M. (1937–8) 'Die Abhängigkeit frühneuenglischer Grammatiken', *Englische Studien* 72 (1937–8), 192–206

LEHNERT, M. (1938) 'Die Anfänge der wissenschaftlichen und praktischen Phonetik in England', *Archiv für das Studium der neueren Sprachen*, Bd. 173, *pp* 163–80; Bd. 174, *pp* 28–35

LEWIS, J. (1735) *Life of the learned and reverend John Wallis S.T.D. . . . collected and written in the year 1735, by John Lewis, Minister of Mergate* (Bodleian MS Rawl. C.978, and on microfilm in Edinburgh University Library)

LINDSAY, W. M. (1894) *The Latin Language*, Oxford

LODWICK, F. (1686) 'Essay towards an Universal Alphabet', *Philos. Trans.* XVI.182, June, 1686

LOWTH, R. (1762) *Short introduction to English Grammar*, London; facsimile reprint, Scolar Press, 1967

LYONS, J. (1968) *Introduction to theoretical linguistics*, C.U.P.

LUCIAN (second century A D) *Works*, ed A. M. Harmon, Heinemann, 1913–

MCINTOSH, M. M. C. (1956) *The Phonetic and Linguistic Theory of the Royal Society School, from Wallis to Cooper*; B LITT thesis, Oxford Univ.

MCKERROW, R. B. (1910) 'Some notes on the letters i, j, u, v', *The Library*, 3rd Series, Vol I.239

MADSEN, J. (1586) *De literis*, Basle; ed C. Møller and P. Skautrup, Acta Jutlandica, II.3 and III.1, 1930–31

MATTINGLY, I. G. (1960) 'The phonetic structure of Nootka', *NSA Technical Journal*: Special linguistic issue, *pp* 75–83

MEYER, E. A. (1903) *Englische Lautdauer*, Uppsala

MICHAEL, I. (1970) *English grammatical categories*, C.U.P.

MICHAUD, L. G. *Biographie Universelle*, Paris, 1842–65

MIEGE, G. (1688) *The English Grammar*, London

MONTANUS, P. (1635) *De Spreeckonst*, Delft; ed Caron, Groningen, 1964; see also VOS (1962)

MONTUCLA, J. E. (1758) *Histoire des Mathematiques*, Paris

MOREL, L. (1895) *De Johannis Wallisii Grammatica Linguae Anglicanae et Tractatu de Loquela*, Thesis, Paris

MUELLER, W. (1909) *Theodor Arnolds Englische Grammatiken*, Dissertation, Marburg

MULCASTER, R. (1582) *Elementarie*; ed E. T. Campagnac, Clarendon Press, Oxford, 1925

MURRAY, J. A. H. (1873) *The Dialect of the Southern Counties of Scotland*, London

NEBRIJA, E. A. DE (1492) *Gramatica sobre la lengua castellana*; ed Gonzalez-Llubera, O.U.P., 1926

NEWTON, I. (1661?) *Phonetic Notes*; see ELLIOTT, R. V. W. (1954)

NICERON, P. (1745) *Mémoires . . . des hommes illustres*, Vol 43, Paris

NICHOLS, J. (1812) *Literary anecdotes of the eighteenth century*, Vol II, London, *p* 445 *ff*

NICHOLS, J. (1828) *Illustrations of the literary history of the eighteenth century*, Vol V, London, *p* 797

OUGHTRED, W. (1631) *Clavis Mathematica*, Oxford

PALMER, L. R. (1954) *The Latin Language*, Faber

PEPYS, S. (1679–) *Private Correspondence and Miscellaneous Papers of Samuel Pepys, 1679–1703*; ed J. R. Tanner, 2 vols, London, 1926

PLOT, R. (1677) *History of Oxfordshire*, Oxford

POLDAUF, I. (1948) *On the History of Some Problems of English Grammar before 1800*, Prague

PORT-ROYAL GRAMMAR see LANCELOT, C. and A. ARNAULD (1660)

PRICE, O. (1665) *The Vocal Organ*, Oxford

PRIESTLEY, J. (1761) *Rudiments of English*, London

PRISCIAN (sixth century AD) *Institutiones Grammaticae*; ed Hertz, *Grammatici Latini*, II–III, Leipzig, 1857–80

QUINTILIAN (first century AD) *Institutio Oratoria*; ed H. E. Butler, 4 vols, Heinemann, 1921

RAMUS, P. (1559) *Scholae Grammaticae*, Paris; see also P. GREAVES (1594), ed Funke

RAMUS, P. (1562) *Gramere*, Paris

RATKE, W. (1959) *Wolfgang Ratkes Schriften zur deutschen Grammatik*, ed Ising, Berlin

ROBINS, R. H. (1951) *Ancient and mediaeval grammatical theory in Europe*, London

ROBINS, R. H. (1957) 'Dionysius Thrax and the western grammatical tradition', *Trans. Phil. Soc.* (1957), *pp* 67–106

ROBINS, R. H. (1967) *A Short History of Linguistics*, Longmans

ROBINSON, R. (1617) *The Art of Pronuntiation*, London; ed E. J. Dobson, *The Phonetic writings of Robert Robinson*, London, 1957 (Early English Text Society, Original Series 238)

SALESBURY, W. (1550) *A playne and familiar introduction*; in ELLIS, A. J., *E.E.P.*, Vol III

SALMON, V. (1961) 'Joseph Webbe: some seventeenth century views on language teaching and the nature of meaning', *Bibliotheque d'Humanisme et Renaissance*, 23, 1961, *pp* 324–340

SALMON, V. (1969) Review of Chomsky, N. *Cartesian Linguistics, Journal of Linguistics*, 5 (1969), *pp* 165–187

SAPIR, E. (1949) *Selected writings of Edward Sapir, in language, culture and personality*, ed David G. Mandelbaum, University of California Press

SCALIGER, J. C. (1540) *De causis linguae Latinae*, Lyons

SCALIGER, J.-J. (1610) *Diatrïba de Europaeorum Linguis*, in *Opuscula Varia*, Paris

SCHEURWEGHS, G. and E. VORLAT (1959) 'Problems of the History of English Grammar', *English Studies*, 40 (1959), *pp* 135–43

SCOTT, J. F. (1938) *The Mathematical Work of John Wallis*, Taylor and Francis

SCOTT, J. F. (1958) *History of Mathematics*, Taylor and Francis

SCRIBA, C. J. (1966) *Studien zur Mathematik des John Wallis . . . Im Anhang: Die Bücher und Handschriften von Wallis in der Bodleian Library zu Oxford*, Wiesbaden

SERGIUS (date unknown) *Explanationes in Donatum*, ed Keil, *Grammatici Latini*, IV.486

SMITH, T. (1568) *De recta et emendata linguae Anglicanae scriptione dialogus*, Paris, ed O. Deibel, Halle, 1913; facsimile reprint Scolar Press 1968

STEINTHAL, H. (1863) *Geschichte der Sprachwissenschaft bei den Griechen und Römern*, Berlin; 2nd ed, 1890–91

STUBBE, H. (1657) *A Severe Enquiry into the late Oneirocrita*, London

STUBBE, H. (1658) *The Savilian Professor's Case Stated*, London

STURTEVANT, E. H. (1940) *The Pronunciation of Greek and Latin*, 2nd edition, Yale

SUNDBY, B. (1952) 'A case of seventeenth century plagiarism', *English Studies*, 33 (1952), *pp* 209–13

SWEET, H. (1888) *A History of English Sounds*, Oxford

SWEET, H. (1932) *A Primer of Phonetics*, 4th edition, Oxford

TERENTIANUS MAURUS (second century AD) *De litteris, syllabis et metris Horatii*, ed Keil, *Grammatici Latini*, VI.325–413

TERENTIUS SCAURUS (second century AD) *Liber de Orthographia*, ed Keil, *Grammatici Latini*, VII.11–33

THORESBY, R. (1832) *Letters of Eminent Men*, London

THUROT, C. (1881–3) *De la prononciation française depuis le commencement du XVIe siecle*. 2 vols, Paris

TRAGER, G. L. and H. L. SMITH (1957) *An Outline of English Structure*, Washington

VAN RIPER, C. G. and IRWIN, J. V. (1958) *Voice and Articulation*, London

VELIUS LONGUS (second century A D) *De Orthographia*, ed Keil, *Grammatici Latini*, VII.46–81

VORLAT, E. (1963) *Progress in English Grammar 1585–1735*, Luxembourg

VOS, A. L. (1962) *Tradition and innovation in Petrus Montanus, The Art of Speech, 1635*, PH D Thesis, Edinburgh

WAINWRIGHT, F. T. (1955) ed *The Problem of the Picts*, Nelson

WALLIS, J. (1657) *Reasons showing the consistency of the place of Custos Archivorum with that of a Savilian Professor*, Oxford; a broadsheet, (Bodleian Lib. – Wood Collection; Edinburgh Univ. Lib. – Dc.1.61, 571)

WALLIS, J. (1662) *Letter to Robert Boyle*, 14 March, *Philos. Trans.* (1670), *pp* 1087–97

WALLIS, J. (1678) *A Defence of the Royal Society*, London

WALLIS, J. (1680) *Letter to Mr Tenison*, 30 November; Bodleian MS Add. D.105, *ff* 70–71

WALLIS, J. (1685) *Letter to Dr Fell*, 8 April; printed in T. Hearne's Works, Vol III, Preface to Peter Langtoft's Chronicle, London, 1810

WALLIS, J. (1688) *Letters to Samuel Pepys*, 20 April; Bodleian MS Rawl. A.171, *ff* 26–7

WALLIS, J. (1697) *Letter to Dr Thomas Smith*, 29 January; Bodleian MSS Smith 31 and Smith 66, *f* 31; also printed in T. Hearne's Works, Vol III, Preface to Peter Langtoft's Chronicle

WALLIS, J. (1698) *Letter to Thomas Beverley*, 30 September; for locations see Introduction *p* 13

WALLIS, J. (1693–99) *Opera mathematica et miscellanea*, 3 vols, Oxford

WALLIS, J. (1700) *Letter to Conrad Amman*, January; printed in the Preface to Amman's *Dissertatio de Loquela*, 1700

WALLIS, W. (1791) *Sermons now first printed from the original manuscripts of John Wallis . . . to which are prefixed memoirs of the author*, London

WARD, S. (1654) *Vindiciae Academiarum*, Oxford

WEBBE, J. (1622) *An appeale to truth*; facsimile reprint, Scolar Press, 1968

WEINGREEN, J. (1948) *A Practical Grammar for Classical Hebrew*, O.U.P.

WELD, R. (1848) *History of the Royal Society*, London

WHARTON, J. (1655) *A New English Grammar*, London

WILIAM, U. (1960) *A Short Welsh Grammar*, Davies (Christopher)

WILKINS, J. (1668) *An Essay towards a Real Character and a Philosophical Language*, London; facsimile reprint, Scolar Press, 1968

WOOD, A. (1674) *Historia Universitatis Oxoniensis*, Oxford

WOOD, A. (1691–2) *Athenae Oxonienses*, London

WOOD, A. (1891) *The Life and Times of Anthony Wood, antiquary, of Oxford, 1632–1695, described by himself*, collected by Andrew Clark (Oxford Hist. Soc. vols XIX, XXI, XXVI, XXX, XL, Oxford, 1891–1900)

WRIGHT, J. (1896) *English Dialect Dictionary*, London, 1896–1905

WRIGHT, J. and E. M. WRIGHT (1924) *An Elementary Historical New English Grammar*, Oxford

ZACHRISSON, R. E. (1913) *Pronunciation of English Vowels 1400–1700*, Göteborg

ZACHRISSON, R. E. (1914) 'Notes on the relation . . . of some early grammars', *Anglia Beiblatt*, 25 (1914), *pp* 247–53

ZACHRISSON, R. E. (1917) Review of C. Müller, 'Die englische Lautentwicklung nach Lediard' etc, *Anglia Beiblatt*, 28 (1917), *pp* 62–82

INDEX

All references are to page numbers. Those in *italic* type refer to the Introduction and to *annotated* pages of the text; references in roman type are to the text alone. Greek letters and Greek or Latin technical terms are indexed separately and follow the main index.

GREEK INDEX

LATIN INDEX